TRUE COLOURS

FOOTBALL KITS FROM 1980 TO THE PRESENT DAY

JOHN DEVLIN

**This book is dedicated with love
to my dear Mum and Dad.**

Published in 2005 by A & C Black Publishers Ltd
37 Soho Square, London W1D 3QZ
www.acblack.com

Copyright © 2005 by John Devlin

ISBN 0 7136 7389 3

A CIP record for this book is available from the British Library.

Note: While every effort has been made to ensure that the content of this book is as technically accurate and as sound as possible, neither the author nor the publisher can accept responsibility for any injury or loss sustained as a result of the use of this material.

A & C Black uses paper produced with elemental chlorine-free pulp, harvested from managed sustainable forests.

Acknowledgements:

Designed and illustrated by John Devlin

Front cover photograph © Getty Images

Textual photographs © Empics

Printed and bound by Butler and Tanner Ltd, Frome and London

CONTENTS

CHARLIE ATHERSMITH, ASTON VILLA, 1895

ARTHUR HITCHINS, TOTTENHAM HOTSPUR, 1936

FACING PAGE – SUNDERLAND FANS, 1999

A brief history of football kit design

When most football clubs formed in the late 1800s/early 1900s, they wore whatever could be cobbled together simply and cheaply from local suppliers. In the early days a cohesive identity was not always an issue, and sometimes the players wore lightweight trousers (often tucked into woollen stockings) and basic working shirts, with the colour of the players' caps being the only effective way to determine who was on which side. Not an inch of bare flesh was seen, to keep out the cold (and prevent cuts and bruises).

The colour selections came from many sources – the colours of the club founder's old school, the colour most associated with the heraldry of the area or even just whatever was available at the time. As the fledgling teams found their footballing feet the designs often changed, with bizarre spots, stars and zigzags all adorning the outfits at times. A few of these older fashions have survived today, for example in Blackburn's halved shirt and Bristol Rovers' quartered version. When several clubs were formed in the same area, colours were carefully selected so as not to clash with their near neighbours, enabling the tribes of players and supporters to be instantly identified. Often blue and red were chosen, as was the case with Liverpool and Everton along with Manchester United and Manchester City. Eventually, however, the fashions settled down; players and supporters became accustomed to a particular hue and the good-old fashioned large woollen jerseys became the choice of the day, paired with large baggy shorts designed for ease of movement (an early FA rule from 1903 stated that 'footballers' knickers must cover the knee'). However, after years of playing in heavy wool tops, cotton shirts became popular and a variety of different button-up collars and fastenings came and went as the years passed.

The basic rules and regulations concerning players' uniforms, which we take for granted today, also came in gradually. In 1908 the Football League ruled for the first time that goalkeepers should wear a different coloured jersey from the rest of the team. In 1924 the concept of change colours was made official; before that, if there was a colour clash it was customary for the away side to don a simple all-white kit (a white shirt being considered the garment most players would already own). Then, in 1928, numbered shirts were introduced, although they did not become compulsory until five years later. At this stage, club badges tended to only be included on shirts for special occasions such as Cup finals or international games.

The biggest change came in 1953 when the Hungarian national side arrived to play England at Wembley. Their lightweight, fitted shirts, shorter shorts and streamlined boots, which were initially ridiculed by the home crowd, highlighted the difference between the Hungarians and the English team, who were still wearing their large, clumsy, heavy jerseys and baggy shorts. The fact that the England side were well beaten led to a drastic change of fashion in football after that game. The English kit was reviewed the following year and soon the team were attired in similar outfits to those worn by the Europeans – although in white, of course.

Given the recent over-the-top criticism of Manchester United and their innovative philosophy regarding football strips, it may not be a surprise to learn that it was United, under the leadership of the great Sir Matt Busby, who first picked up on the new, more fitted, continental style of kit. In 1955 the side, closely followed by everyone else, began sporting the new V-neck short-sleeved shirts that had been worn to great success in the 1954 World Cup. Heavy, cumbersome jerseys were now yesterday's news.

With the arrival of pop culture in the 1960s, football shirts began to adopt an even more stylish approach. In came round crew necks (influenced perhaps by The Beatles' collarless jackets), synthetic materials and the return of long sleeves. A few traditional colour schemes were abandoned as English clubs attempted to emulate the great teams of Europe. The most famous example was Leeds United, who switched from blue and yellow to white in the early 60s under the instruction of Don Revie in homage to the great Real Madrid team of the era.

Up until this point British companies such as Umbro and Bukta had been the driving forces behind kit production, but in the 60s and 70s European brands such as adidas and Puma began to make an impression in the Football League – although, of course, in those days you couldn't tell who had produced the jersey unless you looked at the label. Replica versions were not available and manufacturers' logos did not

appear on shirts until around the 1973–74 season, with the first replica versions sold a few seasons later. Soon the FA introduced strict rules over the sizing of the new manufacturers' logos on the front of the shirt, but before long the logos had ingeniously become an integral part of the trim running down each sleeve, thereby gaining maximum exposure (and bypassing the rules).

After the sophistication of the 60s came the glamour and excess of the 70s. With glam rock, flares and large flamboyant attire commonplace on the terraces, wing collars were added to football shirts as part of the increasingly adventurous designs spearheaded by Admiral, Umbro and adidas. The positioning of the club badges also began to vary between the left-hand side (over the heart, of course) and the centre. World football fashion was also making an impact in Britain during the 70s, and for a while it seemed that every side had adopted yellow as either an away or third colour to emulate the talented Brazilian side who were dominating the global scene.

1979 was a key year in football kit history. Apart from the Scottish national side pre-empting the Premier League by including players' surnames above the shirt numbers, the big news was the arrival of Japanese electrical home entertainment manufacturers Hitachi as shirt sponsors to Liverpool. The inclusion of a third party's logo on the shirt had been something of a contentious issue with the football authorities. Derby County had attempted a deal with the car manufacturers Saab that fell through due to FA regulations,

KEN SHELLITO, CHELSEA, 1959

DENIS LAW, MANCHESTER UNITED, 1970

DAVID JOHNSON, LIVERPOOL, 1980

and a similar situation had occurred at non-League Kettering before Liverpool broke the mould. Other teams followed, of course, and by the mid-80s most League sides had found themselves their own shirt sponsors, with electrical technology companies and breweries comprising a high percentage (although the issue of promoting alcohol has always been a thorny subject – children's replica shirts were, for a long while, sold minus the brewer's logo). It was not until the 1983–84 season that TV companies allowed the logo shirts to be worn during televised games. Until then, unsponsored jerseys were worn whenever the cameras were present.

Aside from sponsorship, in design terms the 80s was a period of modernity led by sophisticated European brands such as Le Coq Sportif, Patrick and Hummel. Heritage went out the window as designers began pushing the boundaries of traditional colours and styles. As the new sharply-dressed casual fashion swept the grounds, the wing collars were gradually faded out and replaced by slick crew or V-necks, often trimmed with recently introduced additional colours. Cotton shirts also disappeared to be superseded by silky, shiny, man-made polyester versions. Loose-fitting shirts were about as unfashionable as flares, and the cut of the kits became tighter and tighter. And to top it all, you couldn't move for pinstripes, shadow stripes or piping as new technology allowed for new embellishments and snazzier designs.

Technology began to drive kit design even more strongly towards the end of the 80s. With the advent of new, lightweight fabrics, the size of the shirt became baggier again as clubs realised that the more 'comfortable' jersey now did not necessarily mean more fabric weight. They also made the players seem larger and more physically intimidating. Slowly, as off-the-pitch fashions became looser and baggier, so did the by now cuffless shirts and shorts. It wasn't long before the cycle of fashion spun again and button-up collars made an unexpected return. Also, new printing techniques allowed for more ambitious, abstract designs to be incorporated into the fabric, and soon almost every club featured material that was flecked, paint-splattered or daubed with all manner of vivid hues.

The marketing of replica shirts, which had already gathered pace in the mid to late 80s, exploded in the early 90s and soon it seemed that everyone owned at least one modern glossy replica shirt of their favourite team. As the pace of fashion increased and clubs realised the income that could be generated from these designs, previously obscure (but necessary) third shirts became popular and the changing of the club's strips was carefully timed so that at least one new design would be available every season. The boom in replica shirts also brought with it some criticism from angry parents writing into the national press to complain about the 'overpriced' kits that were soon out of date. Of course, most sensible fans realised that when a team strip was seen at half-price in the local sports shop, chances were it wasn't going to be around on the pitch for much longer and was due to be replaced the following season. In fact, most fans actually look forward to the unveiling of their club's new kit and eagerly anticipate the potential glory that will accompany it.

However, the criticism sparked the football authorities into action and by the late 90s every kit had to include a 'sell-by date' informing the purchaser of the lifespan of the garment. Price fixing has also been a contentious issue, with a disagreement occurring after several supermarket chains began undercutting official sports shops in the sale of replica apparel. All of these facts did not stop dedicated fans buying the shirts in their thousands.

The rejuvenation of the English national side, which started at Italia 90 and culminated in Euro 96, re-ignited interest in football. The Premier League emerged in 1992 and soon grounds were once again packed to the rafters. Post-modern, retro-influenced fashions had become the flavour of the month. Instigated primarily by Umbro, there was a logical progression from baggy shirts and collars to traditional designs and original features such as lace-up and long 40s-style button-up necks. At the 1991 FA Cup final, the football world gasped (and initially sniggered) as Umbro decked out Tottenham Hotspur in a pair of large fitting, long baggy shorts. The style had indeed gone full circle.

On the pitch it was not all old-fashioned though, as in true post-modern style the traditional look was complemented by the inclusion of large and varied shadow patterns and designs woven into the fabric. Replica retro cotton shirts, which recreated the large collars and heavy fabric from days gone by, were produced by specialist companies purely for the fans and were also popular at this time.

With replica shirt sales at an all-time high, sportswear companies began to design kits specifically with this marketplace in mind, even going as far as to introduce special versions for women. It was a difficult task as companies attempted to create fashions that looked just as good with jeans as they did on the pitch.

The Premiership also introduced squad numbers for players, along with their names, on the backs of shirts, enabling fervent supporters to add their own name or the name of their favourite player to their own replica version. However, critics claimed that this was purely to attract more revenue, as each 'iron-on' letter cost money, with a long surname upping the price of the replica jersey quite considerably.

Once the nostalgic influence had died out, the late 90s saw a design free-for-all. No real trend emerged and the pitches were full of V-necks, collars, round necks, pinstripes, shadow patterns, plain shirts, piping… the variation was incredible! It was not until the pure aesthetics of the kits began to take second place to a new 'form follows function' philosophy, which coincided with the arrival of revolutionary new fabrics, that a new minimal style emerged to replace the busy designs of the 90s. Once again, companies began to introduce kits designed purely for optimum performance on the pitch. This meant reversed seams for a more comfortable fit with no rubbing against the skin, lightweight hi-tech fabrics designed to draw moisture away from the body and keep the body cool, mesh panels for breathability and no superfluous

DUNCAN FERGUSON, EVERTON, 2003

accessories or detail. Every major company launched their own uniquely named version: Nike had their Dri-fit and Cool Motion double-layered shirts, Reebok introduced Play Dry, adidas Climalite and Umbro had Vapatech and later Sportswool (although, with ICI, they were also behind Tactel, a mid-80s fabric that was a forerunner of today's material advancements). Now, technology and science were designing shirts. Soon every side were wearing multi-panelled outfits designed to make them faster, lighter and stronger. To the replica-buying fan there were also advantages, as the new shirts dried a lot more quickly when they were taken out of the washing machine.

Slowly, the fit of the shirts began to get tighter again. Kappa introduced their incredible 'Kombat 2000' range, which was designed to prevent the fad of shirt-pulling – the latest blight on the sport. The range was unlike any shirt seen for many years (not since the Hungarians in 1953), with minimal neck designs, long sleeves and stretchy Lycra fabric that all helped to accentuate the players' impressive physiques and fitness levels, thereby intimidating the opposition. More overweight supporters panicked, though, as they realised that they just might not look as good in the replica versions!

Recent years have seen the large multi-national apparel suppliers such as Nike, Puma and adidas premier their latest kit templates at the major international football events, only for the styles to be absorbed into domestic leagues in the following season. Asymmetrical design began to creep into the English league in 2004, with the irregular placement of trim

and coloured panels upsetting the purists who preferred to see a more balanced array of detail on a shirt.

Although on the whole modern shirt designers do seem to be listening to the fans' pleas for traditional and simple designs, collecting replica shirts from the garish 80s and 90s is at an all-time high with hundreds of shirts offered on sale daily via online auction websites. Contemporary signed shirts are also particularly popular.

There can be little doubt that the restrained and elegant designs of today, fuelled by science and aesthetically minimal (often in only two colours), will be here for a while yet. But as long as science keeps creating new and more marvellous fabrics that assist sports stars in their jobs (and are attractive to supporters), no doubt more adventurous designs will start to creep back in. The last 25 years of kit design have made one thing clear – no football fashion is ever completely obsolete.

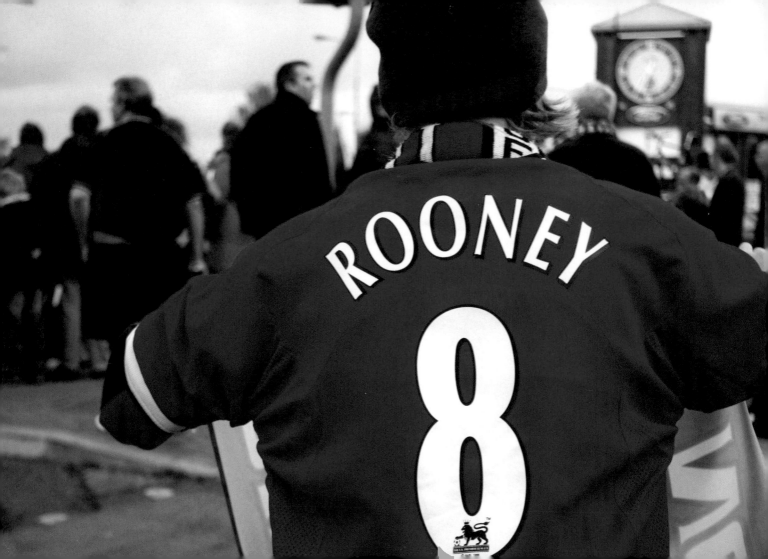

The psychology of football kit design

One of the myths surrounding contemporary football kits is that the constant changing of the design is purely a modern invention, merely a revenue booster aimed at parting parents with their cash in order to frantically keep up to date with the latest kits for their ever-demanding children. Although the selling of replica shirts is obviously a major source of income to the clubs today, this criticism is, on the whole, a fallacy. Although this book takes 1980 – arguably the birth of modern sponsorship in sport – as its starting point, any rudimentary research into football history shows that from day one kit styles were constantly changing from season to season, and also often from colour to colour as fashion developed and clubs attempted to forge their identity.

Today, football supporters choose to show their allegiance to their team by donning a replica jersey. In the 70s it was scarves, bobble hats and rosettes, but now only identical versions of the uniform your heroes wear on the field is enough to indicate that you are a true fan. As recently as the late 80s, replica shirts were still not de rigueur for the hardcore football fan. It is really only since Gazza led the English emotional rollercoaster of Italia 90 and the emergence of the Premier League that the colourful polyester jerseys became more popular and filled terraces throughout the land.

The modern football kit is very complex. For many years it was purely a functional item – a simple means of identifying the team. Then, of course, as more teams joined the Football League, change strips had to be introduced to avoid colour clashes. Gradually, as fashion changed over the years, collars, V-necks, lace-up and button-up collars all came and went and came again. Occasionally, radical innovations would occur, as mentioned above when Hungary played England in 1953 and made the heavy woollen English jerseys look almost prehistoric compared to the relatively lightweight, sleek continental outfits.

However, in the mid-70s, when the first manufacturer's logo appeared on a shirt, the colourful uniform not only had to contain the identity of the club, but also the identity of the company who produced it. When Hitachi signed the first professional shirt sponsor deal with Liverpool in 1979, a third element was thrown into the mix. Now the shirt also had to accommodate the large logo of a third party previously unconnected to the club. As anyone connected with design will confirm, it is no easy job blending these three identities together on a garment in such a way that each is clearly recognisable and does not clash with the other. Throw in the away strips problem when the entire recognised outfit has to be switched to another colour (think Coke/Diet Coke) and the problem is confounded. Also, with the popularity of replica shirts increasing in the early 90s, designers also began to consider not only how the shirt would look on the field but also how it would look off it. Yet another problem!

FACING PAGE – A MANCHESTER UNITED FAN
IN A REPLICA WAYNE ROONEY HOME SHIRT

In very recent years, with the whole professional business side of football jumping up a gear, the kits switched focus back to enhancing performance on the pitch. Hi-tech lightweight fabrics designed to maximise comfort and minimise heat and moisture (handy for those balmy days in Glasgow!) are concerned primarily with the 90 minutes of a match. Of course, replica shirts are still a consideration as they consistently sell in their thousands, but not in the quantities they did in the 90s.

The fit of the shirts has also varied dramatically in recent years, from fairly tight to baggy to frankly enormous and back to tight again! Intimidation is the key here – larger shirts make the players look larger and stronger, but as players' fitness levels increase in the now high-pressure football world, practical skimpier outfits (such as Kappa's Kombat range) allow for the players' own physique to create the threatening image. The combination of multi-panelled hi-tech fabric outfits has also enabled designers to create styles that are intended to subconsciously increase physical presence and to give an almost armour-like impression – perfect for battle on the pitch.

It is easy to draw parallels between modern football kits and army uniforms of the past; both feature bright hues trimmed with all manner of braid, badges, medals and so on and are worn by groups of men proudly displaying their colours before the opponent. The culture of swapping shirts after important matches can also be seen as a modern-day equivalent of claiming a battle-scarred souvenir from the defeated enemy.

Colour choice can also give a psychological advantage. Red is probably the most successful colour in football (think Liverpool, Man Utd and Arsenal) and gives a fearless impression. In nature, animals that are brightly coloured often exude an aggressive and arrogant air – they have no need to camouflage themselves. Natural colour coding, as seen in wasps and bees, may also explain the combination of contrasting warning colours, normally arranged on the shirt in stripes of some form. This amalgamation generally gives a subconscious warning.

The second most popular colour in British football is probably blue. Although not as aggressive as red, it does exude a calming, self-assured air of confidence and loyalty. White, of course, is the colour of heroes – pure and virtuous. For away strips, yellow is another popular choice. This may just come from the fact that there are not many sides that play in yellow and it is therefore a pretty safe selection! Or it may have something to do with Brazil...

The colours that are harder to explain as shirt choices are those that are not as strong, for example pale blue or, worse, grey or even ecru! When one of the primary functions of a football kit is its clear, distinguished visibility, it is astonishing that grey goes through trends in popularity. Of course, its selection in the mid-90s did lead to one of the most incredible events in football fashion, as is explained later in the book, when Alex Ferguson famously blamed his Manchester United side's grey shirts for their poor performances.

FAUSTINO ASPRILLA CELEBRATING A GOAL
FOR NEWCASTLE UNITED, 1996

Gone are the days when the different coloured shirts were simply there to differentiate one team from the other. Of course, this is still a necessity, although even in this sophisticated age games are still occasionally played with both teams forced into wearing their change kits, or donning a training outfit, due to poor kit preparation and an unforeseen colour clash on the pitch.

The kit provides the most visible identity of a football club. After all, every minute of every match is identified and branded by the strip that is worn. As can be seen throughout the main section of this book, when a team is wearing a well-designed kit they often play better and achieve success. Also, when a new strip manufacturer arrives at a club, results can often pick up that season. The most passionate of goal celebrations is often accompanied (well it was, until it was banned by UEFA) by the ripping off of the jersey and waving it in jubilation like a flag of victory, antagonising the opposition and stirring the fervour of your own club's fans.

Modern kit manufacturing and sponsorship deals are incredibly lucrative for the clubs. Manchester United's recent 15-year deal with Nike is said to be worth an incredible £300 million. There is no doubt that these kind of contracts are vital to teams in these days of players' astronomical wages.

The fact that the contemporary football battle dress also now contains the financial benefits of additional sponsorship is a problem solely for the kit designers – not the players, not the fans. To the players it is merely a part of their uniform, good or bad, and to the fans it is an expression of their loyalty and

devotion. These extra logos are not something to be ashamed of as some older supporters claim. Often the brands become intrinsically linked with the club, especially if the relationship lasts for many seasons, although the downside of this is that supporters who have a strong dislike of a certain team have been known to boycott their sponsors' products. For example, how many Spurs fans do you see with a JVC stereo?

Many supporters see the logos as actually enhancing the shirt, adding an extra focal point and helping to pinpoint a time and a place and also to identify with the side. After all, who would happily walk around with a shirt with the logo of an insurance company or photocopier supplier proudly displayed on it unless it meant something a little extra and gave a message out to other people? It is an example of another form of allegiance – joining together with these companies and organisations in the mutual support of a team. It is a mark of authenticity of the club's, and consequently a replica shirt wearer's, place in society. It's all about belonging to a tribe, displaying your battle colours, adopting the rich and wide variety of designs your favourite team has worn, whether it's a solid and traditional home shirt or an outrageous eyeball-scorching away, showing who you follow and, by default, who you don't. It's all about belonging and showing your true colours.

Key:

H Home Kit

A Away Kit

3 Third Kit

C Centenary Kit

E European Kit

Notes on the illustrations:

When a shirt's lifespan encompasses two or more sponsorship deals, the initial sponsor's logo will appear within the main illustration. Subsequent sponsors' logos will be included in the bottom right-hand corner of the illustration box.

It has become common practice for the forthcoming season's new kit design to be premiered during the last match of the previous season. However, for simplicity I have listed only the main period of usage. Similarly, if a kit design is resurrected as an emergency measure due to an unforeseen colour clash in a subsequent season, this too has been omitted from the main period of use.

Arsenal's red and white colours were actually inherited when the club was joined by some ex-Nottingham Forest players in 1895. To save funds, the team were kitted out in the same old red strip that the players had brought with them.

The highly recognisable white sleeves arrived with Herbert Chapman's managerial reign at Highbury in 1925. Legend has it that Chapman was inspired to create the new kit by a man he spotted one day at the ground wearing a red 'tank-top' over a plain white shirt – and so the Gunners' fashion was born. Apart from a couple of years in the mid-60s, the club have favoured white sleeves ever since. Although having such a well-known kit is undoubtedly a benefit for the heritage of the club, such a distinctive style can prove problematic for modern kit designers who struggle to create new and groundbreaking designs that are still sympathetic to the club's tradition.

The early years of the club also saw the team sporting navy-blue socks, and in the mid-80s Umbro brought back navy blue to the Arsenal palette as an integral trim colour within the home kit.

The club have never opted for alternative change shorts when a colour clash occurs with their standard white pair. Instead, they are more than happy to don their away kit, with the preferred colour combination for the club being yellow and blue. It is this tried-and-tested look that reappears every few seasons, most successfully in the 03–04 Nike away kit that managed to perfectly combine the modern with the traditional. In fact, many of the club's greatest moments over the years have been while wearing yellow and blue: the incredible last-minute 3–2 victory over Man Utd in the 1979 FA Cup final; Charlie George's goal that brought the club the League/FA Cup double in 1970–71; and, of course, the dramatic 2–0 victory at Anfield that clinched the Division 1 title in 1989.

Nike arrived at Highbury in 1994, choosing the Gunners to spearhead their assault on the English football kit market, and have been responsible for some wonderful designs over the past 10 years.

As the club prepare for their final season at Highbury, they will be returning once more to the original strip design worn at the ground way back in 1913 with a new, darker red home shirt – minus, for once, the famous white sleeves.

IAN WRIGHT IN THE 96–98 NIKE HOME KIT.

A special edition of the 78–82 Umbro away jersey was produced to commemorate
the club wearing yellow and blue in three consecutive FA Cup finals.

H 1978–79 to 1981–82

Design: UMBRO
Sponsor: JVC (81–82)

Regarded by some as the definitive Arsenal
home shirt, this Umbro outfit had in fact lasted
for pretty much the entire 70s with only very
minor changes. The Umbro logo was added in
78–79, and the only other addition came with
the arrival of the club's first sponsors,
Japanese electronic giants JVC, whose logo
appeared on the shirts in 1981 and started an
extraordinary 18-year relationship with the
club, managed at the time by Terry Neill.

Worn in: The 1980 Cup Winners Cup campaign
and the FA Cup runs of the 78–79 and 79–80
seasons. Good home wins over Spurs (2–0)
and Liverpool (1–0) in the 80–81 season.
Worn by: Liam Brady, Pat Rice, Tony Woodcock,
Frank Stapleton.

A 1978–79 to 1981–82

Design: UMBRO
Sponsor: JVC (81–82)

Yellow and blue have always been favourite
away colours for Arsenal fans. A round-neck
version of this shirt had been worn since the
mid-70s (and featured in the 1978 FA Cup final
defeat to Ipswich), with the collar added in
78–79. A kit with mixed memories for fans, it
was featured in two consecutive FA Cup finals
and the 1980 European Cup Winners Cup
defeat on penalties to Valencia.

Worn in: The incredible 3–2 FA Cup final win
over Man Utd in 78–79 when the club thwarted
a Utd comeback. Also, the amazing win over
Liverpool in the epic 79–80 FA Cup semi-final
that went to three replays, followed by the 1–0
defeat to West Ham in the final.
Worn by: Alan Sunderland, Graham Rix.

H 1982–83, 1983–84

Design: UMBRO
Sponsor: JVC

To the sound of disapproving mutterings, the
white round neck was replaced after almost 20
years with a modern red V-neck design. This
shiny fabric shirt also included navy-blue
piping, with a matching trim on the shorts and
hoops on the socks – an additional colour
going way back to Chapman's Arsenal side of
the 30s, who were the first to introduce multi-
striped socks. After the excitement of recent FA
Cup finals, this was a quiet time for the club
with Don Howe now at the helm.

Worn in: Two tough defeats to Man Utd in the
82–83 cup competitions: 2–1 in the FA Cup
semi-final and 4–2 in the League Cup. Also
worn in a terrific 4–2 victory at Spurs in 83–84.
Worn by: Charlie Nicholas, David O'Leary.

A 1982–83

Design: UMBRO
Sponsor: JVC

The club's enthusiasm for change is well
demonstrated by this next choice of away
colours: green and navy blue. Umbro actually
introduced green as a change colour for
various clubs in the early 80s, but this was
never a popular outfit with the Arsenal faithful
and its services were dispensed with after only
one season. Mirroring the design of the home
shirt, the shirt featured white piping on the
shirt seams.

Worn in: A 3–1 win over West Ham towards the
end of the season – one of the few games won
in this unpopular kit, although it did make an
appearance in good draws at Man Utd,
Middlesbrough and Southampton.
Worn by: Raphael Meade, Tommy Caton.

The 85–86 versions of the both the Umbro home and away shirts were worn
with additional embroidered text marking the club's centenary.

A 1983–84 to 1985–86

Design: UMBRO
Sponsor: JVC

This paler yellow and navy kit was unveiled a season early to replace the unpopular green affair and to appease fans who were calling for a return to more traditional colours. This really nice shirt incorporated a shadow stripe design and red trim on the V-neck and cuffs. The Umbro diamond trim also made its first appearance within an Arsenal kit on the socks turnover. Also worn very occasionally with the white home shorts.

Worn in: The 6–2 win over Aston Villa with five Woodcock goals and the shock 1–0 defeat to York in the 84–85 FA Cup. Also worn at Spurs in 85–86, one of the few times Arsenal have not worn red in a North London derby.
Worn by: Brian Talbot, Paul Davis.

H 1984–85, 1985–86

Design: UMBRO
Sponsor: JVC

Umbro removed the navy blue from the club's next home shirt, but strangely persevered with it as a trim on the shorts and socks. The shirt included quite an elaborate wrap-over round neck trimmed with three red bands, along with subtle shadow pinstripes. The Umbro diamond trim was included on the socks. It was to be the last Umbro kit worn by the club. The side finished seventh in the league both seasons this kit was worn.

Worn in: Some high scoring wins over Stoke (4–0), Watford (4–3) and West Brom (4–0) in the 84–85 season. Also a tremendous 7–2 win vs Hereford in that season's FA Cup third round.
Worn by: Viv Anderson, Paul Mariner, Brian Marwood. Kenny Sansom.

H 1986–87, 1987–88

Design: ADIDAS
Sponsor: JVC

Adidas replaced Umbro as the Gunners' next kit supplier and introduced this typically 80s snug-fitting design. The shirt included adidas' famous three stripes on the white sleeves, a wrap-over V-neck and a shadow pattern of stripes and tiny versions of the club badge. Red pinstripes were added to the shorts along with an AFC monogram replacing the badge. The deal with adidas coincided with the club's rise during the 80s under George Graham.

Worn in: The 86–87 Littlewoods Cup 2–1 victory over Liverpool at Wembley with two goals by Charlie Nicholas, and the following year's unfortunate 3–2 defeat to Luton in the final of the same competition.
Worn by: Steve Williams, Martin Hayes.

A 1986–87, 1987–88

Design: ADIDAS
Sponsor: JVC

Yellow and navy remained for adidas' first away kit for the club and so popular were the colours that they were nearly always worn in away games, even if there was no serious colour clash. The design basically followed that of the home shirt, except that the sleeve colour now matched the body of the jersey. Red was used as a third colour throughout the kit – even as an outline on the JVC logo. The trefoil logo was embroidered on the socks.

Worn in: The 87–88 Littlewoods Cup semi-final first leg victory over Everton (1–0) and the 1–0 league win over Nottingham Forest at the City Ground the same season.
Worn by: Niall Quinn, Kevin Richardson.

Arsenal were not alone in wearing the bruised banana 'acid house' away kit – the RCS (Russian) national side wore a blue and white version.

H 1988–89, 1989–90

Design: ADIDAS
Sponsor: JVC

The Arsenal/George Graham rollercoaster was gathering momentum in the late 80s and reached full speed in this memorable outfit. As with most adidas kits at the time, it changed only slightly from the previous affair. The white sleeves now ran to the neck for the first time, and the cuffs were removed. Also, the overall fit of the shirt was bigger than in previous years. The kit was worn during the club's magnificent Division 1 league title success in 88–89 – their first since 1971.

Worn in: The epic 5–0 win over a high-flying Norwich in the 88–89 season. Also the 1–0 defeat to Liverpool in the following season's Charity Shield.
Worn by: Paul Merson, Tony Adams, Lee Dixon.

A 1988–89 to 1990–91

Design: ADIDAS
Sponsor: JVC

One of the most cherished of all Arsenal strips, worn that fateful night at Anfield when the club clinched the 88–89 championship with Mickey Thomas' last-minute goal. Regarded as a lucky strip, it was often worn at subsequent away games whether there was a clash or not, and was retained for a third season (90–91), which saw the club win the league title again. Like the previous away kit, it simply replicated the design of the home kit in yellow and navy.

Worn in: The incredible 2–0 victory over Liverpool that won the 88–89 Division 1 title. Also an astonishing 6–2 win at Old Trafford vs Man Utd in the 90–91 Rumbelows Cup.
Worn by: Alan Smith, Michael Thomas, Perry Groves.

H 1990–91, 1991–92

Design: ADIDAS
Sponsor: JVC

The club entered the 90s full of optimism and with a new adidas home kit. The wrap-over round neck included the AFC initials on one side, and the cuffless shirt featured an abstract two-tone shadow pattern and a new club shield that replaced the old, simpler, cannon logo. The shorts now featured large red side panels and the kit was trimmed throughout with navy blue. The first season this kit was worn saw the club win the league title again.

Worn in: The dramatic 90–91 FA Cup semi-final 3–1 defeat against Spurs at Wembley. Plus the joyous victory by the same score over Man Utd in the last match of that season, when the club were presented with the Division 1 trophy.
Worn by: Nigel Winterburn, David Rocastle.

A 1991–92, 1992–93

Design: ADIDAS
Sponsor: JVC

Arsenal's next away strip was one of the most outrageous outfits of the 90s and one often brought up in debates about unusual kits. Known among fans as the 'bruised banana' shirt, it typified the arrogance of the brash away kit designs of the time. The shirt fabric was printed with a navy zigzag fading design and topped with a shadow pattern. Also worn with change shorts of yellow, this bold kit became a major fashion must-have in early 90s London.

Worn in: A memorable 3–2 win over Nottingham Forest and a 4–0 trouncing of Southampton at the Dell (both 91–92 season).
Worn by: Anders Limpar, Kevin Campbell.

The Arsenal team have had their fair share of superstitious players over the years. Ian Wright always folded in the lapels of the first Nike home kit collar and Lee Dixon never took to the field showing the stripes on the turnover of his socks.

H 1992–93, 1993–94

Design: ADIDAS
Sponsor: JVC

The last adidas-produced home kit for the club was not one of their best, although the club did achieve Cup success wearing it. Branded with the new adidas equipment logo, the shirt, which was worn during the inaugural season of the Premier League, featured a large chunky V-neck and red and navy stripes across each white sleeve, which seemed to detract slightly from the traditional look of an Arsenal jersey.

Worn in: FA Cup final and Coca-Cola Cup final wins in 92–93 against Sheffield Wed (both 2–1), along with a 1–0 victory in the 93–94 Cup Winners Cup final vs Parma.

Worn by: David Hillier, Stephen Morrow (who broke his arm during celebrations after the Coca-Cola Cup final of 92–93).

A 1993–94

Design: ADIDAS
Sponsor: JVC

Lasting for only one season before the adidas deal ended, this new away kit was another controversial affair as some felt the modern, aggressive adidas branding overshadowed the identity of the club. It was certainly a very striking design, with three large navy-blue stripes running diagonally across the shirt before continuing in amber on the shorts. The socks also saw the return of the cannon logo on the turnover.

Worn in: Arsenal's biggest ever win in Europe: the 7–0 thrashing of Standard Liege (who, incidentally, were wearing a different coloured kit of exactly the same design) in the 93–94 European Cup Winners Cup second leg.

Worn by: Eddie McGoldrick, Ian Selley.

H 1994–95, 1995–96

Design: NIKE
Sponsor: JVC

After eight years as kit suppliers to Arsenal, adidas left Highbury to be replaced by Nike – the US company's first major football contract since the mid-80s. The kit was quite a move on from the last design, with the blue trim removed and the amount of white on the sleeves drastically reduced. The club name was also spelled out in Gothic script on the back of the shirt at the bottom, and could only be seen when the jersey was untucked.

Worn in: The devastating defeat against Real Zaragoza in the 94–95 European Cup Winners Cup (worn without the JVC logo) and the 4–0 win over Aston Villa the same season. Also the epic 1–0 victory over Man Utd in 95–96.

Worn by: David Platt, John Hartson.

A 1994–95

Design: NIKE
Sponsor: JVC

Nike's first away kit for the Gunners followed the design of the home kit but in a radical new colour scheme of navy and turquoise. Like the home kit, the socks were hooped, and a zigzag shadow pattern was included on the shirt. A vastly different shirt for Arsenal, it took fans a little while to get used to it. New manager John Hollins attempted to continue the work started by George Graham, who left the club after a financial scandal in February 95.

Worn in: The vital European Cup Winners Cup quarter-final 1–0 victory over Auxerre, with the Gunners winning 2–1 on aggregate. Also a 3–0 defeat at Anfield in 94–95.

Worn by: Steve Bould, Chris Kiwomya, Stefan Schwarz.

The 96–98 Nike home shirt was worn by Ian Wright as he beat Cliff Bastin's goal-scoring record for the club as part of yet another hat-trick in the 4–1 win over Bolton in September '97.

3 1994–95

Design: NIKE
Sponsor: JVC

Arsenal wore a third strip for the first time in the 94–95 season. The traditional yellow shirt mirrored the design of the home and away jerseys and was paired with the standard shorts and socks of the away kit. It was also trimmed with the lighter turquoise that had appeared in the club's colour range this season. It seems the kit was only worn twice during this year, with the club finishing a disappointing 12th in the Premier League.

Worn in: The 1–0 away defeat to Liverpool at Anfield in the quarter-final of the 94–95 Coca-Cola Cup.
Worn by: Glenn Helder, Andy Linighan.

A 1995–96

Design: NIKE
Sponsor: JVC

Sticking with the same two shades of blue as the previous away kit (a yellow and blue version was apparently prototyped but never worn), the new change shirt featured an astonishingly bold version of the zigzag pattern that had been a feature of the club's earlier Nike kits. A repeated shadow design of the Arsenal badge from the 30s was also incorporated. For the first time, a large Gothic 'A' replaced the badge on the shorts and socks. Bruce Rioch took over as manager.

Worn in: Wins over Middlesbrough (3–2) and West Ham (1–0), but also the 1–0 defeat at Sheffield Utd in the FA Cup third round replay.
Worn by: John Jensen, Dennis Bergkamp, Ian Wright.

H 1996–97, 1997–98

Design: NIKE
Sponsor: JVC

A golden era for the club started with Arsene Wenger's 'French Revolution' and their second League and Cup double in 97–98 – the last season in which this popular home kit was worn. The Nike logo was reduced to just the swoosh, and an intricate shadow pattern made up of the 1930s club badge adorned this really nice strip. Tiny ID tags featuring a 'Gunners' logo were sewn onto the right-hand shirt cuff and the left leg of the shorts.

Worn in: The exciting 97–98 3–2 triumph over Man Utd and two cracking 5–0 wins over Wimbledon and Barnsley. Also the 2–0 win vs Newcastle in the 97–98 FA Cup final.
Worn by: Patrick Vieira, Christopher Wreh, Emmanuel Petit.

A 1996–97

Design: NIKE
Sponsor: JVC

Lasting only one season, the next away kit simply replicated the design of the home version in yellow and navy blue. With Bruce Rioch sacked pre-season, the shirt was worn during a tumultuous time for the club due to a period of managerial unrest and personal problems for inspirational captain Tony Adams. As with the home kit, the socks followed the new simpler design introduced by Nike in the 95–96 season.

Worn in: A good 2–1 win over West Ham. Also the 2–0 FA Cup victory over Sunderland, which included a superb goal by Dennis Bergkamp.
Worn by: Martin Keown, Matthew Upson, Nelson Vivas.

A reversed version of the 97–99 away shirt (navy blue with amber trim) was designed for the club's match with RC Lens but never worn.

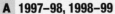
Dreamcast

A 1997–98, 1998–99

Design: NIKE
Sponsor: JVC

This amber and navy-blue ensemble was another wonderful kit for the club. Featuring a fine red trim throughout, the kit also included a series of navy-blue bands across the chest and arms. A nice touch was the addition of the cannon logo on the shorts. This was the first Arsenal shirt to feature Nike's Dri-fit™ material, designed to expel body moisture and keep the wearer cool, and was the club's away strip during their double success of 97–98.

Worn in: A 1–0 win at Old Trafford in 97–98 plus a 6–1 thrashing of Middlesbrough that included an awesome Kanu goal (98–99). Also worn in that year's 3–0 Charity Shield victory over Man Utd.
Worn by: Marc Overmars, Stephen Hughes.

H 1998–99, 1999–2000

Design: NIKE
Sponsor: JVC (98–99), DREAMCAST (99–00)

One of the longest partnerships in football came to an end in the 98–99 season with the departure of JVC, a company by now synonymous in the football world with Arsenal, and the arrival of Sega Europe as new club sponsors, who chose to display the logo of their new games machine, Dreamcast, on the club's home shirts. Although very cool looking (and feeling, due to the Dri-fit fabric), it did not bring much success to the club.

Worn in: Good 3–0 wins over Man Utd and Newcastle, along with a vital 1–0 victory over Chelsea (all 98–99). Also the 99–00 Charity Shield 2–1 win over Utd and the 99–00 UEFA Cup semi-final second leg 2–1 win over Lens.
Worn by: Nicolas Anelka, Ray Parlour.

3 1998–99

Design: NIKE
Sponsor: JVC

The team donned this dark blue strip only once in the 98–99 Champions League against RC Lens, as the French club's kit consisted of red and yellow stripes that managed to clash with both Arsenal's home and away strips at the time. The shirt was very simple in design with just a plain collar and red neck, worn with the home shorts and the alternative white home socks. Not the most memorable of jerseys, its only outing saw a poor Arsenal performance. A replica version was never produced.

Worn in: The Champions League match against RC Lens at Wembley that ended in a bitterly disappointing 1–0 defeat.
Worn by: Gilles Grimandi, Luis Boa Morte.

A 1999–2000, 2000–01

Design: NIKE
Sponsor: SEGA

Nike brought back yellow and navy blue for the next away kit, which was the first to feature the new sponsors' Sega logo. Incorporating a similar design to that of the home kit, it featured a unique V-neck with a subtle pale blue trim throughout. However, the team's results away from home in this jersey were not that impressive, although the team did get a good 1–1 draw with Barcelona wearing this shirt paired with the home white shorts and red socks.

Worn in: The 99–00 UEFA Cup final against Galatasary, which ended in defeat after a penalty shoot-out. The best league result in 99–00 was the 1–0 win at Southampton.
Worn by: Oleg Luzhny, Davor Suker, Silvinho.

Patrick Vieira's playing shirts over the last few years have seldom been seen without a liberal smearing of Vick's Vapor Rub on the chest area to aid his breathing.

H 2000–01, 2001–02

Design: NIKE
Sponsor: DREAMCAST

With its broad navy trim, this was not a million miles away from the previous home shirt. The white side panels were removed and the white sleeve continued across the shoulders to the collar instead. The club finished second in the league for the third year running in 00–01, but achieved an impressive Premier League and FA Cup double the following season wearing this strip. Memorable for a stunning Thierry Henry goal vs Man Utd in 00–01.

Worn in: A good home victory over Man Utd (3–1) in the 01–02 season plus two FA Cup finals: the demoralising 2–1 defeat to Liverpool in 00–01, followed the next season by a 2–0 win over Chelsea.

Worn by: Ashley Cole, Sol Campbell, Kanu.

3 2000–01, 2001–02

Design: NIKE
Sponsor: DREAMCAST

Another Champions League campaign called for another third strip. This new navy blue shirt, trimmed with yellow, caused some problems when first worn in October 2000 at home to Sparta Prague due to its resemblance to the Czech team's dark shirt. The second half saw the Gunners take to the field in their normal yellow away shirt. The shirt was often paired with the away blue shorts and socks, which were reversals of the yellow pairs.

Worn in: A great 4–2 victory over Sparta Prague in stage one of the 00–01 Champions League, but also a nightmare 4–1 defeat to Spartak Moscow later in the competition.

Worn by: Matthew Upson, Sylvain Wiltord, Giovanni van Bronckhorst.

A 2001–02 3 2002–03

Design: NIKE
Sponsor: SEGA (01–02), O2 (02–03)

One of the more fleeting trends in the early 00s was the penchant for metallic-coloured shirts. Arsenal's new gold away kit was an interesting design inspired by the favourite yellow and blue colour scheme. The shirt, which incorporated breathable navy-blue panels under each arm and Nike's Dri-fit fabric, was also worn as a third strip in 02–03 with new sponsor O2's logo replacing that of Sega and the addition of the new club badge. The shirt proved to be very lucky for the team as they were unbeaten in it away from home in 01–02.

Worn in: The opening 4–0 away win of 01–02 vs Middlesbrough and the classic 1–0 win at Old Trafford that clinched the title in 01–02.

Worn by: Freddie Ljungberg, Robert Pires.

H 2002–03, 2003–04

Design: NIKE
Sponsor: O2

More controversy loomed with the introduction of a newly designed crest in 2002 – a move that did not please all supporters of the club. This new home shirt shot the Gunners into the technological world of 21st century kit design with its sleek round neck and Nike's Cool Motion dual-layered fabric design. It also saw the arrival of the mobile phone company O2 as new shirt sponsors, and it was in this shirt that the club embarked on their amazing record-breaking run of 49 games without defeat.

Worn in: The 1–0 FA Cup final victory over Southampton in the 02–03 season. Also worn the following season in the 2–2 draw at Spurs that confirmed the title for the Gunners.

Worn by: Lauren, Francis Jeffers.

The Arsenal captain determines whether the team wears long-sleeved or short-sleeved shirts in a match – whichever he chooses, the entire side have to go along with.

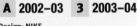

A 2002–03 3 2003–04

Design: NIKE
Sponsor: O2

This stunning kit seemed to abandon all football fashion tradition in favour of a futuristic geometric print on the front of the shirt combined with a subtle blended blue background. A striking red trim and mesh panelling on the shirt completed the outfit, which like the home version incorporated Nike's dual-layered Cool Motion fabric design for breathability and comfort. Worn as a third strip in 03–04.

Worn in: The disappointing 2–0 defeat at Old Trafford in the Premiership, but also the great victory over Utd by the same score in the FA Cup. Plus the superb 4–1 trouncing of Leeds (all 02–03 season).
Worn by: Gilberto, Jeremie Aliadiere, Edu.

A 2003–04 3 2004–05

Design: NIKE
Sponsor: O2

From one extreme to another! Nike issued this great yellow and blue retro-style away kit influenced by the Arsenal side of the 70s, even including a collar with a blue V inset. It was an ingenious blend of tradition and technology, with Nike's space-age fabric blending well with the classic design. It was very popular with the club's fans, especially as it was the kit worn during Arsenal's astonishing undefeated Premier League-winning season of 03–04.

Worn in: Two controversial matches against Manchester Utd – the 1–1 draw in the 03–04 Community Shield (with Utd winning on penalties) and the 0–0 draw at Old Trafford. Also featured in a good 2–1 win at Liverpool.
Worn by: Pascal Cygan, Gael Clichy.

H 2004–05

Design: NIKE
Sponsor: O2

For the first time, yellow was used as a third colour on an Arsenal home shirt. Although some fans weren't keen, this new colour scheme did create a very different and strong design. The jersey combined the traditional white sleeves with Nike's 'Total 90' design of contemporary breathable panels and fabrics along with a dashing asymmetrical design, creating a very intimidating kit that almost resembled a suit of armour.

Worn in: The 5–4 win at Spurs plus the 7–0 thrashing of Everton in the final home game of the season – the last match to see an Arsenal side wear red and white at Highbury. Also the narrow FA Cup final win over Man Utd.
Worn by: Jermaine Pennant, Manuel Almunia.

A 2004–05 3 2005–06

Design: NIKE
Sponsor: O2

Like the home version, this new vibrant blue shirt featured anatomically placed mesh fabric under the arms and down the sides, an asymmetrical Nike swoosh design on the left sleeve and yellow piping. It was worn in another bad-tempered battle at Old Trafford when the Gunners' unbeaten run finally came to an end. A really striking looking kit. The club finished the 04–05 season in second place.

Worn in: A storming 3–1 triumph over Man Utd in the 04–05 FA Community Shield, followed by the hard-fought 2–0 defeat against the same team that ended the Gunners' incredible 49-match unbeaten run of games.
Worn by: Jose Antonio Reyes, Mathieu Flamini, Robin Van Persie, Philippe Senderos.

To promote the commemorative redcurrant home jersey the entire Arsenal side, including manager Arsene Wenger and coaching staff, recreated the club's team photo style from 1913 – complete with flat caps!

H 2005–06

Design: NIKE
Sponsor: O2

To mark Arsenal's last season at Highbury before the move to the brand-new Emirates Stadium, the club have abandoned their familiar red body and white-sleeved shirt and adopted this stunning commemorative jersey based on the one worn by the club way back in 1913 – their first season at Highbury. Research had indicated that the first colour worn at the famous old stadium was in fact a rich dark red and it is this hue (now officially named 'redcurrant') that has been updated into a simple and stylish design for this special kit. Gold embroidered text on the shirt pays tribute to the club's famous old stadium. The shirt was teasingly revealed gradually during the first half of 2005, to much anticipation.

A 2005–06

Design: NIKE
Sponsor: O2

With the club looking to the past with the introduction of their redcurrant home shirt, their traditional yellow away kit also makes a reappearance in 05–06. Rather than being paired with royal blue as the club's previous yellow strip had been, the jersey is now accompanied by a curious shade of dark grey. The shirt design, with its arched shoulder detailing and innovative colour selection, will ensure that the Gunners are one of the best-dressed sides in the Premiership this season. As well as the move from Highbury, the 05–06 Arsenal shirts also mark the end of another era at the club as they are the last to be sponsored by O2 – the club's sponsor for the past four years.

ASTON VILLA

Aston Villa originally wore dark red and blue when they were formed in 1874 as these were the colours associated with the school the founders had attended. After a few experiments with other combinations, such as a red and light blue striped jersey (worn in 1886–87 – the year of the club's first FA Cup final triumph) and brown and light blue halved strips, the colours evolved into the regular claret and light blue. Over the next few years, this colour scheme appeared in stripes, halved shirts and hoops before settling on a primarily claret body with light blue sleeves, which has become the design most commonly linked with the club.

Another highly recognisable fashion trait in the early years was the large light-blue round neck complete with lace-ups, and it was in this design that the club achieved their Cup and League double success of 1896–97. This design was revived successfully by the club in the 40s and 50s and then later by Umbro (complete with retro lace ups) amid the post-modern football kit nostalgia fever that emerged after the Italia 90 World Cup.

The Umbro design of the early 70s, first introduced in the 74–75 Ron Saunders era and featuring highly distinctive striped cuffs and collar, was possibly one of the longest serving designs worn by any club in recent years and is regarded fondly by the Villa faithful today.

Away colours have nearly always revolved around white with claret and blue trim, although several variations in blue and amber have also been worn over the years – most famously in the FA Cup success of 1957 when the team sported a light blue shirt with thin claret stripes.

Villa fans are a traditional bunch when it comes to their team's kit. Most seem to just want the traditional claret body and light blue sleeves, but in the last 25 years they have witnessed a vast array of designs that move far away from the heritage of the club. Even white shorts are not a given, as the 80s Le Coq Sportif claret pair and the Diadora light blue pair of 2000 prove. Recent criticism has also centred around the exact shade of claret, as a distinctly pinker hue as been known to creep in. However, as long as the kits adhere firmly to the heritage of the club, as the most recent designs have, the Villa Park crowd will be happy.

TONY MORLEY IN THE UMBRO HOME STRIP OF 74–81.

A special one-off version of the 81–83 shirt with the Le Coq Sportif logo and club badge positioned on either side of the chest was worn in the 3–0 win over Barcelona in the 82–83 Super Cup.

H 1974–75 to 1980–81

Design: UMBRO
Sponsor: NONE

Give or take a few tweaks, Ron Saunders' Villa side wore this classic Umbro strip for seven seasons! Regarded fondly by fans as one of the club's best-ever designs, it had just enough individuality to make it unique – a striped claret and blue collar and broad trim down the shorts. It was produced in various fabrics over the years, including a mesh material aimed at cooling the body – a forerunner of the hi-tech fabrics that were to arrive 20 years later.

Worn in: League Cup final victories over Norwich in 74–75 and Everton in 76–77. Also worn in a marvellous 5–1 thrashing of Liverpool in the 76–77 season and, of course, the championship-winning season of 80–81.
Worn by: Andy Gray, Gordon Cowans.

A 1974–75 to 1980–81

Design: UMBRO
Sponsor: NONE

The white Umbro away kit was just as fresh and stylish as the home one, and possibly even a little better as it also featured Umbro's trademark diamond trim on the sleeves and shorts. The shorts and socks of the home and away kits were pretty much interchangeable throughout the many seasons in which they were used.

Worn in: A heartbreaking defeat to Johan Cruyff's Barcelona in the 77–78 UEFA Cup quarter-final and a tense 3–3 draw at Old Trafford in the 80–81 season. Also worn at the final game of the 80–81 season at Highbury, when the club clinched the championship.
Worn by: Dennis Mortimer, Colin Gibson, Brian Little, David Geddis.

H 1981–82, 1982–83

Design: LE COQ SPORTIF
Sponsor: DAVENPORTS (82–83)

After their long association with Umbro, Villa turned to Le Coq Sportif for their kit design as the club defended their Division 1 title. The design was radically modernised with the badge placed centrally on the shirt, extended blue panels added down each side and a stylish new V-neck replacing the old faithful wing collar. In the 82–83 season, Davenports brewery became the club's first shirt sponsor. The shirt was often worn with the claret shorts of the away kit.

Worn in: A 2–2 draw with Spurs in the 81–82 Charity Shield. Three 4–0 wins in the 82–83 season against Spurs, Coventry and Stoke.
Worn by: Kenny Swain, Allan Evans, Tony Morley.

A 1981–82, 1982–83

Design: LE COQ SPORTIF
Sponsor: DAVENPORTS (82–83)

Villa hit the 80s with a bang as Le Coq Sportif updated the white away kit. With no light blue in sight, the kit was a sleek blend of white with claret, including widely spaced pinstripes. Replicas of this shirt still sell today on the strength of its appearance (with the home white shorts) in the victorious 1982 European Cup final against Bayern Munich. The following season saw extra embroidery added beneath the club badge on both this and the home kit to mark the triumph.

Worn in: The wonderful 1–0 win over Bayern Munich in the 1982 European Cup final and an awful run of away league matches in the following 82–83 season.
Worn by: Des Bremner, Gary Shaw.

Early versions of the second Le Coq Sportif range of kits featured 'Mita Copiers' as the logo rather than just 'Mita'.

H 1983–84

Design: LE COQ SPORTIF
Sponsor: MITA COPIERS

Opinion is divided about the mid-80s Le Coq Sportif kits – some fans love them, some hate them. Their second home kit featured shadow stripes and the French company's trademark neck design. During its first season of use the shirt was worn with claret (and sometimes blue) shorts, which, bearing in mind the vastly reduced blue content of the shirt, did tend to give the outfit a rather sombre feel. Mita Copiers came in as sponsors in March 1984.

Worn in: An opening derby match-of-the-season 4–3 win over West Brom and the only league home defeat of 83–84, vs Liverpool.
Worn by: Paul Rideout, Brendan Ormsby.

A 1983–84, 1984–85

Design: LE COQ SPORTIF
Sponsor: MITA COPIERS

Amber was added to complement the claret on the next white kit. Widely spaced horizontal pinstripes combined with the extremely snug fit of the shirt certainly made for an interesting effect on the pitch. Early versions saw the Mita logo included in black. The continental look of the strip was worn with panache by Didier Six, the first foreign player to star for the Villa. The shorts, which featured shadow stripes for the first time, alternated between white and claret when a clash occurred.

Worn in: Rare away wins at Man Utd (2–1) and West Ham along with a disappointing 2–1 defeat to Liverpool (all 83–84 season).
Worn by: Peter Withe, Steve McMahon.

H 1984–85

Design: LE COQ SPORTIF
Sponsor: MITA COPIERS

Although Villa had a great run of matches in the 83–84 Le Coq home kit, it was obviously felt that the claret shorts just weren't working. So in the next season the club switched to wearing the white shorts of the away strip with the home shirt. Having said that, the kit was still sometimes worn with the previous season's change blue shorts when required. The standard Le Coq Sportif hooped socks remained the same as before, however. Graham Turner replaced Tony Barton as manager this season.

Worn in: The 3–1 win over Manchester Utd and a superb Mark Walters hat-trick in the 4–0 win over Newcastle Utd.
Worn by: Tony Dorigo, Alan Curbishley.

H 1985–86, 1986–87

Design: HENSON
Sponsor: MITA COPIERS

Goodbye Le Coq Sportif, hello Henson. This little-known Icelandic firm became the new manufacturers of the club's kit and produced quite a controversial outfit. It dispensed with the traditional blue sleeves/side panels and instead featured a horizontal blue and white striped design across the chest and down each sleeve. The badge was removed from the shirt and replaced by the club's initials. Perhaps the kit brought the club bad luck, as the team were relegated under new manager Billy McNeill in 86–87. It was a dark time for the Villa.

Worn in: A tremendous 8–1 thrashing of Exeter in the Milk Cup (85–86) but also an awful 4–1 home defeat to Arsenal (86–87).
Worn by: Martin Keown, Steve Hodge.

Hummel's infamous halved shirts were pioneered by the Danish national side, along with Coventry and Southampton in the English League.

A 1985–86, 1986–87

Design: HENSON
Sponsor: MITA COPIERS

Henson broke with the past with their away kit for the club. The amber jersey, which unlike the home version featured shadow stripes, also included a portion of the claret, light blue and white pattern from the home shirt across the chest. For both this and the home kit, a plainer pair of socks was also sometimes worn – presumably the hooped versions were a little too racy for the mid-80s! This was an interesting period kit-wise for the club, but the Henson era was to last only two seasons.

Worn in: A 4–0 defeat to Man Utd early in the 85–86 season followed by similar humiliations at West Ham (4–1) and Liverpool (3–0).
Worn by: Mark Walters, Steve Hunt.

H 1987–88, 1988–89

Design: HUMMEL
Sponsor: MITA COPIERS

Now down in Division 2, the club stuck with Scandinavian flair for their next choice of manufacturer with the appointment of Danish firm Hummel. One of the more controversial kit designs of the decade was this halved shirt ensemble. Many Villa fans were not happy with the radical approach, even though it was worn by the club as they were promoted back into Division 1 at the first attempt. The 88–89 season often saw the shirt worn with the white shorts of the away kit.

Worn in: The 1–1 draw against Coventry that was just enough to avoid relegation in 88–89. Also worn in wonderful 5–0 and 6–0 wins over Birmingham City (88–89).
Worn by: Alan McInally, Nigel Callaghan.

A 1987–88, 1988–89

Design: HUMMEL
Sponsor: MITA COPIERS

This attractive away kit followed the design of the home one in the now familiar white, light blue and claret combination. As with the home kit, the word 'Copiers' was added to the Mita logo and, for the first time, the kit supplier's logo appeared on the socks. This kit was often worn with the claret shorts from the home design. These Hummel outfits are a perfect example of 80s football culture controversially attempting to break with tradition. Graham Taylor arrived at the club in 87–88 with the task of lifting the Villa back to Division 1.

Worn in: A superb 3–2 win over Arsenal and a thrilling 3–3 draw at Middlesbrough. Best not to mention the 4–0 drubbing by Forest though!
Worn by: Kevin Gage, Derek Mountfield.

H 1989–90

Design: HUMMEL
Sponsor: MITA COPIERS

Any ill feeling the Villa faithful may have felt towards Hummel was surely gone after this wonderful effort. Returning after many years to a traditional claret body and pale blue sleeves, this was a really nice kit that was minimal in design, with the Hummel chevrons trim reduced to just a single pair on each sleeve. 'AVFC' appeared down one side of the shorts and the club badge was included on the socks. A great kit and a great team – Villa finished runners up in Division 1 this season.

Worn in: An amazing 3–0 win over Man Utd along with splendid thrashings of Everton (6–2) and Coventry (4–1).
Worn by: Kent Nielsen, Paul McGrath, Ian Ormondroyd, Stuart Gray.

The 1991 Umbro catalogue shows that the home and away designs as worn by Villa in the early 90s were officially entitled 'Aston'.

A 1989–90

Design: HUMMEL
Sponsor: MITA COPIERS

Although essentially the same design as the home kit, the away kit remained white although it was now strangely coupled with black and trimmed with purple. Unusual colour scheme aside, the only real problem with this set of strips was the tendency to mix and match the shorts of the home and away – not normally a problem with Villa kits, but in this case it just looked wrong. Both kits lasted just one season as the Hummel deal came to a conclusion.

Worn in: A tight 1–1 draw with Nottingham Forest in the opening game of the season and also a good 2–0 win over Manchester City.
Worn by: Tony Cascarino, Mark Blake, Chris Price.

H 1990–91, 1991–92

Design: UMBRO
Sponsor: MITA COPIERS

After ten years away Umbro returned to the fold at Villa Park and brought the club that staple of early 90s kits – a collar! The shirt, perhaps in response to fans' comments, maintained the traditional look but was enhanced by a subtle shadow pattern. Taylor left to manage England in 1990 and the team again began to struggle. Club hero Gordon Cowans returned once more to Villa Park.

Worn in: The first European match in England since Heysel – a 2–0 win for Villa over Inter Milan in the 90–91 UEFA Cup. A tight 3–2 win at Sheffield Wed in new manager Ron Atkinson's first league game in charge (91–92).
Worn by: David Platt, Tony Daley, Cyrille Regis (who scored on his debut at Hillsborough).

A 1990–91 to 1992–93

Design: UMBRO
Sponsor: MITA COPIERS

White and black remained the central colours of the club's next away kit, although this time it was perhaps more logically trimmed with pale blue. The shirt's subtle shadow pattern was almost identical to that worn by the England team in their Umbro kit of the time. Dr Josef Venglos became the club's new manager in 90–91, but was replaced after a poor season by Ron Atkinson.

Worn in: A 2–1 defeat to Liverpool at Anfield (91–92) and a good 1–1 draw at Old Trafford in the same season. The unlucky 3–2 defeat to Inter Milan in the 90–91 UEFA Cup second round. A great 1–0 win over Arsenal (92–93).
Worn by: Dalian Atkinson, Paul Mortimer, Ian Olney, Kevin Richardson.

3 1991–92, 1992–93

Design: UMBRO
Sponsor: MITA COPIERS

For the first time in the club's history an official third shirt was issued and it proved quite an eye-catching design. This amber shirt, trimmed with a sophisticated claret and blue collar, featured a large off-centre shadow pattern of the club badge in a typical fashion of the time. In the 92–93 season, although still regarded as a third shirt, it was worn many times, possibly even more than the standard away strip. 92–93 was a brilliant season for the revived club, who managed to finish second under Atkinson's reign.

Worn in: The 91–92 1–0 defeat at Liverpool in the FA Cup sixth round and a 2–0 defeat at Nottingham Forest later that season.
Worn by: Ray Houghton, Dean Saunders.

The 92–93 season saw a new version of the famous Umbro logo with capital letters introduced across all their kits.

ASTON VILLA

H 1992–93

Design: UMBRO
Sponsor: MITA COPIERS

With nostalgia dominating the football kit world, the team took to the field in the inaugural Premier League season in a strip unashamedly influenced by classic Villa kits from the past. The shirt included a large light blue hoop around a white lace-up neck – laces that, incidentally, were often removed by players before kick-off. A new design of club crest was also introduced, replacing the familiar round badge worn since the early 70s.

Worn in: The 5–1 win over Middlesbrough that saw the club move to the top of the League for a short period. Plus the 4–2 triumph over Liverpool – with Dean Saunders grabbing his revenge over his ex-club!
Worn by: Steve Staunton, Steve Frogatt.

H 1993–94, 1994–95

Design: ASICS
Sponsor: MÜLLER

Asics replaced Umbro as kit supplier with a short-term deal. Their home kit seemed to be inspired by the kit worn by the club in the 1957 FA Cup final victory and comprised thin blue stripes on a slightly pinker claret shirt. The jersey also featured a large button-up collar. Towards the end of the 93–94 season the dairy company Müller became club sponsor.

Worn in: The epic penalties win over Tranmere in the semi-final of the 93–94 Coca-Cola Cup followed by the triumphant 3–1 win over Man Utd in the final. Also the 1–1 draw vs Norwich that saved the club from relegation (94–95).
Worn by: Andy Townsend, Gordon Cowans.

A 1993–94, 1994–95

Design: ASICS
Sponsor: MÜLLER

The Asics away kit divided the Villa faithful and accompanied the team as they hit a slight decline in form. Some fans loved the bold red, black and green striped shirt while others loathed this strange new concoction – but at least the Müller logo didn't clash too much with this shirt. It was certainly unlike any other modern kit worn by the club. A bad run in the 94–95 season saw the departure of Ron Atkinson as manager and the arrival of ex-Villa player Brian Little as boss.

Worn in: An emphatic 2–1 win over Arsenal in the 93–94 season and a great 2–1 victory over Nottingham Forest the following season.
Worn by: Guy Whittingham, Shaun Teale, John Fashanu.

3 1994–95

Design: ASICS
Sponsor: MÜLLER

A design that did please the purists among the Villa crowd was this seldom-worn, all-white third strip introduced by Asics in the second season of their deal with the club. With the club back in European action, it was first worn in the match against Trabzonspor and was paired with the white shorts and socks of the home strip. It may have also been worn in some Premier League games, as the standard away outfit did cause some problems as it clashed with the referee's green kit.

Worn in: The 2–1 win over Trabzonspor at home in the UEFA Cup second round second leg. However, Villa still went out of the competition on away goals.
Worn by: Earl Barrett, Garry Parker.

Strangely, Aston Villa supporters have a reputation for not being as keen on wearing replica shirts as fans of some other Premiership sides.

H 1995–96, 1996–97

Design: REEBOK
Sponsor: AST COMPUTER

It was all change on the kit front in 95–96 – not only did the club now sport a kit produced by Reebok, their shirts also featured the logo of a new club sponsor, AST Computer. The shirt, which saw the return of the traditional light blue sleeves, featured a nice amber trim on the collar and a shadow stripe pattern incorporating the lion from the club's crest. It also coincided with a great renaissance 95–96 season under manager Brian Little.

Worn in: A brilliant 3–1 win over Man Utd in the opening match of 95–96 and later that season another Coca-Cola Cup final victory, this time 3–0 over Leeds with a superb Milosevic goal.
Worn by: Ian Taylor, Julian Joachim, Tommy Johnson.

A 1995–96 3 1996–97

Design: REEBOK
Sponsor: AST COMPUTER

Fans were dubious about Reebok's first away kit for the club, mainly because it fell into the old trap of being primarily a colour associated with a local rival – in this case blue and Birmingham City! The design mirrored that of the home kit, with a pale blue and claret trim, and it graced the backs of the team during some important wins away from home in 95–96. The shirt was also maintained as a third choice in the 96–97 season with the club still pushing for top spot in the top flight.

Worn in: Good wins in 95–96 against West Ham and Middlesbrough (4–1 and 3–0 respectively). Also the 95–96 FA Cup match vs Sheffield Utd with Yorke's cheeky penalty.
Worn by: Gareth Southgate, Savo Milosevic.

A 1996–97 3 1997–98

Design: REEBOK
Sponsor: AST COMPUTER

Possibly reacting to the feedback from fans, Reebok returned to tradition and introduced this fine new white away kit for the 96–97 season. It included the same shadow pattern as the previous kit and a turquoise AST logo. It was also sometimes worn with the shorts and socks from the home kit. Reebok also announced the re-signing of their deal with Villa in April '97. They would now supply the club's kit until the 99–00 season.

Worn in: The 2–0 win over West Ham and respectable draws against both Arsenal and Man Utd (96–97) plus a dreadful 3–0 loss at Anfield that season.
Worn by: Mark Draper, Dwight Yorke, Gary Charles.

H 1997–98

Design: REEBOK
Sponsor: AST COMPUTER

The next home kit resembled the team's kit from the 50s with a simple design, topped with a V-neck and a unique thin zigzag shadow pattern 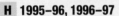 throughout the fabric. The socks were a striking design though – claret and blue hoops with white turnovers. The kit was also worn with blue change shorts. After a dreadful start, John Gregory replaced Brian Little as manager, the club eventually finishing seventh.

Worn in: A great 4–1 win over Spurs at home and an even more impressive 4–1 victory over Everton at Goodison Park (both 97–98).
Worn by: Fernando Nelson, Stan Collymore.

Aston Villa first wore stripes of matching thickness way back in 1886-87, the year of the club's first FA Cup success.

A 1997-98

Design: REEBOK
Sponsor: AST COMPUTER

Modelled by long-term Villa fan Stan Collymore when he joined the club, the new away kit was a very bold design that proved popular with fans. The shirt was primarily light blue with a large white panel at the bottom, topped with a claret band. The collar was also a unique design and included a curious wrap-over design on the neck. The trim on the white shorts (strangely the same colour as the home pair) moved from the sides to the bottom. Also worn with the blue change shorts that accompanied the equivalent home shirt.

Worn in: Some good wins away from home: 3–0 at Barnsley and 2–1 vs Southampton.
Worn by: Alan Wright, Sasa Curcic, Scott Murray.

H 1998-99

Design: REEBOK
Sponsor: LDV VANS

After only one season a new home kit appeared, along with another new sponsor – the long-term football supporters LDV Vans. This dashing kit saw another new collar design (although similar to the version on the first Reebok home shirt) combined with a new, much lighter blue. The club badge was also now housed within a new shield design. Shorts and socks returned to a much more restrained design, displayed proudly by new signing Paul Merson.

Worn in: Two storming 3–2 home wins over Tottenham and Arsenal (98–99).
Worn by: Alan Thompson, Fabio Ferraresi.

A 1998-99   3 1999-2000

Design: REEBOK
Sponsor: LDV VANS

Another blue away kit! This rather uninspired outfit was trimmed with black and white, with not a splash of claret in sight (apart from on the badge, of course). It was a standard Reebok design that was also worn in a more effective colour combination by Liverpool at the same time. The 98–99 season saw John Gregory's side finish sixth in the Premiership, causing waves of optimism for the new campaign at Villa Park.

Worn in: The storming 4–0 triumph over Middlesbrough in the 99–00 season.
Worn by: Riccardo Scimeca, Steve Watson, Colin Calderwood.

H 1999-2000

Design: REEBOK
Sponsor: LDV VANS

Reebok's last home strip for Villa really broke with tradition and was unlike any other worn in recent years by the club. Featuring a pretty basic design, the striped shirt included a simple V-neck and minimal embellishments. The Reebok and LDV logos were centralised, along with the club badge, and claret shorts and socks were reintroduced.

Worn in: A great 2–1 win at Leeds. Also the 99–00 FA Cup semi-final penalty shoot-out triumph over Bolton, followed of course by the disappointing 1–0 defeat to Chelsea in the final. Plus the incredible 4–2 win over Spurs – Villa fighting back after being 2–0 down.
Worn by: Benito Carbone, Steve Stone.

Gareth Southgate admitted in an interview at the launch of the 99–00 away kit that he never looks forward to appearing in new strip promotional photoshoots.

A 1999–2000

Design: REEBOK
Sponsor: LDV VANS

Although white is always a popular away choice for Villa fans, this away kit was something special even though it yet again shared design similarities with Liverpool's away shirt of the time. The jersey featured a large claret and blue diagonal band across the body and a compact claret and blue collar. The shorts, like the home pair, were very simple in design with just a tiny claret panel on each leg. The 99–00 season was the last sponsored by LDV Vans.

Worn in: A dismal 3–0 defeat to Manchester Utd at Old Trafford and a tense 1–1 draw at West Ham.
Worn by: George Boateng, Ugo Ehiogu, Gareth Barry.

H 2000–01

Design: DIADORA
Sponsor: NTL

New kit supplier Diadora's first strip for the club went back to the traditional claret body and blue sleeves. Again, all logos were placed centrally (including that of new sponsors, the communications company NTL). The shirt also featured white piping – flavour of the month in kit embellishment at this time. For the first time in recent years, blue shorts were worn as first choice.

Worn in: A 4–1 home thrashing of Derby County followed by a good 1–0 win over Newcastle at Villa Park in the third round of the FA Cup. Also worn in the 2–1 win vs Ipswich at Portman Road – a victory tainted by the horrific broken leg suffered by Luc Nilis.
Worn by: Lee Hendrie, Dion Dublin.

A 2000–01

Design: DIADORA
Sponsor: NTL

Not since the club's early years had they appeared in black, but the colour had proved popular with contemporary football fans since the abolishment of black referees' jerseys with the arrival of the Premier League. The shirt was nicely trimmed with claret and blue, with the badge standing out well against the dark fabric alongside the purple and green of the NTL logo. The first range of Diadora Villa kits was promoted by Gareth Barry, who had also just signed an endorsement deal with the Italian company.

Worn in: A 2–0 defeat at Old Trafford against Manchester United and a thrilling 3–3 draw with Charlton Athletic at the Valley.
Worn by: Mark Delaney, Paul Merson.

3 2000–01

Design: DIADORA
Sponsor: NTL

This season Diadora also decided to introduce a third kit, which was white with black and blue trim – a colour scheme that had appeared three times in the last 10 years. The seldom-worn strip included black panels under the arms and down the side of the shirt, along with an interesting, although slightly outdated, V-neck design. Also worn with the blue shorts from the home kit.

Worn in: A 1–1 draw with West Ham at Upton Park with an equalising goal from Lee Hendrie.
Worn by: David Ginola, Alpay Ozalan.

Paul Merson adopted the Patrick Vieira idea of smearing vapour rub on his shirt in 01–02 to assist his breathing.

ASTON VILLA

H 2001–02

Design: DIADORA
Sponsor: NTL

Another unusual shirt, this was all claret (although a pinker hue than normal) with just the merest hint of blue on the V-neck and cuffs, which were also trimmed with yellow. The baggy shorts returned to a more standard white, while the socks remained the same as the previous design. Although Villa started well this year, John Gregory left the club in January after a difficult period.

Worn in: The 2–0 defeat by Leicester that saw the end of Ginola's Villa career after being sent off, plus the end-of-season 2–1 win over Coventry with Angel's first goal for the club.
Worn by: Darius Vassell, Hassan Kachloul.

A 2001–02

Design: DIADORA
Sponsor: NTL

With the football kit world going metallic mad, Villa decided to don this silver shirt with navy-blue panels and navy and fluorescent green trim (similar in fact to Man City's away shirt at the time). It was a daring look which, when combined with the home shirt, saw a real move away from traditional Villa outfits. The silver shirt soon began to look greyer by the game, however, as a poor run of away matches saw Villa win only four of their games away from Villa Park leading to Graham Taylor returning to replace John Gregory.

Worn in: A great victory at Anfield (3–1) but losses against Arsenal, Man Utd and Blackburn as the team struggled with their away form.
Worn by: Moustapha Hadji, Juan Pablo Angel.

H 2002–03

Design: DIADORA
Sponsor: MG ROVER

Yet another shirt sponsor change saw Midlands-based car manufacturers MG Rover drive into Villa Park as part of a last-minute deal with the club. With its dependable multi-striped V-neck, this kit was clearly influenced by the classic Villa kit of the 50s. It was an extremely minimal looking kit, although really striking and popular with the fans. Points were minimal too this season, as the club struggled to 16th place in the Premiership, leading to Taylor's resignation.

Worn in: The 2–0 home defeat to Birmingham with Dion Dublin sent off during a bad-tempered and eventful match. Also a tight 3–2 win over Everton at Villa Park.
Worn by: Peter Crouch, Stefan Moore.

A 2002–03

Design: DIADORA
Sponsor: MG ROVER

MG Rover decided to split their branding over the home and away shirts – Rover on the home and MG on the away. The club's away kit reverted to white, now trimmed with an elegant light blue and black combination. Worn with blue shorts that seamlessly doubled with the home kit where necessary, the shirt featured a large collar and delicate blue piping across the chest and arms.

Worn in: The impressive 5–2 away win at Middlesbrough – the club's only away win this season – and the hard-fought 1–1 draw with Manchester Utd at Old Trafford.
Worn by: Thomas Hitzlsperger, Jlloyd Samuel, Liam Ridgewell.

True Colours   **35**

MG Rover produced a special claret and blue car in 2002 entitled the 'Aston Villa Rover 25' as a competition prize to celebrate their sponsorship deal with the club. Let's hope the winner didn't park it near St Andrew's...

H 2003–04

Design: DIADORA
Sponsor: MG ROVER

From the slightly old-fashioned to the thoroughly modern, Diadora's last home kit for the club combined all the elements that were trendy in kit design at the time: minimal round neck, reversed seams and a combination of breathable mesh fabrics. It was a really stylish design, geared for high performance, which took the club firmly into contemporary fashion while fully acknowledging the tradition of the club colours – the heart of good kit design.

Worn in: A 3–2 triumph over Chelsea at Villa Park, plus two good wins over Leicester: 3–1 at home and 5–0 away.
Worn by: Olof Mellberg, Ulises De la Cruz.

A 2003–04

Design: DIADORA
Sponsor: MG ROVER

It had been 10 years since the club last took to the field in amber. This new away kit was certainly very vivid and saw the amber trimmed not with claret and blue, but black. As in the previous season, it featured the MG logo with the Rover logo appearing on the home shirt. Dynamic, sleek black panels ran down each sleeve and underarm. After a disappointing 02–03 season, new manager David O'Leary's team consolidated and finished an impressive sixth in the Premiership.

Worn in: Two splendid 2–1 wins in the Premiership away from home at Charlton and Middlesbrough with the winning goal in the 'Boro game coming from Peter Crouch.
Worn by: Gavin McCann, Ronny Johnsen.

H 2004–05

Design: HUMMEL
Sponsor: DWS INVESTMENTS

To mixed reactions, prodigal sons Hummel reappeared at Villa Park as kit manufacturers, along with a new club sponsor, DWS Investments. The Hummel kit was not a million miles away from the previous home strip, apart from the addition of the Danish company's bold chevron trim – which you either love or hate. A new design of the trim was also included on the socks. The shirt was also worn with the light blue away shorts.

Worn in: A comprehensive 4–2 win over Newcastle and a 3–0 victory over Norwich. Also another home defeat to rivals Birmingham City – this time 2–1 (all 04–05).
Worn by: Martin Laursen, Nolberto Solano, Peter Whittingham.

A 2004–05

Design: HUMMEL
Sponsor: DWS INVESTMENTS

Memories of the 80s flooded back with Villa's next away kit – not just due to the return of Hummel, but with the introduction of a straightforward kit that simply mirrored the style of the home strip in traditional white with claret and blue trim. Whether you were in favour of the Hummel kits or not, it was good to see the club back in this more familiar colour scheme. The blue shorts were occasionally worn with the home claret and blue shirt.

Worn in: Some poor away defeats in the 04–05 season: 3–0 vs Charlton, 3–1 vs Arsenal and 3–0 vs MIddlesbrough.
Worn by: Carlton Cole, Vaclav Drobny, Thomas Sorensen.

After several years of two-colour strips, third colours were beginning to be introduced again in the mid-00s and away kit design once more closely resembled the home versions.

H 2005–06

Design: HUMMEL
Sponsor: DWS INVESTMENTS

After just one season Hummel have updated the Villa kit. Launched in May 2005 and featuring a similar slick cut to the previous design, the shirt now removes the chevron trim from the sleeves and instead runs it down each side. A new round neck has been introduced along with amber piping – the first time the colour has been worn as an integral part of a Villa home strip since the Reebok design of 95–97. A broad claret strip has also been included on each leg of the shorts along with light blue chevrons.

A 2005–06

Design: HUMMEL
Sponsor: DWS INVESTMENTS

The home kit may have only received a slight update but the away kit has been radically overhauled. For the first time the club sport a pale amber and navy blue outfit, providing a vivid change from the debonair white kit of the previous season. The strip essentially follows the design of the home – the only real difference being the inclusion of a unique and intricate collar design. Although O'Leary's men experienced a distinctly average 04–05 campaign, at least this new change strip will liven up away games during the club's next assault on the Premiership.

BIRMINGHAM CITY

Given their nickname, the traditional colour of Birmingham City will come as no surprise to all football fans. The Blues, formed in 1875 under the rather unwieldy name of Small Heath Alliance, have sported the confidence-enhancing royal blue strip through their entire football career. The nearest the side came to ditching this particular aspect of their heritage came in the mid-70s, when the famous 'penguin' strip was worn – a design with blue sleeves and sides but a broad white panel down the front of the shirt. It was a fashion that was revived briefly by Pony in 1997.

Although they have remained true to blue and white throughout their existence, the club have experimented with various colour combinations of shirts, shorts and socks. All-blue outfits have been popular and in 02–03, with the club in the Premiership for the first time, a unique blend of blue shirt, blue shorts and white socks was worn. However, blue shirts and white shorts is the combination most associated with the club.

Since the 90–91 season the club have changed both their home and away strip every year, an act that has attracted criticism from some quarters. However, they have worn some superb designs since then that have accompanied the side as they fought their way out of financial turmoil and Division 3 to become the respected Premiership side they are today.

With such regular changes of kit, it is natural that away colours have varied enormously for the club. Yellow is a recurrent theme, but the club have also occasionally sported white, silver and black in recent years. Red strips have also appeared many times, often in some important wins for the club, earning a reputation as a lucky colour for the Midlands side. The club are also famous for one of the most bizarre away strips of the past few years in the bold yellow, red and black shirt they sported in the mid-70s – a design resembling the German flag!

When the club were owned by the Kumar brothers in the early 90s, they were in the unusual position of wearing a kit produced by one of their owners' other companies (Influence Sportswear).

Now a solid Premiership side, the club will no doubt continue aiming to confound their critics by remaining in the top flight – and, of course, walk out at St Andrew's with a fresh new look every season.

MUZZY IZZET IN THE 04–05 DIADORA HOME KIT.

The now familiar Blues' club badge consisting of two globes appeared for the first time on a Blues shirt in the 76–77 season as part of a one-year kit deal with Umbro before adidas arrived at the club in 77–78.

H 1980–81, 1981–82

Design: ADIDAS
Sponsor: NONE

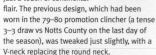

Birmingham entered the decade fresh to Division 1 and with a classic adidas kit. It was simple in style with just a touch of continental flair. The previous design, which had been worn in the 79–80 promotion clincher (a tense 3–3 draw vs Notts County on the last day of the season), was tweaked just slightly, with a V-neck replacing the round neck.

Worn in: A superb 80–81 opening day 3–1 win over Coventry, plus two well-earned draws later in the season: 1–1 vs Liverpool and 0–0 vs Man Utd. Also a good 1–0 win vs Wolves.
Worn by: Frank Worthington, Colin Todd, Archie Gemmill.

A 1980–81

Design: ADIDAS
Sponsor: NONE

Featuring the same basic design as the home kit, this yellow and blue ensemble was worn for just one season. It was based on the previous yellow shirt but, like the home kit, was updated to include a V-neck. Jim Smith's team more than held their own in their first season back in the top flight and proved very hard to beat. The shirt was occasionally worn with the change blue shorts from the home kit.

Worn in: A good 1–0 win over Manchester City at Maine Road, along with some vital draws vs Brighton (2–2), Everton (1–1) and West Brom (2–2).
Worn by: Alan Ainscow, Kevin Dillon, Mark Dennis, Joe Gallagher.

A 1981–82

Design: ADIDAS
Sponsor: NONE

A curious change in 81–82 saw the yellow and blue away strip become yellow and black. It was a turn of events that happened with several clubs at this time – yellow was such a popular change colour in the late 70s/early 80s that sometimes only the trim would change. Also, as with all adidas kits of the era, the position of their trefoil logo on the shorts would vary from leg to leg.

Worn in: An exciting 3–2 defeat to Ipswich Town in the league at Portman Road, only three days after the Blues had lost by the same score to the East Anglian side in the FA Cup. Also an entertaining 2–2 draw at West Ham.
Worn by: Pat Van den Hauwe, David Langan, Kevan Broadhurst.

H 1982–83 to 1984–85

Design: PATRICK
Sponsor: ANSELLS (84–85)

After five seasons with adidas the club switched to Patrick, one of the French sportswear designers who were making inroads into the English kit market in the early 80s. The badge was centrally placed with Patrick logos on each sleeve. Two other important changes were the introduction of red socks to the kit and the arrival of the club's first ever sponsor in the 84–85 season, local brewery Ansells.

Worn in: A classic Christmas match vs Aston Villa in 82–83 that ended in a 3–0 win for the Blues. Also a great 3–0 win over Oxford.
Worn by: Noel Blake, Mick Harford (who scored a hat-trick in the 4–0 win over Derby in the 83–84 Milk Cup second round second leg).

The second set of Patrick kits were identical in style to those worn by Southampton at the time.

A 1982–83 to 1984–85

Design: PATRICK
Sponsor: ANSELLS (84–85)

For their first away kit Patrick opted for white rather than yellow in a simple reversed version of the new shiny home kit design. It was a fine-looking strip with an imaginative use of piping and a dynamic diagonal flash on the right leg of the shorts, which were interchangeable with the white pair of the home kit. The club were relegated to Division 2 at the end of 83–84.

Worn in: A couple of great victories against Ipswich (2–1) and Leicester (3–2) in the otherwise disappointing 83–84 season.
Worn by: Wayne Mumford, Martin Kuhl, Gerry Daly, Howard Gayle.

3 1982–83

Design: PATRICK
Sponsor: NONE

When white is chosen as an away colour, it is nearly always essential to have a third strip for those matches against teams who play in a white striped shirt. For one season only Patrick issued this all-yellow outfit, which followed the same design as the home and away strips. The arrival of Patrick in 82–83 coincided with the arrival of Ron Saunders, replacing previous manager Jim Smith. Also worn with unique blue and yellow shorts.

Worn in: An unfortunate 2–0 defeat to local rivals West Bromwich Albion at the Hawthorns.
Worn by: Mick Halsall, Tony Morley, Mark McCarrick.

3 1983–84, 1984–85

Design: PATRICK
Sponsor: ANSELLS (84–85)

After just one season Birmingham replaced their yellow third strip with this all-red version, which again mirrored the design of the other kits in the range. After effectively dismantling the underachieving side of the previous season and spending 84–85 in Division 2, Ron Saunders and his team gained promotion back to the top flight at the end of the season.

Worn in: A great 2–1 win over West Bromwich Albion followed by an unfortunate defeat by the same score to QPR at Loftus Road in the 83–84 season.
Worn by: Brian Roberts, Ken Armstrong, Ray Ranson.

H 1985–86

Design: PATRICK
Sponsor: NONE

With the club back in Division 1, Patrick updated their kit with a new design featuring two-colour shoulder panels and a multi-striped V-neck and cuffs. Red was much more prominent in this range of kits than it had been in the previous design. The socks remained the same as those from the previous home kit. Also worn with the blue shorts from the away version.

Worn in: A good 1–0 opening day win over West Ham at St Andrew's followed closely by a 3–1 victory over Oxford United. Also a shocking 2–1 defeat to non-league Altrincham in the 85–86 FA Cup third round.
Worn by: Des Bremner, Andrew Kennedy, Mark Jones.

Aston Villa's controversial 86–87 Hummel kit didn't only cause problems for Birmingham; Liverpool also had to create a one-off third kit to avoid a colour clash.

A 1985–86

Design: PATRICK
Sponsor: NONE

As with the previous design, Patrick's next away kit mirrored that of the home one, with red now given prominence over blue in the trim hierarchy. The shorts from this kit were also worn with the home kit and vice versa. This away kit also made a surprise appearance in the 87–88 season at the away game at Aston Villa. Villa's Hummel half claret/half light blue shirt was felt to clash with both Blues kits at the time, so this Patrick outfit was worn instead – no doubt to the displeasure of the then official suppliers, Matchwinner.

Worn in: A 4–1 drubbing at the hands of Everton at Goodison Park and a rare 1–0 away win at Ipswich.
Worn by: Brian Roberts, Robert Hopkins.

3 1985–86

Design: PATRICK
Sponsor: NONE

This last range of Patrick kits lasted for only one season and included another all-red third strip. Featuring the same design as the home and away outfits, the only difference was the omission of stripes on the legs of the shorts. Birmingham's stay in the 1st division was short-lived, however; they had a poor season, eventually finishing 21st and being relegated yet again back to Division 2 – further enhancing their reputation as a yo-yo club. The kit also made a surprise appearance in the 86–87 season vs Portsmouth.

Worn in: A tight 3–2 victory over Bristol Rovers in the 85–86 Milk Cup.
Worn by: Nicky Platnauer, Jim Hagan, Billy Wright.

H 1986–87, 1987–88

Design: MATCHWINNER
Sponsor: CO-OP MILK (86–87)

Back in Division 2 and now with a new manager in John Bond, the Blues turned to Matchwinner to produce their new kit. It was quite a change from the previous affair. Red was ditched and a wrap-over round neck and piping were introduced, along with shadow stripes and a large horizontal white band across the chest. The club's initials were also embroidered onto the socks turnover. Co-op Milk became the shirt sponsor mid-season and cheekily included a smaller version of their logo on each sleeve.

Worn in: An astonishing 4–0 defeat away to Leeds Utd (86–87), but also a fine 4–1 win over Crystal Palace that season.
Worn by: Julian Dicks, Tommy Williamson.

A 1986–87, 1987–88

Design: MATCHWINNER
Sponsor: CO-OP MILK (86–87)

John Bond completely overhauled the team sheet in an attempt to lift the club. Things were also shaken up on the kit front with the issue of this new silver/grey away strip, which replicated the design of the home outfit. The mid-80s saw a brief fad of silver kits with many teams sporting the unusual colour as an away choice. The shirt was unsponsored in the 87–88 season, with the club now managed by Garry Pendrey.

Worn in: A series of dismal defeats in the 86–87 season. The best results were a 2–0 win over Millwall and a fine 1–0 triumph over Ipswich in the 86–87 FA Cup third round.
Worn by: Vince Overson, Steve Whitton, Tony Rees, Kevin Ashley.

Unusually, a Blues team photo session was held before the 89–90 season with the players all sporting the amber away kit.

H 1988–89, 1989–90

Design: MATCHWINNER
Sponsor: EVANS HALSHAW (88–89)
MARK ONE (89–90)

For their second home kit for the club, Matchwinner removed the white chest band and instead included two large white shoulder panels. Both the shirt and the shorts (which were still a typically 80s skimpy fit) incorporated a chequerboard shadow pattern within the material. Local car dealers Evans Halshaw became the club's new shirt sponsor.

Worn in: A rare home win in the 88–89 season, 3–2 vs Sunderland. Also worn in the away game at Barnsley in 88–89 that saw the club relegated.
Worn by: Ian Clarkson, Paul Tait, Carl Richards.

A 1988–89, 1989–90

Design: MATCHWINNER
Sponsor: EVANS HALSHAW (88–89)
MARK ONE (89–90)

The club sported a striking new amber away kit for the final two seasons of the decade. Unusually, the Evans Halshaw logo was reversed out of the shirt. The arrival of this second Matchwinner kit proved quite ironic as 88–89 was a truly awful season for the Blues, who actually won very few matches. Their slow decline continued with relegation to Division 3. The 89–90 season saw the arrival of Dave Mackay as manager and the kit sponsored by clothing retailers Mark One.

Worn in: Two defeats in 88–89 to Aston Villa that Blues fans would rather forget: 5–0 in the Littlewoods Cup and 6–0 in the Simod Cup.
Worn by: Kevin Langley, John Trewick.

H 1990–91

Design: MATCHWINNER
Sponsor: MARK ONE

Since the 1990–91 campaign, Birmingham have launched a new kit every season. The first in this sequence was perfectly in keeping with the fashion of the turn of the decade. The shirt utilised new printing techniques that allowed more complex and painterly patterns to be incorporated into the fabric. An increasingly baggy fit and an attractive old-fashioned collar completed the look. A subtle yellow band was included on the socks.

Worn in: The great 1–0 win at Brentford in the Leyland Daf Cup Area Final 2nd leg followed by the thrilling 3–2 win over Tranmere in the Wembley final.
Worn by: Trevor Aylott, Dennis Bailey.

A 1990–91   3 1991–92

Design: MATCHWINNER
Sponsor: MARK ONE

Yellow remained the colour of Matchwinner's next away kit, although it was now a much paler shade than the previous outfit. The kit, which featured an abstract marble-like print and blue piping on the shirt, was sometimes worn with the white shorts from the home kit, and also made an appearance in the 91–92 season as a third kit due to further colour clashes.

Worn in: The great 12-match unbeaten run through September and October. Also a good 1–0 win at Chester later in the 90–91 season.
Worn by: Nigel Cleghorn, Phil Robinson, Trevor Mathewson.

The club badge was rendered in colour for the first and only time on the 92–93 home and away kits.

H 1991–92

Design: INFLUENCE
Sponsor: MARK ONE

Blues owners the Kumar brothers were making quite an impact at St Andrew's: they were also behind Influence Sportswear, who were now producing the Blues kit, and club sponsors, Mark One, were customers of theirs. The shirt dispensed with a collar and brought in a simple wrap-over V-neck, as well as introducing a pattern of dynamic white flashes throughout the fabric. The shorts and socks remained the same as the previous design. 91–92 saw the club, under manager Terry Cooper, finally lift themselves out of Division 3.

Worn in: A superb 4–0 win over Exeter followed by some good wins over Luton, Preston and Stockport later in the season.
Worn by: Martin Hicks, Louie Donowa.

A 1991–92

Design: INFLUENCE
Sponsor: MARK ONE

This distinctive and flashy away kit was worn by the Blues in their promotion-winning 91–92 season. It was a bold design with large blue and yellow bands running over the right sleeve and across the front of the shirt. Unusually, however, the Influence logo did not appear on the shirt. The kit often included the white shorts from the home outfit.

Worn in: A glorious 1–0 win over local rivals West Brom at The Hawthorns and a desperately unlucky 1–1 draw at Crystal Palace in the Rumbelows Cup third round, which saw the Blues in front until four minutes from the end.
Worn by: Paul Mardon, Dean Peer, Ian Rodgerson.

H 1992–93

Design: INFLUENCE
Sponsor: TRITON SHOWERS

With the creation of the Premier League, the club found themselves in the newly renamed Division 1 at the start of the 92–93 season, accompanied by one of the most daring and controversial football kits in recent years. Known to fans as the 'paintbox' kit, Influence introduced daubs of vivid yellow and green to the now all-blue strip along with a red trim on the socks. It was certainly a bold and arrogant design that was not popular with all Blues fans at the time. Triton Showers became the club's sponsor in a new three-year deal.

Worn in: An opening day 1–0 win over Notts County; also an encouraging 2–0 home triumph over Southend Utd.
Worn by: Darren Rogers, David Rennie.

A 1992–93

Design: INFLUENCE
Sponsor: TRITON SHOWERS

In contrast to the typically busy early 90s design of the home strip, the next away kit was a much more classy and restrained effort. Minimal in design, with a unique V-neck enhanced by a nice 'Blues' graphic, it was a really nice-looking strip – although it didn't bring the club too much luck on the pitch. The 92–93 season was to prove tough for the club who, now under new ownership after the Kumar brothers' financial problems, just managed to escape relegation.

Worn in: Two dismal 4–0 defeats this season, to Portsmouth and later to Southend.
Worn by: Darran Rowbotham, Jason Beckford, Simon Sturridge.

With the collapse of the Kumars' fabric industry in March 93, the club switched mid-season to the new Admiral kit. This design was worn in the last game of the 92–93 season, which saw a 1–0 win over Charlton save the Blues from relegation.

3 1992–93

Design: INFLUENCE
Sponsor: TRITON SHOWERS

Another Influence shirt that mysteriously omitted their logo was this yellow third strip worn as the club struggled in Division 1. A really striking design, it comprised two blue bands on each sleeve, a centralised badge and the same customised V-neck as the away kit. It was worn with identical yellow socks to the 90–91 Matchwinner away kit.

Worn in: The good 2–2 draw with Newcastle Utd at St James' Park.

Worn by: John Frain, Paul Moulden, John Gayle.

H 1993–94

Design: ADMIRAL
Sponsor: TRITON SHOWERS

After the colourful extravaganza of the last Influence home kit, long-established firm Admiral arrived as the new kit suppliers. Their first home outfit reverted to basic blue and white, but embellished the sleeves with a lively white abstract design. The fabric also featured an Admiral logo shadow pattern. The shorts, which had reverted to white, also included a blue version of the sleeve pattern on one side. This kit actually made some early appearances towards the end of the 92–93 season.

Worn in: The thrilling 2–2 draw with Wolves early in the season followed by good wins over Charlton (1–0) and West Brom (2–0).

Worn by: Paul Peschisolido, Ted McMinn, George Parris.

A 1993–94

Design: ADMIRAL
Sponsor: TRITON SHOWERS

The club returned to yellow for their away colours in 93–94. It was another unconventional design with the stripes from the shirt continuing, albeit now reversed out, on the shorts. A nice touch on this otherwise quite gaudy strip was the subtle inclusion of 'Blues' on the button-down collar and the shorts. New MD Karren Brady brought in Barry Fry as manager, but the club could not improve their status in the league and were relegated to Division 2.

Worn in: A solid 2–2 draw at Leicester, but also crushing defeats at Southend's Roots Hall (3–1) and the Den against Millwall (2–1).

Worn by: Steve McGavin, Richard Dryden, Andy Saville.

H 1994–95

Design: ADMIRAL
Sponsor: TRITON SHOWERS

The club may have been back in Division 2, but they were at least determined to look good with this nice all-blue Admiral outfit. It was one of the best strips the club had worn for years, with a perfect blend of the traditional and the modern. The large collar included a shield marking the club's founding year, 1875. Inspired by this great kit the club had a superb season, finishing up as Division 2 champions and Auto Windscreen Shield winners.

Worn in: The Auto Windscreen Shield final 1–0 victory over Carlisle, Tait scoring the vital goal. Also the 7–1 thrashing of Blackpool and the 2–1 win vs Huddersfield that clinched the title.

Worn by: Steve Claridge, Scott Hiley, Dave Regis.

Perhaps inspired by events north of the border, the 95–96 Blues home kit was remarkably similar to the design worn by Rangers at about that time.

A 1994–95

Design: ADMIRAL
Sponsor: TRITON SHOWERS

It had been nearly ten years since Birmingham had last sported an all-red outfit, but Admiral decided to revive the colour with this dashing design. The kit featured many of the elements of the home strip, but combined them with a bold navy and white diagonal pattern along the bottom of the shirt. The baggy shorts were also much longer in length than previous seasons. This kit was often worn at away games by Fry's side whether there was a colour clash or not.

Worn in: The incredible 5–3 away win at Peterborough with the Blues goals scored by Bull, Dominguez and a hat-trick by Jonathan Hunt. Also a good 1–0 win over Brighton.
Worn by: Gary Poole, Liam Daish, Chris Whyte.

H 1995–96

Design: ADMIRAL
Sponsor: AUTO WINDSCREENS

The club reverted to a more traditional blue shirt/white shorts combination for the 95–96 season, which found them full of confidence and in Division 1 once again. It was quite a move on in design terms and had a more contemporary feel, including a stylish polo neck that incorporated an Admiral logotype, forming a very attractive outfit. Like the away version, the socks were hooped.

Worn in: The brilliant opening day home 3–1 win over Ipswich and a shock 2–0 win over Premiership side Middlesbrough in the Coca-Cola Cup fourth round.
Worn by: Richard Forsyth, Martin Grainger, Gary Breen, Jose Dominguez.

A 1995–96

Design: ADMIRAL
Sponsor: AUTO WINDSCREENS

Encouraged by some great results in the previous season's red strip, Admiral opted for the colour again for the club's next away design. It was another bold and innovative style with navy blue and white horizontal stripes and a shadow pattern made up of 'BCFC' and 'Blues'. A rather swish navy and white trim adorned the left leg of the shorts. Car windscreen specialists Auto Windscreens became the new shirt sponsor, replacing Triton Showers after three years.

Worn in: Some good away wins in the league: 1–0 over Portsmouth and 1–0 against Reading.
Worn by: Ken Charlery, Andy Edwards, John Cornforth, Jonathan Hunt.

3 1995–96

Design: ADMIRAL
Sponsor: AUTO WINDSCREENS

Birmingham also wore this special third strip for Cup away matches. Unique cup stripes are common on the continent, but have not been a regular feature in the English game – although some clubs have dabbled with the idea. It was an unconventional looking strip, with the black and grey striped shirt and blue shorts both embellished with the same shadow pattern as the home and away kits. The team finished the season in 15th place with Blues favourite Trevor Francis becoming the new manager in May 96.

Worn in: The disappointing 3–0 defeat to Leeds Utd in the semi-final second leg of the 95–96 Coca-Cola Cup.
Worn by: Michael Johnson, Ricky Otto.

The club produced a special 90-inch replica shirt of the 97–98 home kit for 48-stone Blues fan Barry Austin – Britain's heaviest man!

H 1996–97

Design: PONY
Sponsor: AUTO WINDSCREENS

After three years and seven kits, Birmingham switched from Admiral to American apparel company Pony. Their first kit was a clean and simple design with a distinctly 70s retro feel. Euro 96 had instigated a celebration of football shirt culture and bygone design elements were finding their way on to modern kits. This Blues shirt included a retro-influenced inset collar and a monogram club badge, last worn by the club in the mid-70s.

Worn in: The FA Cup fifth round game vs Wrexham, which saw a 10-man Blues crash out 3–1. Also worn in a 1–0 win over Crystal Palace on the opening day of the season and a great 2–0 victory over Manchester City.
Worn by: Steve Bruce, Michael Johnson.

A 1996–97

Design: PONY
Sponsor: AUTO WINDSCREENS

For the third season in a row Birmingham sported a red away strip, now in this strong, striped design. The shirt featured the same inset collar design as the home kit along with the new club badge, which was based around the club's initials. Simple black shorts and red socks completed the look. Francis' side finished 10th in Division 1 this season.

Worn in: A run of away draws: 1–1 vs QPR, Southend, Portsmouth and Ipswich. Also the Coca-Cola Cup match vs Coventry that ended in... a 1–1 draw.
Worn by: Paul Furlong, Jason Bowen, Kevin Francis.

3 1996–97

Design: PONY
Sponsor: AUTO WINDSCREENS

The club also sported this unusual new third kit in the 96–97 season. Similar in style to the away version, it incorporated a 60s-influenced round neck and centralised badges and logos. As the main colour was blue, albeit a much lighter shade than any worn by the club previously, it was felt to be a rather superfluous outfit, but nevertheless it was another nice design from Pony.

Worn in: The away game at Lou Macari's Stoke that ended in a 1–0 defeat for the (now sky) Blues.
Worn by: Matthew Jackson, Chris Holland, Barry Horne.

H 1997–98

Design: PONY
Sponsor: AUTO WINDSCREENS

Pony's retro trend continued with their next home kit, which was a throwback to the famous white and blue 'penguin' strip of the early 70s worn by Trevor Francis, who was of course now manager. It was a bold move and quite a change from the more familiar all-blue shirt. To further enhance the retro feel, it might have made sense to include the previous season's penguin badge design, but instead the club reverted to the more familiar version.

Worn in: A barnstorming 4–1 win over Stockport including a Furlong hat-trick. Plus a superb 7–1 triumph at Oxford Utd. Also the 0–0 draw vs Charlton in the last game – not quite enough for City to qualify for the play-offs.
Worn by: Jon McCarthy, Simon Charlton.

The late 90s saw a brief trend in retro-style logo trims on kits. As well as the 98–99 Le Coq Sportif design, Umbro also reintroduced their diamond trim of the 70s. Of course, some designs – like the classic adidas three-stripe trim – never really went away.

A 1997–98

Design: PONY
Sponsor: AUTO WINDSCREENS

97–98 saw yellow and black return to the Blues' wardrobe after 15 years. This stylish ensemble featured a simple wrap-over V-neck, trimmed with just a little blue, and the same textured fabric as the home strip. It was a fine-looking kit and was worn by the club in some vital away games. The Blues' league form was improving season on season and 97–98 saw them finish seventh in Division 1 – their highest position in 12 years!

Worn in: The fantastic 7–0 thrashing of Stoke that included another Furlong hat-trick. Also the last-minute 1–0 victory over Manchester City at Maine Road.
Worn by: Darren Wassall, Chris Marsden, Gary Ablett, Dele Adebola.

H 1998–99

Design: LE COQ SPORTIF
Sponsor: AUTO WINDSCREENS

After only two years with Pony, Le Coq Sportif became Birmingham's new kit supplier in 98–99. Their first home outfit abolished the 70s stylings of the previous kit and went straight for a contemporary feel, as the club aimed to better the previous season's final position. A suave shirt, it included a collar, a subtle logo trim on the sleeves, differing fabrics and a two-tone blue colour scheme.

Worn in: A thrilling 4–2 win over Bristol City and the dramatic play-off semi-final second leg vs Watford, with Blues losing in a nail-biting penalty shootout.
Worn by: Martin O'Connor, Steve Robinson.

A 1998–99

Design: LE COQ SPORTIF
Sponsor: AUTO WINDSCREENS

Le Coq Sportif's new away kit owed little to tradition, but was nevertheless a very striking outfit. The shirt featured a Le Coq Sportif logo trim, a workmanlike collar and two black vertical stripes that faded gradually as they reached the neck. Black shorts and white socks finished off this strong kit. With the club stable financially and ambitious on the pitch under Trevor Francis, it was a good time to be a Bluenose.

Worn in: A tense Worthington Cup first round second leg 1–1 draw with Millwall – enough for Blues to go through 3–1 on aggregate. Also the 4–2 defeat to Leicester in the FA Cup third round.
Worn by: Peter Ndlovu, Chris Holland.

3 1998–99, 1999–2000

Design: LE COQ SPORTIF
Sponsor: AUTO WINDSCREENS

This fine all-red third strip, complete with white button-up collar, logo trim and underarm/side panels, was actually almost identical to the strip Le Coq Sportif produced for Charlton Athletic at the same time. It was a good-looking design that saw the club reap the benefits of wearing their lucky away kit colour many times. Unlike most Blues kits of the era, this popular all-red affair lasted for two seasons and was worn many times.

Worn in: Also a 1–0 win over QPR in the 98–99 season and a superb 3–0 triumph over West Bromwich Albion the following year.
Worn by: David Holdsworth, Isaiah Rankin, Bryan Hughes, Gary Rowett.

As with many Le Coq Sportif kits at the time, their logo was split over the outfit, with the triangular marque on the shirt, and the logotype appearing on the shorts.

H 1999–2000

Design: LE COQ SPORTIF
Sponsor: AUTO WINDSCREENS

One of the most distinctive kits the club has worn in recent years was launched by Le Coq Sportif for the 99–00 season. Loosely influenced by the famous white and blue outfit that had inspired Pony a couple of seasons earlier, the shirt now featured audacious white stripes on the central area of the jersey. Blue shorts and a white round neck were introduced, as well as white side panels.

Worn in: An exciting 2–2 draw with Fulham at St Andrew's, with Stan Lazaridis equalising for the Blues with only five minutes left. Also the 5–1 thrashing of Crewe, plus the two matches with Barnsley in the play-off semi-final that ended in a 5–2 aggregate defeat for the Blues.
Worn by: Stan Lazaridis, Marcelo.

A 1999–2000

Design: LE COQ SPORTIF
Sponsor: AUTO WINDSCREENS

Another stunning kit – and one formed from simplicity itself. In an age where more and more away kits were a million miles away from the home design, Birmingham sported a straightforward red and white version of their multi-striped home kit. This was a striking look that completed an impressive set of kits this season as the Blues attempted once again to push for the Premiership – eventually finishing fifth in the table.

Worn in: A fine 1–0 win against Ipswich at Portman Road and a hard-fought 2–2 draw with Portsmouth at Fratton Park.
Worn by: Graham Hyde, Andrew Johnson, Steve Robinson.

H 2000–01

Design: LE COQ SPORTIF
Sponsor: AUTO WINDSCREENS

After the excesses of the previous season, Le Coq Sportif went for a more elegant and restrained approach for their next home kit. The design had a distinctly traditional feel with a simple white V-neck and white piping running from the sleeves. The conventional white shorts also made a return. It was a fitting outfit to accompany a strong and stylish Birmingham side in one of their best seasons to date.

Worn in: The Blues' first major cup final for 38 years: the Worthington Cup defeat to Liverpool after a penalty shoot-out. It was nevertheless a superb performance from Francis' men. Also worn in a fine 4–1 thrashing of Barnsley.
Worn by: Danny Sonner, Gary Charles.

A 2000–01

Design: LE COQ SPORTIF
Sponsor: AUTO WINDSCREENS

With optimism rife at St Andrew's, away games found the team sporting this extremely vivid, almost fluorescent yellow kit. The outfit was trimmed with navy-blue bands down each sleeve and featured a simple collar and centrally placed badges and logos. The shorts included a neat navy waistband. 2000–01 saw the end of the club's six-year relationship with Auto Windscreens.

Worn in: Good 2–1 wins over Gillingham, Nottingham Forest and Huddersfield this season, but also a shocking 3–1 defeat to Wimbledon at Selhurst Park.
Worn by: Geoff Horsfield, Nicky Eaden.

The 01–02 design was the club's second yellow away kit in a row. In recent years, teams issuing a new away kit every season have tended to ensure that the colour is different from that of the previous season, giving them an emergency third strip if required.

H 2001–02

Design: LE COQ SPORTIF
Sponsor: PHONES 4U

New sponsors Phones 4u, whose bright red logo stood out well on the blue shirt, replaced Auto Windscreens in a two-year deal. The 01–02 season saw a chunky collar featuring the Le Coq Sportif logo added to the home shirt, along with white reversed seams and black panels under the arms and down the sides. A wonderful 01–02 season saw the club, now managed by Steve Bruce after Trevor Francis' surprise departure, finally promoted to the Premiership after success in the play-offs.

Worn in: An important 2–0 win vs Sheffield Utd. Also the tense play-off final with the club beating Norwich City at the Millennium Stadium after a penalty shoot-out.
Worn by: Stern John, Paul Devlin, Jerry Gill.

A 2001–02

Design: LE COQ SPORTIF
Sponsor: PHONES 4U

The confusion at St Andrew's was quite understandable when City revealed another bright yellow, very baggy away kit. New sponsors Phones 4u had previously sponsored Watford, whose last kit was, at first glance, very similar to the Blues' new away outfit. The shirt featured a new style collar and neck ensemble and, like the home kit, the shorts were in Le Coq Sportif's new lightweight athletic style.

Worn in: A dreadful 3–1 defeat to Wimbledon on the opening day of the season, but also of course the superb 1–0 win over Millwall at the Den in the second leg of the play-off semi-final.
Worn by: Tommy Mooney, Darren Carter, Curtis Woodhouse.

H 2002–03

Design: LE COQ SPORTIF
Sponsor: PHONES 4U

With Steve Bruce's men in the Premiership, the club opted for a radical overhaul to the kit. The home outfit now comprised a blue shirt and shorts and white socks, à la Chelsea. It was an intimidating and relentlessly stylish shirt, with no white trim other than minimal piping and a strong combination throughout of three shades of blue. It was a good season in the top flight, with the club eventually finishing 13th.

Worn in: Glorious double victories over local rivals Aston Villa: a bad-tempered 2–0 win at Villa Park and 3–0 at St Andrew's. Plus a superb 2–1 win at home to Liverpool. It wasn't all good though – there was also a dreadful 2–0 defeat to Manchester City.
Worn by: Christophe Dugarry, Robbie Savage.

A 2002–03

Design: LE COQ SPORTIF
Sponsor: PHONES 4U

If the club went for an intimidating look with their first choice kit, they certainly hammered their point home with the away strip! For the first time, Birmingham sported a dark and mysterious all-black kit. Following a similar design to the home kit, including a slick V-neck, it showed the Premiership that the club meant business. An elegant blue trim completed the look.

Worn in: 1–1 draws at Everton and Blackburn, a 3–0 defeat to Chelsea at Stamford Bridge and a 1–0 loss to Manchester City. This little black number was not a lucky shirt for the club!
Worn by: Matthew Upson, Martin Grainger, Aliou Cisse, Clinton Morrison.

Diadora also included their striking two-colour curved panel trim on kits for West Bromwich Albion, Crystal Palace, Sunderland and Leeds in the 04–05 season.

H 2003–04

Design: LE COQ SPORTIF
Sponsor: FLYBE.COM

It was back to traditional blue shirts, white shorts and blue socks for 03–04, which saw Steve Bruce's Birmingham consolidate their position in the Premiership with a final position of 10th. The last home shirt to be produced by Le Coq Sportif was a flamboyant effort, with curved white trim from each shoulder down to the sides of the shirt. A slightly clumsy-looking collar with a large white neck was also introduced.

Worn in: A good 1–0 win over Spurs in the first home game of the season and a great 3–0 victory over Everton later in the season.
Worn by: David Dunn, Jamie Clapham.

A 2003–04

Design: LE COQ SPORTIF
Sponsor: FLYBE.COM

Le Coq Sportif's last away kit exactly mirrored the style of the home strip but in yellow trimmed with blue. As with the home shirt, a neat shadow stripe pattern was incorporated into the front panel. Both kits were also worn with blue change shorts when necessary. Low-cost airline Flybe.com replaced Phones 4u as the new shirt sponsor. The club started superbly this season and managed to finish the campaign in 10th position.

Worn in: A 2–0 win over Leicester and a respectable 0–0 draw at Stamford Bridge against Chelsea.
Worn by: Stephen Clemence, Darren Purse, Christophe Grondin, Mikael Forssell.

H 2004–05

Design: DIADORA
Sponsor: FLYBE.COM

After six years and numerous wonderful kits, Le Coq Sportif departed St Andrew's. They were replaced by Italian company Diadora (previously known for their footwear), whose designs several top clubs were wearing this season. It was another good strip that included a simple slick collar (complete with Diadora's trademark asymmetrical two-colour bands) and breathable mesh panels for comfort.

Worn in: Two great victories over Liverpool (and revenge for Heskey!): 1–0 at Anfield and 2–0 at St Andrew's. Also a great 4–0 thrashing of West Brom and a 2–1 triumph over the Villa.
Worn by: Emile Heskey, Dwight Yorke.

A 2004–05

Design: DIADORA
Sponsor: FLYBE.COM

With simpler, more functional away strips back in vogue, Diadora opted for a basic 'lucky' red version of their excellent home design. Unlike the last time the side had worn red (the Le Coq Sportif third strip of 98–00), the kit also included a distinguished black trim as a counterpoint to the white. As with the home kit, the Flybe.com logo was amended slightly this season, which saw the side finish the campaign in 12th position.

Worn in: A 1–1 draw vs Portsmouth and a thrilling 3–3 draw at Blackburn Rovers. Also an unfortunate 2–0 defeat to Chelsea. Perhaps not such a lucky colour after all!
Worn by: Mario Melchiot, Jesper Gronkjaer, Kenny Cunningham, Muzzy Izzet.

The new Lonsdale kit arrived at City's training ground for the launch via helicopter, personally couriered by Club President David Gold.

H 2005–06

Design: LONSDALE
Sponsor: FLYBE.COM

As was the case a little further north at Sunderland, City parted company with Diadora after just one season and signed a new kit deal with English firm Lonsdale. With the biggest revamp seen to a Birmingham kit in a number of years, Lonsdale have introduced this smart new strip including one of their standard neck designs (as also worn by Sunderland) and curved white panels that dominate each sleeve, creating a vastly different look for the side. For the first time since the early 80s adidas kit, the team will also sport white shorts and socks.

A 2005–06

Design: LONSDALE
Sponsor: FLYBE.COM

The 05–06 season will bring a relatively rare sight for Blues fans watching the side play away from home – their team playing in all white, as for the first time since the Le Coq Sportif away kit of 1999–2000 (which incidentally also featured a healthy dose of red) white has been selected as the Blues' change colour. A relatively simple design, the shirt features red panels under each arm and down each side, accompanied by red piping. The club badge has been embroidered in red, although the Flybe.com logo switches to blue, creating a welcome contrast to the rest of the shirt. Unusually, this new kit includes the same colour shorts and socks as the home outfit.

BLACKBURN ROVERS

Once upon a time the league was full of halved shirts: Newton Heath (aka Man Utd) favoured green and yellow, Liverpool opted for blue and white and Bolton wore red and white, to name but three. However, only one club has retained this early example of football kit fashion for over 125 years and that club is, of course, Blackburn Rovers.

Rovers were formed in 1874 and, aside from some early all-blue or quartered outfits, the club's blue and white halved shirts have become one of the most recognisable in the Football League. However, early days saw the use of a much lighter blue, a style that was revived in the late 80s to a lukewarm response – although, apart from the Jack Walker/Kenny Dalglish era in the 90s, spearheaded by Alan Shearer and accompanied by a stylish Asics outfit, the lighter blue saw halcyon days for the club.

Soon enough, though, the blue darkened in shade, and the only difference from then on was in the style of collar or the colouring of the sleeves; although the halved shirts have been consistent throughout, whether or not the sleeves match their respective half of the shirt is often up for debate with kit designers.

Umbro introduced red into the kit as a third colour in the 70s with a V-neck and cuffs alongside a trim on the shorts and socks and, apart from a few seasons here and there, the colour has been a refreshing addition to the Blackburn palette ever since. Favoured away kits normally fall into the red and black colour scheme, although for a while the club did turn out in an all-yellow outfit.

The club's long relationship with Spall in the 80s was quite extraordinary in that both the home and away kits barely changed over a seven-year period. Clearly, having such a distinctive kit can prove problematic to designers desperate to keep the style fresh, but despite this handicap Rovers are also no stranger to innovation. At the turn of the new millennium, Italian company Kappa solved the quandary of breathing new life into the traditional outfit by decking Rovers out in their latest lightweight, skin-tight jerseys designed for optimum performance on the field. 2004 saw Rovers attired in a brilliant new kit (including a switch to blue shorts) from famous sportswear firm Lonsdale – their first major professional football strip contract.

Despite mixed fortunes in recent years on the pitch, there can be no doubt that Blackburn have benefited by firmly establishing such a distinguished playing kit style.

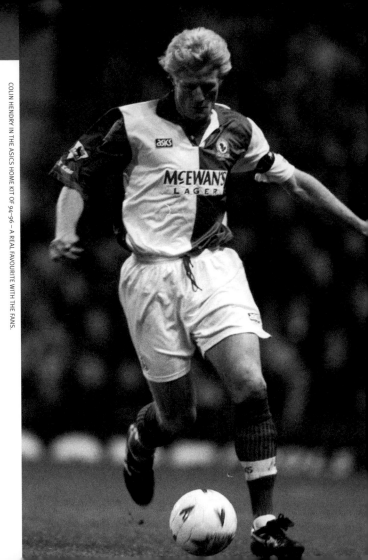

COLIN HENDRY IN THE ASICS HOME KIT OF 94–96 – A REAL FAVOURITE WITH THE FANS.

Until the mid-80s, most Umbro shorts only included the diamond element of the Umbro logo, omitting the company's name.

H 1978–79 to 1980–81

Design: UMBRO
Sponsor: NONE

Rovers entered the 80s in Division 2 having been promoted in the 79–80 season under player-manager Howard Kendall. The following season almost saw them achieve promotion two years running. The club's kit was produced by Umbro, with the only change to the previous design being the addition of a red V-neck. The Umbro diamond trim appeared only on the shorts, in a rare two-colour version.

Worn in: A shock 1–0 triumph over Division 1 Coventry in the 79–80 FA Cup. Also a superb 3–0 win over Newcastle (80–81).
Worn by: Simon Garner, Noel Brotherston, Duncan McKenzie, Derek Fazackerley.

A 1978–79 to 1980–81

Design: UMBRO
Sponsor: NONE

Umbro's away kit for the club was in the favoured red and black combination. The shirt, with its matching V-neck and cuffs, was quite a unique design, let down only by its clumsy addition of the club badge within a large white oval. As with the home kit, the classic Umbro trim appeared on the shorts and now also on the red socks. Although the club did also play all in yellow in the late 70s, red and black were reinstated as away colours as they were felt to have been lucky in the 79–80 season!

Worn in: The 2–1 win at Bury at the end of the 79–80 season that confirmed the club's promotion to Division 2. Also a storming 2–1 victory away to Cardiff early in 80–81.
Worn by: Roger De Vries, Mick Speight.

H 1981–82 to 1983–84

Design: SPALL
Sponsor: NONE

With a kit so steeped in tradition it is difficult to come up with original designs that are still true to the heritage of the club. In 1981 the club signed a deal with Spall to produce their kit and for the next seven years the design remained virtually the same, with just minor amendments made here and there. In fact, the first Spall strip was almost identical to the last design. Bobby Saxton was now manager and led the team up to sixth in Division 2 in 83–84.

Worn in: An impressive 4–1 win vs Newcastle in 81–82. Also a 5–1 mauling of Derby County in 83–84, with all five goals coming from Simon Garner.
Worn by: Kevin Stonehouse, David Mail, Norman Bell, Mark Patterson.

A 1981–82 to 1983–84

Design: SPALL
Sponsor: NONE

Spall abandoned the lucky red and black colour scheme and instead opted for an all-yellow kit trimmed with blue, featuring the most fashionable of early 80s trends: pinstripes. The 70s, and to some extent the 80s, were the years of the yellow away kit as many teams opted for the colour as their change strip. As with the home version, this outfit was to change only subtly over the next few years.

Worn in: A good 3–0 win over Oldham Athletic in 81–82 and a controversial 2–2 draw vs QPR at Loftus Road the following season. Also a horrendous 6–0 humiliation at the hands of Manchester City in 83–84.
Worn by: Jim Branagan, John Lowey.

Spall also produced kits for Wimbledon and Wolverhampton Wanderers in the 1980s.

3 1981–82 to 1983–84

Design: SPALL
Sponsor: NONE

A real rarity! Possibly worn only once or twice, this all-red kit dates from the early 80s and shows the club in a Spall-manufactured version of the fans' favourite away colour shirt. What is curious about the kit is the fact that the shirt is paired with red Umbro shorts. Loyalty and exclusivity to a specific brand in the early 80s was not what it is today.

Worn by: Marshall Burke, Glen Keeley, Colin Randall.

H 1984–85, 1985–86

Design: SPALL
Sponsor: ICI PERSPEX

By the mid-80s shirt sponsorship was commonplace and very few clubs were without an additional company logo on the front of their jersey. It must have come as no surprise to the Ewood faithful when the Blackburn shirt succumbed to this modern invention midway into 84–85. The club's first sponsors were the chemical giants ICI, who chose to promote their famous Perspex on the shirt.

Worn in: A 4–0 thrashing of Carlisle in 84–85. Also the memorable 3–2 victory over Nottingham Forest in the 85–86 FA Cup third round replay and the 3–1 win over Grimsby in the last game of that season, which saved the club from relegation.

Worn by: David Hamilton, Jimmy Quinn.

A 1984–85, 1985–86

Design: SPALL
Sponsor: ICI PERSPEX

As with the home kit, the 84–85 season saw ICI Perspex become the team shirt sponsor. It was the start of a relationship that was to last seven years. As with the home shirt, early versions of the logo were contained within a blue panel. Later in the season the more familiar variation of the logo appeared on the shirts. After a few good seasons, 85–86 saw a dip in form and the club finished a lowly 19th in Division 2.

Worn in: A great 2–0 win at Birmingham in the 84–85 season, but some awful away defeats in 85–86: 3–1 to Brighton, 5–0 to Wimbledon and 3–0 to Portsmouth.

Worn by: Simon Barker, Mick Rathbone, Ian Miller.

H 1986–87

Design: SPALL
Sponsor: ICI PERSPEX

The 86–87 season only saw minor changes to the Rovers kit but a major change in managers, with Don Mackay replacing Bobby Saxton at Christmas 1986. The Spall logo was updated to a new red version, shadow pinstripes were added to the shorts and the socks switched to a distinctly lighter blue than before. The rest of the kit design remained exactly as it had done for the past few seasons.

Worn in: A great 6–0 thrashing of Sunderland in the 86–87 season, plus a rare Wembley outing later that year in the 86–87 Full Members Cup final against Charlton Athletic. The game ended in a great 1–0 win for the Rovers with a goal by Colin Hendry.

Worn by: Alan Ainscow, Chris Thompson.

Blackburn sponsors ICI worked closely with sportswear giants Umbro in the late 80s to create Tactel, a futuristic fabric designed to transport moisture away from the skin – a forerunner of today's hi-tech materials.

A 1986–87

Design: SPALL
Sponsor: ICI PERSPEX

This slightly remodelled version of the away kit was worn for just one season. As with the home kit, the Spall logo was updated and shadow pinstripes added to the shorts. The socks remained as before. The club finished 12th this season, after being bottom of the table at one point earlier in the campaign.

Worn in: A poor series of away matches, the only real successes of note in this shirt being the 2–1 win over Huddersfield and the tight 1–0 win over West Brom late in the season.
Worn by: Chris Sulley, Sean Curry, Chris Price.

H 1987–88

Design: SPALL
Sponsor: ICI PERSPEX

Spall's last home kit for the club once again featured only very few changes to the previous design. Red cuffs were added to the shirt and a small BRFC monogram included on the shorts left-hand leg, with the Spall logo moving to the right. Otherwise, the kit was identical to the one worn by the club in 86–87. Long-sleeved versions of the shirts included an additional Spall logo on each arm. On the pitch the club's momentum under Mackay continued and they finished the season in 5th place.

Worn in: A superb 3–2 victory over Aston Villa along with some vital wins over Millwall (2–1), Sheffield Utd (4–1) and Manchester City (2–1) as the club pressed for promotion.
Worn by: John Millar, Ally Dawson.

A 1987–88

Design: SPALL
Sponsor: ICI PERSPEX

Considering that there had hardly been any change in style over the years since Spall began manufacturing the Rovers' kit, and bearing in mind that there was only a year left of their deal with the club, it was curious that Spall decided to make their first major alterations to the Blackburn shirt for the 87–88 season. Gone were the pinstripes and in came classy diagonal shadow stripes, which were very much in vogue at the time. The shorts and socks remained the same except for the addition of the club's initials on the shorts.

Worn in: Another vital 1–0 win over West Brom and a brilliant 4–1 triumph at Millwall that ensured Rovers reached the play-offs.
Worn by: Steve Archibald, Ossie Ardiles.

H 1988–89, 1989–90

Design: ELLGREN
Sponsor: ICI PERSPEX

After seven seasons at Ewood Park, Spall moved on and local sportswear company Ellgren, who produced a few other English football strips but mainly manufactured rugby apparel, took over the kit production. The red cuffs were retained and a diagonal shadow pattern incorporated into the shirt fabric. The shorts included a blue and red side flash and the Ellgren logo replaced that of Spall.

Worn in: A classic 5–4 win over Crystal Palace (88–89) and the sad 2–1 defeat in the play-off semi-final second leg vs Swindon (89–90).
Worn by: Andy Kennedy, Howard Gayle, Keith Hill.

BLACKBURN ROVERS

The lighter shade of blue selected by Ribero in 90–91 was actually much closer in shade to the club's original home kit design than the royal blue most fans have become accustomed to.

A 1988–89, 1989–90

Design: ELLGREN
Sponsor: ICI PERSPEX

Ellgren remained true to the 80s penchant for yellow Rovers away kits. Their change strip design incorporated the same shadow pattern as the home strip and introduced a thick blue trim to the shorts and a blue turnover on the socks. The 89–90 season saw the club's Lancashire rose badge replaced by the now familiar club crest on both the home and away kits.

Worn in: A great 2–1 opening day win over Chelsea at Stamford Bridge in 88–89 – the only game won in the league that year in this strip.
Worn by: Tony Finnigan, Ronnie Hildersley, Mark Atkins.

H 1990–91

Design: RIBERO
Sponsor: ICI PERSPEX

Rovers started the 90s with a new kit supplier, Ribero, who introduced a new larger fitting shirt that now included an old-fashioned button-up collar. Gone were the modernist, minimal V-necks of the 80s as the early part of the 90s saw a trend for all things retro as far as football kit design was concerned. Ribero's switch to a much lighter blue did not go down too well with the club's fans, who preferred the more familiar shade. Also, a blue left sleeve was introduced for the first time, effectively dividing the entire shirt into distinct halves.

Worn in: A solid 4–1 thrashing of Leicester and an impressive 3–2 win over Wolves. Also a good 1–0 win over Middlesbrough (90–91).
Worn by: Kevin Moran, Frank Stapleton.

A 1990–91

Design: RIBERO
Sponsor: ICI PERSPEX

The 90–91 season saw Don MacKay's team in freefall following the disappointment of missing out on promotion the season before. The first Ribero away kit retained the cut of the home version, but in the now conventional all-yellow colour scheme. As with the home kit, the shorts included neat triangular blue panels on each leg and the Ribero logo on the socks. A delicate shadow pattern was also included on the shirt and shorts.

Worn in: A good 3–1 win at Leicester, but also several poor defeats in the league with the club going down 3–2 to Portsmouth and 2–1 to Ipswich early in the season.
Worn by: Lee Richardson, Lenny Johnrose, Philip Starbuck, Jason Wilcox.

H 1991–92

Design: RIBERO
Sponsor: McEWANS LAGER

Ribero hoped for a change of fortune with this new kit, which revived a slightly darker shade of blue and discarded red. Contrasting sleeves and a halved collar were also

introduced. The poor 90–91 season led to the departure of Mackay and set the scene for a Rovers renaissance with Jack Walker and Kenny Dalglish's arrival leading the club to promotion.

Worn in: The brilliant comeback vs Derby in the play-off semi-final first leg: from 2–0 down, Rovers eventually won 4–2. Also Dalglish's first match in charge, a 5–2 win vs Plymouth Argyle.
Worn by: David Speedie (who scored a hat-trick in the 3–1 win over Newcastle).

McEwan's Lager, produced by The Scottish and Newcastle Brewery, also sponsored Newcastle United and Notts County at about the same time as their deal with Blackburn.

A 1991–92

Design: RIBERO
Sponsor: McEWAN'S LAGER

Rovers remained in yellow for their wonderful 91–92 season. With its much baggier fit, the shirt was similar in design to the home one, except for some additional trim on the collar and piping running from the collar to under the arm. McEwan's Lager were introduced as new shirt sponsors following the end of the ICI deal.

Worn in: The nerve-wracking play-off semi-final second leg against Derby, with Rovers holding on to win the second match 2–1 and progress to the final, in which they beat Leicester 1–0 in a joyous afternoon, also in this strip.
Worn by: Scott Sellars, Mike Newell (who scored the decisive goal at Wembley vs Leicester in the play-off final).

H 1992–93, 1993–94

Design: ASICS
Sponsor: McEWAN'S LAGER

Blackburn were back in the top flight for the first time since the mid-60s and were also part of the first Premier League. To accompany them

was a new kit deal with Asics, who were making big inroads into the football apparel market at the time. It was a confident-looking strip, which matched the ambitions of the club. Red was incorporated on the trim. 92–93 saw the McEwan's Lager logo placed on the shirt without a white background.

Worn in: Alan Shearer's goal-scoring debut – the 3–3 draw vs Crystal Palace – plus the great 7–1 thrashing of Norwich (both 92–93).
Worn by: David Batty, Kevin Gallacher.

A 1992–93, 1993–94

Design: ASICS
Sponsor: McEWAN'S LAGER

For the first time in ten years, a now high-scoring Rovers side were back in red and black with this traditional-looking strip from Asics. Featuring the larger fit of shirt and longer shorts of the home kit, it was a solid design that pleased the many fans who were keen to see the revival of the familiar away colour scheme. The shirt incorporated the same collar design as the home jersey, along with an intricate shadow pattern. The shorts simply followed Asics' standard design of the time.

Worn in: A 2–1 triumph over Chelsea on the opening day of the 93–94 season followed by a 2–0 win over Manchester City and a wonderful 3–0 victory at Everton later in the season.
Worn by: Alan Wright, David May.

3 1992–93

Design: ASICS
Sponsor: McEWAN'S LAGER

Asics introduced a seldom-worn third strip for the 92–93 season. Simple in design, it saw a return to yellow and blue and matched the style of the home and away kits, with just a little extra yellow trim on the collar. The fabric incorporated a faint paint-splattered effect, similar to a style featured on the Newcastle Utd away kit at the time. The 92–93 season saw Rovers have a brilliant start to the club's Premier League life, and they eventually finished fourth in the table.

Worn in: The superb 1–0 win vs Arsenal at Highbury.
Worn by: Richard Brown, Tim Sherwood, Stuart Ripley.

BLACKBURN ROVERS

3 1993–94, 1994–95

Design: ASICS
Sponsor: McEWAN'S LAGER

As the marketing of official replica third strips increased in the early 90s, many sides began introducing alternative away colours. Asics replaced the stop-gap all-yellow strip of the previous season with this dynamic yellow and black affair. Improvements all round on last season, not only in the design of the third kit but also in the Premier League, where the club finished second.

Worn in: The unfortunate 1–0 defeat to Tottenham in the Coca-Cola Cup.
Worn by: Gordon Cowans, Roy Wegerle.

H 1994–95, 1995–96

Design: ASICS
Sponsor: McEWAN'S LAGER

This must be one of the most memorable of all Rovers shirts, primarily because it was worn during the magnificent 94–95 Premier-League winning season. Asics had done a good job in updating the previous design, adding a new ribbed collar with a red inset panel and the club motto 'Arte et Labore' on each sleeve – a nice touch.

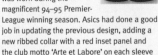

Worn in: The 2–0 defeat to Man Utd in the 94–95 Charity Shield. Also the exciting climax to that season, with Rovers losing 2–1 to Liverpool but still clinching the championship.
Worn by: Chris Sutton (who scored his first goal for the club in the 3–0 win over Leicester).

A 1994–95

Design: ASICS
Sponsor: McEWAN'S LAGER

Since arriving in the Premier League, Blackburn had been pushing for the title every season, accompanied by some marvellous Asics kits. Premier League referees had now ditched their traditional outfits, leaving teams free to wear black for the first time – and Rovers did so with this slick-looking design complete with thin red stripes and woven red collar. The shorts, now much longer in length than in previous years, featured minimal trim.

Worn in: A 2–1 victory at Chelsea early in the season, followed by a convincing 3–0 win over Ipswich Town. Also the 2–2 draw at Trelleborgs that saw the Rovers crashing out of Europe.
Worn by: Paul Warhurst, Ian Pearce, Robbie Slater.

A 1995–96

Design: ASICS
Sponsor: McEWAN'S LAGER

One of the best away kits worn by the club was this red and black outfit used in the 95–96 season. A large shadow design marking the previous season's championship triumph was incorporated onto the front of the shirt, with the shorts and socks pretty much reversals of the previous season's away kit. With Ray Harford now in control as manager, the 95–96 season saw the club's form drop away, and they could only manage seventh place.

Worn in: The Champions League match at Spartak Moscow that included a bizarre fight between Rovers team-mates David Batty and Graeme Le Saux. Also a shocking 5–0 defeat away to Coventry.
Worn by: Garry Flitcroft, Martin Dahlin.

Despite manufacturing some superb kits throughout the early 90s, Asics withdrew from the English football strip market towards the end of the decade and switched their main focus back to sports footwear.

H 1996–97, 1997–98

Design: ASICS
Sponsor: CIS INSURANCE

With Shearer gone, the heart of the team seemed to disappear and the side suffered a disappointing season. The new home kit

was a much plainer affair than that of the previous two designs, with no red trim and a simple button-up 'grandad' neck. The socks also switched to white rather than blue. New sponsors CIS Insurance replaced McEwan's.

Worn in: The 4–1 win over Sheffield Wed that guaranteed Rover's top flight survival in 96–97. Also an amazing 3–1 win vs Arsenal the following season and a superb 4–0 away win at Aston Villa with a hat-trick by Gallacher.
Worn by: Stephane Henchoz, Lars Bohinen.

A 1996–97

Design: ASICS
Sponsor: CIS INSURANCE

After the success of all the Asics away kits to date, Blackburn fans were a bit taken aback by this new yellow and navy away design. It featured a rather cluttered pattern based on abstract renderings of the club badge on the left sleeve and down the right-hand side. With the team in decline this season, this arrogant-looking shirt did not manage to boost the confidence of the players and, after a poor start to the campaign, Ray Harford resigned.

Worn in: The great 2–0 win over Everton at Goodison Park – Rovers' only league away win this season. Also appeared in two 1–1 draws, at Chelsea and Leicester.
Worn by: Billy McKinlay, Jeff Kenna.

A 1997–98

Design: ASICS
Sponsor: CIS INSURANCE

Another unusual away design, but one with real character and style. The shirt was orange with a simple shadow stripe pattern and a silver-coloured collar. As with a majority of designs at this time, away strips gave the designers a chance to let their hair down a bit after the rigidity of following tradition for the home version. This vivid outfit coincided with a revival in the club's fortunes under new manager Roy Hodgson.

Worn in: The 1–0 victory away to Wimbledon and a brilliant 1–0 win over Chelsea at Stamford Bridge. Also a good 3–0 win over Sheffield Wednesday in the FA Cup fourth round.
Worn by: Gary Croft, Chris Coleman.

H 1998–99, 1999–2000

Design: UHLSPORT
Sponsor: CIS INSURANCE

After six eventful years Rovers and Asics parted company and Uhlsport, a company known in the UK mainly for their goalkeeping equipment, became the new kit supplier. Their arrival coincided with a further downturn in the club's fortunes, which culminated in relegation and the eventual sacking of Roy Hodgson. The new kit seemed a little over-complicated, with intricate elements of trim throughout. All logos were placed centrally on the shirt.

Worn in: The 99–00 FA Cup fourth round shock win over Liverpool at Anfield. A great 3–1 win at Aston Villa (98–99) and the 0–0 draw vs Man Utd that relegated the club in that season.
Worn by: Kevin Davies, Damien Duff, Christian Dailly.

A 1998–99, 1999–2000

Design: UHLSPORT
Sponsor: CIS INSURANCE

Yellow and blue returned as the club's away colours, but that was about as far as tradition went with this bold new design. The shirt featured blue vertical stripes reaching down from the right shoulder and up from the left-hand side. The shirt and shorts featured a complex shadow stripe pattern incorporating the Uhlsport logo. Brian Kidd replaced Roy Hodgson as manager, but unfortunately arrived too late to stop the club from being relegated. After spending six years in the top flight, Rovers were back in Division 1.

Worn in: Plenty of draws for the club away from home in 98–99, vs Chelsea, Wimbledon, Leicester and Coventry.
Worn by: Darren Peacock, Sebastien Perez.

3 1999–2000

Design: UHLSPORT
Sponsor: CIS INSURANCE

This stunning limited edition away shirt was produced by Uhlsport to commemorate 125 years of Blackburn Rovers and, although it didn't conform with convention, it was arguably their best design for the club. The purple design with red diagonal band was quite unlike anything previously worn by the team. Events on the pitch were not going the club's way, and Brian Kidd was sacked mid-season to be replaced (eventually) by Graeme Souness. With the club unsettled, they could only manage 12th position in their first season back in Division 1.

Worn in: An unlucky 3–2 defeat at Huddersfield.
Worn by: Nathan Blake, Marlon Broomes, Jason McAteer.

H 2000–01, 2001–02

Design: KAPPA
Sponsor: TIME COMPUTERS

With Souness at the helm, in came Kappa with their own unique brand of continental cool – the Kombat 1. It was a great-looking kit and one of the most forward-thinking and contemporary designs the club have ever worn. Simple but effective, it had an intriguing round collar, navy panels on each side of the shirt and navy trim on the shorts.

Worn in: The superb 2–1 Worthington Cup final triumph over Spurs in the 01–02 season. Worn with black armbands vs Norwich following the news of the sad death of Jack Walker in August 2000.
Worn by: Stig Bjornebye, Mark Hughes.

A 2000–01 3 2001–02

Design: KAPPA
Sponsor: TIME COMPUTERS

Rovers returned to red and black as they battled for promotion back from Division 1. The kit had essentially the same design as the home strip, with stripes added to the body, and the shirt was made of the same quick-drying fabric. A simple but effective kit, it accompanied the club in some vital promotion/relegation matches in the two seasons it was worn. Computer company Time became the club's new sponsor.

Worn in: The 1–0 win at Preston that confirmed the club's promotion back to the Premiership in the 00–01 season. Also the 2–1 win at Everton the following season that virtually guaranteed the Rovers safety from relegation.
Worn by: Henning Berg, Tugay, Craig Short.

Shirt-pulling had become commonplace in world football by the early part of the 21st century. One of the reasons Kappa created their skin-tight Kombat range was to try to thwart this problem.

A 2001–02

Design: KAPPA
Sponsor: TIME COMPUTERS

Rovers were back in the Premiership! Considering the club's home colours are blue and white, it was unusual to select one of those (albeit in a much darker shade) to form the primary colour of their away strip. Still, it gave the team plenty of opportunities to wear the nice red and black striped kit from the previous season as well. The shirt, which was trimmed with sleek white piping, was also occasionally worn with the home kit's white shorts.

Worn in: Poor defeats at Derby County (2–1) and Leeds United (3–1).
Worn by: Keith Gillespie, Andy Cole, Craig Hignett.

H 2002–03, 2003–04

Design: KAPPA
Sponsor: AMD PROCESSORS (02–03)
HSA (03–04)

After two seasons Time moved on and another computer company, AMD Processors, became shirt sponsors. This second Kappa kit was even cooler than their first and brought bold flashes of red back into the strip. Designed for additional comfort, reversed seams were also incorporated on each sleeve.

Worn in: The club's UEFA cup exploits of 02–03, most notably the unfortunate 3–0 defeat to Celtic in the eagerly anticipated tie. Also a great 2–0 win over Arsenal the same season.
Worn by: David Dunn, Brett Emerton, Egil Ostenstad.

A 2002–03

Design: KAPPA
Sponsor: AMD PROCESSORS

Another excellent Kappa kit was this new red and black away strip. It featured essentially the same stitching patterns and design of the home kit with white visible seams and black underarm panels. Like the home kit, the shorts incorporated a unique fold-over fabric design on each leg. All Kappa Kombat series kits were produced from skin-tight and stretchable Lycra for optimum performance – and to prevent shirt tugging! 02–03 saw the club finish sixth in the Premiership – a glorious return to form.

Worn in: A triumphant 2–1 win over Chelsea and the superlative 4–0 victory at Tottenham, which guaranteed European football for the club the following season.
Worn by: Lucas Neill, Martin Taylor.

A 2003–04

Design: KAPPA
Sponsor: HSA

After one season in red, yellow – or more correctly a vibrant amber – became the new change colour. It featured an updated version of the intimidating Kombat design that was also worn at the time by Spurs. Private health insurance company HSA became the new shirt sponsor and replaced AMD after just one season. A nice touch was the inclusion of the club's initials, BRFC, on the back of the neck. Hooped socks and smart black shorts completed the kit.

Worn in: The brilliant 4–3 away win vs Fulham and a 2–1 result at Portsmouth early in the season.
Worn by: Matt Jansen, Craig Short, Lorenzo Amoruso.

Although already a long-established sportswear brand, the 05–06 season sees Lonsdale beginning to make inroads into football apparel with kits for Premiership clubs Sunderland and Birmingham City as well as Blackburn.

E 2003-04

Design: KAPPA
Sponsor: HSA

The early part of the 00s saw several teams releasing new versions of their home kit colours specially designed for European competitions. Obviously hoping to imitate Umbro's unique European kit success for Manchester Utd a few seasons earlier, many of the other teams unfortunately fell at the first hurdle, Blackburn included. The kit design followed the style of the 03–04 skin-tight away kit. The club badge was placed centrally with a Kappa logo on each sleeve.

Worn in: The two matches against Genclerbirligi, a dismal 3–1 defeat away from home followed by 1–1 at home, which was not enough to see Rovers go through.
Worn by: Dino Baggio, James McEveley.

H 2004–05

Design: LONSDALE
Sponsor: HSA

Overweight Rovers fans could breathe out again at last! After four years with Kappa, the club turned to Lonsdale (famous for their classic boxing sportswear) to produce their new outfit – the company's first kit deal with a major club. The home version was quite a change from any the club had worn in recent years. It featured a new, slightly lighter, shade of blue, a body-mapped sleeve design, separate underarm panels and an elegant use of red piping. The biggest change was the introduction of blue shorts rather than white.

Worn in: The 3–0 defeat to Arsenal in the FA Cup semi-final at The Millennium Stadium.
Worn by: Paul Dickov, Dominic Matteo, Javier de Pedro, Barry Ferguson.

A 2004–05

Design: LONSDALE
Sponsor: HSA

Lonsdale's first away kit was another real classic, moving back to the favoured red and black. With a similar basic design to that of the home kit, it featured a red body with black sleeves and stylish white underarm panels. Other changes this season were the introduction of a new version of the HSA logo and, more importantly, Mark Hughes, who replaced the outgoing manager Souness. It was a tough season for the club, but at least they wore a couple of superb-looking kits to see them through it.

Worn in: A controversial 1–0 win at Portsmouth, a 2–0 triumph at Fulham and a 1–0 result at Bolton – good shirt, good results.
Worn by: Martin Andresen, Jonathan Stead.

H 2005–06

Design: LONSDALE
Sponsor: LONSDALE

Unveiled to the Blackburn fans after the introduction of the new black away kit, the 05–06 home design sees Mark Hughes' Rovers revert

to a more traditional colour combination of royal blue and white. The more familiar white shorts have also made a comeback. Other than the change of shade, the design of the shirt differs only slightly from the previous outfit. A new standard Lonsdale neck design has been introduced along with two dynamic red flashes on each sleeve. The club's two-year relationship with HSA ended at the close of the 04–05 season and kit suppliers Lonsdale have now also taken over as main shirt sponsors.

A 2005–06

Design: LONSDALE
Sponsor: LONSDALE

After the great kits Lonsdale produced for the
Rovers the previous season, 05–06 sees the
company go one step further with a stunning
design for the club's next away outfit,
modelled by Robbie Savage in pre-season
promotional photos. Quite unlike any other kit
around, the mean and menacing all-black affair
is offset with blue piping and a highly
distinctive large curved silver panel around the
neck. With Lonsdale's famous logo proudly
displayed on the shirt at a larger size as part of
their new deal as shirt sponsor, the company
can be assured of maximum impact from this
revolutionary new design.

BOLTON WANDERERS

Bolton's long involvement with football is rivalled only by their long association with white shirts and navy blue shorts. However, the club's early years saw the team turn out in red shirts, red and white quarters and even a white shirt with large red spots in the 1884–85 season – dispelling the myth that outrageously gaudy kits are a purely modern invention!

Originally formed as a local church team in 1874 (which perhaps goes some way towards explaining their pure white shirts), the club have worn their famous colours since the 1890s. Occasionally, the side have sported an all-white kit, as reintroduced in the 03–04 season, but the late 60s and early 70s also saw the team ditch the navy shorts for the heroic Real Madrid look.

Possibly in acknowledgement of their origins, red often crops up on Bolton's strips. In fact, for a long period from the mid-80s to the late 90s it was included as a third colour on their home kit and also formed the basis for numerous away kits, but it seems that pale blue is a favourite away colour among Trotters fans – red of course being the colour of a certain nearby team that play at Old Trafford!

Recent years have seen the club form a solid bond with local sportswear company Reebok, culminating in the sponsoring and naming of their new ground in 1997. Reebok have produced the kit since 93–94, but in fact appeared as a shirt sponsor three years before that as part of a wonderful set of Matchwinner kits that were streets ahead of their time in design terms. This range of outfits really bucked the contemporary trend for garishly printed, eye-watering kits. Instead, the Trotters turned out in debonair plain white shirts with an old-fashioned blue collar, the club badge placed over the heart as expected and restrained Matchwinner logos on the left sleeve. Even the confident and swish away kit in a fine navy and white check pattern incorporated sophisticated design.

In acknowledgement of their heritage, the 2002–03 season saw the club sporting a one-off kit based on an early outfit to celebrate their 125th anniversary.

Secure in the Premiership under Sam Allardyce, the club's current standing must be a relief to Bolton fans who, despite their club's bright white shirts, remember the dark days of the 80s when the club were a regular fixture in the old Division 3.

JASON McATEER IN THE REEBOK HOME KIT USED FROM 93–95.

Green has never been a popular colour in the English game and is often considered to be unlucky. The only Football League side who regularly play in green home shirts is Plymouth Argyle.

H 1977–78 to 1980–81

Design: UMBRO
Sponsor: KNIGHT SECURITY (80–81)

Umbro commanded a large percentage of the football kit market in the late 70s and early 80s and most featured their famous diamond trim, including this Bolton home shirt. The shirt was slightly unusual in that the collar and cuffs were not contrasting but matched the colour of the shirt, which was also worn with the white shorts of the away kit to create a dazzling all-white strip. Local firm Knight Security became the club's first ever shirt sponsor in 80–81. This season saw Stan Anderson managing the club, who were now mid-table in the old Division 2.

Worn in: A 4–0 thrashing of Newcastle, a 6–1 demolition of Cambridge and the thrilling 3–3 draw with Forest in the FA Cup (80–81).
Worn by: Neil Whatmore, Brian Kidd.

A 1977–78 to 1980–81

Design: UMBRO
Sponsor: KNIGHT SECURITY (80–81)

As with most kits of the time, the away design featured the same styling as the home but in a different colour scheme. Red is a long-established Bolton away colour and, like the home outfit, this shirt also featured matching collar and cuffs. Never a particularly lucky shirt for the club, it was worn during many defeats in the 80–81 season.

Worn in: The epic 2–2 draw with Spurs in the 77–78 FA Cup third round. Also the storming 3–1 win over QPR at Loftus Road the following year. Plus thrilling away draws in 79–80: 2–2 at Leeds and 4–4 at West Bromwich Albion.
Worn by: Phil Wilson, Gerry McElhinney, Mike Graham, Ian Brennan.

H 1981–82

Design: UMBRO
Sponsor: BOLTON EVENING NEWS

Bolton obviously felt a little out of date with their wing-collared shirt, so for the 81–82 season they made a tiny tweak to their home strip and replaced the collar with a tidy V-neck. Knight Security were replaced as sponsors by Bolton Evening News, who bizarrely decided to include their acronym 'BEN' on the shirts – much to the bewilderment of anyone outside the Bolton area! The upgrades to the shirt made little difference to the club's form as they continued to struggle in Division 2, narrowly avoiding relegation.

Worn in: Good league wins over Barnsley (2–1), Charlton (2–0) and Wrexham (2–0), plus a solid 3–1 victory over Derby in the FA Cup.
Worn by: Jeff Chandler, Alan Gowling.

A 1981–82

Design: UMBRO
Sponsor: BOLTON EVENING NEWS

Umbro attempted to start a trend for green shirts in the early 80s, with both Bolton and Arsenal sporting this slightly unorthodox strip colour. However, this kit was never popular with fans and did not seem to last long in the club's dressing rooms. This simple design essentially mirrored that of the amended home shirt, with matching V-neck and cuffs and the Umbro diamond trim. Also worn with the navy shorts from the home kit if required.

Worn in: A superb 2–0 away win at Derby County, but also defeats against Orient, Luton and Crystal Palace.
Worn by: Len Cantello, Peter Reid, Dave Hoggan.

H 1982–83 to 1984–85

Design: UMBRO
Sponsor: TSB (82–83) HB ELECTRONICS (83–85)

After just one season Umbro updated the club's kit design again, but this time it was a more comprehensive overhaul. However, it was not enough to stop the side being relegated to Division 3. The V-neck remained, but was now in a contrasting navy blue with two white stripes. Blue piping ran from the collar to under the arm. The Trustees' Savings Bank (TSB) became the club's new shirt sponsor in 82–83, before being replaced by local company HB Electronics the following season.

Worn in: A superb 3–1 win over Newcastle at Burnden Park (82–83) and the incredible 8–1 thrashing of Walsall the following season, in which Tony Caldwell scored five times.
Worn by: Steve Whitworth, Mike Doyle.

A 1982–83 to 1984–85

Design: UMBRO
Sponsor: TSB (82–83) HB ELECTRONICS (83–85)

With the club fighting for survival in Division 2 in 82–83, the mysterious green kit was replaced after only one season by this nice red outfit, which followed the same design as the home shirt. The kit was sometimes worn with the home strip's navy shorts. As with the home shirt, HB Electronics became the sponsor in the 83–84 season.

Worn in: A battling draw with Blackburn (82–83) and a crushing 4–0 defeat to Fulham early in the same season. Also, a nightmare 6–1 away defeat to Notts County in the third round of the 84–85 Milk Cup.
Worn by: Simon Rudge, Wayne Foster, John McGovern (player-manager).

H 1985–86 to 1987–88

Design: UMBRO
Sponsor: HB ELECTRONICS (85–86)
NORMID SUPERSTORES (86–88)

Bolton's next home kit was actually very similar to that of the previous design. A subtle white pinstripe was added to the fabric, and the stripes on the V-neck and cuffs were now red in an attempt to add some flair to the two-colour kit. The shorts and socks remained the same as in previous seasons. HB Electronics' three-year deal ended and Normid Superstores became the new sponsor as the side slumped.

Worn in: The 85–86 Freight Rover Cup 3–0 defeat to Bristol City, plus the two-leg play-off loss to Aldershot that saw the side fall to Division 4 in 86–87. Also the promotion-clinching 1–0 win over Wrexham (87–88).
Worn by: George Oghani, Warren Joyce.

A 1985–86 to 1987–88

Design: UMBRO
Sponsor: HB ELECTRONICS (85–86)
NORMID SUPERSTORES (86–88)

The club's long-term relationship with Umbro was due to come to an end and the last away kit the company produced for the club was in a refreshing pale blue. It was in the same design as the home kit, now trimmed with white. This era saw the team boosted by the arrival of Asa Hartford and new manager Phil Neal, who attempted to lift the struggling club to past glories.

Worn in: A 3–1 victory over Swansea in the 85–86 season and possibly the best win for the club in that year's campaign – a 4–2 away win over Fulham at Craven Cottage.
Worn by: Tony Caldwell, Dave Sutton, Steve Thompson, Robbie Savage.

With the advent of baggier fitting shirts towards the end of the 80s, cuffs disappeared from many clubs' jerseys – Bolton's 90–93 strip being a rare exception.

H 1988–89, 1989–90

Design: MATCHWINNER
Sponsor: NORMID SUPERSTORES

Newly promoted back to Division 3, Bolton took to the field in probably their boldest set of kits up to that point. They were produced by smaller sportswear firm Matchwinner and featured a chequerboard shadow pattern on both the shirt and shorts. Dynamic flashes of navy and red ran from collar to seam and on the left leg of the shorts. The home kit was also worn with the white shorts from the away version.

Worn in: The glorious 4–1 win over Torquay in the 88–89 Sherpa Van Trophy final at Wembley, plus great wins over Birmingham (3–1) and Reading (3–0) the following season.
Worn by: Mark Winstanley, Paul Comstive, Trevor Morgan.

A 1988–89, 1989–90

Design: MATCHWINNER
Sponsor: NORMID SUPERSTORES

As with all Trotters kits up to this point, the away design mirrored that of the home. The shirt returned to red and was paired with either white or red shadow-patterned shorts. Optimism returned to Burnden Park in the 89–90 season that saw Neal's Bolton finish sixth in the division.

Worn in: A 2–2 draw with Fulham and an amazing 3–1 victory over Tranmere in the 89–90 season. Also worn in the well-earned 0–0 draw at Swansea that saw the club reach the play-offs that season.
Worn by: Dean Crombie, David Reeves, Stuart Storer.

H 1990–91 to 1992–93

Design: MATCHWINNER
Sponsor: REEBOK

With local sportswear company Reebok on Bolton's doorstep, it was surely only a matter of time before they became involved with the club, and they finally became Bolton's new shirt sponsors in 90–91. This was quite possibly one of the best shirts the club has ever worn – cool, classy and understated. It was a design that really stood out amid the gaudy fashions that were common at the time. Also worn with the white shorts of the away kit.

Worn in: Goals galore at Burndean in 92–93: 4–0 vs Burnley and 5–0 against Bradford. Also a hard-fought 2–2 draw vs Liverpool in the FA Cup and the defeat to Tranmere in the 90–91 play-off final at Wembley.
Worn by: Alan Stubbs, Andy Walker.

A 1990–91 to 1992–93

Design: MATCHWINNER
Sponsor: REEBOK

The second series of Matchwinner kits saw the club maintain the same design for three seasons. Matchwinner were striving to be different – not only did they favour minimalism in a time of football kit excess, they also confidently included their logo on the left sleeve of the shirt only and issued this away kit in a fine fabric printed with a tiny navy and white chequerboard pattern – giving the appearance at a distance of a pale blue. Bruce Rioch and Colin Todd become joint managers.

Worn in: A superb 4–1 win over Fulham (92–93) with goals by Lee, Stubbs and Walker.
Worn by: Jason McAteer, Tony Kelly, Phil Brown, John McGinlay.

To have the same company producing a club's kit and being the main shirt sponsor at the same time is relatively rare. Leeds with Admiral in the early 90s and later Derby with Puma are two examples.

3 1990–91 to 1992–93

Design: MATCHWINNER
Sponsor: REEBOK

Having the innovative blue chequerboard shirt as the away strip was bound to cause some colour-clash problems, so the club issued this all-yellow third kit to alleviate the problem. It followed the same design as the home and away kits, including the blue collar and the Matchwinner logo on the sleeve. The 92–93 season saw the formation of the Premier League, so therefore the Trotters now found themselves in Division 2. The club finished second that season after a wonderful year and were promoted to Division 1.

Worn in: A 1–1 draw vs Fulham at Craven Cottage (91–92).
Worn by: Mark Seagraves, Mark Patterson, David Lee.

H 1993–94, 1994–95

Design: REEBOK
Sponsor: REEBOK

Three years after becoming Bolton's sponsor, Reebok began producing their kit as well – the company's first venture into the football strip world. The shirt, by now much baggier than previous designs, contained a diagonal shadow stripe pattern, a centralised badge and large navy and red bands on each sleeve. Unique white shorts were also produced for the first time. Reebok's arrival as supplier coincided with a great era for The Trotters.

Worn in: FA Cup shock victories over Arsenal, Aston Villa and Everton (93–94). The 94–95 season saw the club defeated 2–1 in the Coca-Cola Cup final by Liverpool, but victorious over Reading by 4–3 in the Division 1 play-off final.
Worn by: Jimmy Phillips, Scott Green.

A 1993–94   3 1994–95

Design: REEBOK
Sponsor: REEBOK

The first Reebok away kit included the same shorts and socks as the home – an unusual state of affairs. Of course, the alternative white versions of both – also worn with the home kit – were available, but it was a strange choice nonetheless. The kit was worn as a third choice in the 94–95 promotion season. The 93–94 campaign was a triumph for John McGinlay, who scored over 30 goals for Bolton.

Worn in: A 2–0 win over Luton Town at Kenilworth Road – the only decent result while wearing this shirt in the 93–94 season.
Worn by: Owen Coyle, Alan Kernaghan.

3 1993–94

Design: REEBOK
Sponsor: REEBOK

A seldom-worn yellow third strip was also produced by Reebok in their first season as kit suppliers. It featured exactly the same collar as the home and away kits and also utilised the diagonal shadow pattern. The club had a great run in the FA Cup this season, but could only manage 14th place in Division 1.

Worn in: The 0–0 draw away to Portsmouth at Fratton Park.
Worn by: Robert Fleck, Alan Thompson.

The 95–97 Reebok home kit accompanied the team in their first season in the Premiership culminating in relegation later that year, followed by a storming 96–97 campaign that saw them clinch the Division 1 title.

A 1994–95 3 1995–96

Design: REEBOK
Sponsor: REEBOK

After two yellow third kits in a row, the club again selected the colour (albeit in a slightly richer hue) as their preferred away kit colour for the 94–95 season. With a strange stitched neck/collar ensemble unlike any other worn at the time and pairs of pinstripes, it was certainly a unique design, and accompanied the club as they reached the top flight for the first time since 1980 following a superb season in Division 1. Rioch left the club to become manager of Arsenal at the end of 95–96.

Worn in: The superb 3–0 win over Ipswich at Portman Road in the 94–95 Coca-Cola Cup. Also an unfortunate 1–0 defeat to Manchester City the following season.
Worn by: Richard Sneekes, Sasa Curcic.

H 1995–96, 1996–97

Design: REEBOK
Sponsor: REEBOK

The Premiership new boys took to the field in a new kit. On initial inspection the strip was not vastly different from the previous outfit. Gone were the bands of colour on each sleeve, replaced by simple blue cuffs and navy piping.

Worn in: Fine victories over Arsenal (1–0) and Blackburn (2–1) in the Premiership. Also the 1–0 defeat to Southampton that brought relegation in 95–96. In 96–97 it was worn as Bolton humiliated Spurs 6–1 in the Coca-Cola Cup fourth round, beat QPR 2–1 to win the Division 1 title and thrashed Charlton 4–1 in the last ever game at Burnden Park.
Worn by: Neil McDonald, Mixu Paatelainen.

A 1995–96 3 1996–97

Design: REEBOK
Sponsor: REEBOK

Another unique colour combination for the club, pale blue and navy blue, emerged with their new away kit. However, the design itself was not unique – a virtually identical kit was worn by Aston Villa at the same time. Neat red piping was added to the shadow-striped shirt and shorts. The club never adjusted to life in the Premiership under new manager Roy McFarland in 95–96 and, after being anchored near the foot of the table for much of the season, were finally relegated.

Worn in: A fight-back 2–2 draw with Spurs after falling two goals behind and an unlucky 1–0 defeat to Southampton at The Dell.
Worn by: Scott Sellars, Gerry Taggart, Nathan Blake, Gudni Bergsson.

A 1996–97

Design: REEBOK
Sponsor: REEBOK

With the club now back in Division 1 and under Colin Todd's control, Reebok provided them with another unorthodox away kit. It was

an old-fashioned looking outfit, all dark green with red and white trim (including really nice detailing on the button-up collar). The badge moved to the left-hand side of the shirt and a large version of the full Reebok logo advertised the company as both shirt sponsor and shirt manufacturer. The kit was also worn with its own unique pair of white shorts.

Worn in: A thrilling 2–2 draw with Tranmere Rovers in the last game of the 96–97 season.
Worn by: Jamie Pollock, Chris Fairclough.

The 99–00 season saw squad numbers introduced on the players' shorts for the first time.

H 1997–98, 1998–99

Design: REEBOK
Sponsor: REEBOK

After the retro look of the previous season's away kit, Bolton were brought bang up to date with a stunning new home design. They also had a new home in the Reebok Stadium and were back in the Premiership. A sleek, round-neck collar with navy triangle detail, curved navy side panels with red piping and very long shorts were the main features of this kit.

Worn in: The 2–0 defeat to Chelsea (97–98) that saw the club relegated. Back in Division 1, the 98–99 play-offs saw the kit worn in the semi-final victory over Ipswich and the sad 2–0 defeat to Watford in the final.
Worn by: Peter Beardsley, Mike Whitlow.

A 1997–98

Design: REEBOK
Sponsor: REEBOK

Obviously determined to make an impact on their return to the Premiership, the Trotters' new away kit was a bold purple ensemble. Worn with either purple or white shorts (trimmed with red), the shirt featured the Reebok logo within a large oval on the front with a smaller logo on the left sleeve. Purple was not lucky for the club and they were relegated this season after a 2–0 defeat to Chelsea.

Worn in: A string of defeats: 5–0 to Sheffield Wed, 3–1 to Blackburn, 1–0 to Spurs and 4–0 to Derby in the 97–98 season. The club didn't hit much of a purple patch in this kit.
Worn by: Dean Holdsworth, Franz Carr.

A 1998–99   3 1999–2000

Design: REEBOK
Sponsor: REEBOK

Yet again the Trotters were back in Division 1. They had a pretty good season though, finishing sixth and qualifying for the play-offs. The new away kit saw a return to yellow, now trimmed with navy and white in an identical style to the away kit worn by Liverpool at the time. As in the previous season, the badge was centralised and accompanied by the Reebok logo. Also worn as an emergency third kit vs Stockport in the 2000–01 season.

Worn in: A 2–0 defeat to QPR and a 2–1 defeat to Bury. Also worn in the 2000–01 season in a thrilling 4–3 defeat to Stockport, Bolton coming back from three goals down only to lose in the final seconds.
Worn by: Gudni Bergsson, Nicky Spooner.

H 1999–2000, 2000–01

Design: REEBOK
Sponsor: REEBOK

The club sported a bold and attractive new design for the 99–00 season. A wrap-over V-neck replaced the previous design's round neck, and the shirt also included a large blue band running across the shoulders and ending in a smaller red panel. The shirt was made from a horizontal-weave fabric and was worn during the promotion-winning 00–01 season.

Worn in: The 99–00 FA Cup semi-final penalty shoot-out disappointment vs Aston Villa, along with the 2–2 draw with Ipswich in the 99–00 play-off final followed by a 5–3 loss at Portman Road. Plus an impressive 2–0 win over Portsmouth the following year.
Worn by: John O'Kane, Franck Passi, Robbie Elliott.

Last-minute call-up Djibril Diawara had to borrow the replica shirt of Bolton fan Lee Houghton when the club realised that they hadn't brought his shirt for the match at Arsenal in the 01–02 season.

A 1999–2000

Design: REEBOK
Sponsor: REEBOK

For the first time in four seasons the club turned out in a blue kit, this time in a particularly rich shade. It was a confident outfit with a navy and white diagonal flash across the front of the shirt – an identical style to that worn by both Liverpool and Aston Villa at the time. The shirt also included the full Reebok logo. With Sam Allardyce becoming club manager, the side finished sixth in Division 1 for the second year running.

Worn in: An awful 3–0 defeat to Tranmere in the 99–00 Worthington Cup, but a good 2–1 win over Derby earlier in the tournament. Also a goal-fest 4–4 draw at West Bromwich Albion.
Worn by: Bo Hansen, Ricardo Gardner.

A 2000–01

Design: REEBOK
Sponsor: REEBOK

For the third season running, the design for the club's away kit was identical to that worn by Liverpool at the time – a fact that did not please some fans of the club. Reebok retained blue as the main colour, although it was now a lighter shade, and added navy panels under the arms and down the sides. Worn with navy or light blue shorts, it was a popular kit that was worn many times in the 00–01 season as Sam Allardyce's team raced up the Division 1 table.

Worn in: The memorable 3–0 win over Preston in the 00–01 Division 1 play-off final that saw the club once again back in the top flight.
Worn by: Per Frandsen, Gareth Farrelly.

H 2001–02, 2002–03

Design: REEBOK
Sponsor: REEBOK

You would have thought that Bolton would have celebrated their return to the Premiership with kits awash with colour. In fact, they took to the pitch this season in virtually monochrome designs. The new lightweight home kit reverted to simply white and navy blue with all traces of red removed, apart from the extended ribbons now added to the badge.

Worn in: An incredible 5–0 thrashing of Leicester away in the first game of the 01–02 season followed by a great win at Man Utd. Also the vital 2–1 win over Middlesbrough in 02–03 that saved the side from relegation.
Worn by: Henrik Pedersen, Paul Warhurst.

A 2001–02 3 2002–03

Design: REEBOK
Sponsor: REEBOK

Continuing the rather sombre approach to the season. the club's next away kit was a simple two-tone navy blue with white piping. Unusually, the shirt was worn with the same blue shorts as the home (although, like the home shirt, it was paired with white shorts if there was a colour clash). To the surprise of many people, Bolton actually topped the Premiership early on in the 01–02 season, before sliding down the table and just managing to escape the drop into Division 1.

Worn in: Worthy draws at Leeds and Southampton, but disappointing defeats against Fulham (3–0) and Derby (1–0).
Worn by: Michael Ricketts, Bruno N'Gotty, Dean Holdsworth, Jay Jay Okocha.

Recent years have seen a spate of special kits celebrating anniversaries of clubs' important milestones.

A 2002–03 3 2003–04

Design: REEBOK
Sponsor: REEBOK

Aside from the flashy navy panels on the sleeves, this was a fairly pedestrian but stylish away kit. It featured a simple V-neck and the new style Reebok logo that had been introduced on the equivalent home kit a season earlier. Still, it was nice to see a vivid splash of colour after the muted shades of the club's return to the top flight.

Worn in: The disappointing 4–1 defeat to Fulham in the first game of the 02–03 season – not a good start for this strip, although things improved with a storming 4–2 win over Leeds later in the season (worn with the blue shorts from the home kit).

Worn by: Youri Djorkaeff, Kevin Davies, Bernard Mendy.

C 2002–03

Design: REEBOK
Sponsor: REEBOK

To commemorate Bolton's 125th anniversary, the club turned out in this special one-off home kit based on a design worn by the side in the 1885–86 season. Special dispensation was granted by the Premiership to wear the unique shirt, which featured striking red, navy blue and white stripes and a sleek V-neck. In order to maintain the historical integrity of the kit, Reebok decided to include only the smaller version of their logo. The shirt was worn with the standard white socks and change white shorts of the home kit.

Worn in: A 0–0 draw at home to Fulham – the only league match the shirt was worn in.

Worn by: Ivan Campo, Kevin Nolan.

H 2003–04, 2004–05

Design: REEBOK
Sponsor: REEBOK

A big change at the Reebok Stadium occurred with the launch of this all-white home kit. Gone were the traditional navy shorts – now the team resembled Real Madrid in their heroic new strip. The shirt featured Reebok's Play Dry moisture-management technology, visible navy seams, a shadow pinstripe and a minimal neck. The shirt was sometimes also worn with the navy shorts from the away kit. The club surprised many with sixth place in the Premiership in a very successful 04–05 season.

Worn in: A 4–1 win vs Charlton on the opening day of 04–05. Plus the wonderful 1–0 win over champions Arsenal in the same season.

Worn by: Stelios Giannakopoulos, Gary Speed, Fernando Hierro.

A 2003–04 3 2004–05

Design: REEBOK
Sponsor: REEBOK

Red has never been the most popular away kit colour with Bolton fans due to its close association with Man Utd, and it had been 10 years since Bolton had last worn red as part of an away kit. It was not a bad-looking strip though – like the new home strip it was produced in Play Dry fabric and was minimal in aesthetics, with just the merest hint of white as trim. In fact, it was reminiscent of the club's first ever kit from 1881. Also worn with red shorts.

Worn in: The 1–0 win over Spurs and a 2–0 triumph over Leeds (03–04).

Worn by: Nicky Hunt, Simon Charlton, Julio Cesar Santos.

Slightly different versions of Reebok's new range of asymmetrical kits were also worn by West Ham and Manchester City in the 05–06 season.

A 2004–05 3 2005–06

Design: REEBOK
Sponsor: REEBOK

One of the most warmly received away kits in recent years was this lightweight pale blue ensemble. Possibly the only drawback was its extremely close resemblance to the West Ham away kit launched this season. A recent phenomenon is the desire among fans for their club to have totally unique kits – gone are the days of the 70s and 80s when many kits were similar in design with only colour separating them. This new kit also featured the hi-tech Play Dry fabric and breathable white panels under each arm.

Worn in: Another good win at White Hart Lane over Spurs, this time 2–1.
Worn by: Michael Bridges, Les Ferdinand, Anthony Barness.

H 2005–06, 2006–07

Design: REEBOK
Sponsor: REEBOK

Worn for the first time in the last game of the 04–05 season (a superb 3–2 win over high-flying Everton), Reebok's new Wanderers kit follows the all-white trend of the previous design. This time round, however, it has been sculpted into a very different look. With asymmetrical design all the rage, the shirt features a large navy panel highlighted with a flash of red on the right sleeve. A curious stitching pattern runs downwards across the chest, accompanied by sweeping diagonal shadow stripes. The shorts also feature a 'lop-sided' trim design.

A 2005–06

Design: REEBOK
Sponsor: REEBOK

If the home kit looks a little unbalanced at first glance, the club's new away outfit favours a more conventional symmetrical look. The strip reverts to all navy with an elegant silver/grey collar and panels under each arm. Thin white panels of breathable fabric run from under each arm to the collar and a fine vertical pinstripe design spreads across the chest. Sam Allardyce's side finished the 04–05 season in a highly impressive 6th place – enough to earn Bolton a position in the 05–06 UEFA Cup.

CHARLTON ATHLETIC

Charlton Athletic were formed in 1905 but didn't join the Football League until 1920. The first Addicks team (with an average age of just 15) sported red and white and the club have remained true to these colours ever since, apart from a short period in the 1920s when a proposed merger with Catford Southend saw the side dressed in light and dark blue stripes. The scheme didn't take off, however, and Charlton reverted to their favoured red.

The first half of the twentieth century saw the side sporting an almost Manchester United-style red shirt, white shorts and black socks with a red and white turnover, although red and white hooped socks were favoured in the 1940s and 50s.

In the mid-60s a strange event occurred concerning the team's home kit. Although they remained loyal to red and white, the balance of the two colours was switched and the team took to the field in a crisp new white home kit with a very distinctive red yoke (a design worn by the side as their change strip in the 50s and 60s). The reasons for the change are unclear, but it was not long before the colours switched again and the all-white outfit was relegated to just an away strip.

The modern history of Charlton has been dominated by their homelessness in the mid-80s when they left the Valley, their ground since 1919, and shared first with Crystal Palace at Selhurst Park and then later with West Ham. When the club returned to the ground seven years later in 1992, a special commemorative kit was produced by Ribero and the team celebrated their homecoming with a fine win over Portsmouth.

White seems to be the preferred away colour for the team, and it was in white that the club achieved their major success to date – the 1947 FA Cup final triumph over Burnley. Blue and yellow also make regular appearances in the Charlton wardrobe, and for a while in the mid-90s the team were attired in combinations of white, green and purple as Quaser attempted to shake up the club's traditional colours. Recent years have seen a glut of fine kits with continental flair courtesy of Le Coq Sportif and Spanish company Joma – their first venture into the English football world.

Charlton are built on loyalty and tradition and, despite numerous traumas over the past 25 years, still attract a loyal fan base who are ever-hopeful that success will soon come back to the red and white Valley.

WITH THANKS TO MICHAEL EVERETT.

'SUPER' CLIVE MENDONCA IN THE 98–00 LE COQ SPORTIF HOME STRIP.

Due to a colour clash, the adidas 82–83 kit was also worn for at least one match in the Osca-supplied 83–84 season – an event that would not be permitted today due to stricter exclusivity deals between clubs and kit manufacturers.

H 1980–81, 1981–82

Design: ADIDAS
Sponsor: FADS (81–82)

1980 was not a good time to be a Charlton fan as the club had been relegated to Division 3 the previous season. Kit suppliers Bukta were replaced by adidas, who started their three-year deal as the club prepared for the 80–81 season. A classic 70s style, it seemed a little out of date when compared to some of the striking new kit designs that were beginning to appear. DIY chainstore FADS became the club's first shirt sponsor in 81–82.

Worn in: A 5–0 thrashing of Brentford in the 80–81 League Cup first round second leg, overcoming the 3–1 deficit of the first leg. Also a 2–2 draw at Chelsea with both goals by Paul Walsh.
Worn by: Leighton Phillips, Derek Hales.

A 1980–81, 1981–82

Design: ADIDAS
Sponsor: FADS (81–82)

In the days when a club's away kit nearly always followed the design of the home, Charlton sported a yellow and blue version of their first choice outfit. Unusually, the colours of the club badge were not changed to match the away colour scheme, instead remaining red and white. The 80–81 season saw the club gain promotion to Division 2 after a superb 15-match unbeaten run under manager Mike Bailey. When Bailey resigned in June 81 Alan Mullery took over.

Worn in: A hard-fought 4–3 defeat away to Exeter and an impressive 3–1 win at Reading (both 80–81).
Worn by: Paul Walsh, Lawrie Madden, Colin Powell.

H 1982–83

Design: ADIDAS
Sponsor: FADS

In the final year of the adidas deal the club succumbed to fashion and both the home and away shirts witnessed a small but important addition – pinstripes! The 80s had arrived at the Valley. Otherwise the kit remained the same as the one worn for the past two years. As with most early 80s adidas kits, the position of the logo on the shorts varied from leg to leg.

Worn in: A superb 3–0 win vs Fulham and a 3–2 defeat to Ipswich in the FA Cup third round. Also a 2–0 home win over Luton in the Milk Cup second round second leg, Charlton eventually going out 3–2 on aggregate.
Worn by: Allan Simonsen, Les Berry, Steve White, Billy Lansdowne.

A 1982–83

Design: ADIDAS
Sponsor: FADS

The yellow and blue away kit was also remodelled to include pinstripes, but like the home kit remained essentially the same as before. Although the club were holding their own in Division 2 they weren't exactly setting it alight, perhaps due to the high managerial turnover. However, stability arrived in the year this strip was worn with the appointment of Lennie Lawrence in November 82, replacing short-term manager Ken Craggs.

Worn in: The 3–0 defeat against Middlesbrough at Ayresome Park, plus the horrific 7–1 thrashing at Burnley earlier in the season.
Worn by: Terry Bullivant, Paul Curtis, Carl Harris, Paul Elliott.

The Osca 84–86 home kit was worn by the club in their last match at The Valley against Stoke in September 1985, which Charlton won 2–0.

H 1983–84

Design: OSCA
Sponsor: SUNLEY (PART SEASON)

When smaller sportswear manufacturer Osca took over from adidas the club were in dire straits and on the brink of extinction. Local housing developers The Sunley Group stepped in with a rescue deal and saved the club. For a short period this season the company's logo appeared on the shirts, making them the club's second ever sponsor. The Osca kit changed little from the previous design, but the collar was replaced by a standard 80s V-neck. Also worn with the away kit's black shorts.

Worn in: A good 1–0 win over Crystal Palace and fine victories over Portsmouth (2–0) and Manchester City (1–0).
Worn by: Keith Dickenson, Steve Gritt, Steve Dowman.

A 1983–84 to 1985–86

Design: OSCA
Sponsor: SUNLEY (PART 83–84 SEASON)
THE WOOLWICH (84–86)

Osca ditched yellow and blue in favour of a more traditional white shirt with red trim. The shirt was a straightforward reversal of the home and was paired with black shorts and white socks, although it was often worn with the white shorts from the home kit. The jersey was sponsored by Sunley for a short while in 83–84, before featuring the logo of The Woolwich in 84–86. After four years of mediocrity in Division 2, 85–86 saw the club promoted to the top flight.

Worn in: Defeats at Barnsley (3–2) and Middlesbrough (1–0) in 83–84 – the club did not win a game in this strip that season.
Worn by: John Pearson, Mike Flanagan.

H 1984–85, 1985–86

Design: OSCA
Sponsor: THE WOOLWICH

Although the early part of the 84–85 campaign saw the club once again sporting unsponsored shirts, The Woolwich Building Society arrived midway through the season and commenced a long relationship with the club. To accommodate their logo, the kit was updated to include a large white panel. Other than that the design remained the same, except for the reintroduction of black socks – last worn by the Addicks in the 60s.

Worn in: A warmly remembered match that saw the club beat Barnsley 5–3 after being 3–1 down at half time. Also, of course, the 3–2 win over Carlisle in 85–86 that saw the club achieve promotion to Division 1.
Worn by: Paul Friar, Robert Lee, Phil Walker.

H 1986–87, 1987–88

Design: ADIDAS
Sponsor: THE WOOLWICH

A return to adidas saw the Addicks, now playing at Selhurst Park, dressed in this typical 80s kit that featured a wrap-over V-neck and the adidas three stripes trimmed with black. Unusually for the club, the socks now became white. The black shorts from the white third kit were also worn with this shirt. The 87–88 season saw the wrap-over V-neck mysteriously replaced by a plainer design.

Worn in: The impressive 3–2 win over Everton at home (86–87). Also a rare outing at Wembley for the 86–87 Full Members Cup final vs Blackburn, which sadly ended in a 1–0 defeat. Plus the crucial 1–1 draw with Chelsea that kept the Addicks in Division 1 in 87–88.
Worn by: Jim Melrose, Steve Thompson.

Other teams sporting grey in the 80s included Liverpool, Newcastle Utd and Birmingham City.

A 1986–87, 1987–88

Design: ADIDAS
Sponsor: THE WOOLWICH

There was quite a change for the next away kit, which was all blue with white and black trim. The design followed that of the home version. The last time adidas had been kit supplier at the Valley, Charlton were in Division 3; now it was a different story as the club were proudly in the top flight. A new one-colour version of the club badge was included on all three of the adidas kits of the time.

Worn in: An early season 2–0 defeat to Liverpool and the exciting 2–2 vs Southampton at the Dell as Charlton fought to retain their Division 1 place in the 86–87 season.

Worn by: Mark Aizlewood, Mark Stuart (who scored the winner in an outstanding 1–0 win over Man Utd at Old Trafford in 86–87).

3 1986–87, 1987–88

Design: ADIDAS
Sponsor: THE WOOLWICH

In 86–87 and 87–88 the club also sported a third kit in the traditional white, red and black. Like the away kit it mirrored the design of the home, although this time it was a simple reversal with red and black trim. The shirt fabric of all three kits at this time featured a diagonal shadow stripe pattern similar to that worn by Manchester Utd and Ipswich, among others. Like the home version, this shirt was produced with two different neck designs.

Worn in: A tight 1–1 draw against West Ham at Upton Park (87–88).

Worn by: Andy Jones, David Campbell, Paul Miller, Ralph Milne.

H 1988–89

Design: ADMIRAL
Sponsor: THE WOOLWICH

The 80s ended with the club stuck in the bottom half of Division 1 and with a new Admiral-produced set of kits. More snug-fitting than any previous designs, the shirt introduced a wrap-over round neck, a small Admiral logo trim to the shoulder and a chequerboard shadow pattern. Curiously, the kit was occasionally worn with red shorts even if there was no colour clash.

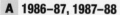

Worn in: A dramatic 1–0 win over Man Utd at Selhurst Park late in the season. Also a vital 1–0 victory over Wimbledon that helped the club remain in the top flight.

Worn by: Paul Mortimer, Steve MacKenzie.

A 1988–89

Design: ADMIRAL
Sponsor: THE WOOLWICH

With grey all the rage in the late 80s, Charlton also took to the field in this rather sombre colour. The away kit replicated the design of the home with a red, black and white trim lifting the overall drab feel of the kit. For the first time a shadow pattern crept onto the shorts. Although Admiral signed a four-year deal with the club, this set of designs was replaced after just one season. This outfit was worn as Charlton triumphed at the Guinness 'Soccer 6' championship in Manchester.

Worn in: A 3–0 humbling at Old Trafford against Man Utd in 88–89, followed later in the season by a 2–0 defeat at Liverpool.

Worn by: John Humphrey (club player of the year 88–89), Colin Pates.

Following their introduction in the 90–91 season, Football League badges could be purchased and sewn on to each sleeve by fans keen to add extra authenticity to their replica shirts.

3 1988–89

Design: ADMIRAL
Sponsor: THE WOOLWICH

Admiral also issued a third kit for the club in 88–89, which once again followed exactly the design of the existing home and away strips. The outfit was yellow with red and black trim – a unique colour scheme for the club. After spending the majority of the season near the bottom of the table, the club escaped relegation after a series of battling performances throughout Spring 89.

Worn in: Another defeat for the Addicks in this tough year – this time away to Millwall. A happier occasion saw this strip worn in a 3–1 victory over West Ham with two goals by Paul Williams. Also a fine 2–2 draw at Arsenal.
Worn by: Carl Leaburn, Andy Peake, Robert Lee.

H 1989–90, 1990–91

Design: ADMIRAL
Sponsor: THE WOOLWICH

After only one season the club introduced a new set of kits with just a few tiny tweaks to the previous design – the cuffs were removed and a new button-up round-neck collar introduced, along with a new shadow pattern. The overall size of the shirt was a little larger too. The shorts and socks were retained from the previous design (although a new pair of change red shorts were also worn).

Worn in: A real high point of the 89–90 season, the 2–0 home win over Man Utd – the second season in a row that the Red Devils had been defeated by Charlton at Selhurst Park. Also that season a 4–2 defeat to Southampton.
Worn by: Colin Walsh, Tommy Caton, Garth Crooks.

A 1989–90, 1990–91

Design: ADMIRAL
Sponsor: THE WOOLWICH

A new blue kit was released in 89–90 to replace the previous grey outfit. Like all of Admiral's kits to date, it maintained the design of the home and changed only the colour scheme with the shirt now trimmed in red and white. Not the luckiest of kits, it saw the club fall to many defeats away from home in the 89–90 season that eventually spelled relegation for Lennie Lawrence's side.

Worn in: Away defeats to Liverpool and Arsenal (both 1–0) and Nottingham Forest (2–0) as the club found the going too tough in 89–90 and were relegated to Division 2. Also worn in a tough 2–2 draw with Hull the following year.
Worn by: Joe McLaughlin, Scott Minto.

3 1989–90

Design: ADMIRAL
Sponsor: THE WOOLWICH

This third kit is a bit of a curiosity, as it would appear to have been worn only once, against Charlton's landlords at the time (and of course bitter local rivals) Crystal Palace. The change was made necessary due to Palace's blue and red striped kit, which caused major clash problems with The Addicks' first two choices. It followed the same design as the home and away kits and was worn with black shorts and red socks.

Worn in: The 2–0 defeat away to Crystal Palace (although technically still at home, of course, as both teams were sharing the same ground at the time!)
Worn by: Kim Grant, Alex Dyer, Simon Webster.

The 91–92 Admiral kits were actually also worn (without a sponsor) up until December 92 of the following season, when the club celebrated their return to the Valley with the launch of the brand-new Ribero strip.

H 1991–92

Design: ADMIRAL
Sponsor: THE WOOLWICH

The 91–92 season saw the conclusion of the club's kit deal with Admiral and also their long relationship with The Woolwich. It also found Charlton ground-sharing with West Ham, although this was soon to change. This last Admiral home kit was much more ample in size than the last one and included a collar for the first time since the early 80s adidas kit. Bold white and black panels adorned each sleeve. Steve Gritt and Alan Curbishley became joint managers in July 1991, replacing Lawrence.

Worn in: Excellent wins against Portsmouth (3–0), Newcastle (4–3) and Leicester (2–0), which helped the club into the Division 1 play-off positions.
Worn by: Stuart Balmer, Alan Pardew.

A 1991–92

Design: ADMIRAL
Sponsor: THE WOOLWICH

In an era when away shirts were becoming more and more outrageous, the club donned this blue and black affair. It utilised the same collar design as the home shirt, but also included an adventurous black horizontal pattern, on top of which lay a shadow design. The shorts featured the standard Admiral trim of the time. Like the equivalent home strip, this kit was actually worn up until December 92.

Worn in: A solid away win at Swindon (2–1), but poor defeats to Middlesbrough (2–0) and Barnsley (1–0) plus a 3–1 humbling at Sheffield United in the FA Cup fourth round.
Worn by: Darren Pitcher, David Whyte.

H 1992–93

Design: RIBERO
Sponsor: NONE

A kit that holds special memories for all Charlton fans, this was worn as the club returned at last to their home ground. Unusually, Ribero had replaced Admiral as suppliers mid-season in December 92 and their first home kit was everything a good football shirt should be: stylish, functional and traditional. It was back to basic red and white with a conventional button-up collar. A nice touch was the 'Back at the Valley' script added beneath the club badge.

Worn in: The first game back at the Valley – a 1–0 win over Portsmouth in December 92.
Worn by: John Robinson, Lee Power, Colin Walsh (who scored the club's first goal back at their traditional ground).

A 1992–93

Design: RIBERO
Sponsor: NONE

With baggy shorts and shirts back in fashion in the early 90s, the days of skimpy shorts and skin-tight tops were long gone. The club's new away kit followed the design of the home, complete with shadow pattern, but in a powder blue colour trimmed with white and paired with black shorts. The shirt also included the 'Back at the Valley' logo.

Worn in: A 1–1 draw with Watford at Vicarage Road, John Robinson scoring the only Addicks goal.
Worn by: Alex Dyer, John Bumstead.

3 1992–93

Design: RIBERO
Sponsor: NONE

White has always been a preferred away colour for the club, and in fact for a short while in the 60s white (with a red yoke) was selected as the first choice home kit before the club reverted to the more familiar red. This plain and simple white version of the 92–93 kit was also worn in that memorable season. The red shorts from this kit were occasionally paired with the home strip when necessary.

Worn in: A 2–2 draw at Swindon Town.
Worn by: Paul Williams, Steve Gatting.

H 1993–94

Design: RIBERO
Sponsor: VIGLEN COMPUTERS

After the excitement of the Addicks' return to the Valley, the following season saw the team in a remodelled Ribero kit. Pretty much the same as their first design, the new kit added a red trim to the collar and sleeves and also included a red flash on the left-hand side of the shorts. Also worn with the red shorts from the away kit. The kit was unsponsored until November 93 when computer manufacturers Viglen became the club's new shirt sponsors.

Worn in: Three consecutive home wins (vs Birmingham, Tranmere and Bolton) and an exciting 4–3 goal-fest against Southend.
Worn by: Phil Chapple, Peter Garland, Garry Nelson (who scored a hat-trick in this strip vs Peterborough).

A 1993–94

Design: RIBERO
Sponsor: VIGLEN COMPUTERS

For the next away kit Ribero decided on a straightforward reversed version of the home outfit – a simple white shirt with red trim. Normally worn with red shorts, it also appeared with the white shorts from the home kit and also a change pair in black. Early versions of the kit included the Viglen logo in their official corporate pale blue colour.

Worn in: A humiliating 4–0 defeat at Roker Park vs Sunderland. Also an honourable 1–1 draw against Ancona in the Anglo–Italian Cup and the end to that season's good FA Cup run: a quarter-final defeat to Man Utd (3–1).
Worn by: Alan McLeary, Shaun Newton.

H 1994–95, 1995–96

Design: QUASER
Sponsor: VIGLEN COMPUTERS

A new kit era was ushered into the Valley in 94–95, provided by new suppliers Quaser. All of Quaser's kits were very bold, confident outfits, and this was no exception. The shirt included a unique chunky button-up collar design that also featured a small Quaser logo. All-over abstract shadow prints were popular at this time, and the one incorporated into this kit was based around the club badge. The jersey was also worn with the black shorts from the away kit if necessary. The sponsorship deal with Viglen was extended this season.

Worn in: A dismal 3–0 defeat to Chelsea in the FA Cup third round, but also good wins over Sunderland, Bristol and Watford (all 94–95).
Worn by: Richard Rufus, Jamie Stuart.

Despite their lively and innovative designs, Charlton were one of the very few top-flight sides for whom sportswear brand Quaser produced a kit.

A 1994–95, 1995–96

Design: QUASER
Sponsor: VIGLEN COMPUTERS

Quaser's first away kit for The Addicks was very distinctive – the stunning-looking shirt retained the same collar and shadow print of the home, but added stylish red and black horizontal bands on which the logo was placed. Worn with black shorts, it was also paired with the home white pair when necessary. In June 1995 Alan Curbishley took sole managerial control of the club.

Worn in: Two unfortunate away defeats in the 94–95 season: 2–1 against Barnsley and 1–0 to Middlesbrough. Also a narrow 2–1 defeat at Anfield in the 95–96 FA Cup fifth round.
Worn by: Stuart Balmer, David Whyte, Keith Jones.

3 1995–96, 1996–97

Design: QUASER
Sponsor: VIGLEN COMPUTERS

A vivid new colour scheme was introduced in the mid-90s by Quaser – green, purple and white, which was to feature in two of their kits in the forthcoming season. This outfit saw a predominantly green shirt with purple and white stripes. In a time when more was more, the shadow print from the home and away kit was overlaid over the colours. It was another bold and controversial design move.

Worn in: Not the luckiest of strips, it was worn in a tough 3–0 defeat away to Sheffield Utd and a close-fought 1–0 loss to Stoke City (both 96–97 season).
Worn by: Gary Poole, Anthony Barness, Kevin Lisbie.

H 1996–97, 1997–98

Design: QUASER
Sponsor: VIGLEN COMPUTERS

The second Quaser home kit had a slightly retro feel. All badges were now placed centrally on the shirt and a new shadow pattern was

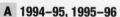

added, again based around the club badge. Large red panels appeared on the shorts along with Quaser's own distinctive dotted-line trim. Rather than switching to the away kit when there was a shorts colour clash, the team often wore a pair of alternative change red shorts.

Worn in: A 4–2 win over Forest at home in 97–98 and then later in the season the thrilling play-off semi-final success over Ipswich.
Worn by: Brendan O'Connell, Bradley Allen, Matt Holmes.

A 1996–97, 1997–98

Design: QUASER
Sponsor: VIGLEN COMPUTERS

With the club finding themselves mid-table in Division 1, a new away strip was launched. It retained the colour scheme from the previous season's third kit, although the shirt was now predominantly white with vertical green and purple bands down the left-hand side. It also featured the same 'grandad'-style button-up neck and intricate shadow pattern of the home kit. A nice touch was the addition of an old-fashioned CAFC shield design on the socks.

Worn in: The 4–1 defeat to Liverpool in the 96–97 Coca-Cola Cup third round replay. Also another big defeat, this time 5–2 to Nottingham Forest the following season.
Worn by: Phil Chapple, Kevin Nicholls.

CHARLTON ATHLETIC

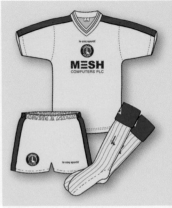

3 1997–98

Design: QUASER
Sponsor: VIGLEN COMPUTERS

Quaser's last kit for Charlton was this extraordinary outfit introduced for one season only. It was in a new darker shade of green and included brash white horizontal panels trimmed with red and topped with the same complex shadow pattern as the home and away kits. It was a curious style that was very distinctive but bore little resemblance to Charlton tradition. A prototype version was unveiled towards the end of the previous season with a slightly different design.

Worn in: A good 2–1 win over Stoke City but a dreadful 4–1 thrashing at Sheffield United.
Worn by: Danny Mills, Mark Kinsella.

H 1998–99, 1999–2000

Design: LE COQ SPORTIF
Sponsor: MESH COMPUTERS

Another much-loved Addicks shirt is this first outfit from French company Le Coq Sportif. It was premiered at the end of the 97–98 season and graced the back of 'Super' Clive Mendonca as he scored a hat-trick in one of the great Wembley matches – the 97–98 Division 1 play-off final vs Sunderland. It was quite ahead of its time, with white panels down each side.

Worn in: The 97–98 Division 1 play-off final 3–3 AET, which the Addicks won on penalties. Also the 1–0 home defeat to Sheffield Wed in 98–99 that saw the team relegated from the Premiership, plus the match vs Ipswich the following season that saw the club presented with the Division 1 title.
Worn by: Steve Jones, John Barnes.

A 1998–99

Design: LE COQ SPORTIF
Sponsor: MESH COMPUTERS

As the UK football world went ecru-mad in the late 90s, Charlton launched their own kit in the curiously-named colour. Essentially following the style of the home kit – minus the panels under the arm – it accompanied the team in their first venture into the Premier League. Unfortunately, the club struggled and were relegated back to Division 1 at the end of the season. Mesh Computers became the club's new sponsor and a Le Coq Sportif logo trim was included on the sleeve and shorts.

Worn in: A thrilling 3–3 draw with Liverpool, a 0–0 draw with Arsenal and a good 1–0 win over Nottingham Forest.
Worn by: Clive Mendonca, Neil Redfearn, Mark Bright.

A 1999–2000

Design: LE COQ SPORTIF
Sponsor: MESH COMPUTERS

This more conventional colour scheme found the club back in yellow and blue and back in Division 1. Not a bad-looking kit, although perhaps a little pedestrian, the Le Coq Sportif logo was now reduced to a text-only version placed centrally on the shirt. The socks included the sword graphic from the club badge – a stylish touch that was to continue on later kits. 99–00 was a great season for the side, who bounced back after the relegation disappointment of the previous year to take Division 1 by storm.

Worn in: The 1–1 draw at Blackburn that saw the club crowned as Division 1 champions and back in the top flight after just one season.
Worn by: Greg Shields, Eddie Youds.

Prior to the instigation of the Premier League in 1992 and the new striped green referees' shirts that were introduced, black kits had not been permitted. Since then, almost every Premiership side has worn black at some time or other.

*DUE TO COPYRIGHT REASONS THE REDBUS LOGO IS UNABLE TO BE INCLUDED.

H 2000–01, 2001–02

Design: LE COQ SPORTIF
Sponsor: REDBUS*

A typically stylish Le Coq Sportif kit, this new home kit (at first glance similar to the previous season's) saw the club back in the Premiership and eventually finishing ninth. Investment company Redbus became the club's new sponsor. The shirt was worn with the red shorts and white socks from the away kit when necessary. A nice touch was the 'Addicks' text included in the red triangle on the left leg of the shorts.

Worn in: The amazing 4–4 home draw with West Ham (01–02) along with good wins over Chelsea and Everton the same season. Also, the 2–0 home win over Leicester in 00–01 that included a great goal by Shaun Bartlett.
Worn by: Chris Powell, Andy Hunt.

A 2000–01, 2001–02

Design: LE COQ SPORTIF
Sponsor: REDBUS*

For the first time in six years Charlton turned out in a fresh white kit trimmed with red and black. It was a good solid design with a fabric comprising a delicate weave pattern and was paired with reversed shorts and socks to those of the home choice, enabling them to be interchanged with ease. The kit was not worn as often as it could have been in the second season of its life (01–02) due to the popularity of the all-black strip that was also introduced that year.

Worn in: Consecutive 2–0 defeats at Liverpool and West Ham towards the end of the 01–02 season.
Worn by: Paul Konchesky, Mark Fish.

3 2000–01

Design: LE COQ SPORTIF
Sponsor: REDBUS*

Le Coq Sportif introduced this fine-looking blue and black striped shirt for two matches only in the 00–01 season: the games away at Southampton and Sunderland. The change was made necessary as both clubs' home kits comprised red and white stripes. This simple, workmanlike kit was possibly influenced by an early Addicks kit dating from the 1920s.

Worn in: A 0–0 draw with Southampton followed by a 3–2 defeat to Sunderland in the last away game of the season.
Worn by: Scott Parker, Claus Jensen, Radostin Kishishev.

3 2001–02 A 2002–03

Design: LE COQ SPORTIF
Sponsor: REDBUS* (01–02) ALLSPORTS (02–03)

The club issued a new third strip early in the 01–02 season and it was a real classic. Made from an incredibly shiny fabric, it was all black with a fine horizontal pinstripe and red patches under each arm and on the shorts. This kit was such a success that it was promoted to the standard away kit for the 02–03 season, where the logo of new sponsors Allsports replaced that of Redbus, whose deal with the club had finished early.

Worn in: An absolute classic 4–2 win over Arsenal (01–02) and the exciting 1–0 triumph over Manchester City the following season.
Worn by: Matt Svensson, Luke Young, Jonatan Johansson.

Joma also produce the team kit for Spanish club Deportivo La Coruna, as well as the Costa Rica and Honduras national sides.

H 2002–03

Design: LE COQ SPORTIF
Sponsor: ALLSPORTS

The final kit of Le Coq Sportif's five-year stint at Charlton saw the launch of this simple and stylish home design. Two options were revealed towards the end of the 02–03 season for fans to decide which they preferred. Although to the neutral supporter they were both strong, the Addicks fans felt there was too much black in both, so a new version was created that was a loose amalgamation of both designs – minus the black! Sportswear chain Allsports became new shirt sponsors.

Worn in: The exciting 4–4 draw with West Ham and the 3–1 victory over Spurs at home. Also the awful 6–1 thrashing by Leeds.
Worn by: Jason Euell, Martin Pringle, Shaun Bartlett.

H 2003–04, 2004–05

Design: JOMA
Sponsor: ALLSPORTS

Apart from the arrival of Paolo Di Canio from West Ham, the other major continental arrival at the Valley in 2003 was that of Spanish sportswear manufacturers Joma who took over as the club's new kit suppliers. The home shirt featured some of the better elements of recent Charlton kits, combined with a new sleek, contemporary neck design, centralised badges and white piping.

Worn in: The 4–2 home win over Chelsea in 03–04 followed by a 3–2 triumph over Liverpool, featuring a cracking Lisbie goal.
Worn by: Graham Stuart, Chris Perry, Matt Holland.

A 2003–04, 2004–05

Design: JOMA
Sponsor: ALLSPORTS

Joma's first away kit saw a return to yellow, a colour last worn during the 99–00 season. Now the colour was in an extremely bright and vibrant hue and trimmed with black. The shirt incorporated a different collar design from that of the home kit, along with unique stitched side panels. In what proved to be a very successful season for the club, the side eventually came seventh in the 03–04 season.

Worn in: A well-earned 1–0 win over Liverpool at Anfield and another good 1–0 win against Blackburn, plus a 2–1 win over Birmingham (all 03–04).
Worn by: Danny Murphy, Jerome Thomas, Jonathan Fortune, Paolo di Canio.

C 2004–05

Design: JOMA
Sponsor: ALLSPORTS

To celebrate the club's centenary year, a one-off home kit was launched. It was given special dispensation by the Premiership to be worn just once in a league fixture, the home match vs Newcastle. The kit included a smaller Allsports logo and a white vertical band on which was the legend '1905–2005'. Each limited-edition replica shirt was numbered, and every fan who bought one was included on a special roll of honour.

Worn in: The 1–1 home draw against Newcastle United, with another important Kevin Lisbie goal equalising for the Addicks. Also worn in the 2–1 defeat to local rivals Crystal Palace in the Carling Cup third round.
Worn by: Dennis Rommedahl , Francis Jeffers.

Despite the forthcoming introduction of the club's new white kit, the team chose to don the previous Joma yellow away kit for the 05–06 pre-season friendly against Morecambe.

H 2005–06

Design: JOMA
Sponsor: ALLSPORTS

Charlton do battle in 05–06 in another competent design from Joma created from the company's breathable DUAL Comfort System fabric, which is incredibly light and totally waterproof. The jersey features a unique pointed neck design trimmed with red, along with contrasting red and white cuffs and white breathable fabric panels down each side. The club badge and sponsor's logos remain in a central position. The shorts have changed little from the previous design and the socks see a return to red and white hoops. 04–05 saw the Addicks finish the season in 11th place in the Premiership – a slight drop from the previous campaign's 7th position.

A 2005–06

Design: JOMA
Sponsor: ALLSPORTS

The Addicks were one of the last Premiership clubs to unveil their 05–06 kits, preferring to don the previous yellow and black outfit for the majority of their pre-season friendlies. This new away strip sees the side return to predominantly white and black for the first time in 10 years. Worn for the first time in one of the club's last friendlies before the start of the new campaign (against AEK Athens), this classy kit brings a really fresh new look to Alan Curbishley's side.

CHELSEA

Blue is the colour, football is the game – Chelsea are as famous for their blue shirts as they are for their links to a certain Russian businessman. They are in fact one of the few clubs in the football league who have never deviated from their original home colour choice. The reason behind the famous blue strip is fairly straightforward: when Chelsea's founder, Gus Mears, formed the club in 1905, he simply chose Lord Chelsea's racing colour of blue as the most logical visual identity for his team.

Although the tradition of blue shirts had been long established, it wasn't until the mid-60s that the club began to wear the matching blue shorts (with just a single white stripe on each leg) that have become synonymous with the club. Prior to then, as with many clubs at the time, white shorts were the norm, with red, yellow or white being the preferred palette of away colours. The club have never shied away from donning their away kits, often opting to wear them even when there is only a shorts colour clash.

In recent years the team's kit has also been distinctive due to the club's preference for white socks, although this tradition was discontinued for a while in the mid-80s before being revived in 1993.

The first manufacturer's logo to appear on a Chelsea shirt was Umbro's in the mid-70s and, with the exception of a few years in the 80s, they have been involved with the Blues' kits ever since. However, 1986 witnessed an unusual and revolutionary state of affairs at Stamford Bridge with the team sporting a kit branded as 'The Chelsea Collection' and apparently produced by the players and club themselves. The facts surrounding the kit are unclear, although it would appear that Umbro were involved to some extent with the supply as the tracksuits and training kit at the time featured the Umbro logo. In fact, the very next season the famous diamond motif also returned to the playing kit. The last few seasons' designs have seen a re-emergence of minimal and effective styles, echoing the simple all-blue shirt and shorts from the 60s and early 70s.

2005 sees the centenary of the club's formation and, to commemorate the event, the 80s-designed club badge is being replaced by an updated version of the most famous Chelsea crest, which was based on the borough's coat of arms. It may well be that this milestone in Chelsea's life could also herald the dawn of a new highly successful era for the West London club.

GIANFRANCO ZOLA IN THE 99-01 UMBRO HOME KIT.

Earlier 70s away kits saw the team sporting an all-red strip.

CHELSEA

H 1977–78 to 1980–81

Design: UMBRO
Sponsor: NONE

The start of the 80s found Chelsea in the old Division 2, just missing out on promotion in the 79–80 season. The kit at the time was a fondly remembered, classic royal blue Umbro affair. It was paired with the traditional white socks and had accompanied the club through a tough couple of seasons in Division 1 at the end of the 70s, before they eventually dropped down to Division 2 in 78–79.

Worn in: A hard-fought 4–3 win over Bolton in 78–79, a rare highlight in a dismal season. Three excellent consecutive wins over London clubs in 79–80: 7–2 vs Orient, 2–1 over West Ham and 3–1 vs Charlton. Also a brilliant 6–0 thrashing of Newcastle (80–81).
Worn by: Ray Wilkins, Clive Walker.

A 1978–79 to 1980–81

Design: UMBRO
Sponsor: NONE

With the Brazilian national side creating such a stir worldwide in the 70s, it was no surprise to see elements of their influential kit infiltrating the English market. Many clubs at the time toyed with the famous Brazil yellow and green colour scheme and Chelsea were no exception, although the original outing of this strip in 77–78 saw the outfit trimmed with blue rather than green. The kit was a straightforward copy of the home design and was also worn with green shorts.

Worn in: A 5–1 thrashing by Ipswich in the relegation season of 78–79 and a 3–2 win over Man City – the club's only away triumph of 78–79. Also a 2–2 draw with QPR in 79–80.
Worn by: Eamonn Bannon, Mickey Droy.

H 1981–82, 1982–83

Design: LE COQ SPORTIF
Sponsor: NONE

French sportswear manufacturers Le Coq Sportif invaded Division 1 in the early 80s and brought continental flair to traditional English apparel. Their first kit for Chelsea was a smart pinstripe affair, with the badge placed centrally on the shirt and Le Coq Sportif logos on each sleeve. Red trim was added to the V-neck and cuffs. The two seasons in which this kit was worn found the club still struggling to make an impact in Division 2 under new manager John Neal.

Worn in: The stunning 6–0 home win over Cambridge Utd in the 82–83 season and a great 2–0 win over Liverpool in the 81–82 FA Cup fifth round.
Worn by: Gary Locke, Mike Fillery.

A 1981–82, 1982–83

Design: LE COQ SPORTIF
Sponsor: NONE

Yellow was retained for Chelsea's away kit, but was now trimmed with red and blue – a curious colour combination. The new silky-feel kit followed the design of the home. Unusually for this period, both kits were unsponsored. In fact, it was not until the arrival of Commodore in 87 that the club found a regular long-term shirt partner. Despite these dashing outfits, the 82–83 season saw the side drifting towards possible relegation to Division 3.

Worn in: A 2–0 triumph over London rivals QPR in 81–82. The 82–83 season's run of poor away defeats against Leicester, Blackburn (both 3–0) and Carlisle Utd (2–1).
Worn by: Gary Chivers, Kevin Hales, Dale Jasper, Paul Canoville.

Chelsea's appearance in the 85–86 Full Members Cup final match vs Manchester City was unusual in that it saw both sides wearing their away colours.

3 1981–82, 1982–83

Design: LE COQ SPORTIF
Sponsor: NONE

This white kit formed a seldom-seen third choice for the Blues in the early 80s. A very plain design with no embellishment at all except for a bold red, white and blue V-neck and cuffs, it was worn on only a few occasions, normally with the home kit's change blue socks. 82–83 saw the club at their lowest ebb for many seasons, finishing 18th in Division 2, but a revival was on its way the following year.

Worn in: A dismal 1–0 defeat away to Shrewsbury Town in the 81–82 season.
Worn by: Bryan 'Pop' Robson, Alan Mayes, Peter Rhoades-Brown.

H 1983–84, 1984–85

Design: LE COQ SPORTIF
Sponsor: GULF AIR (83–84)

Le Coq Sportif set the football kit world ablaze in the early 80s and their slim-fitting shirts, unique round neck and inset design featured on several kits at the time. This two-tone blue strip also featured white and red horizontal pinstripes and shadow stripes on the shorts. Gulf Air became the club's first sponsor in December 84, but the shirt was unsponsored the following year. Also worn with white shorts.

Worn in: A great 6–2 home win over Coventry in 84–85 along with a 3–2 defeat to Sunderland in the semi-final of that year's Milk Cup. Also the fine 5–0 win over Leeds a season earlier.
Worn by: Nigel Spackman, Colin Pates.

A 1983–84 3 1984–85

Design: LE COQ SPORTIF
Sponsor: GULF AIR (83–84)

83–84 saw Chelsea finally gain promotion to the top flight after five years in Division 2, with the team finishing that season as champions. For away games they wore this rather gaudy yellow kit trimmed with red and blue. It followed a similar design to the home, but with wider-spaced horizontal stripes. It was an extraordinary kit that featured in some extraordinary matches in the 83–84 season.

Worn in: A superb 5–3 win at Fulham in the 83–84 season and a 3–3 draw at Cardiff later that season, with the Blues coming back from 3–0 down with only six minutes left! Plus the goal that clinched the Division 2 title vs Grimsby on the last day of 83–84.
Worn by: Mickey Thomas, Gordon Davies.

A 1984–85 3 1985–86

Design: LE COQ SPORTIF
Sponsor: NONE

84–85 found the Blues back in Division 1, but after only one season the brash yellow away kit was relegated to third choice and this more sedate white kit was introduced. The shirt saw the return of a standard V-neck paired with horizontal blue and red pinstripes, highlighted with a silvery shadow line. Although still a highly decorated strip, it was definitely more restrained than the previous design. Also worn with the normal home blue shorts on occasion.

Worn in: Chelsea's first ever Wembley victory: a thrillingly memorable 5–4 victory over Man City in the 85–86 Full Members Cup final.
Worn by: Joe McLaughlin, Doug Rougvie, Colin Lee, Pat Nevin.

The arrival of The Chelsea Collection also brought with it a newly
designed club badge based around the lion motif and the club's initials.

H 1985–86

Design: LE COQ SPORTIF
Sponsor: NONE

Le Coq Sportif's last home kit for the club was
this marvellous outfit – perhaps one of the
best the club has ever worn. Minimal and
classy, it was a welcome relief after the
excesses of the first half of the decade. The
shirt featured a blue V-neck and cuffs with
white trim and vertical shadow stripes that
incorporated, for the first time, the Le Coq
Sportif logo. The athletics-style shorts were cut
away at the sides and were much skimpier
than in previous seasons.

Worn in: A great 2–1 home win over defending
champions Everton. Also worn in a memorable
3–1 victory at Newcastle where it was worn
with the white shorts from the away kit.
Worn by: Darren Wood, Kerry Dixon.

A 1985–86

Design: LE COQ SPORTIF
Sponsor: NONE

After five years, Le Coq Sportif were set to
move on from Stamford Bridge and, due to a
suitable yellow fabric not being available,
their last kit for Chelsea saw the club wearing
red for the first time since the mid-70s. The kit
mirrored the design of the home (including the
smaller-fitting shorts), with the exception of a
contrasting V-neck and cuffs, and featured
heavily in Le Coq Sportif's ads at the time.
Since being promoted, Chelsea had more than
held their own in the top flight, finishing sixth
two years running under manager John Hollins.

Worn in: A closely fought 1–1 draw against
Sheffield Wednesday on the opening day of
the 85–86 season.
Worn by: Keith Dublin, Joey Jones.

H 1986–87

Design: CHELSEA COLLECTION
Sponsor: BAI LIN TEA, GRANGE FARM, SIMOD
(all for short periods)

The mid-80s were an uncertain time for the
club and for one season only they wore a
range of kits branded under the name 'Chelsea
Collection'. It was the first time a club had
taken over the production of their own strip,
but it was not a popular design among the
club's supporters. Other apparel the club wore
at the time seemed to be produced by Umbro,
so it is highly likely that the Chelsea Collection
was linked in some way with them.

Worn in: An amazing 5–3 defeat at West Ham;
also a 6–2 win over Nottingham Forest.
Worn by: Robert Isaac, Roy Wegerle,
John Millar.

A 1986–87

Design: CHELSEA COLLECTION
Sponsor: BAI LIN TEA, GRANGE FARM, SIMOD
(all for short periods)

The Chelsea Collection saw the first
appearance of the unusual blue/green colour
officially named 'jade'. The kit followed the
design of the home, with a simple V-neck and
broad grey trim along each sleeve. The shorts
were the same athletic style as the previous Le
Coq Sportif design. Without a regular shirt
sponsor for the third consecutive season, the
home and away jerseys both featured the
logos of three different companies for short
periods, each towards the end of the season.

Worn in: A thrilling 2–2 draw at Leicester City
featuring a spectacular Bumstead goal.
Worn by: Steve Clarke, Mickey Hazard.

With its diamond pinstripe pattern, the Chelsea home kit design of 87–89 was almost identical to Manchester City's kit of the same era.

H 1987–88, 1988–89

Design: UMBRO
Sponsor: COMMODORE

Umbro returned to the Bridge at the start of the 87–88 season – the beginning of a long relationship with the club. The new shirt included a diagonal white pinstripe pattern, white piping and a wrap-over V-neck that saw red returning to the home colour scheme. Computer company Commodore signed a sponsorship deal with the club in 87–88, and early versions of the kit saw a large white panel sewn to the front of the shirt on which their logo was placed.

Worn in: The 2–0 defeat to Middlesbrough in the 87–88 play-off final first leg that all but saw the side relegated. Also a good 2–1 win over Leicester the following season.
Worn by: Tony Dorigo, Clive Wilson.

A 1987–88, 1988–89

Design: UMBRO
Sponsor: COMMODORE

The club continued with the mysterious and enigmatic jade away strip in 87–88. Like the home kit this new design featured a wrap-over V-neck and white piping, but was now trimmed with grey and featured a shadow diagonal pinstripe pattern. The shorts were the standard Umbro issue of the time. As with the previous Chelsea Collection jade kit, questions were raised about the legitimacy of the new kit – after all, in certain lights the colour was not vastly different from the blue of the home kit.

Worn in: A superb 3–0 win at newly-promoted Portsmouth in its first league appearance, followed by unfortunate defeats at Derby (2–0) and Everton (4–1).
Worn by: Graham Roberts, Colin West.

3 1987–88

Design: UMBRO
Sponsor: COMMODORE

This all-red outfit was a rare third kit that was worn only once during the 87–88 season. Similar in design to that of the home, but actually more like Umbro's Everton kits of the time, the shirt included a large diamond shadow pattern and white piping. Although Chelsea had some level of business stability for the first time thanks to their sponsorship deal with Commodore, on the pitch it was a different story; despite finishing 18th this year, the club were relegated to Division 2 due to the play-off final defeat to Middlesbrough.

Worn in: A 2–2 draw at Wimbledon with both Chelsea goals scored by Gordon Durie.
Worn by: Steve Wicks, Billy Dodds, Alan Dickens, Gareth Hall.

3 1988–89 A 1989–90

Design: UMBRO
Sponsor: COMMODORE

A boldly uncompromising red and white hooped kit was introduced as an alternative to the problematic jade away strip. It featured a typical Umbro button-up round neck and thin diagonal shadow stripes. The shorts followed the design of the home pair, complete with a chequerboard shadow pattern. The 88–89 season again saw the side capture the Division 2 title and gain promotion to the top flight, where this strip became the primary away choice.

Worn in: A 4–1 thrashing of Birmingham at St Andrew's with two goals each from Durie and Dixon (88–89). Also a superb 1–0 win over Everton the following season.
Worn by: Kevin Wilson, Graeme Le Saux.

Vinnie Jones took to cutting off the bottom few inches of his pair of longer-style home shorts from the 91–93 season as he preferred a shorter length.

H 1989–90, 1990–91

Design: UMBRO
Sponsor: COMMODORE

With the team back in the top flight, Chelsea's next home kit followed a standard Umbro design (entitled 'Nederlande') of light blue pinstripes combined with a printed diamond pattern. The shorts included a spear-like trim on each leg and the shirt featured a trendy new button-up collar (complete with red neck). Umbro were among the first manufacturers to reintroduce this old-school collar on late 80s shirts.

Worn in: The 89–90 Zenith Data Systems Cup final 1–0 win vs Middlesbrough. Plus an astonishing 10-goal thriller vs Derby, ending in a 6–4 win for Chelsea, and the brilliant 4–2 win over Liverpool (both in the 90–91 season).
Worn by: Gordon Durie, Graham Stuart.

3 1989–90

Design: UMBRO
Sponsor: COMMODORE

Another rare kit, this all-white outfit was worn for one game only against Crystal Palace at Selhurst Park – Palace's red and blue striped home kit proving just too close to Chelsea's two standard strips. This conventional and rather plain white shirt was a common Umbro design also worn by several other clubs at the time as a spare third kit. It featured a small chevron shadow pattern and blue wrap-over V-neck. 89–90 saw the side finish fifth in their first season back in the top division.

Worn in: The 2–2 draw at Crystal Palace in December 89 with Graeme Le Saux equalising for the Blues with seconds to go – a match that was also notable for Dennis Wise's sending off.
Worn by: Kevin McAllister, David Lee.

A 1990–91, 1991–92

Design: UMBRO
Sponsor: COMMODORE

Bobby Campbell's Blues sported another flashy away kit with this dazzling red and white geometric design, which, according to the Umbro catalogue of the time, was named 'Sampdoria'. The jersey originally featured the Commodore logo flush on the shirt. However, questions were raised over the logo's visibility and later versions remedied this by placing it within a separate white panel.

Worn in: The thrilling 3–2 result vs Portsmouth in the 90–91 Worthington Cup third round replay with Chelsea coming back from 2–0 down to win, followed by a fine 2–1 victory over Oxford in the next round.
Worn by: Jason Cundy, Kenneth Monkou.

H 1991–92, 1992–93

Design: UMBRO
Sponsor: COMMODORE

Many of Umbro's kits in the early 90s featured asymmetrical graphics on the right sleeve of the shirt, which were also repeated on the left leg of the shorts (now much longer in length than in previous years). This new Chelsea shirt not only adopted this trend, but also incorporated a two-tone shadow pattern throughout the fabric and a new design of button-down collar. Ian Porterfield took over as manager in the 91–92 season.

Worn in: The great 1–0 win over Everton in the 91–92 FA Cup fourth round. Also the 2–1 win over Liverpool at Anfield and the 2–0 win over Spurs the following season.
Worn by: Andy Townsend, Clive Allen, Dennis Wise, John Bumstead.

The 91–93 yellow third kit, which was identical to Everton's away strip at the time, was an Umbro design officially named 'Porto'.

3 1991–92, 1992–93

Design: UMBRO
Sponsor: COMMODORE

To combat any colour clashes caused by both the blue home and white and red away kit, this rather swish all-yellow outfit was introduced. It had an aggressive array of geometric shapes and an asymmetrical design running across the chest and sleeves. The shirt featured the same simple button-up collar as the home kit and an abstract shadow pattern. The shorts and socks were the standard Umbro issue of the era.

Worn in: The 2–0 defeat away to Blackburn Rovers at Ewood Park (92–93) and the 1–0 win away to Coventry (91–92).
Worn by: Paul Elliot, Vinnie Jones, Andy Myers, Erland Johnsen, Tony Cascarino.

H 1993–94, 1994–95

Design: UMBRO
Sponsor: COMMODORE AMIGA (93–94)
COORS* (94–95)

The famous white socks were back after eight long years! The new home kit featured a little more red than previous designs, along with a nice reinvention of the Umbro diamond trim. The strip was topped off with a dynamic shadow pattern. Commodore decided to promote its new Amiga computer on the shirts, but in its second season the jersey was sponsored by American brewery Coors. Glenn Hoddle took over as manager in 94–95.

Worn in: A superb 1–0 win away at Man Utd in 93–94, but also the 4–0 defeat to the same team in the FA Cup final later the same season. Plus a thrilling 4–3 win over Spurs in 93–94.
Worn by: Frank Sinclair, Paul Furlong.

A 1992–93, 1993–94

Design: UMBRO
Sponsor: COMMODORE

This rather curious new white away outfit was a popular strip for the club. Paired with red shorts – which featured a broad white and blue trim – and red socks, the shirt incorporated a retro round lace-up neck. The cut of the outfit was a lot baggier than before. Pairs of fine blue pinstripes ran through the fabric. It was a great-looking design and another good example of tradition and modernity meeting up in kit fashion.

Worn in: A good 1–0 win over Everton at Goodison in the 92–93 season. Not a fortunate shirt the following year – the club didn't win a game in it, including a 4–2 defeat to Everton.
Worn by: Mark Stein, John Spencer, Michael Duberry.

3 1993–94

Design: UMBRO
Sponsor: COMMODORE AMIGA

With the retro look fully in vogue in the early 90s, Umbro issued this striking series of third shirts for various clubs. They all featured large button-up collars and thin vertical bars combined with pinstripes. A shadow pattern was the only nod to contemporary fashion. Chelsea's version was this unique yellow and black outfit, with a baggy shirt and even baggier shorts. The Amiga and Umbro logos curiously remained in white, which made them slightly difficult to see on the light fabric.

Worn in: The FA Cup fourth round replay win vs Sheffield Wednesday 3–1 AET (1–1 at 90 minutes).
Worn by: Eddie Newton, Craig Burley, David Rocastle.

...mbro 95–97 home shirt, which introduced yellow into the club's home kit, ...e of the designs most fondly remembered by many Chelsea fans.

*DUE TO COPYRIGHT REASONS THE COORS LOGO IS UNABLE TO BE INCLUDED.

A 1994–95, 1995–96

Design: UMBRO
Sponsor: COORS*

One of the most outrageous kits of recent years, and one not fondly remembered by most Chelsea fans, was this eyeball-burning outfit. Officially graphite and tangerine in colour, it combined a silvery-grey speckled pattern with orange panels and navy trim. Its main claims to fame were that it was worn in the superb 94–95 win over Bruges and that it was the first Chelsea shirt worn by Ruud Gullit (in a 95–96 pre-season friendly at Gillingham).

Worn in: The home 2–0 win over Bruges in the 94–95 European Cup Winners Cup, overcoming a 1–0 deficit from the first leg, and also the poor 3–0 away defeat to Real Zaragoza in the semi-final first leg of the same competition.
Worn by: Scott Minto, Glen Hoddle.

H 1995–96, 1996–97

Design: UMBRO
Sponsor: COORS*

After eight years, red was removed from the Chelsea home kit. Instead, yellow was introduced for the logos and as trim on the collar, which also featured a new design of button-up neck. The shorts included a white triangular trim on each leg and the fabric featured a shadow pattern of the Umbro logo and the Chelsea badge. Ruud Gullit became manager in May 96, replacing Hoddle.

Worn in: The 5–0 win vs Middlesbrough in 95–96 with a hat-trick by Gavin Peacock. Plus the wonderful 4–2 comeback from 2–0 down in the FA Cup vs Liverpool in 96–97. Also that season the 2–0 FA Cup final win over Boro – the club's first major honour for 26 years!
Worn by: Ruud Gullit, Mark Hughes.

A 1996–97, 1997–98

Design: UMBRO
Sponsor: COORS* (96–97) AUTOGLASS (97–98)

Traditional yellow was brought back as the club's primary away colour in 96–97, incorporated into a dazzling new design with light and royal blue stripes on the sleeves and a delicate light blue chest panel. All logos and badges were placed centrally on the shirt. The trim on the shorts matched that of the shirt, and light blue turnovers adorned the socks. 96–97 saw the club finish sixth with some brilliant football under Gullit.

Worn in: An early away victory 2–0 against Wimbledon followed by the emphatic 4–1 triumph over Sheffield Wednesday at Hillsborough in the 97–98 season.
Worn by: Frank Leboeuf, Dan Petrescu, Roberto Di Matteo.

H 1997–98, 1998–99

Design: UMBRO
Sponsor: AUTOGLASS

Obviously intending to revitalise the Chelsea home strip, a new shade of blue was introduced. However, this decision was not a hit with the club's supporters. The new lighter hue was combined with white underarm panels trimmed with navy and yellow and a broad shadow stripe design. 98–99 saw Vialli take charge as manager.

Worn in: The 97–98 Coca-Cola Cup final 2–0 win over Middlesbrough. Also the wonderful 1–0 win over VFB Stuttgart in the European Cup Winners Cup final that same year with a goal from Zola. A 1–0 win over Leeds in 98–99 helped the club finish third.
Worn by: Gianfranco Zola, Gianluca Vialli, Jody Morris.

In the five-year period between 97–98 and 01–02, Umbro change[d] design of its logo on the Chelsea kits an incredible tir[ee]

Fly Emirates

A 1998–99, 1999–2000

Design: UMBRO
Sponsor: AUTOGLASS

The 98–99 season brought another Chelsea away kit and another change to the Umbro logo, with the famous diamond graphic returning. This new white shirt was very slick, with elegant blue and yellow piping and a smart collar. All logos were placed centrally on the vertically-patterned shirt, which was often worn with the home blue shorts. The only criticism levelled at the outfit was its similarity to the Everton away kit at the time.

Worn in: The entertaining 3–2 win at Valerenga in the 98–99 Cup Winners Cup quarter-final second leg, along with a 4–2 victory over Leicester at Filbert Street that same season.
Worn by: Celestine Babayaro, Tore Andre Flo, Gustavo Poyet.

3 1998–99, 1999–2000

Design: UMBRO
Sponsor: AUTOGLASS

Like Man Utd and Everton, Chelsea took to the field in a standard Umbro training kit design for their third kit this season. Utilising the latest hi-tech fabric, with reversed seams for comfort and anatomically inspired side panels, this range of kits was an unusual addition to the football world in the late 90s. The classic diamond trim was included on the shorts and socks.

Worn in: The thrilling 98–99 4–3 win at Ewood Park vs Blackburn and a brilliant 3–0 win over Aston Villa later that season. Also the bad-tempered defeat to Sheffield Wednesday the following year.
Worn by: Pierluigi Casiraghi, Brian Laudrup, Bernard Lambourde.

H 1999–2000, 2000–01

Design: UMBRO
Sponsor: AUTOGLASS

For the first time since the launch of the Chelsea Collection in the mid-80s, the team took to the field in a simple blue and white home strip. On first inspection the kit was basic in design with its neat round neck and white piping. However, a closer look revealed a hi-tech combination of ribbed fabrics and patterns. With the side still failing to live up to its potential, Vialli was sacked as manager in 00–01 with Claudio Ranieri replacing him.

Worn in: The 99–00 FA Cup final 1–0 triumph over Aston Villa with a goal by Di Matteo. Also, earlier that season, a 5–0 victory over Man Utd. Also a 2–0 win over the Red Devils in the 00–01 Charity Shield at The Millennium Stadium.
Worn by: Marcel Desailly, Alberto Ferrer.

A 2000–01   3 2001–02

Design: UMBRO
Sponsor: AUTOGLASS (00–01)
EMIRATES AIRLINES (01–02)

This amber and blue kit was one of the more memorable recent Chelsea outfits and set a precedent for some excellent forthcoming away

kits. It shared the 'training shirt' design of Man Utd's third kit that season, and included visible blue seams and a horizontal shadow stripe design. In the 01–02 season it was worn with the logo of new sponsors Emirate Airlines.

Worn in: The 4–2 win over Gillingham in the 00–01 FA Cup fourth round. Also a 2–1 win over Man City in the last game of the season.
Worn by: Chris Sutton, Didier Deschamps, Gabriele Ambrosetti, Samuele Dalla Bona.

The Umbro 03–05 home shirt replica also included a darker blue 'leisure shirt' on the inside, creating the first ever reversible jersey formed from just one layer of fabric.

H 2001–02, 2002–03

Design: UMBRO
Sponsor: EMIRATES AIRLINES

With high-scoring Chelsea full of optimism for the future, the 01–02 season saw two new kits launched, each with the logo of Emirates Airlines who had replaced Autoglass as club sponsors. This rather workmanlike but still intimidating home strip, made from Umbro's new Vapatech fabric, resembled a suit of armour with its curved sleeve panels. It also featured a nifty two-layered collar: blue on the outside, white on the inside.

Worn in: A series of superb wins over Liverpool (4–0), Man Utd (3–0) and West Ham (5–1) in the 01–02 season. Also the 2–0 defeat to Arsenal in the FA Cup final of the same year.
Worn by: Jimmy Floyd Hasselbaink, Manu Petit, William Gallas.

A 2001–02   3 2002–03

Design: UMBRO
Sponsor: EMIRATES AIRLINES

The club's second new kit of the 01–02 season was this sleek white affair. It was a good example of how an away shirt design can borrow elements from the home (in this case the armour-like sleeves and seams) and yet still be very different. The shirt featured a V-neck, blue piping and a subtle double shadow pinstripe effect, while the shorts and socks were just simple reversals of the home versions. Also worn with the blue home shorts.

Worn in: A good 3–2 win over Leicester but also dismal 0–0 draws against Ipswich and Everton in 01–02. The club only managed sixth place in the league this year.
Worn by: Frank Lampard, Mikael Forssell, Jesper Gronkjaer, Eidur Gudjohnsen.

A 2002–03   3 2003–04

Design: UMBRO
Sponsor: EMIRATES AIRLINES

Chelsea looked mean, moody and menacing in this new all-black (or 'carbon') away strip. Regarded as a lucky shirt for the club, it incorporated Umbro's heat-managing Vapatech fabric and breathable mesh panels under the arms. The shirt was topped off with a blue round neck and sleeve trim. Another great Umbro kit, although Chelsea were the only Premiership side wearing the Cheshire-based company's apparel at the time.

Worn in: The great 3–1 away win at Everton in 02–03. Also that season a 3–2 win over Blackburn at Ewood Park and a 3–0 victory over Manchester City.
Worn by: Celestine Babayaro, Carlton Cole, Wayne Bridge, Mario Melchiot.

H 2003–04, 2004–05

Design: UMBRO
Sponsor: EMIRATES AIRLINES

Taking into consideration the fans' requests for simple and traditional designs, the next Chelsea strip was still just blue and white with minimal embellishments and not vastly different from the previous. However, it made maximum use of modern fabric technology to create a lightweight and comfortable outfit that accompanied the side to the Premiership title in 04–05. A nice touch was a 'CFC' monogram on the back of the neck.

Worn in: A great 4–0 win over Lazio in 03–04 and the 2–1 Carling Cup win over Liverpool the following year. Also, of course, the 2–0 win at Bolton that finally clinched the long-awaited 04–05 Premiership crown.
Worn by: Damien Duff, Mario Stanic, Geremi.

The Umbro 03–05 home shirt was actually premiered in the last home match of the 02–03 season vs Liverpool. It was also the last Chelsea shirt to be worn by Gianfranco Zola before he parted company with the club.

A 2003–04   3 2004–05

Design: UMBRO
Sponsor: EMIRATE AIRLINES

The club returned to white for their away kit this season, but in a strikingly different design. With its plain and simple blue and black vertical stripes down the centre of the shirt, it resembled a typical kit from the 70s. The shirt featured the same Vapatech technology as the home kit, with mesh panels under the arms and reversed seams. The Blues finished second with big-spending new owner Roman Abramovich now on board.

Worn in: A narrow 1–0 win in 03–04 vs Everton and a 4–0 victory over Leicester. Also, a superb 3–0 win over PSG in the 04–05 Champions League.
Worn by: Scott Parker, Hernan Crespo, John Terry.

A 2004–05   3 2005–06

Design: UMBRO
Sponsor: EMIRATE AIRLINES (04–05)
SAMSUNG MOBILE (05–06)

Under new manager Jose Mourinho, this was the season when it all came right for Chelsea. After the success of the club's last black kit they returned to the colour again for this daunting new away strip. The shirt included Umbro's X-Static fabric technology, which is designed to warm you when cool and cool you when hot. The jersey also featured air vents under each arm. The jersey will be worn in 05–06 with the new sponsor's logo and badge.

Worn in: A great 2–0 win over Portsmouth. Plus a narrow 2–1 defeat at Porto in the Champions League (all 04–05).
Worn by: Mateja Kezman, Arjen Robben, Didier Drogba, Joe Cole.

H 2005–06

Design: UMBRO
Sponsor: SAMSUNG MOBILE

As the club prepare for the defence of their Premiership title they also prepare to switch kit suppliers and sponsors, ending their 18-year association with Umbro and meaning that the 05–06 season will be the last time Chelsea wear the famous diamond logo. Samsung also arrive as new shirt sponsors. Umbro go out with a bang with this superb new kit commemorating the club's centenary – in comes a stylish collar, rich gold X-Static trim on each shoulder and sleeve and a more traditional Chelsea crest. As champions it is certainly fitting gold is used to trim the club's new outfit, and the colour certainly freshens up a home strip that has been solely blue and white for the past six years.

A 2005–06

Design: UMBRO
Sponsor: SAMSUNG MOBILE

A more unusual away colour combination has been chosen to end Chelsea's Umbro connection: silver/sky blue and black – a selection that raised plenty of eyebrows around Stamford Bridge. As with all Umbro jerseys this season, a new innovation sees the reproduction of the club badge at a large scale on the inside of the jersey. The shirt itself retains all of the hi-tech characteristics of the home, with a slightly different rendering of the Umbro X-Static trim. In selecting the same colour as the home jersey for the away choice (albeit in a different shade), it's safe to say that there will be plenty of outings in 05–06 for the previous season's black away kit – one of the most popular Chelsea outfits of recent years.

Formed as St Domingos in 1878, the first incarnation of an Everton team took to the field in blue and white. However, rather than the all-blue shirt and white shorts that the team wear today, this first side sported stripes. In fact, it was to be another 23 years before the club adopted the familiar outfit supporters recognise in the modern game.

In the club's early years, any new players joining the side from outside the area each brought their own kit. The club did not want the expense of purchasing a new outfit, so the players simply dyed all their various kits black and sewed a red diagonal sash on top, earning the newly renamed Everton Football Club their first nickname – 'The Black Watch'.

After a rent disagreement at their previous home Anfield, which eventually led to the formation of Liverpool Football Club, Everton moved to Goodison Park in 1892. The first kit worn at their new home was the infamous salmon pink and navy blue concoction that was to be revived 100 years later by Umbro – to a mixed reaction by fans.

From 1901 onwards the club have remained in royal blue, the only changes being the normal fashion trends that occurred throughout the next 100+ years. For the majority of Everton fans, the favoured style is the one worn in the 60s – a simple white round neck and cuffs on the royal blue shirt, white shorts and white socks – which saw success in the 1966 FA Cup final. It was a shirt design resurrected by Puma in 2003 to great acclaim.

The club have donned a large array of away colours over the years: white, grey, black and, of course, salmon pink! But yellow is the colour most associated with Everton away from home.

Despite some excellent kits from both Le Coq Sportif and Puma in recent years, the club always seem to return to Umbro. The Cheshire-based company have produced Everton's kit over no less than three separate stints in the last 25 years, the most recent being the 'form follows function' approach of hi-tech fabrics and performance-driven attire launched in 2004. Newly equipped with the revived Umbro range (complete with white socks) and after a decade of under-performance, the side once again showed the potential they possess in the 2004–05 season under David Moyes, hoping for a return to the glory days of the mid-80s.

GRAEME SHARP IN THE LE COQ SPORTIF HOME SHIRT FROM 83–85.

Everton were actually the first club in Britain to introduce a stripe on the leg of the shorts, way back in the 1920s.

H 1978–79 to 1981–82

Design: UMBRO
Sponsor: HAFNIA (80–82)

Everton started the decade with the same kit they had worn for the previous two seasons – a classic 70s affair with a white wing collar and the traditional Umbro diamond trim on the sleeves and shorts. Like their Merseyside rivals Everton were quick to embrace the potential of sponsored shirts, with Danish canned meat producers Hafnia becoming the first company to feature their logo on the famous blue jersey.

Worn in: The 2–2 draw with Manchester City in the 80–81 FA Cup sixth round and also that season the epic 2–2 match with Liverpool.
Worn by: Asa Hartford, Bob Latchford, Alan Biley.

A 1978–79 to 1981–82

Design: UMBRO
Sponsor: HAFNIA (80–82)

The club's first away kit of the 80s was in the old Everton favourite colour combination of yellow and blue and followed the same design as the home. Occasionally, the shirt was also worn with yellow shorts. As with the home kit, earlier versions of the Hafnia logo were slightly different from the more familiar design shown here. Although not a hugely familiar name in the UK at that time, in these early days of sponsorship the Hafnia brand became instantly associated with the club.

Worn in: The 80–81 FA Cup semi-final replay vs Man City that saw Everton beaten 3–1.
Worn by: John Gidman, Imre Varadi.

H 1982–83

Design: UMBRO
Sponsor: HAFNIA

As the football kit design revolution kicked in, Umbro introduced this new silky, shiny shirt for the club, which would be worn for one season only. Of a similar design to that worn by Leeds United and the Scottish national team at the time, the strip abandoned the collar and replaced it with a simple V-neck. White piping ran from the collar to under the arms. The shirt was also worn, where necessary, with the blue shorts from the away kit.

Worn in: The 5–0 humiliation at the hands of local rivals Liverpool in 82–83 and a great 2–0 win over Spurs in that season's FA Cup fifth round. Also two impressive 5–0 victories against Aston Villa and Luton.
Worn by: John Bailey, Steve McMahon.

A 1982–83

Design: UMBRO
Sponsor: HAFNIA

The corresponding white away kit was a plain and simple reversal of the home design, with blue piping and a blue V-neck complete with white stripe. The shirt was also worn with the white home shorts where necessary. The kits appeared at a time when the club, now under the managerial control of Howard Kendall, finished seventh in the league and were just beginning to show the promise that was to threaten the top-placed clubs in the league within the next two seasons.

Worn in: A fine 2–0 victory over a good Ipswich side and a 0–0 draw with Manchester City.
Worn by: Mick Lyons, Peter Eastoe.

In an interview in the 90s, Liverpool legend Robbie Fowler (a childhood Everton fan) admitted that his favourite football kit as a young boy was the Everton Le Coq Sportif 83–85 home design.

3 1982–83

Design: UMBRO
Sponsor: HAFNIA

The second set of Umbro strips worn in the 80s was complemented by this yellow third strip. Worn with the same shorts and socks as the standard away kit, this shirt was sported in those awkward games against teams whose kits featured large areas of blue and white in one form or another. Utilising the same design as the home and away shirts of the period, this strip is one of the rarest worn by the club.

Worn in: The 2–2 draw with West Bromwich Albion at the Hawthorns in the 82–83 season.
Worn by: Andy King, Kevin Sheedy, Derek Mountfield.

H 1983–84, 1984–85

Design: LE COQ SPORTIF
Sponsor: HAFNIA

The club's deal with Umbro ended in 1983 and in came Le Coq Sportif, who in the early 80s were redefining modern kit aesthetics. Their first outfit for the club was stunning and coincided with the greatest period in the club's history. The shirt featured the unique Le Coq Sportif continental neck design, a new version of the club badge and vertical shadow stripes. Also worn with the third kit blue shorts.

Worn in: Two consecutive FA Cup finals: a 1–0 win over Watford in 83–84 and a 1–0 defeat the next year vs Man Utd. Also the epic 3–1 victory over Bayern Munich in the 84–85 Cup Winners Cup semi-final, followed by success in the final vs Rapid Vienna.
Worn by: Andy Gray, Adrian Heath.

A 1983–84, 1984–85

Design: LE COQ SPORTIF
Sponsor: HAFNIA

Away kit colours often come in trends and in the early 80s grey became the hue of choice, as demonstrated by this Le Coq Sportif outfit. The design replicated that of the home kit, with the silver/grey replacing the blue. As the primary function of football kit design is to ensure the players are distinctly visible, it is curious that grey has had moments of popularity as a shirt colour. Still, a magnificent Everton side won the Division 1 title in the 84–85 season while wearing this kit away from home, so it can't be all bad!

Worn in: A good 1–0 win over Ipswich in the 84–85 FA Cup quarter-final replay and a 1–0 win at Chelsea later that season.
Worn by: Kevin Ratcliffe, Peter Reid.

3 1983–84, 1984–85

Design: LE COQ SPORTIF
Sponsor: HAFNIA

Having grey as an away colour can cause some clash problems, but the Toffeemen always had this neat yellow shirt to fall back on. Seldom worn, when it did appear it was paired with blue shorts and trademark Le Coq Sportif-style blue hooped socks. Perhaps the strip's greatest night was the European Cup Winners Cup quarter-final success in 84–85 against Fortuna Sittard. The shirt also saw the distinctive Le Coq Sportif neck replaced by a more conventional design.

Worn in: A competent 2–1 win over Leicester at Filbert Street and the awful 4–1 defeat at Coventry (both 84–85).
Worn by: Graeme Sharp, Gary Stevens, Paul Bracewell, Trevor Steven.

By keeping the home shirt introduced in 86–87 for three years while changing the away version after only two, Umbro were able to instigate a pattern of launching at least one new design for Everton every season.

H 1985–86

Design: LE COQ SPORTIF
Sponsor: NEC

One of the most unpopular kits in Everton's history was this home outfit, which was worn for only one season and completed the end of the three-year deal with Le Coq Sportif. Although the shirt featured a nice shadow stripe pattern comprising the Le Coq Sportif logo, it was the large white panel across the chest that made it so unpopular with the club's fans.

Worn in: Two amazing 6–1 wins over Arsenal and Southampton. Also the 85–86 FA Cup final 3–1 defeat to Liverpool.
Worn by: Gary Lineker (in his only season at Goodison Park, when he scored an incredible 30 goals in 41 league appearances).

A 1985–86

Design: LE COQ SPORTIF
Sponsor: NEC

The club returned to their old favourite yellow as their away colour for this season with a design that mirrored the essential elements of the home kit – minus the controversial chest panel. This second range of Le Coq Sportif kits also saw the birth of a new sponsorship deal with Hafnia being replaced by NEC (the electronics company) after five years with the club. The new kits were tight fitting, with the athletics-style shorts being particularly skimpy. The shirt was also occasionally worn with the plain blue change shorts of the home kit.

Worn in: The brilliant 5–1 thrashing of Sheffield Wednesday and the thrilling 4–3 triumph over Ipswich Town at Portman Road.
Worn by: Ian Wilson, Wayne Clarke.

H 1986–87 to 1988–89

Design: UMBRO
Sponsor: NEC

After three years the club returned to Umbro for their kit supply in 1986. The new design was a stylish and minimal affair that included a diamond shadow pattern and just the merest hint of white on the wrap-over collar, cuffs and piping. The shorts featured the standard Umbro design of a shadow pattern combined with a coloured diagonal corner panel. The socks also included the Umbro logo.

Worn in: The 1–0 win vs Norwich in 86–87 with a goal by Pat Van den Hauwe that won the title for the club. Also the 88–89 all Merseyside FA Cup final loss vs Liverpool and the Simod Cup 4–3 defeat to Forest in 88–89.
Worn by: Tony Cottee (who scored a hat-trick on his debut for the club in the 88–89 season).

A 1986–87, 1987–88

Design: UMBRO
Sponsor: NEC

Umbro's new away kit for the club was a lighter shade of yellow than previous years and featured the same design as the home. For a short while, though, the shirt was worn with a contrasting blue collar and cuffs rather than the standard yellow. Also worn with yellow change shorts. This was a transitional period for the club, which saw them win the title again but eventually lose Kendall, who was replaced by Colin Harvey.

Worn in: A 5–0 thrashing of Sheffield Wed in the 87–88 FA Cup third round second replay after two closely-fought draws.
Worn by: Paul Power, Alan Harper, Allan Clarke.

The 1991 Umbro catalogue reveals that the home design used by Everton in 89–91 was officially named 'Goodison' and the away strip for 90–92 'Porto'.

A 1988–89, 1989–90

Design: UMBRO
Sponsor: NEC

The previous yellow away strip was replaced after two seasons by this white and grey striped outfit. The shirt was a swaggering, confident and controversial design that heralded a new explosion in football kit fashion. It introduced a basic button-down collar and grey stripes outlined with blue. It also featured blue shorts with a chequerboard shadow pattern, which were also worn with the blue home shirt when necessary.

Worn in: A solid 2–1 win over Millwall and a 2–2 draw with Oldham in the fifth round of the FA Cup (both 89–90).
Worn by: Pat Nevin, Dave Watson, Neil McDonald, Norman Whiteside.

3 1988–89, 1989–90

Design: UMBRO
Sponsor: NEC

The new grey and white striped away shirt caused some clash problems, so Umbro produced this all-yellow third kit for the club in a design that would also be used for the club's next home strip. The larger-fitting shirt included a good old-fashioned button-up collar and a zigzag shadow pattern throughout the fabric. The shorts featured large white and blue panels on each leg. The cuffs maintained the two-coloured design from the standard away kit.

Worn in: The 1–1 draw at Sheffield Wednesday (88–89). Also, the following season, a 2–1 win over Wednesday in the FA Cup fourth round.
Worn by: Ian Snodin, Martin Keown, Stefan Rehn.

H 1989–90, 1990–91

Design: UMBRO
Sponsor: NEC

Umbro's next home kit followed the larger-sized design from the previous season's third shirt, complete with button-up collar and an elaborate 'cracked ice' shadow pattern design. A third colour, grey, was also included within the outfit. The kit was actually debuted at the end of the 88–89 season during the FA Cup final 3–2 defeat against Liverpool. Another twist in the managerial tail occurred in 90–91 when Howard Kendall returned to the club, replacing Colin Harvey.

Worn in: The classic 4–4 draw with Liverpool in the 90–91 FA Cup. Also the 4–1 defeat to Crystal Palace in the Zenith Data Cup final.
Worn by: Stuart McCall, Neil Pointon, Mike Newell.

A 1990–91, 1991–92

Design: UMBRO
Sponsor: NEC

The 90–91 season saw the introduction of this dazzling yellow and blue away strip. It was a standard early 90s bold and rather abstract design with blue bars across the shirt and sleeves, which typified Umbro's adventurous approach to kit fashion at the time. To many fans, however, it summed up the problems of excessively garish modern away shirts. Also worn on occasion with the yellow shorts from the previous third kit.

Worn in: Two exciting matches against Chelsea: a good 2–1 win on New Year's Day 1991 and the 91–92 FA Cup fourth round 1–0 defeat, with Tony Cottee missing a penalty.
Worn by: John Ebbrell, Andy Hinchcliffe, Peter Beagrie.

The 93–95 home shirt was worn in Joe Royle's first game in charge at Everton – the 2–0 win over Liverpool with a thundering goal from Duncan Ferguson.

3 1992–93

Design: UMBRO
Sponsor: NEC

For the first time in eight years the Toffeemen turned out in a simple white shirt. It was a conventional design (officially entitled 'Napoli' by Umbro) with a blue and white striped wrap-over V-neck and a chevron shadow pattern fabric that was featured on many shirts at the time. The shirt was worn with blue shorts, which doubled as a change pair for the home kit when required.

Worn in: The unlucky 2–1 defeat to Aston Villa at Villa Park.
Worn by: Robert Warzycha, Barry Horne.

H 1991–92, 1992–93

Design: UMBRO
Sponsor: NEC

In the early 90s Umbro's kits were generally very busy designs packed with various graphic elements, and their next Everton shirt was typical of the era. It included an all-over shadow pattern based around the club's initials and the Umbro logo, along with a neat asymmetrical shoulder flash on the right sleeve and on the (now much longer) shorts. The club badge also underwent a change and reverted to a more traditional crest design.

Worn in: A brilliant 3–1 victory over Arsenal at home in 91–92 with two goals by Mark Ward and one by Tony Cottee, and a 4–0 win over West Ham the same season.
Worn by: Mo Johnston, Peter Beardsley.

A 1992–93, 1993–94

Design: UMBRO
Sponsor: NEC

The 92–93 season brought with it one of the most controversial away kits in the club's history – the salmon pink and navy blue outfit. Its roots were firmly intertwined with Everton's, as it was based on the first strip the team wore after their move to Goodison Park 100 years earlier. However, it was just a little bit too close to red for most fans' liking! The retro feel was completed with a wing collar and full button-up neck. Also worn with salmon pink shorts.

Worn in: A 3–2 win over Blackburn and the brilliant 5–2 triumph over Manchester City in the last game of the season (both 92–93).
Worn by: Gary Ablett, Mark Ward.

H 1993–94, 1994–95

Design: UMBRO
Sponsor: NEC

This attractive kit was full of interesting little details: a small motif of the tower from the club's badge was added within the neckpiece of the collar, and small ID tags featuring the club's name were added to the sleeves and shorts. A dramatic shadow pattern was woven into the shirt, featuring diagonal pinstripes along with an abstract version of the Umbro diamond.

Worn in: The dramatic comeback against Wimbledon in the last game of 93–94 that saved the club from relegation, Everton winning 3–2. Also the superb 4–1 win over Spurs in the 94–95 FA Cup semi-final.
Worn by: Graham Stuart, Matt Jackson.

Shirt sponsors NEC included an updated version of their logo across all Everton kits in 93–94.

3 1993–94

Design: UMBRO
Sponsor: NEC

This white shirt with 50s-style thin navy blue stripes was introduced as a third kit for one season only. It was a retro-influenced design that Umbro used for several of their teams at the time. The shirt retained the collar design and baggier size of the standard away outfit and also incorporated a similar shadow pattern throughout the material. As with the away kit, the club crest was now housed within a further shield motif. A poor season saw the club escape relegation and Mike Walker replace Howard Kendall.

Worn in: The convincing 4–1 win over Crystal Palace in the League Cup.
Worn by: David Unsworth, Paul Rideout.

A 1994–95, 1995–96

Design: UMBRO
Sponsor: NEC (94–95) DANKA (95–96)

An even more outrageous away strip emerged this season with a dynamic grey and black pattern. Away kit designs at the time seemed to be moving further away from tradition than ever and, although the garishly patterned replicas were popular with younger fans, the older supporters expressed disapproval. New sponsors Danka, a photocopier and fax machine company, appeared on the shirt in 95–96, replacing long-term shirt sponsors NEC.

Worn in: The 95–96 Charity Shield 1–0 victory over Blackburn, possibly the kit's most memorable appearance. Also a great 3–0 win again over Rovers with a lovely Andrei Kanchelskis goal.
Worn by: Vinny Samways, Anders Limpar.

H 1995–96, 1996–97

Design: UMBRO
Sponsor: DANKA

Joe Royle had become the club's new manager in 94–95 and his fresh approach led Everton to the FA Cup final that year, in which this new

home kit was first worn (complete with outgoing sponsors NEC's logo – the only major match in which it appeared on this kit). It was another complex design that included a striped collar and button-up neck. Black was added throughout the strip, most noticeably on the new hooped socks.

Worn in: The 1–0 victory over Man Utd in the 94–95 FA Cup final, along with a 2–1 win over Liverpool in 95–96.
Worn by: Duncan Ferguson, Nick Barmby.

A 1996–97, 1997–98

Design: UMBRO
Sponsor: DANKA (96–97) ONE 2 ONE (97–98)

96–97 saw the issue of an amazing new away strip – a yellow and black striped shirt with a subtle blue flash fading across the chest. The badge was placed centrally and sat below a new style Umbro logo. An interesting addition to the shirt was the repeated 'Everton' text shadow pattern. Also worn with the change shorts of the 97–98 home kit. The following season saw the logo of new shirt sponsors One 2 One replacing that of Danka.

Worn in: An awful 4–0 defeat at Wimbledon (96–97) and the only two Premiership away games the club won in the 97–98 season: 1–0 vs Leicester and 3–1 vs Crystal Palace.
Worn by: Francis Jeffers, Gary Speed, Daniel Amokachi, Andrei Kanchelskis.

The high collar of the 97–99 home shirt did not please everyone. Duncan Ferguson regularly customised it with a small cut to make it more comfortable to wear.

H 1997–98, 1998–99

Design: UMBRO
Sponsor: ONE 2 ONE

It was a year of royal(e) exits at Goodison Park; Joe was out as manager (replaced by Howard Kendall in his third stint at the club) and royal blue was replaced throughout the kit by a much lighter shade – an unpopular decision with the fans. An 'Everton' logo was incorporated into the collar. Mobile phone giants One 2 One became the new sponsors.

Worn in: A sweet 2–0 win over Liverpool in 97–98 and the 1–1 draw with Coventry that kept the club in the Premiership that year, but couldn't keep Kendall in a job. Also a great 6–0 home win over West Ham in 98–99.
Worn by: Michael Ball, Slaven Bilic.

A 1998–99

Design: UMBRO
Sponsor: ONE 2 ONE

By the 98–99 season the club itself was undergoing a period of crisis, with a power struggle at board level and the sale of Ferguson causing uproar. This stylish white away kit was introduced in the midst of the chaos. Worn by John Collins when he signed for the club, the kit saw the famous Umbro diamond trim return to the sleeves. It was also worn with matching change shorts to form a slick all-white outfit.

Worn in: A 2–0 defeat to Leicester in the club's first away game of 98–99, but also a 2–1 win over Wimbledon later in the season.
Worn by: Mickael Madar, John Spencer, Danny Cadamarteri, John Oster.

3 1998–99

Design: UMBRO
Sponsor: ONE 2 ONE

A new yellow and navy third kit was also worn in the tough 98–99 season under new manager Walter Smith. It was in a generic style that Umbro marketed at the time as a 'training kit', with Chelsea and Man Utd wearing similar designs. It had a neat collar and was one of the first designs to explore high-performance sportswear styles and new fabric technology, with the addition of ribbed material under each arm and down the side of the shirt. Despite looking good, the team still failed to impress in the Premiership.

Worn in: A 2–1 win over Blackburn at Ewood Park, but also a dismal 3–0 defeat vs Coventry.
Worn by: John Collins, Olivier Dacourt, Marco Materazzi.

H 1999–2000

Design: UMBRO
Sponsor: ONE 2 ONE

With retro influences now yesterday's news and the new millennium dawning, Umbro launched a home kit that was one of the most modern and technologically advanced outfits the club have ever worn. It incorporated a white V-neck and the Umbro ribbed 'Vapatech' fabric, designed to regulate body heat. The kit only lasted one season, as the club's 12-year relationship with Umbro ended this year.

Worn in: The brilliant 5–0 thrashing of Sunderland and the 2–0 win over Birmingham in the FA Cup fourth round. Also this season a convincing 4–0 victory over Bradford.
Worn by: Don Hutchison, Richard Gough.

An embarrassing incident occurred at Highbury in 00–01 when a disgruntled Everton fan offered to swap shirts with Alex Nyarko, believing that he could do better on the pitch than the player!

A 1999–2000

Design: UMBRO
Sponsor: ONE 2 ONE

For the final season of their deal with Everton, Umbro also released this slightly unnecessary new away kit. The kit was bright yellow and, like the previous third outfit, it followed the generic 'training kit' design that was also worn by several other clubs at the time. Produced in Umbro's Vapatech fabric, the kit featured ribbed fabric panels under each arm and black piping along each sleeve and on the sides of the shorts.

Worn in: A 2–0 win over Sheffield Wednesday and a brilliant 4–0 drubbing of West Ham at Upton Park.
Worn by: Stephen Hughes, Mitch Ward, Richard Dunne.

H 2000–01, 2001–02

Design: PUMA
Sponsor: ONE 2 ONE

New kit suppliers Puma totally revitalised the home shirt, but couldn't revitalise the team's fortunes on the pitch. The new shirt, which was also worn with blue shorts, saw the return of a collar and the introduction of white mesh breathable fabric panels down each side of the shirt. 'Everton' was added in large type beneath the badge. Paul Gascoigne posed in the shirt after he had signed for the club in 2000.

Worn in: Gazza's last match for Everton, the 3–0 defeat to Middlesbrough in the 01–02 FA Cup quarter-final. Also that season, the 5–0 thrashing of West Ham (01–02).
Worn by: Alan Stubbs, Duncan Ferguson.

A 2000–01

Design: PUMA
Sponsor: ONE 2 ONE

Puma knew how to win over the Goodison faithful and for their first away kit returned to the old favourite colour combination of yellow/amber and blue. A simple and classic look, the shirt included the new larger-size club badge and blue piping. Finishing it off with a neat minimal round neck definitely made it a favourite among the fans. Also worn with matching amber shorts.

Worn in: An awful 5–0 drubbing at Manchester City but also a good 3–1 win over Coventry City at Highfield Road.
Worn by: Gary Naysmith, Michael Ball, Steve Watson, Alec Cleland.

3 2000–01

Design: PUMA
Sponsor: ONE 2 ONE

A third kit was also promoted at the time, but it is not certain if it was ever worn in a competitive match. Puma issued a new third kit for every season they were involved with the club. The shirt featured a floppy collar design with a button-up neck alongside a large horizontal blue panel coupled with black stripes above and below. Black shorts and white socks completed the outfit. The 00–01 season found the club still languishing close to the relegation zone.

Apart from Kejian mobile phones, the other major arrival from the Far East in the 02–03 season was Chinese player Li Tie.

A 2001–02

Design: PUMA
Sponsor: ONE 2 ONE

For their next away kit Puma studied the history books and turned up with a silver/grey shirt obviously reminiscent of the classic Everton away kit of the mid-80s. Unfortunately, unlike that great side the 01–02 team did not win a single league game wearing it. On first inspection it was a very minimal style, but a closer look at the shirt revealed, aside from its new holographic-style badge, an intricate design of reversed seams and different contemporary fabrics.

Worn in: A worthy 2–2 draw at Leicester and a 3–0 whipping at Stamford Bridge by Chelsea.
Worn by: Tony Hibbert, Niclas Alexandersson, Kevin Campbell, David Weir.

3 2001–02

Design: PUMA
Sponsor: ONE 2 ONE

Puma's nostalgic look into the past continued with the style of this seldom-worn third kit. The shirt borrowed the salmon pink colour of the club's away shirt from the early 90s, which was in turn inspired by one of the club's earliest strips from the 1800s (which may explain this kit's unfeasibly long shorts). The shirt featured black sleeves and pink piping from collar to cuff. New manager David Moyes replaced Walter Smith late in the season and managed to save the club from relegation yet again.

Worn in: The disappointing 1–0 defeat to Blackburn at Ewood Park.
Worn by: Scott Gemmill, Abel Xavier, Thomas Graveson.

H 2002–03

Design: PUMA
Sponsor: KEJIAN

The club's next home strip was a real gem. This new tight-fitting shirt was produced to mark the club's 100 years in the top flight

and included a nice commemorative logo on the right-hand sleeve, featuring an image of club hero Dixie Dean. The shirt had a blue continental collar and white reversed seams that mapped an elegant design across the shirt. Also worn with blue change shorts.

Worn in: The 2–1 win over Arsenal at Goodison Park and the Worthington Cup triumph on penalties over Newcastle (3–3 AET).
Worn by: Wayne Rooney (when he scored a wonderful late goal in the 2–1 win vs Arsenal).

A 2002–03

Design: PUMA
Sponsor: KEJIAN

After four years as shirt sponsor One 2 One (who had recently been bought by T Mobile) were replaced by another mobile phone company, Kejian, forging a link between the club and China. An unfussy strip, it was simple and stylish and included a vertical blue line down each side of the shirt and a unique V-neck design. It also featured the 100-years motif on the right-hand sleeve.

Worn in: A heavy 4–1 defeat to Chelsea in the Worthington Cup. Also the humiliating 2–1 defeat to Shrewsbury in the FA Cup 3rd round. Not a lucky shirt for the club.
Worn by: Peter Clarke, Joe-Max Moore.

The 03–04 Puma home shirt was actually premiered at the last home game of the 02–03 season vs Manchester United, which ended in a 2–1 defeat for the Toffeemen.

3 2002–03

Design: PUMA
Sponsor: KEJIAN

The final kit of the club's commemorative 02–03 season was this daringly unorthodox little black number, which was inspired by the club's early kit and 'Black Watch' nickname from the late 1800s. The kit followed the design of the home kit exactly, with its white reversed seams designed to accentuate the players' physique. Like the home kit, it was very tight fitting to discourage shirt-pulling. Perhaps one of the best kits produced by Puma, it inspired the club to seventh place in the Premiership.

Worn in: Good wins at Blackburn (1–0) and West Brom (2–1), but another awful 4–1 defeat at Chelsea – this time in the Premiership.
Worn by: Li Tie, Lee Carsley, Juliano Rodrigo.

H 2003–04

Design: PUMA
Sponsor: KEJIAN

One of the most popular of Everton's recent kits was this home outfit. It was another commemorative edition, this time to celebrate the 125th anniversary of the club, and marked the end of Everton's deal not only with Kejian but also with Puma. It featured all the classic elements the Goodison faithful wanted to see: a simple yet stylish design, white round neck and cuffs and no distracting elements (other than the hi-tech combination of reversed seams and thin breathable fabric strips). Also worn with the blue shorts from the away kit.

Worn in: The amazing 4–3 defeat to Man Utd at Goodison Park along with a great 4–0 win over Leeds earlier in the season.
Worn by: Alessandro Pistone, Alex Nyarko.

A 2003–04

Design: PUMA
Sponsor: KEJIAN

Puma's last away kit for the Toffeemen mirrored the design of the home, a relatively rare event in the modern game. However, the kit did attract some criticism for being too close to Puma's first Everton away kit three years earlier. Like the equivalent home shirt, it was a slightly more generous fit than the previous style. The shirt was also worn with matching amber change shorts.

Worn in: A 2–1 win over Portsmouth – the only League victory in this shirt. Plus a 5–1 drubbing at the hands of Manchester City in the last match of the season.
Worn by: Lee Carsley, Tomasz Radzinski.

3 2003–04

Design: PUMA
Sponsor: KEJIAN

In Puma's final year with the club they issued another mystery superfluous third kit. It was actually quite a pleasant-looking concoction of silver/grey and navy. Extremely retro in style with its 70s V-inset collar and sleeve stripe trim, it was not warmly received by fans and, like the 00–01 season third kit, it does not appear to have been worn in a competitive league match. It was a dismal season for the Toffeemen, which saw them just missing out on relegation by finishing 17th. Perhaps this silver kit should have been given a chance, given some of the dismal results gained in the standard yellow away shirt.

Once a dominant force in football kit design, Umbro produced kits for just two clubs in the English top flight in 04–05: Everton and Chelsea.

H 2004–05

Design: UMBRO
Sponsor: CHANG BEER

In a remarkable turn of events, Umbro returned once more to Goodison Park as Everton's kit suppliers – their third stint at the club. They pulled out all the stops with this home kit – an ultra-modern layered V-neck, breathable fabric panels and cooling air vents under each arm. Another popular move was the reintroduction of plain white socks. Like the last Umbro home outfit four years earlier, it epitomised contemporary kit design. The club's new sponsors again originated from the Far East – Thailand's Chang Beer.

Worn in: A great 1–0 win over Liverpool at home and a close 3–2 win over Bolton.
Worn by: Marcus Bent, Eddy Bosnar, James Beattie, Nick Chadwick.

A 2004–05

Design: UMBRO
Sponsor: CHANG BEER

Umbro reverted to a nice and simple white and blue colour scheme for the first away kit of this era. The shirt included a different neck design from that of the home strip and dynamic blue panels on each sleeve. Like many of Umbro's recent kits, the shirt included their X-Static fabric technology designed to warm you when cool and cool you when hot. The shorts and socks were reversals of the home styles and were designed to effortlessly mix and match.

Worn in: A superb 3–1 win at Crystal Palace in the first away game of 04–05 and a good 1–0 win over Man City, spoiled only by Tim Cahill's sending off for pulling his shirt over his head in celebration after his winning goal.
Worn by: Tim Cahill, Kevin Kilbane.

3 2004–05

Design: UMBRO
Sponsor: CHANG BEER

Following the popularity of the 02–03 all-black Puma kit, Umbro released their own version in 04–05. The shirt featured similar breathable fabric panels to the home kit with special blue inserts under each arm. The blue worked well with the black, which was offset with just a subtle white trim. The return of Umbro coincided with a remarkable season that saw the club flying high, eventually finishing in fourth place and surprising many people with their strong team spirit under manager David Moyes.

Worn in: The 0–0 draw with Blackburn Rovers at Ewood Park.
Worn by: James McFadden, Leon Osman.

H 2005–06

Design: UMBRO
Sponsor: CHANG BEER

The promotional campaign for Everton's 05–06 home kit centred around airports, planes and travel, aptly commemorating the club's fantastic return to European football. The design itself is remarkably similar to the previous year's. At first glance the shirt is basic in design, but a closer inspection reveals a neat little collar and curved white mesh panels gracing each side, along with, of course, Umbro's state of the art X-Static fabric technology. The back of the shirt also includes a fine mesh fabric designed to easily expel excess body heat. The plain white shorts and socks are adorned with the merest hint of blue.

A 2005–06

Design: UMBRO
Sponsor: CHANG BEER

The club return to silver for the 05–06 season
in this slick and hi-tech new outfit. Worn for
the first time in the pre-season friendly against
Fenerbahce (which ended in an awful 5–0
defeat for The Toffeemen), the shirt features
black and blue trim and includes Umbro's Skin
Effect Body fabric along with mesh fabric
panels. As with all Umbro designs this season,
special zonal underarm ventilation panels
assist temperature regulation. A third kit will
also be introduced later in the campaign.

FULHAM

Despite being one of the smaller clubs in London and living in the shadow of their more famous neighbours Chelsea, Fulham have always had a glamorous side. After all, how many clubs can boast of a West London home, a celebrity fan in Wolfie 'Citizen' Smith and the likes of Bobby Moore, George Best and Rodney Marsh in their line-up at one time or another? It is therefore perhaps strange that the club's kit is based on one of the most basic and workmanlike football outfits imaginable: a simple white shirt and black shorts. This was the outfit originally selected when the club formed as St Andrew's in 1879, and has been the strip of choice at Craven Cottage ever since.

Favourite away colours for the side are undoubtedly red and black. In fact, an exact replica of the home kit in this colour combination formed the standard away outfit for the club for the entire 1980s. Since the DMF Sportswear phase in the early 90s, however, a more varied palette of colours has been worn by the club. Light blue, yellow and even a vivid green have all made appearances, but the more traditional red and black colour scheme still regularly makes a reappearance.

The club kit has remained fairly consistent over the years, although the badge worn on the shirt has gone through several changes. A more regal crest was popular in the Johnny Haynes era of the 50s and 60s (and made a comeback in 1995), with a simple monogram more popular in the 70s and a distinctive shield in the 80s and early 90s. Today the club sport a highly contemporary crest that is perfectly in step with their cosmopolitan image and which was introduced with relatively little fuss in 2001.

After the club's golden era in the 50s and 60s they dropped down the league. In the late 90s adidas began to concentrate on supporting clubs in the lower divisions and their arrival at Craven Cottage (with some snazzy new kits) coincided with Mohammed Al Fayed's patronage of the club and, of course, the managerial reign of both Keegan and Wilkins – a series of events that no doubt inspired the team. The club's confidence and success has grown in tandem with the design aesthetics of their recent kits, culminating in the revolutionary series of Puma kits the club currently wear.

Perhaps along with Wimbledon, the story of Fulham has been one of the biggest rags to riches stories of the past 25 years. However, fans of the Cottagers will be hoping that the club do not fall into decline as Wimbledon have done.

LUIS BOA MORTE IN THE 03–05 PUMA HOME KIT.

Osca also produced kits for Charlton Athletic and Derby County in the early 80s.

FULHAM

H 1977–78 to 1980–81

Design: ADIDAS
Sponsor: NONE

In the 70s Fulham was a haven for superstars in the latter days of their career and it was arguably the greatest, George Best, who appeared in this shirt – a swish adidas kit – in the 77–78 season. It was a classic adidas design with a wing collar and the trademark three-stripe trim that superseded the previous Umbro outfit. As with almost all adidas kits from this era, there were slight variations over the four years it was in use – notably in the size of the collar and the positioning of the logo on the shorts.

Worn in: The epic 1–1 draw with Man Utd in the 79–80 FA Cup fourth round. Also the 4–3 win over Swindon in the 80–81 season.
Worn by: Dean Coney, Robert Wilson.

A 1977–78 to 1980–81

Design: ADIDAS
Sponsor: NONE

For a long period the standard Fulham away kit was simply the home design reproduced in red and black, and the club's first adidas away affair was no different. After nine seasons in Division 2 the club were relegated to Division 3 at the end of the 79–80 season, and the 80–81 season saw ex-player Malcolm McDonald attempting to lift the club back to past glories. The club badge was now based around a shield design, replacing the simple FFC monogram that had graced the previous shirt.

Worn in: Two dreadful defeats in the 79–80 season: 4–1 to Swansea and 4–0 to Luton. Plus a 2–1 win over Reading in the 80–81 FA Cup first round.
Worn by: John Beck, Brian Greenaway.

H 1981–82, 1982–83

Design: OSCA
Sponsor: NONE

After just one set of kits, the deal with adidas ended and smaller sportswear company Osca became the club's new kit suppliers. A London-based company, Osca specialised in kits for lower league teams throughout the early 80s. This unique design of white shirts and black shoulders was worn by Malcolm McDonald's young team and is fondly remembered by Fulham fans. The side gained promotion to Division 2 in the 81–82 season, and so nearly went up to Division 1 the following year.

Worn in: A solid 4–1 victory over Wimbledon (81–82) and the 1–1 draw at home against Lincoln City later in the season that was good enough to secure promotion.
Worn by: Sean O'Driscoll, Roger Brown.

A 1981–82, 1982–83

Design: OSCA
Sponsor: NONE

The club's early 80s renaissance saw Fulham accompanied away from home by a red and black version of the Osca home kit. The kits had a contemporary feel and were good, functional outfits. As with all Osca kits the club badge did not appear on the shorts, which only featured a simple trim.

Worn in: An emphatic 4–0 win over Grimsby in 82–83, but arguably the greatest match of that season was the 4–1 win over Keegan's Newcastle at St James' Park with a sterling performance from Ray Houghton.
Worn by: Gordon Davies, Kevin Lock, Dale Tempest, Tony Gale.

Umbro's shorts from the 84–87 kit with their broad white trim were almost exactly the same style as the last pair the company had produced for the club, way back in the mid-70s.

H 1983–84

Design: OSCA
Sponsor: NONE

Osca's last home kit for the club followed the company's standard design of the time: a simple contrasting wrap-over V-neck and pinstripes. The shorts and socks remained exactly the same as the previous outfit. The only other change was the badge, which was now housed in a round design rather than the traditional shield.

Worn in: A superb 5–0 win over Swansea at Craven Cottage, followed the next week by an even more exciting 5–3 defeat to local rivals Chelsea – a match in which Gordon Davies scored a hat-trick yet still ended up on the losing side.
Worn by: Jeff Hopkins, Ray Houghton, Clifford Carr.

A 1983–84

Design: OSCA
Sponsor: NONE

As the club attempted to reproduce the success of the previous two seasons, away games were played in this striking red and black strip. Again, it followed the design of the home kit, but with white pinstripes rather than black creating an attractive contrast. As with the home strip, the shorts and socks were identical to those worn with the previous kit. Fulham reserves continued to wear these Osca kits well into the 84–87 deal with Umbro.

Worn in: An unlucky 2–1 defeat away to Grimsby Town. Also a thrilling encounter at St James' Park with Fulham suffering a 3–2 defeat to Newcastle.
Worn by: Paul Parker, Sean O'Driscoll, Ray Lewington.

H 1984–85 to 1986–87

Design: UMBRO
Sponsor: WILLIAM YOUNGER (84–85)
PRESTIGE TRAVEL (85–86)

After seven years away from Craven Cottage, sportswear giants Umbro took over Fulham's kit production once again in 84–85 as part of a three-year deal. Their home kit was one of the smartest designs the company produced and one of the best worn by the club. The shirt included red for the first time, as well as black piping and a shadow stripe pattern. The shirt was sponsored by the beer brand William Younger before being replaced a season later by coach company Prestige Travel.

Worn in: A good 4–2 win over Bolton (86–87), but also the nightmare 10–0 defeat to Liverpool in the 86–87 Milk Cup second round.
Worn by: Keith Oakes, Jim Hicks.

A 1984–85 to 1986–87

Design: UMBRO
Sponsor: WILLIAM YOUNGER (84–85)
PRESTIGE TRAVEL (85–86)

No surprises with Umbro's next away kit – it was the same design as the home in red and black with just a hint of white, incorporating exactly the same V-neck and cuffs. The classic Umbro diamond trim adorned the sock turnovers. It was a difficult time for the club, who had been relegated in 85–86 and found themselves in Division 3 under player-manager Ray Lewington in 86–87.

Worn in: A superb 3–2 victory away to Notts County (86–87) followed by a defeat by the same score to Bolton later that season.
Worn by: Kenneth Achampong, John Marshall, Brian Cottington.

...combination, the mysterious Fulham third shirt
...rpool's kit from the previous season.

3 1986–87

Design: UMBRO
Sponsor: NONE

A real anomaly in Fulham's wardrobe was this seldom-seen yellow third shirt. The fact that it was worn without a club badge indicates that it was probably an unofficial emergency shirt worn due to a difficult colour clash in the game vs Brentford (who of course play in red and white stripes, thus clashing with both Fulham's kits at the time). The shirt was a standard Umbro design of the time with shadow pinstripes and piping and was worn with unique yellow socks and the red and black shorts from the away kit.

Worn in: A classic 3–3 encounter away to local rivals Brentford at Griffin Park with goals from Kenneth Achampong, Peter Scott and Cliff Carr.
Worn by: Wayne Kerrins, Kevin Hoddy.

H 1987–88

Design: SCORELINE
Sponsor: NONE

After the three-year deal with Umbro ended, Fulham turned to Scoreline to manufacture their next range of kits. Scoreline outfits are what all good football strips should be: contemporary, functional and intimidating, yet still traditional. The shirt featured thin shadow stripes, a central badge, Scoreline logos on each sleeve and black side panels – a trend that was not to come into fashion until 10 years later. Once again there was no major sponsor, although Emirates did appear on the shirt a few times at the end of the season.

Worn in: A 4–0 thrashing of Doncaster at Craven Cottage and another high-scoring win – this time 5–0 against Grimsby Town.
Worn by: Michael Cole, Jeff Eckhardt.

A 1987–88

Design: SCORELINE
Sponsor: NONE

The first away kit produced by Scoreline was once again a straightforward red and black version of the home. The kit was usually worn with red or white shorts (which doubled as change shorts for the home kit) but also with the first choice black pair. The Scoreline logo also appeared on each side of the shorts in a unique design. The team's fortunes improved this season even though they were still in Division 3, and they eventually finished ninth.

Worn in: An awful 5–1 hammering at Notts County, but also a good 3–1 win at Wigan.
Worn by: Justin Skinner, Richard Langley, Wayne Kerrins, Leroy Rosenior.

H 1988–89, 1989–90

Design: SCORELINE
Sponsor: TELECONNECT

Scoreline's kits tended to evolve gradually season by season rather than undergoing huge changes. For this next home strip, the fabric and side panels remained the same, but the V-neck developed into a wrap-over design and the badge moved to the traditional left breast with the Scoreline logo now on the right. Towards the end of the season telecommunications company Teleconnect became the new shirt sponsor, signing a deal that was to last until the end of 90–91.

Worn in: Brilliant home wins over Aldershot (5–1) and Northampton (3–2) in 88–89. Also a 4–0 thrashing of Wigan the following year.
Worn by: Andy Sayer, Colin Gordon, Glen Thomas.

A 1988–89, 1989–90

Design: SCORELINE
Sponsor: TELECONNECT

The next away kit underwent the same minor changes as the home version, with the Scoreline logo now also appearing on the socks. Another difference was the addition of white piping to highlight the black trim on the shorts. The 89–90 season found the club in dire straits, lucky to have escaped relegation to the dreaded Division 4.

Worn in: The disappointing 2–0 defeat to Swansea, followed by a closely fought 1–0 win over Notts County (both 88–89).
Worn by: Gary Elkins, Clive Walker, Gary Barnett.

H 1990–91

Design: RIBERO
Sponsor: TELECONNECT

With the club still struggling at the bottom end of Division 3 another smaller sportswear company, Ribero, began producing the team's kits. Football shirts were following the world of high-street fashion and becoming bigger and baggier, with the sleeve length creeping down towards the elbow. The first Ribero kit was a great-looking design, with the return of a large collar and piping running from the cuffs and down each side of the shirt. The shorts featured a triangular white trim on each leg.

Worn in: The awful first three home games of 90–91 against Cambridge, Huddersfield and Wigan – all played without a win for Fulham.
Worn by: Stacey North, Martin Pike.

A 1990–91

Design: RIBERO
Sponsor: TELECONNECT

The equivalent Ribero away kit retained the design of the home but now of course in red. White trim was used instead of black, making a refreshing change for the club's away matches. The Teleconnect logo also changed and now appeared in a black rectangular panel. As with the home shirt, a subtle abstract shadow pattern was added to the fabric. The side, now managed by Alan Dicks, finished 21st in Division 3 – their lowest ebb for many years.

Worn in: 1–0 defeats to Preston North End and Reading – the club's away form this season was no better than their home.
Worn by: Mark Newson, Graham Baker, Peter Scott.

H 1991–92

Design: RIBERO
Sponsor: NONE

The home kit for 91–92 saw only a subtle move on from the previous style. Ribero added a nice splash of red to the black collar, moved the piping to run from the collar to under the arm and introduced a new shadow pattern. The deal with Teleconnect had ended the previous season, so the club spent 91–92 unsponsored once again. The shorts featured a new red and white Umbro-esque spear-like trim and a shadow pattern. Two different designs of socks were worn: a pair with three black stripes as shown here, along with the red and black trimmed pair from the previous kit.

Worn in: Encouraging early-season wins over Bradford (4–3) and Swansea (3–0).
Worn by: Julian Hails, Andy Cole, Kelly Haag.

Apart from a simplified V-neck and cuffs combination, the mysterious Fulham third shirt of 86–87 was exactly the same as Liverpool's kit from the previous season.

3 1986–87

Design: UMBRO
Sponsor: NONE

A real anomaly in Fulham's wardrobe was this seldom-seen yellow third shirt. The fact that it was worn without a club badge indicates that it was probably an unofficial emergency shirt worn due to a difficult colour clash in the game vs Brentford (who of course play in red and white stripes, thus clashing with both Fulham's kits at the time). The shirt was a standard Umbro design of the time with shadow pinstripes and piping and was worn with unique yellow socks and the red and black shorts from the away kit.

Worn in: A classic 3–3 encounter away to local rivals Brentford at Griffin Park with goals from Kenneth Achampong, Peter Scott and Cliff Carr.
Worn by: Wayne Kerrins, Kevin Hoddy.

H 1987–88

Design: SCORELINE
Sponsor: NONE

After the three-year deal with Umbro ended, Fulham turned to Scoreline to manufacture their next range of kits. Scoreline outfits are what all good football strips should be: contemporary, functional and intimidating, yet still traditional. The shirt featured thin shadow stripes, a central badge, Scoreline logos on each sleeve and black side panels – a trend that was not to come into fashion until 10 years later. Once again there was no major sponsor, although Emirates did appear on the shirt a few times at the end of the season.

Worn in: A 4–0 thrashing of Doncaster at Craven Cottage and another high-scoring win – this time 5–0 against Grimsby Town.
Worn by: Michael Cole, Jeff Eckhardt.

A 1987–88

Design: SCORELINE
Sponsor: NONE

The first away kit produced by Scoreline was once again a straightforward red and black version of the home. The kit was usually worn with red or white shorts (which doubled as change shorts for the home kit) but also with the first choice black pair. The Scoreline logo also appeared on each side of the shorts in a unique design. The team's fortunes improved this season even though they were still in Division 3, and they eventually finished ninth.

Worn in: An awful 5–1 hammering at Notts County, but also a good 3–1 win at Wigan.
Worn by: Justin Skinner, Richard Langley, Wayne Kerrins, Leroy Rosenior.

H 1988–89, 1989–90

Design: SCORELINE
Sponsor: TELECONNECT

Scoreline's kits tended to evolve gradually season by season rather than undergoing huge changes. For this next home strip, the fabric and side panels remained the same, but the V-neck developed into a wrap-over design and the badge moved to the traditional left breast with the Scoreline logo now on the right. Towards the end of the season telecommunications company Teleconnect became the new shirt sponsor, signing a deal that was to last until the end of 90–91.

Worn in: Brilliant home wins over Aldershot (5–1) and Northampton (3–2) in 88–89. Also a 4–0 thrashing of Wigan the following year.
Worn by: Andy Sayer, Colin Gordon, Glen Thomas.

A 1988–89, 1989–90

Design: SCORELINE
Sponsor: TELECONNECT

The next away kit underwent the same minor changes as the home version, with the Scoreline logo now also appearing on the socks. Another difference was the addition of white piping to highlight the black trim on the shorts. The 89–90 season found the club in dire straits, lucky to have escaped relegation to the dreaded Division 4.

Worn in: The disappointing 2–0 defeat to Swansea, followed by a closely fought 1–0 win over Notts County (both 88–89).
Worn by: Gary Elkins, Clive Walker, Gary Barnett.

H 1990–91

Design: RIBERO
Sponsor: TELECONNECT

With the club still struggling at the bottom end of Division 3 another smaller sportswear company, Ribero, began producing the team's kits. Football shirts were following the world of high-street fashion and becoming bigger and baggier, with the sleeve length creeping down towards the elbow. The first Ribero kit was a great-looking design, with the return of a large collar and piping running from the cuffs and down each side of the shirt. The shorts featured a triangular white trim on each leg.

Worn in: The awful first three home games of 90–91 against Cambridge, Huddersfield and Wigan – all played without a win for Fulham.
Worn by: Stacey North, Martin Pike.

A 1990–91

Design: RIBERO
Sponsor: TELECONNECT

The equivalent Ribero away kit retained the design of the home but now of course in red. White trim was used instead of black, making a refreshing change for the club's away matches. The Teleconnect logo also changed and now appeared in a black rectangular panel. As with the home shirt, a subtle abstract shadow pattern was added to the fabric. The side, now managed by Alan Dicks, finished 21st in Division 3 – their lowest ebb for many years.

Worn in: 1–0 defeats to Preston North End and Reading – the club's away form this season was no better than their home.
Worn by: Mark Newson, Graham Baker, Peter Scott.

H 1991–92

Design: RIBERO
Sponsor: NONE

The home kit for 91–92 saw only a subtle move on from the previous style. Ribero added a nice splash of red to the black collar, moved the piping to run from the collar to under the arm and introduced a new shadow pattern. The deal with Teleconnect had ended the previous season, so the club spent 91–92 unsponsored once again. The shorts featured a new red and white Umbro-esque spear-like trim and a shadow pattern. Two different designs of socks were worn: a pair with three black stripes as shown here, along with the red and black trimmed pair from the previous kit.

Worn in: Encouraging early-season wins over Bradford (4–3) and Swansea (3–0).
Worn by: Julian Hails, Andy Cole, Kelly Haag.

Ribero also produced designs for Coventry, Norwich, Blackburn, Charlton and Crystal Palace in the early 90s.

A 1991–92

Design: RIBERO
Sponsor: NONE

Red remained the away kit colour in 91–92 and the strip was remodelled by Ribero into a slick, modern and streamlined affair. It was also the first main away kit worn by the club in recent years that didn't simply replicate the style of the home, as it featured a wrap-over round neck instead of a collar. The red shorts were also worn with the white home shirt on occasion. Don Mackay took over the reins at the club after the departure of Dicks.

Worn in: A 3–1 drubbing at Darlington that saw manager Alan Dicks resign after the match. Also a superb 3–2 win over West Brom later in the season.
Worn by: Sean Farrell, Mark Kelly, Udo Onwere.

H 1992–93

Design: DMF SPORTSWEAR
Sponsor: NONE

With the arrival of the Premier League in 1992, Fulham now found themselves 'promoted' to the renamed Division 2. They also sported a new kit by little-known company DMF Sportswear. As with most Fulham kits over the past few years, there were only slight changes to the previous design – the main differences being the incorporation of the club badge into a lively shadow pattern throughout the fabric and the addition of large red panels to the shorts, upon which sat the club's initials: 'FFC'.

Worn in: A 3–1 win over Plymouth Argyle and a nail-biting 3–3 draw with Hull at the Cottage.
Worn by: Lee Tierling, Gavin Nebbeling, Martin Ferney, Martin Thomas.

A 1992–93

Design: DMF SPORTSWEAR
Sponsor: NONE

DMF dramatically livened up the red away kit this season in a bold change from the recent designs the club had worn. White stripes ran across each sleeve and in an asymmetrical pattern on the left leg of the shorts. As with the home kit, the Fulham badge appeared on the shorts for the first time since the last set of Umbro kits. The FFC initials were included on the socks, which were also worn with the white home shirt on occasion.

Worn in: The wonderful 2–0 win at Brighton with goals from Martin Pike and Julian Hails. Also a stunning 4–1 away victory at high-flying Bolton Wanderers.
Worn by: Simon Morgan, Leon Lewis, Mark Tucker.

3 1992–93

Design: DMF SPORTSWEAR
Sponsor: NONE

For the first time the club issued an official third strip, which was this rather nice all light blue outfit trimmed with navy. It was the first time in over 15 years that the club had officially worn anything other than white or red, excluding of course the obscure, unofficial Umbro yellow third shirt in 86–87. The shirt had the same unique striped sleeves of the away kit, but unlike both the home and away strips it featured a button-up round neck rather than a collar. The shorts followed the design of the home pair. The shirt remained unsponsored for the second season running.

Worn in: The dismal 2–0 defeat to Brentford in the second round of the 92–93 Coca-Cola Cup.
Worn by: Junior Lewis, Paul Sheldrick.

The club crest introduced in the 95–96 season was last worn by the club in the 50s and 60s.

H 1993–94

Design: VANDANEL
Sponsor: GMB

There were plenty of changes at Craven Cottage in the 93–94 season. Vandanel started supplying the team kit (a very nice, restrained and traditional affair with the only daring element arguably being the white flash on the shorts), the GMB (Britain's general union) became the club's new shirt sponsors and manager Don Mackay departed after another poor season, which saw the team sliding rapidly down the league.

Worn in: Another crushing defeat to Liverpool – this time 5–0 in the Coca-Cola Cup second round. Also a thrilling 3–2 win over Blackpool in the League.

Worn by: Duncan Jupp, Ara Bedrossian, Robert Herrera.

A 1993–94

Design: VANDANEL
Sponsor: GMB

A new look for Fulham was created with this new red and black striped shirt issued by Vandanel. With football kit nostalgia at its peak, many older fashions were coming back to influence modern kits. This outfit featured the baggiest shorts worn by the club for many years, complete with an unusual but innovative striped trim across each leg. The shorts were also worn with the home shirt a couple of times during the season.

Worn in: A narrow 1–0 defeat away to Reading. Plus a tight win over Bristol Rovers in the Autoglass Cup, the match finishing 2–2 with Fulham winning 4–3 on penalties.

Worn by: Terry Angus, Peter Baah.

3 1993–94

Design: VANDANEL
Sponsor: GMB

With yet another relegation-facing season in full swing, Fulham also sported this seldom-worn blue third shirt. It included the same simple collar design as the home and away shirts and was worn with the white shorts and red socks from the standard change outfit. The 93–94 season was another dark time for the club as they were relegated to Division 3.

Worn in: A cracking 10-goal thriller away to Exeter, which ended in a 6–4 defeat for Fulham.

Worn by: Paul Kelly, Alan Cork, Micky Adams.

H 1994–95, 1995–96

Design: VANDANEL
Sponsor: GMB

The next Vandanel home kit changed very little from their first outfit. A new collar design was introduced, which included a miniature version of the club badge, as was a shadow pattern made up of pinstripes and the Vandanel logo. A red waistband was introduced to the shorts, again with a small club badge in the centre, along with white piping down each leg. A new, more regal, crest was introduced as the club badge in 95–96.

Worn in: A 4–2 win over Mansfield in the first game of the 95–96 season, followed by the 7–0 triumph over Swansea in the FA Cup. Also the infamous away defeat that season at bottom-of-the-table Torquay.

Worn by: Mike Conroy, Gary Brazil.

In 98–99 the adidas logo on the home shirt was updated from the text-only version used on the 97–98 version.

A 1994–95, 1995–96

Design: VANDANEL
Sponsor: GMB

The mid-90s is an era most Fulham supporters will want to forget: low attendances, no cash and staring non-league football in the face. Accompanying them during these grim times was this interesting red and black halved shirt. As with the home shirt, a new club badge was introduced in the 95–96 season with a hope to inspire the side back to better days. Ex-player Micky Adams took charge of the team and began to push for the future.

Worn in: A thrilling 3–2 defeat to Preston in 94–95 and some unfortunate losses to Bury (3–0) and Hereford (1–0) in the 95–96 season.
Worn by: Rory Hamill, Nick Cusack.

H 1996–97

Design: LE COQ SPORTIF
Sponsor: GMB

Strangely, a change of kit supplier can often coincide with good fortune for a club, and so it was in 96–97 with Fulham finishing the season second in Division 3 and gaining promotion – their first for 15 years. The Le Coq Sportif strip kept to tradition with the only real embellishment being the tiny chequerboard trim on the shirt cuffs and down each leg of the shorts. A stylish shadow pattern was also included on the shirt.

Worn in: The 6–0 triumph vs Darlington and a 3–2 vs Colchester earlier in the season, along with good 2–0 wins over Brighton and Hull City. Plus the great 2–1 win at Carlisle that virtually secured promotion from Division 3.
Worn by: Glenn Cockerill, Rob Scott.

A 1996–97

Design: LE COQ SPORTIF
Sponsor: GMB

If Le Coq Sportif were restrained with the home kit, they let their hair down a little with the away outfit. The colour scheme was familiar, but was now fashioned into a large chequerboard pattern – a favourite trend of Le Coq Sportif at the time. A chequerboard trim was also included on the shorts, which strangely were black rather than red (although a change pair of white was worn with both this and the home outfit).

Worn in: The vital 2–0 win over Darlington and a good 2–1 win over Swansea.
Worn by: Steve Hayward, Paul Watson, Rod McAree.

H 1997–98, 1998–99

Design: ADIDAS
Sponsor: GMB (97–98)
        DEMON INTERNET (98–99)

97–98 saw many new arrivals at Craven Cottage: a new major shareholder in the form of Mohammed Al Fayed, a new managerial duo in Kevin Keegan and Ray Wilkins and a swish new kit courtesy of adidas, who had last been linked with the club in 80–81. The shirt was sponsored in its second season of use by internet provider Demon.

Worn in: The 3–1 win over Oldham and the 3–0 win over Gillingham that confirmed Fulham as Division 2 98–99 champions.
Worn by: Danny Cullip, Matthew Lawrence, Richard Carpenter, Darren Freeman.

FULHAM

A 1997–98

Design: ADIDAS
Sponsor: GMB

The late 90s saw sportswear giants adidas focusing on several smaller teams in the English league. Their first Fulham away kit was another unique style for the club – red and black hoops. Combined with central logos and the classic three-stripe trim, it was a classy design. The shorts, now even longer than in previous seasons, featured the trademark trim along each leg. Ray Wilkins surprisingly left the club shortly before the play-offs this season.

Worn in: The 1–0 defeat to Grimsby in the second leg of the 97–98 play-off final. A good 2–0 win over Chesterfield and the unlucky 3–1 defeat to Spurs in the FA Cup third round.
Worn by: Geoff Horsfield, Wayne Collins, Paul Peschisolido, Paul Brooker.

A 1998–99

Design: ADIDAS
Sponsor: DEMON INTERNET

Now managed by Keegan, 98–99 was a wonderful season for Fulham. As they steamrollered Division 2 and gained promotion to Division 1, they also had a new yellow and black away strip. Internet providers Demon replaced GMB as shirt sponsor. With a three-stripe shadow pattern and unique trim along each sleeve, it was a self-assured and bold-looking kit. Also worn with yellow adidas 'Opio Cup' shorts.

Worn in: A shock 2–0 win at Premiership Aston Villa in the 98–99 FA Cup fourth round, along with a stunning 4–0 thrashing of Luton.
Worn by: Steve Hayward, Kit Symons, John Salako, Peter Beardsley.

H 1999–2000, 2000–01

Design: ADIDAS
Sponsor: DEMON INTERNET

With the club freshly promoted to Division 1 for 99–00, they sported this fresh new adidas home kit, although in truth it was actually fairly similar to the previous design. Keegan left to manage England and Paul Bracewell came in as new boss, before being eventually replaced himself by Jean Tigana.

Worn in: A brilliant 3–1 win over Spurs in the 99–00 Worthington cup. Also the 1–1 draw with Sheffield Wednesday with a great Sean Davis equaliser a minute from the end that clinched the 00–01 Division 1 title for Fulham.
Worn by: Stan Collymore, Karl-Heinz Riedle, Mark Blake.

A 1999–2000

Design: ADIDAS
Sponsor: DEMON INTERNET

Sunglasses were needed at grounds throughout the country as Fulham came to town in this incredibly bright, shiny green strip. However, it was a strip that was not popular with the Craven Cottage faithful. The shirt featured a conventional collar, a three-stripe trim and large navy panels running across each sleeve. Also worn with navy shorts.

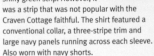

Worn in: The superb 3–0 victory over Luton in the FA Cup second round replay and a solid 2–0 away performance at Port Vale – the only really positive results in this garish strip.
Worn by: Stephen Hughes, Gus Uhlenbeek, Kevin Ball, Terry Phelan.

Shirt sponsors Demon Internet updated their brand logo for the 00–01 away shirt.

A 2000–01

Design: ADIDAS
Sponsor: DEMON INTERNET

After two fairly vivid strips, the club launched a more sedate new design for their next assault on Division 1. It was back to red, although now combined with a white yoke and sleeves. The shirt also featured a new adidas collar design and black piping. The shorts remained white, but were now trimmed with an elegant red and black design. A highly successful season found Jean Tigana's men winning the Division 1 title at a canter with an astonishing 101 points.

Worn in: A good 2–0 win over local rivals QPR and a 4–1 thrashing of Tranmere Rovers. Plus, of course, the 2–1 win at Huddersfield that finally confirmed Fulham's promotion.
Worn by: Louis Saha, Paul Trollope.

H 2001–02, 2002–03

Design: ADIDAS
Sponsor: PIZZA HUT (01–02)
BETFAIR.COM (02–03)

Worn in the club's first ever season in the Premiership, Fulham's final adidas home shirt was much simpler than previous affairs and saw the return of a plain white shirt (with black side and underarm panels) and a restrained use of red as a third colour. Pizza Hut became the club's new sponsor and to top it all off there was also a newly designed modern club badge. Also worn with white shorts.

Worn in: The 2–0 win over Sunderland in the club's first Premiership home game. The 01–02 FA Cup semi-final defeat to Chelsea. A great 3–0 home triumph over Charlton and a thrilling 3–2 win over Liverpool (both 02–03).
Worn by: Barry Hayles, John Collins.

A 2001–02

Design: ADIDAS
Sponsor: PIZZA HUT

After the club's superb 00–01 season in Division 1, optimism was high at Craven Cottage for the new campaign and, although they didn't set the Premiership alight, they were consistent enough to earn a respectable final position of 13th. The away kit saw the return of black and red stripes, now coupled with black sleeves. The shirt was also worn with the alternative home white shorts.

Worn in: Solid 1–0 wins over Derby and Leeds, but a dreadful 4–0 defeat to Spurs.
Worn by: Steve Finnan, Steve Malbranque, Sean Doherty, Luis Boa Morte.

A 2002–03

Design: ADIDAS
Sponsor: BETFAIR.COM

With Tigana's Fulham aiming to build on their great first season in the Premiership, this attractive black and white shirt was introduced.

The shirt featured white mesh panels and a slick V-neck. Online betting company Betfair.com became the club's new sponsor. The kit, which marked the end of the club's six-year association with adidas, was also worn with a unique pair of black change shorts.

Worn in: The 1–1 draw at Spurs that saw the Cottagers down to 10 men. Plus a great 3–0 win over Sunderland early in the season.
Worn by: Zat Knight, Rufus Brevett, Chris Coleman.

Fulham were forced to don their black away kit in their 03–04 home game vs Newcastle as the Magpies had only brought their grey third strip, which was deemed too close to the Fulham outfit by match officials.

H 2003–04, 2004–05

Design: PUMA
Sponsor: DABS.COM

With Chris Coleman now in charge of the side, they sported surely one of the most exciting and trendsetting ranges of kits in the modern era. Produced by Puma and including an ultra-modern asymmetrical design and reversed seams, it was a real classic. It was daring and inventive from the dynamic red trim on the shorts to the central badge/right-hand side Puma logo layout, and was a design that divided Fulham fans. 04–05 saw the club return to Craven Cottage after two seasons ground sharing at Loftus Road.

Worn in: A 3–2 win over Middlesbrough in the first home game of the 03–04 season. Also the 6–0 win vs Norwich in the final game of 04–05.
Worn by: Steve Marlet, Andy Melville.

A 2003–04

Design: PUMA
Sponsor: DABS.COM

A great season for Chris Coleman's team as they finished in ninth place in the league and reached the quarter-final of the FA Cup. Puma's first away kit was another stunner, with red seams and red mesh breathable fabric panels down each side. With rapid advancements in fabric technology driving football kit design, all of Fulham's Puma kits incorporated the company's Micro-lite material that was designed to keep the players cool on the pitch.

Worn in: Great 2–0 wins over Blackburn and later Bolton in the last match of 03–04 .
Worn by: Sylvain Legwinski, Jon Harley, Steed Malbranque, Sean Davis.

3 2003–04, 2004–05

Design: PUMA
Sponsor: DABS.COM

Although Puma had decked the team out in a marvellous set of home and away outfits, they also introduced this splendid new red third kit mid-season. It followed exactly the design of the away and was worn with that kit's black (or red) shorts and black socks. Inspired by these three great kits, the side consolidated their position in the Premiership in 03–04 and finished the campaign in ninth place. Online computer and home electronics suppliers Dabs.com replaced Betfair after just one season.

Worn in: The 3–1 defeat to Newcastle in 03–04 – the only time this shirt was worn that season.
Worn by: Alain Goma, Junichi Inamoto, Lee Clark.

A 2004–05

Design: PUMA
Sponsor: DABS.COM

After just one season the black away kit was replaced by another dynamic affair, this time in a distinctive pale blue colour. With its breathable fabric panels and reversed seams, the lightweight shirt was designed for optimum performance and completed a very strong set of outfits yet again as an energetic Fulham side aimed to improve further on their Premiership form. The side eventually finished 13th in the table.

Worn in: A superb 4–1 thrashing of Newcastle at St James' Park in 04–05 – a glorious return for ex-Magpie Andy Cole. Also that season a thrilling 3–3 draw with Southampton.
Worn by: Collins John, Andy Cole, Claus Jensen, Papa Bouba Diop.

The 05–06 Puma template as worn by Fulham is also sported by Stuttgart and Hamburg in the German Bundesliga and Metz in French Ligue 1 this season.

H 2005–06

Design: PUMA
Sponsor: PIPEX

The internet service provider Pipex arrives at Craven Cottage in 05–06 as part of a massive deal as the Cottagers' new shirt sponsor. In a unique move to promote the kit, the club organised a competition for fans to model the new home design in an exclusive pre-season photoshoot. The strip was eventually promoted using these photographs in the club's biggest ever kit launch. The design features the innovative coupling of contrasting coloured sleeve trim: red on the right sleeve and black on the left. A design decision so effective and simple it is a mystery why no other shirt has included it previously in the English League.

A 2005–06

Design: PUMA
Sponsor: PIPEX

Red makes its habitual return to the Fulham away wardrobe for 05–06 after being promoted from the previous two seasons' third choice to the primary away selection. The strip follows exactly the design of the home minus the contrasting sleeve trim – the away sees a safer choice of simply white. After suffering some heavy defeats in 04–05, Chris Coleman's side will no doubt hope for some degree of consolidation in the Premiership in the forthcoming campaign.

3 2005–06

Design: PUMA
Sponsor: PIPEX

Fulham will also wear this little black number in the 05–06 season. A strikingly simple but effective shirt, it has so far only been pencilled in for one game: the away fixture at Sunderland, whose red and white stripes will create a colour clash with both of Fulham's standard kits. The reversed seam design follows the template of both the home and away versions.

Liverpool's traditional red shirts, shorts and socks has to be one of the most well-known kits in modern football, made famous during the club's dominance of the 70s and 80s. However, up until the mid-60s the team actually wore their famous red shirts with white shorts.

The club was formed when Everton left their then home ground of Anfield in 1892 due to a ground rent dispute. The players who remained founded Liverpool FC and took up residence at the stadium. Originally, the club played in blue and white quarters or halves, a kit chosen to differentiate themselves from local rivals Everton who at the time played in a shade of reddy-pink. At the turn of the century this all changed, of course – the teams switched colours and it was red at Anfield from then on.

For a long period until the 50s the shirts were nearly always all red with no contrasting collar or cuffs, before a white V-neck arrived in 1957. The socks were black in the 1920s and 30s, before changing to a red and white hooped design. After several changes to collars, fabrics and length of shorts, Bill Shankly introduced the all-red outfit in the 64–65 season in an attempt to make his side seem larger and more intimidating to the opposition. It worked.

The glory that Liverpool have achieved in the years since the shorts colour change has been phenomenal, with the club winning several European Cup, FA Cup and League Cup titles, not to mention numerous League championship titles. The fearsome all-red kit has now become synonymous with success.

For away colours, Liverpool have traditionally worn white shirts with red trim and black shorts, and this combination accompanied some magnificent triumphs in the 70s and early 80s. It is still a favourite with the Kop today, although in recent years yellow, grey and even green have made appearances as Liverpool's change colour.

Liverpool also hold a special place in the history of English kit design as theirs was the first jersey ever to boast the logo of a sponsor, that of Japanese electronics company Hitachi. Once again, they set the trend from which the rest of the Football League clubs have never looked back.

KING KENNY IN AN UNSPONSORED VERSION OF THE FAMOUS UMBRO HOME STRIP OF 76–82.

In an early 80s game at Watford, Liverpool sported a curious ensemble of red shirts, black shorts and white socks – one of the few occasions in recent years that have seen the red shirt worn with anything other than red shorts.

H 1976–77 to 1981–82

Design: UMBRO
Sponsor: HITACHI (79–82)

Liverpool's all-red kit from the late 70s and early 80s was one of the most important strips of the modern age. Not only did it accompany the side during an era of unparalleled success, but it was also the first in professional English football to include a sponsor's logo – that of Japanese hi-fi and TV manufacturers Hitachi in 1979. With its simple white V-neck and cuffs and yellow club badge, the kit is regarded as a classic by Liverpool fans.

Worn in: Two European Cup final victories (77–78 and 80–81) and four successful league titles (76–77, 78–79, 79–80 and 81–82). Also the League Cup final 3–1 win vs Spurs in 81–82.
Worn by: Emlyn Hughes, Kevin Keegan, Ray Kennedy, David Johnson.

A 1976–77 to 1981–82

Design: UMBRO
Sponsor: HITACHI (79–82)

This was a real golden era for the club fashion-wise. Not only did they wear one of the best home kits ever, but also one of the most distinctive aways. This white, black and red change strip is fondly remembered by Liverpool fans. Like the home strip, it evolved gradually from a round-neck version and sported the logo of sponsors Hitachi from 78–79 onwards. Also worn with red socks.

Worn in: The 2–1 victory over West Ham in the 80–81 League Cup final replay. Also worn in the 77–78 League Cup final defeat against an impressive Nottingham Forest.
Worn by: Jimmy Case, Kenny Dalglish (who scored his first goal for the club in this kit at Middlesbrough in the 77–78 season).

3 1976–77 to 1980–81

Design: UMBRO
Sponsor: HITACHI (79–81)

A real rarity was this seldom-worn all-yellow third strip. One of the most basic kits the club has ever worn, it did not even feature a contrasting collar and cuffs. It is difficult to ascertain exactly how many times it was worn, but its most notable showing was against Manchester Utd in the FA Cup semi-final in 78–79. A replica version was never produced.

Worn in: The titanic FA Cup tie against Man Utd (78–79), which ended in a 2–2 draw (Liverpool eventually losing the replay 1–0). Also a great 2–2 draw with Southampton at The Dell in the 80–81 season.
Worn by: Phil Thompson, Terry McDermott, Graeme Souness, Alan Hansen.

H 1982–83 to 1984–85

Design: UMBRO
Sponsor: CROWN PAINTS

The 82–83 season saw a huge change of kit design for the club. The previous plain and simple red shirt now included the usual early 80s fashion necessity: pinstripes. The shorts and socks also included white trim. Crown Paints became the club's next sponsor and their logo appeared on the shirts in two different versions in subsequent years. The last two seasons in which the kit was worn again saw the club collect the Division 1 title.

Worn in: A 5–0 thrashing of Everton in 82–83 and the 2–1 Milk Cup final triumph over Man Utd in 82–83, when Bob Paisley collected the trophy in his last year as manager. Also a 1–0 win vs Everton in the 83–84 Milk Cup final.
Worn by: Ian Rush, Michael Robinson.

The 85–87 adidas home shirt was premiered (without the Crown Paints logo) in the tragic European Cup final in Heysel at the end of the 84–85 season.

3 1981–82
A 1982–83, 1983–84

Design: UMBRO
Sponsor: CROWN PAINTS (82–84)

Obviously feeling that the club's pitch-side fashion was looking a little old-fashioned, a bold new all-yellow away strip was introduced – the first major deviation from the club's usual away colour scheme of white and black. The shirt, which was actually premiered as a third strip in 81–82, also included pinstripes. The 83–84 season saw Joe Fagan replace Paisley.

Worn in: A great 3–0 victory over West Ham in the 82–83 season. Also the 3–1 win over Aston Villa the following year, which included an Ian Rush hat-trick that featured in *Match of the Day*'s opening sequence for some time.
Worn by: Alan Kennedy, Mark Lawrenson.

A 1984–85

Design: UMBRO
Sponsor: CROWN PAINTS

With standard pinstripes starting to become yesterday's news, Umbro introduced a new away kit design officially entitled 'World Cup' that featured a pale shadow pinstripe incorporated into the fabric along with an intricate V-neck. It was Umbro's last kit for the club and was worn for just one season. Due to FA size restrictions concerning the amount of space a sponsor's name could take up on a shirt, the Crown Paints logo appeared on just one line in a new simpler style.

Worn in: The dramatic 2–2 84–85 FA Cup semi-final match against Manchester United, with Paul Walsh equalising for the Reds (or Yellows in this case) with just a few seconds to spare.
Worn by: John Wark, Kevin MacDonald.

H 1985–86, 1986–87

Design: ADIDAS
Sponsor: CROWN PAINTS

After a long association with Umbro, Liverpool signed a new deal with sportswear giants adidas. Their first design was a really nice kit, although very snug fitting – just ask Jan Molby – and featured white rather than yellow club badges and adidas logos. A shortened version of the famous three-stripe trim ran just to the sleeves. For the first time, the fabric also contained an intricate shadow stripe pattern of the Liver Bird motif and adidas logo.

Worn in: The 1–0 win at Chelsea that sealed the title and the FA Cup final victory over Everton (85–86) that clinched the double that year. In 86–87 it starred in a tremendous 10–0 win against Fulham in the Littlewoods Cup.
Worn by: Paul Walsh, Sammy Lee.

A 1985–86, 1986–87

Design: ADIDAS
Sponsor: CROWN PAINTS

In a straightforward reversal of the home strip, adidas' first away kit for the club reverted to white and featured the same shadow pattern as the home, along with an identical V-neck and cuffs. A real favourite kit with fans, the shirt was also worn in 86–87 with black shorts – creating an updated version of the classic Liverpool away kit of the 70s. Liverpool legend Kenny Dalglish became player-manager in 85–86, replacing Joe Fagan.

Worn in: The 86–87 Littlewoods Cup final defeat to Arsenal (2–1) – the first match Liverpool lost that Ian Rush had scored in.
Worn by: Gary Gillespie, Craig Johnston.

The adidas home kit of 85–86 and 86–87 was the last worn by outgoing star Ian Rush in a 1–0 win over Watford before he left Liverpool to join Juventus.

3 1985–86, 1986–87

Design: ADIDAS
Sponsor: CROWN PAINTS

For the first time the club introduced an official third strip – previous third kits were never officially launched or marketed. This all-yellow kit featured all the trappings of the home and away designs and completed a brilliant debut set of adidas kits for the club. However, this strip was seldom worn during the two seasons it was in use. The Crown Paints logo varied in design on all the club's kits in the 85–86 season as the company once again began to experiment with the most effective way to display their brand on the shirts.

Worn in: The 2–1 defeat to Southampton at The Dell in the 86–87 season.
Worn by: Barry Venison, Steve McMahon, Jim Beglin, Ronnie Whelan.

H 1987–88, 1988–89

Design: ADIDAS
Sponsor: CROWN PAINTS (87–88)
              CANDY (88–89)

There were only a few changes to the next Liverpool home kit, but all of them were quite important. For the first time in over 10 years there was no yellow present on the strip at all – it had been replaced by grey, which was also to become the new away kit colour. The V-neck was superseded by a new wrap-over round neck and the Liver Bird now stood within a larger shield to comprise the club badge.

Worn in: The shock 1–0 defeat to Wimbledon in the 87–88 FA Cup final that thwarted another league and cup double for the club. Also the emotional post-Hillsborough FA Cup final vs Everton (88–89) that the Reds won 3–2.
Worn by: John Aldridge, John Barnes.

A 1987–88, 1988–89

Design: ADIDAS
Sponsor: CROWN PAINTS (87–88)
              CANDY (88–89)

Grey became the new away colour in 87–88, replacing the previous season's white design. As with the home shirt, the new away jersey retained the same shadow stripe design as the first set of adidas kits. An adidas logo was now also included on the socks. The Crown Paints logo was originally printed in white outlined with red, switching to solid red mid-season, before being replaced altogether by new sponsors Candy the following season.

Worn in: The 2–1 victory over Arsenal on the first day of the 87–88 season with goals by Aldridge and Nicol. Also a 3–1 defeat at Manchester Utd in 88–89.
Worn by: Nigel Spackman, Peter Beardsley.

3 1988–89

Design: ADIDAS
Sponsor: CANDY

One of the few Liverpool outfits worn in only one match, this white shirt popped up in the 88–89 season. The shirt was a straightforward reversal of the standard away version trimmed with red and grey, and was worn with the red shorts and socks of the home kit. It also included the logo of new sponsors Candy, the electrical white goods company. The only match in which it appeared was that season's away game at Aston Villa, whose Hummel kit of half claret and half light blue made the change necessary. A replica version was never issued.

Worn in: The 1–1 draw at Aston Villa in 88–89.
Worn by: Steve Nicol, Gary Ablett, Jan Molby.

Not only was the white-flecked adidas home kit of 89–91 the last shirt worn by a Championship-winning Liverpool side, it was also the last worn by Kenny Dalglish in the 1–0 win over Derby in the 89–90 season.

H 1989–90, 1990–91

Design: ADIDAS
Sponsor: CANDY

One of the more controversial of Liverpool's kits was this next home outfit. It retained the same round neck and classic three-stripe trim as the previous design, but the fabric was now speckled with white flecks to create a paint-splattered effect. The shirt was also much baggier than in previous years. The shorts now included large white side panels and the socks featured a white turnover.

Worn in: The incredible 89–90 season 9–0 thrashing of Crystal Palace, with Aldridge scoring in his last match for the club. Also the classic FA Cup 4–4 draw with Everton (90–91) – the final match before Kenny Dalglish's shock resignation as manager.
Worn by: Glenn Hysen, David Burrows.

A 1989–90, 1990–91

Design: ADIDAS
Sponsor: CANDY

The last away kit of the 80s was just as contemporary as the home outfit. Like the red shirt, it retained the round neck and trim of the previous outfit, but the fabric now incorporated a faded diamond design. Grey is always a risky choice of kit colour as it does reduce visibility on the pitch; however, this didn't stop the club winning Division 1 again in 89–90. The following season saw Graeme Souness replacing Dalglish as manager.

Worn in: A vital 2–1 win over Man Utd in the 89–90 season, plus revenge for Palace as they beat Liverpool 4–3 in a nail-biting FA Cup semi-final (89–90). Also the 1–0 win over Arsenal in the 89–90 Charity Shield.
Worn by: Ronnie Rosenthal, David Speedie.

H 1991–92

Design: ADIDAS
Sponsor: CANDY

This kit attracted criticism from some quarters at Anfield, mainly due to the inclusion of three large white stripes over the right shoulder (an adidas design common on the continent at this time) that many people felt gave adidas' identity prominence over the club's. The kit was produced with an 'adidas Equipment' logo replacing the famous trefoil as the company rebranded themselves. The other main change was the length of the shorts, which were now considerably longer than in previous seasons.

Worn in: The return of the club to European action – the fantastic 3–0 win over Auxerre at Anfield. Also worn in the FA Cup final victory over Sunderland (2–0).
Worn by: Steve Staunton, Dean Saunders.

A 1991–92

Design: ADIDAS
Sponsor: CANDY

Another dramatic change occurred with this green away strip. The kit followed the same basic design as the home and was worn with

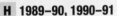

either white or green shorts. It was the last year of the club's four-year deal with Candy, and some speculated that this kit was prepared knowing that Carlsberg would be the new sponsor, as green was their corporate colour. An unlucky kit for the club, they didn't win once in the league in this strip.

Worn in: Four awful consecutive away defeats: Crystal Palace (1–0), Sheffield Utd (2–0), Aston Villa (1–0) and Arsenal (4–0).
Worn by: Ray Houghton, Mike Marsh.

For the first time since the early 80s, long-sleeved replica shirts were marketed in conjunction with the new Premier League, although they didn't become commonplace in club shops for nearly 10 years.

H 1992–93

Design: ADIDAS
Sponsor: CARLSBERG

92–93 marked Liverpool's centenary and, while Souness made his presence felt as manager in the inaugural Premier League, Danish brewery Carlsberg arrived as new sponsors. Combined with the introduction of a new club shield (a complex design produced to commemorate the centenary season), this necessitated a [...] to the previous home strip [...] new position for the adidas logo as [...] V-neck. Other than that, the [...] same as the 91–92 kit.

[...]2–0 defeat at home to [...]nd the great 6–2 victory [...] the season. [...]rk Wright.

A 1992–93

Design: ADIDAS
Sponsor: CARLSBERG

Like the home strip, the away kit changed very slightly from that of the previous season. The new club badge and Carlsberg logo (now sitting proudly on the company's corporate colour) were introduced and the adidas logo was moved. Both this and the home strip also saw the club badge included on the socks for the first time. The club endured another poor season, partly due to their dismal away form.

Worn in: Spartak Moscow's crushing 4–2 victory over the Reds in the European Cup Winners Cup second round and a great 1–0 win over Arsenal at Highbury.
Worn by: Don Hutchison, David Burrows.

H 1993–94, 1994–95

Design: ADIDAS
Sponsor: CARLSBERG

The adidas branding went one step further with the next home kit and fans once again voiced disapproval at the amount of white now present on the strip. Green was added for the first time as a trim colour and shadow stripes returned. Although the kit saw Robbie Fowler's debut in the 3–1 win over Fulham in the Coca-Cola Cup, the strip did not coincide with a happy period at the club and was worn when Grobbelaar argued with McManaman in the 2–0 away defeat at Everton (93–94).

Worn in: The thrilling 3–3 draw with Man Utd, when the club came back from being 3–0 down (93–94). Also the 94–95 Coca-Cola Cup final victory over Bolton (2–1).
Worn by: Neil Ruddock, Nigel Clough.

A 1993–94, 1994–95

Design: ADIDAS
Sponsor: CARLSBERG

With Liverpool struggling under Souness, green remained integral to the next away shirt, which was loosely based on the design of the home. However, the shirt was predominantly white with a black symmetrical pattern on either side. The club badge was also rendered in green and black rather than being identical to that on the home. Old boot-room boy Roy Evans took charge after Souness resigned. It was this shirt that Fowler once wore back to front after celebrating a goal, earning himself a booking.

Worn in: A thrashing of Swindon (5–0) in 93–94. Also worn in the 94–95 Coca-Cola Cup semi-final 1–0 victory over Crystal Palace.
Worn by: John Scales, Phil Babb, Mark Walters.

The 93–94 season saw the introduction of squad numbers and players' names on the back of shirts. It was not until 97–98, however, that a uniform typeface was introduced by the Premiership authorities.

3 1994–95, 1995–96

Design: ADIDAS
Sponsor: CARLSBERG

For only the second time ever, Liverpool marketed an official third shirt. The jersey was gold and black, with a faint black pattern made up of the club badge and the adidas logo. With the adidas Equipment brand losing ground due to the increase in popularity of old-school adidas gear on the high street, the logo was replaced by a simple type-only version. The neat button-up round neck also incorporated a white LFC monogram.

Worn in: A disappointing 2–1 defeat to Middlesbrough in the 94–95 season. Also a good 3–1 win over Southampton in the following league campaign.
Worn by: Julian Dicks, Steve McManaman, Michael Thomas, Stig Inge Bjornebye.

H 1995–96

Design: ADIDAS
Sponsor: CARLSBERG

This shirt was only used for one season and it marked the end of the club's long association with adidas. 95–96 saw a real return to form, not only in kit design but also on the pitch, with the club finishing third. The shirt reintroduced a simple white V-neck (albeit a very large one) and the famous adidas three-stripe trim down each arm. The club badge was housed within an additional shield and a broad shadow stripe pattern introduced.

Worn in: The 3–0 victory over Blackburn that included a stunning Collymore goal, and the nail-biting 4–3 victory over Newcastle in one of the matches of the decade.
Worn by: Stan Collymore, Robbie Fowler (who scored a superb hat-trick vs Arsenal in 95–96).

A 1995–96

Design: ADIDAS
Sponsor: CARLSBERG

Adidas again looked to bygone Liverpool kits for inspiration for their last away kit. The club had worn a quartered shirt way back in the 1890s, although in those days the colours were white and blue. To hammer the retro look home, the shirt also featured a round 'grandad' collar complete with button-down neck. Thin shadow stripes were the only concession to modernity.

Worn in: A great 3–0 win over Aston Villa in the 95–96 FA Cup semi-final, followed by the disappointing 1–0 defeat to Man Utd in the final courtesy of a deflected Cantona goal – Ian Rush's last game in a Liverpool shirt.
Worn by: Rob Jones, Jamie Redknapp, Jason McAteer.

H 1996–97, 1997–98

Design: REEBOK
Sponsor: CARLSBERG

After 10 years with adidas the club had a new kit supplier, British sportswear manufacturer Reebok. Their first home kit for the team was a classy affair with just a tiny amount of white on the collar and cuffs. The club badge was also now housed within an oval shape, a respe[...] nod to the team's outfit of the 60s. Insp[...] this kit, 97–98 was a great season for [...] who finished third.

Worn in: Another amazing 4–3 w[...] Newcastle (96–97) along with [...] 2–0 victory over Paris Saint [...] that same season. Plus a [...] Arsenal, this time 4–0 i[...]
Worn by: Michael Ow[...] in this strip vs Wim[...]

ADIDAS, THE ADIDAS LOGO, THE TREFOIL LOGO AND THE 3-STRIPE TRADEMARK ARE REGISTERED TRADEMARKS OF THE ADIDAS-SALOM[...]

Liverpool kit launches in the late 90s had a distinctly musical theme, with the club dressing as the Beatles to promote the 96–97 ecru kit and Spice Girl Mel C proudly posing in the new white away kit of 98–99.

A 1996–97

Design: REEBOK
Sponsor: CARLSBERG

Liverpool were one of the first clubs to introduce an ecru (otherwise known as beige) away kit in the mid-90s. The shirt featured an

interesting round neck design and the same Liver Bird shadow pattern as the home jersey. Worn with red-trimmed black shorts or, occasionally, a matching ecru pair.

Worn in: The 3–3 draw at the Riverside that saw Ravanelli equalise three times for Boro in his first game for the club, and the awful 3–0 defeat to Paris Saint Germain in the European Winners Cup semi-final first leg.
~~~ by: Patrick Berger, Jamie Carragher,
~~~ Matteo, Danny Murphy.

A 1997–98   3 1998–99

Design: REEBOK
Sponsor: CARLSBERG

Reebok's next away design was a great-looking kit – all yellow with red and black trim, with the red subtly fading into the wrap-over V-neck and cuffs. The baggy shorts also included a red waistband. It was a real back to basics approach to Liverpool kits, a theme that would continue with the forthcoming Reebok designs. The late 90s saw the club lacking consistency in their performances – capable of brilliant displays one week and disastrous ones the next.

Worn in: An early season 2–1 loss at West Ham, but a great 1–0 win at Arsenal. Also worn as the club crashed out of the Coca-Cola Cup 2–0 vs Middlesbrough at the semi-final stage.
Worn by: Paul Ince, Oyvind Leonhardsen.

H 1998–99, 1999–2000

Design: REEBOK
Sponsor: CARLSBERG

Another gem from the Reebok camp was the Reds' 98–00 home kit. Proudly influenced by the great Shankly team of the 60s, this simple design featured a round neck and basic white trim on the shorts and socks. There were also light red horizontal mesh stripes of different thicknesses across the chest. It was a kit designed to inspire Anfield and bring back memories of the glory days. Gerard Houllier became joint manager with Roy Evans in 98–99, but Evans left a couple of months later.

Worn in: The memorable 4–1 win over Newcastle in Gullit's first match in charge at St James' Park and an amazing 7–1 thrashing of Southampton at Anfield (both 98–99).
Worn by: Karlheinz Riedle, Vegard Heggem.

A 1998–99   3 1999–2000

Design: REEBOK
Sponsor: CARLSBERG

Although possibly not the most successful era in Liverpool's history, the late 90s certainly saw a glut of classic kits. The team

reverted to white shirts for 98–99 which, when worn with black shorts, brought back fond memories of Keegan and Dalglish. Similar to the previous season's away shirt, it also included broad red stripes down each sleeve and a very subtle horizontal weave fabric.

Worn in: A sweet 3–1 win over Middlesbrough. Also a comprehensive 5–1 rout of Nottingham Forest and a 4–2 win over Aston Villa that included a Robbie Fowler hat-trick.
Worn by: Erik Meijer, David Thompson.

The 00–01 season actually saw Liverpool playing in four different kits: red at home, amber away, green for the Bradford game and a preview of the next season's white kit against Barcelona in the UEFA Cup.

A 1999–00 3 2000–01

Design: REEBOK
Sponsor: CARLSBERG

The golden era of on-the-field fashion couldn't last and this green, navy and white design was not one of the most popular strips the club has worn. However, it did feature in some vital wins. The shirt contained centrally placed badges and a diagonal navy and white band – an identical design to that worn by both Bolton and Aston Villa at the same time. The kit also made an appearance as a third strip in the 00–01 season, when the club's away game at Bradford saw both the home and away strips clashing.

Worn in: Some good wins in the league in 99–00: 2–0 at Sunderland, 1–0 at Arsenal and 3–2 at Watford.
Worn by: Titi Camara, Rigobert Song.

H 2000–01, 2001–02

Design: REEBOK
Sponsor: CARLSBERG

It all came together for Liverpool both on the pitch and in the dressing room in the 00–01 season, with three trophies and a classy home strip (Reebok's third for the club). It saw a collar return to the shirt, along with white piping running down to each cuff. The two elements of the Reebok logo were split across the shirt and shorts, and a shiny fabric panel was used to house the Carlsberg logo.

Worn in: The 00–01 Worthington Cup final win over Birmingham and the extraordinary UEFA Cup final 5–4 triumph over Alaves the same season. Also worn in the 2–1 Charity Shield triumph over Man Utd in 01–02.
Worn by: Gary McAllister, Nicolas Anelka, plus a farewell to Robbie Fowler.

A 2000–01 3 2001–02

Design: REEBOK
Sponsor: CARLSBERG

A rich amber was introduced as the club's away colour for the glorious 00–01 season. A very deep navy (almost purple) was used as a secondary colour on the kit, which made many important appearances this season as the club rampaged through the FA, League and UEFA Cups. Some Liverpool fans, eager for the club to wear unique kits, were not happy as once again the design was worn in another colour scheme by Bolton in the same season.

Worn in: The triumphant 2–1 win over Arsenal in the 00–01 FA Cup final with Owen scoring twice in the last seven minutes. Also the UEFA Cup fourth round first leg 2–0 win vs Roma.
Worn by: Nick Barmby, Stephen Wright, Emile Heskey.

A 2001–02 3 2002–03

Design: REEBOK
Sponsor: CARLSBERG

This shirt was actually previewed towards the end of the 00–01 season in the European match against Barcelona. For the third season running, blue was present in Liverpool's away kit (were Reebok secret Evertonians?) but this was another classy kit. The blue panels were trimmed with amber, as were the shorts (a white pair was also worn.)

Worn in: The 4–2 defeat to Bayer Leverkusen that ended Liverpool's 01–02 European campaign, and the great 1–0 win at Man Utd. Also the Super Cup victory vs Bayern Munich.
Worn by: Vladimir Smicer, John Arne Riise, Milan Baros.

Most major cup finals in recent years that Liverpool have appeared in have seen an embroidered Liver Bird logo included in the centre of the shirt accompanied by text commemorating the match.

E 2001–02, 2002–03

Design: REEBOK
Sponsor: CARLSBERG

The club celebrated their return to the Champions League with a unique home strip. With a few modern trappings here and there, it was essentially designed to resemble the classic Liverpool kits of the 70s – the team's European peak. All logos were embroidered in yellow, and four stars were placed above the club badge to signify their four European Cup triumphs. Some fans were also hoping for the reintroduction of the classic Liver Bird logo.

Worn in: A 3–1 home defeat to Barcelona, but also the 2–0 win over Roma that saw a wonderful night of European football at Anfield again (both 01–02). Plus the epic matches vs Celtic in the UEFA Cup the following season.
Worn by: Steven Gerrard, Jari Litmanen.

H 2002–03, 2003–04

Design: REEBOK
Sponsor: CARLSBERG

The only retro element of the club's next home kit was the wrap-over round neck, which resembled that of the adidas kits of the late 80s. The rest of the design was bang up to date: visible seams, hi-tech fabrics and a more dynamic Reebok logo. Not a bad-looking kit, it didn't bring much luck to the side as the promise shown just two seasons earlier began to fade, with the club eventually finishing fifth in 02–03.

Worn in: The emphatic 2–0 win over Manchester Utd in the 02–03 Worthington Cup final at the Millennium Stadium. Also the 6–0 thrashing of West Brom that same season.
Worn by: Salif Diao, Dietmar Hamann (who scored a brilliant goal vs Pompey in 03–04).

A 2002–03 3 2003–04

Design: REEBOK
Sponsor: CARLSBERG

02–03 was the first season Liverpool had ever played in a black strip. The away shirt design, with a visible horizontal seam and grey shoulder patches, combined well with the hi-tech Play Dry fabric to give an intimidating look. The shirt was actually similar to that of the home kit, but included a slim-line V-neck rather than a round one.

Worn in: The 1–0 defeat to Arsenal in the 02–03 Community Shield match. Also 1–0 wins over Aston Villa and Southampton – the only league away matches won in this strip – plus a great 3–1 win over Spartak Moscow.
Worn by: Harry Kewell, Bruno Cheyrou.

A 2003–04 3 2004–05

Design: REEBOK
Sponsor: CARLSBERG

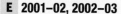

Reebok again returned to the tried and tested white shirts and black shorts combination. The shirt included many interesting features, including breathable mesh panels, red and black piping and a faint shadow pinstripe. The Carlsberg logo was included in their corporate colour. This strip was promoted by a nice Reebok ad campaign linking the shirt with the lyrics of 'You'll Never Walk Alone'.

Worn in: A 1–0 win over Manchester Utd – the only league away match won in this strip. Also a 4–2 defeat to Arsenal at Highbury.
Worn by: El-Hadji Diouf, Steve Finnan, Djimi Traore, Stephen Warnock.

Rumours are that Liverpool will sport a brand-new all-red kit for the 05–06 Champions League campaign to mark the side's marvellous triumph in the 04–05 final.

H 2004–05, 2005–06

Design: REEBOK
Sponsor: CARLSBERG

The most recent Liverpool home kit saw the smallest amount of white in recent years, with the colour restricted to just small white breathable panels under each arm. The fabric was Play Dry, a hi-tech moisture-management material. It featured a curious seamed collar and a diagonal shadow pattern, which was common on some Reebok shirts of the time.

Worn in: A 5–0 thrashing of West Brom and a great 2–1 win over Arsenal (all 04–05 under the command of new manager Rafael Benitez); however, the kit's most important appearance has to be the glorious 04–05 Champions League win on penalties over AC Milan.
Worn by: Djibril Cisse, Josemi, Antonio Nunez, Sami Hyypia.

A 2004–05 3 2005–06

Design: REEBOK
Sponsor: CARLSBERG

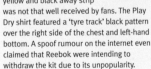

Both the home and away kits were very contemporary designs, although it has to be said that this new pale yellow and black away strip was not that well received by fans. The Play Dry shirt featured a 'tyre track' black pattern over the right side of the chest and left-hand bottom. A spoof rumour on the internet even claimed that Reebok were intending to withdraw the kit due to its unpopularity.

Worn in: The dismal 1–0 defeat to Burnley in the FA Cup third round. Also the impressive 3–1 win over Bayer Leverkusen in the Champions League (both 04–05).
Worn by: Florent Sinama-Pongolle, Neil Mellor.

A 2005–06

Design: REEBOK
Sponsor: CARLSBERG

As anticipation grew for the first official glimpse of the 05–06 away kit, Liverpool surprised many by wearing it for the first time in the July 2005 pre-season friendly against Wrexham. The general consensus about the outfit among the Anfield fans is positive, although some have mentioned its uncanny similarity to the white away kit of two seasons previously. It is a simple and dashing design – a white shirt with a red neck and red trim running along each sleeve. The main body of the shirt features red flashes pointing downwards, each met by a mirrored black flash. Also worn with white change shorts.

MANCHESTER CITY

Most Manchester City fans like to see their team in just two colour schemes: a sky blue home shirt and a red and black striped away shirt. However, some of the club's most glorious moments have seen them sporting other colours. In fact, two of their four FA Cup final triumphs were accompanied by maroon shirts – a colour that also featured on the club's socks in the late 1960s and made a re-emergence in the late 1980s.

City were formed in 1887 and their first outfit saw them in... red and black stripes, which perhaps goes some way to explaining the reason behind the choice of this colour scheme as the club's preferred change outfit. The side played under various names in their early years, but when they finally settled on Manchester City in 1894, sky blue was chosen as the colour for the new kit. Blue has been worn ever since, although not always in this lighter shade.

Dark socks (either black or navy blue) were a unique feature of the early City kits throughout the 1920s and 30s, a trend that was revived in the mid-80s by Umbro. The 1970s and 80s saw the club ditch their traditional white shorts in favour of blue, but this was short-lived and it was not long before the white shorts and dark socks were back.

Umbro and Manchester City enjoyed the longest sportswear supply deal in football – an incredible 63 years. The Cheshire-based company produced the club's kit from 1932 up until 1995, when Italian firm Kappa took over. The Kappa era coincided with a low point performance-wise for the club, who found themselves relegated twice in three seasons. It was at this time that City decided to move away from sky blue to a deeper and more vivid shade entitled 'laser blue'. It was a bold decision and a style that was to last for six years, before Reebok arrived at The City of Manchester Stadium in 2003 and brought back the more familiar shade.

Although the club have stuck rigidly to blue as their first choice, a wide variety of designs and colour combinations has been worn for the away strips. Apart from red/black and maroon, yellow, white with red and a black diagonal sash and even purple have featured alongside outlandish designs such as the Le Coq Sportif silver affair and the Kappa fluorescent kit. But it is blue that remains central to the hearts of the team and their supporters in Manchester, so often unfortunately overshadowed by their nearby red neighbours.

SHAUN WRIGHT-PHILLIPS IN THE 04–06 REEBOK HOME KIT.

Early versions of the 82–83 home shirt featured the Saab logo in black type.

H 1977–78 to 1980–81

Design: UMBRO
Sponsor: NONE

Manchester City and Umbro enjoyed one of the longest-running sports sponsorship relationships in history. Cheshire-based Umbro had been producing the club's kits since 1934. With its large collar and diamond trim combination, this standard Umbro design is a piece of 70s football fashion history. Later seasons saw the shirt produced in new synthetic fabrics, but it was still a style that was starting to look dated as the 1980s began.

Worn in: The 80–81 FA Cup final against Spurs – 1–1 in the first game followed by a 3–2 defeat for City in the replay. Also that season a great 2–2 draw with Man Utd.
Worn by: Paul Power, Phil Boyer, Peter Barnes, Tommy Hutchison.

A 1979–80 to 1981–82

Design: UMBRO
Sponsor: NONE

The club started the 80s with a standard away kit in their preferred colour choice of red and black stripes, simply trimmed with a white V-neck and cuffs. The Umbro diamond trim adorned the black shorts and socks. It was a welcome return to tradition following the flamboyant white away shirt with a red and black diagonal sash that the side had been sporting towards the end of the 70s.

Worn in: The nerve-wracking 1–0 win over Ipswich in the 80–81 FA Cup semi-final with a great free kick from Paul Power. Also a battling 1–0 win vs Everton at Goodison Park (81–82).
Worn by: Ray Ranson, Tommy Caton, Graham Baker, Trevor Francis, Dave Bennett.

H 1981–82, 1982–83

Design: UMBRO
Sponsor: SAAB (82–83)

It was all change at Maine Road in 81–82. Not only did the club have a fashionable slick and shiny new home kit with a trendy V-neck and white piping, they also sported a revived round City badge last seen in the early 70s. The Umbro diamond embellishments were gone (except for on the socks, which remained the same as the previous kit's) and were replaced by minimal white trim. Swedish car manufacturer Saab became the club's first ever shirt sponsor. 82–83 saw the side relegated.

Worn in: The thrilling 3–2 home win over Coventry City, a good 2–2 result at Old Trafford but also the dismal Milk Cup third round replay 4–0 defeat to Southampton (all 81–82).
Worn by: Kevin Reeves, Asa Hartford.

A 1982–83, 1983–84

Design: UMBRO
Sponsor: SAAB

John Bond's City replaced the favourite red and black striped kit after three seasons with this very 80s-looking design. However, it was only the shirt that was updated, the shorts and socks remaining the same as the previous design. The shirt was now white with red and black paired pinstripes.

Worn in: Unfortunate defeats away to Everton (2–1) and Ipswich (1–0) during the 82–83 relegation season. Also a superb 2–1 win over Portsmouth at Fratton Park the following season with the club now in Division 2.
Worn by: Kevin Bond, Bobby McDonald, Dennis Tueart, Nicky Reid, David Cross.

Although they are never popular with fans, chequerboard shirts do crop up from time to time and had also been worn around this time by Coventry, Fulham and Walsall.

H 1983–84, 1984–85

Design: UMBRO
Sponsor: SAAB (83–84) PHILIPS (84–85)

Umbro's next home kit was arguably one of the best worn by the club in the 80s, although it unfortunately coincided with the club's arrival in Division 2 after 17 years in the top flight. Shadow stripes were introduced to create a really solid and functional outfit. The socks design remained the same – the club had now worn the same footwear for an incredible eight years! New boss Billy McNeil replaced Bond.

Worn in: The astonishing 6–0 victory over Blackburn Rovers at home with a hat-trick by Derek Parlane (83–84). Also the 4–2 win over Blackpool in the Milk Cup the following year after being 2–0 down at one point.
Worn by: Andy May, Neil McNab, Mick McCarthy, David Phillips.

A 1984–85, 1985–86

Design: UMBRO
Sponsor: PHILIPS

The home strip was now complemented by this remodelled version of the classic red and black striped away kit, creating a very smart look for the club in 84–85. The skimpy shorts featured a short-lived Umbro trend of a flared trim down each leg. Electronic appliances giant Philips became the club's sponsor in the 84–85 season after signing a three-year deal and immediately brought the club some good fortune – they were promoted back to Division 1 in 84–85.

Worn in: A brilliant 3–0 win over Cardiff in 84–85. Also the exciting 5–4 defeat to Chelsea in the 85–86 Full Members Cup final. Plus a great 2–0 win over Spurs in 85–86.
Worn by: Duncan Davidson, Derek Parlane.

H 1985–86, 1986–87

Design: UMBRO
Sponsor: PHILIPS

Earning their reputation as a yo-yo club with their arrival back in Division 1, City took to the field in this refreshing new kit. The shiny shirt was now in a very light shade of blue and was trimmed with a white wrap-over round neck. The jersey was now paired with white shorts, just like the classic City kits of the 60s. A new sock design was also introduced with simple white turnovers. However, an awful 86–87 season found the club once again relegated to Division 2.

Worn in: A hard-fought 2–1 win over Spurs early in the 85–86 season, followed by a dreadful 3–0 defeat to rivals Man Utd at home.
Worn by: Jim Melrose, Mark Lillis, Kenny Clements.

A 1986–87, 1987–88
3 1988–89

Design: UMBRO
Sponsor: PHILIPS (86–87) BROTHER (87–89)

The club's most controversial kit of the decade! Red and black remained the colours of the new away kit, but that was all that was familiar about the design. The colours were now combined into a bold all-over chequerboard pattern. Although very distinctive, some fans found it difficult to get used to. A triangular corner trim was included on the shorts. Electronic office equipment suppliers Brother sponsored the shirt from 87–88 onwards.

Worn in: Defeats to Ipswich (3–0) and Blackburn (2–1) in 87–88, but also a good 1–0 win over Millwall the same season.
Worn by: Ian Brightwell, David White.

The 89–90 Umbro catalogue reveals that the shorts style worn with the 87–89 home kit was named 'Wembley' and the yellow third kit from 89–90 came from a standard Umbro range entitled 'Napoli'.

H 1987–88, 1988–89

Design: UMBRO
Sponsor: BROTHER

With the club now back in Division 2, Jimmy Frizzell became manager. Umbro updated City's kit, bringing back the more familiar shade of blue but adding a new wrap-over V-neck and a white diamond pinstripe design. A third colour, navy blue, was added to the home shirt, and also became the new colour of the socks. Also worn with sky blue shorts.

Worn in: A stunning 10–1 thrashing of Huddersfield in 87–88 with hat-tricks by White, Stewart and Adcock. Plus wins over Millwall (4–0) and Ipswich (2–0) later that same season.
Worn by: Imre Varadi, Steve Redmond, Paul Simpson.

A 1988–89, 1989–90

Design: UMBRO
Sponsor: BROTHER

The somewhat mixed reaction to the last away kit obviously didn't deter Umbro from producing another challenging design for the club's next change outfit. Maroon, a colour famously associated with the club's FA Cup final successes of 1934 and 1956, was reintroduced. The shirt featured a 'grandad' button-up neck and thin stripes. The decidedly retro-looking shorts were also worn with the home shirt when necessary. The club were again promoted to the top flight at the end of 88–89 after finishing second in Division 2.

Worn in: A 2–0 win over Birmingham (88–89) and a good 1–1 draw with Chelsea (89–90).
Worn by: Gary Megson, Alan Harper, Mark Ward, Paul Stewart.

3 1989–90

Design: UMBRO
Sponsor: BROTHER

With the club back in Division 1 under Howard Kendall, this rare all-yellow kit trimmed with navy blue was worn by the club for one game only, away to Arsenal in the difficult 89–90 season. Replica versions of the shirt were not sold. The jersey followed a standard Umbro design of contrasting wrap-over V-neck and chevron shadow pattern.

Worn in: The away game at Highbury against Arsenal in October 89 that ended in an abysmal 4–0 defeat.
Worn by: Ian Bishop, Brian Gayle, Tony Morley.

H 1989–90, 1990–91

Design: UMBRO
Sponsor: BROTHER

City's next home kit coincided with their arrival back in Division 1. It was a classic late 80s Umbro design in an era when the Cheshire-based company dominated the UK football scene. A button-up collar returned along with a lively zigzag shadow pattern. The shorts featured Umbro's normal spear trim of the era, although the navy blue socks remained the same as the previous kits. Worn with the away claret shorts when necessary.

Worn in: An opening day 3–1 defeat at Anfield in the 89–90 season, but the highlight of the season was surely the magnificent 5–1 thrashing of Man Utd at Maine Road.
Worn by: Colin Hendry, Wayne Clarke, Clive Allen.

The 90–92 maroon away shirt made an early appearance in the 89–90 season. Possibly a prototype version, it featured the same round neck as the striped away jersey and brought the number of kits worn that year by City to four!

A 1990–91, 1991–92

Design: UMBRO
Sponsor: BROTHER

Maroon became the main colour of the next away kit, creating a similar look to the kit the club wore in the 1934 FA Cup final. A more popular outfit than the previous one, the design mirrored that of the home kit with the addition of large blue and white panels on the shorts. Like the home shirt, the jersey included a two-tone shadow pattern. The two seasons in which this strip was officially in use inspired the club to fifth place on both occasions.

Worn in: A good 1–0 win away at Coventry on the opening day of the 91–92 season, followed by a 2–1 win at Everton and a 5–2 win over Oldham the same season.
Worn by: Mark Brennan, Peter Reid.

3 1990–91

Design: UMBRO
Sponsor: BROTHER

Another seldom-worn outfit was this white kit, which lasted for only one season. Similar in style to the previous yellow third outfit, and in fact virtually identical to a kit that Chelsea also wore at the time, it was nevertheless a smart-looking shirt. It was worn with blue shorts that doubled as a change pair for the home kit. The jersey was the first City third shirt to be sold as a replica.

Worn in: The stunning 5–1 win over Aston Villa at Villa Park towards the end of 90–91.
Worn by: Paul Lake, Adrian Heath.

H 1991–92, 1992–93

Design: UMBRO
Sponsor: BROTHER

City's good run in the league continued, as did their choice of excellent home kit designs. With Umbro using asymmetrical patterns on many of their early 90s kits, the new City shirt incorporated a navy flash design on the right sleeve along with another on the left leg of the shorts (which were now much longer than in previous seasons). An extravagant two-tone shadow pattern comprising the Umbro logo, 'MCFC' monogram and thick bands of blue was also printed over the shirt. Also worn with the blue shorts from the third kit.

Worn in: The amazing 2–1 win over Liverpool in the first home game of the 91–92 season. Also a 4–0 win over Leeds the following season.
Worn by: Steve McMahon, Keith Curle.

3 1991–92, 1992–93

Design: UMBRO
Sponsor: BROTHER

Yet another great City outfit was this elegant white third strip – one of the most popular issued by the club up to that point. It was pretty much a straightforward reversal of the home affair, now in white with navy and light blue trim. Worn either with blue shorts or the standard home white pair.

Worn in: A 1–1 draw with Crystal Palace in the 91–92 season along with an unfortunate 3–1 defeat to Aston Villa later in the season. Also a 1–0 win over Wimbledon in the following campaign.
Worn by: Michael Vonk, Niall Quinn, Mike Sheron.

Although obviously purple and not claret, the 92–94 away kit was similar in design to the kit the club wore in their FA Cup final success of 1956.

A 1992–93, 1993–94

Design: UMBRO
Sponsor: BROTHER

The City faithful were faced with another uncompromising away kit design in 1992. With nostalgia heavily influencing fashion on the field, Umbro issued a range of kits across almost all of the sides they supplied that was blatantly inspired by another age. The design itself was very striking, with an old-fashioned collar and thin white stripes – it was just the audacious colour scheme of vivid purple that had the fans in two minds.

Worn in: A 1–0 defeat at Spurs in 93–94, but also a good 2–1 win over QPR in the 92–93 FA Cup fifth round. Plus an exciting 3–2 defeat to Leeds the following season.
Worn by: Andy Hill, Michael Hughes, Fitzroy Simpson.

3 1993–94, 1994–95

Design: UMBRO
Sponsor: BROTHER

And so it went on! For the third season running the club sported another unique white third kit. This one followed the retro stylings of the purple away strip, with its large 1940s-style collar and baggy shorts. Coupled with navy blue, it was another popular strip that was worn on the cover of the NME by a certain Liam Gallagher, a confirmed City fan. As with the away shirt, the Brother logo was outlined to make it easier to read against the stripes.

Worn in: The 3–1 defeat away to West Ham at Upton Park in the 93–94 season. Also the shock 1–0 defeat to Cardiff in the fourth round of the 93–94 FA Cup.
Worn by: Terry Phelan, David Brightwell.

H 1993–94, 1994–95

Design: UMBRO
Sponsor: BROTHER

With standard collars becoming just a little passé, Umbro introduced the next home shirt with a slick new design coupled with a round neck. A dynamic shadow pattern made up of abstract renderings of the Umbro diamond logo and a fine diagonal pinstripe gave the shirt some character. A re-evaluated version of the famous diamond trim appeared on each cuff, which also included a small 'City' ID tag. Brian Horton became manager in 93–94.

Worn in: A solid 4–1 victory over Leicester in the third round of the 93–94 FA Cup. Also that season a great 2–1 win at home to Newcastle. Plus a good 4–0 win over Everton in 94–95.
Worn by: Peter Beagrie, Paul Walsh, Nicky Summerbee.

A 1994–95, 1995–96

Design: UMBRO
Sponsor: BROTHER

With the club spending the last few seasons hovering dangerously around the relegation area of the Premiership, it was obviously felt that a little City heritage was needed to inspire the side back to greatness. So it was the return of the favoured black and red stripes, although they were now much narrower and combined with a curious new chest panel. Topped with a new collar design and stripes on the bottom of the long shorts, it is debatable whether it was a successful contemporary reworking of the traditional City away strip or not.

Worn in: The brilliant 3–2 win over Blackburn in 94–95 and a 2–2 draw vs Coventry in the 95–96 FA Cup fourth round.
Worn by: Garry Flitcroft, Steve Lomas.

The 95–97 Umbro home kit was worn under four managers: Alan Ball (who quit Maine Road after the club were relegated in May 96), Steve Coppell (who left the post after just 32 days), Phil Neal and finally Frank Clark.

H 1995–96, 1996–97

Design: UMBRO
Sponsor: BROTHER

This kit was a milestone for City in many ways. Not only was it the last Umbro home strip produced for the club – the end of a relationship that had lasted an incredible 63 years – it was also the shirt that Alan Ball's City wore in their relegation season after seven years in the top flight. The kit itself was a typically busy mid-90s affair, with an intricate shadow print and unique collar, but its associations with the sad 95–96 season mar its memory with City fans.

Worn in: A 2–1 win over Southampton with a blinding Kinkladze goal. Plus the 2–2 draw with Liverpool in the last game of the season.
Worn by: Uwe Rosler, Nigel Clough, Adie Mike.

A 1996–97

Design: UMBRO
Sponsor: BROTHER

With a depressed Maine Road once again hosting Division 1 matches, this final Umbro kit ensured the deal ended with an eyebrow-raising high point. Certainly one of the most unusual and outrageous kits of the past 25 years, it was popular with celebrity City fan Noel Gallagher who was spotted wearing the jersey. It was an extraordinary combination of white, maroon, navy blue, amber and pink, but unfortunately was worn with the club in crisis as they struggled in the lower division.

Worn in: The good 3–2 win over Southend Utd, but defeats against Portsmouth (2–1), Birmingham (2–0) and Ipswich (1–0).
Worn by: Paul Dickov, Georgiou Kinkladze.

H 1997–98, 1998–99

Design: KAPPA
Sponsor: BROTHER

With the departure of Umbro and the arrival of Kappa, the continental wind of change blew around Maine Road. In an attempt to shake the club from its torpor a new vivid 'laser blue' shade was introduced, which was much richer than the traditional sky blue. With the Kappa logo forming an elaborate trim down the sleeves and shorts and a new regal club badge, this kit aimed to spark a City revival. It didn't work, however, and the end of the 97–98 season found the club relegated yet again – this time to Division 2.

Worn in: A 6–0 win over Swindon at home – the best result of the season – plus a solid 3–1 victory at Nottingham Forest.
Worn by: Shaun Goater, Tony Vaughan.

A 1997–98

Design: KAPPA
Sponsor: BROTHER

Kappa's first change kit for the club was an unconventional design, but nevertheless quite pleasing to the eye. A white body with navy blue chest and sleeves was trimmed with maroon and the Kappa logo. The navy blue shorts were worn with the home kit when necessary. Manager Frank Clark was sacked mid-season, but his replacement Joe Royle was unable to stop the club sinking into relegation. It was a dark time for the club.

Worn in: The dismal 1–0 defeat away to Ipswich, but a superb 3–0 win over Portsmouth.
Worn by: Kit Symons, Gerry Creaney, Craig Russell, Eddie McGoldrick.

The Kappa away kit of 98–99 was the last to feature the logo of Brother, who had been City's shirt sponsor for the past 12 years.

The Kappa away kit of 98–99 was the last to feature the logo of Brother, who had been City's shirt sponsor for the past 12 years.

The Kappa away kit of 98–99 was the last to feature the logo of Brother, who had been City's shirt sponsor for the past 12 years.

The Kappa away kit of 98–99 was the last to feature the logo of Brother, who had been City's shirt sponsor for the past 12 years.

The Kappa away kit of 98–99 was the last to feature the logo of Brother, who had been City's shirt sponsor for the past 12 years.

The Kappa away kit of 98–99 was the last to feature the logo of Brother, who had been City's shirt sponsor for the past 12 years.

The Kappa away kit of 98–99 was the last to feature the logo of Brother, who had been City's shirt sponsor for the past 12 years.

The Kappa away kit of 98–99 was the last to feature the logo of Brother, who had been City's shirt sponsor for the past 12 years.

The Kappa away kit of 98–99 was the last to feature the logo of Brother, who had been City's shirt sponsor for the past 12 years.

The Kappa away kit of 98–99 was the last to feature the logo of Brother, who had been City's shirt sponsor for the past 12 years.

The Kappa away kit of 98–99 was the last to feature the logo of Brother, who had been City's shirt sponsor for the past 12 years.

The Kappa away kit of 98–99 was the last to feature the logo of Brother, who had been City's shirt sponsor for the past 12 years.

The Kappa away kit of 98–99 was the last to feature the logo of Brother, who had been City's shirt sponsor for the past 12 years.

The Kappa away kit of 98–99 was the last to feature the logo of Brother, who had been City's shirt sponsor for the past 12 years.

The Kappa away kit of 98–99 was the last to feature the logo of Brother, who had been City's shirt sponsor for the past 12 years.

The Kappa away kit of 98–99 was the last to feature the logo of Brother, who had been City's shirt sponsor for the past 12 years.

3 1997–98

Design: KAPPA
Sponsor: BROTHER

The third kit worn during the heartbreaking 97-98 relegation season was this bright amber and black affair. It featured a unique design of vertical stripes trimmed with white, black shorts and black socks. It may not have been the club's finest hour, but Kappa had provided them with a stunning range of new and challenging kits. Frank Clark was sacked in February 98 with Joe Royle replacing him in the manager's seat.

Worn in: A 2–0 defeat at Loftus Road to QPR in October, followed by a dreadful 3–0 defeat at Reading a couple of months later.
Worn by: Ged Brennan, Gerard Wiekens, Richard Edghill, Kevin Horlock.

A 1998–99

Design: KAPPA
Sponsor: BROTHER

Kappa's final kit for the club at last saw some success return to the blue half of Manchester. Stuck in Division 2, Joe Royle's team sported this outrageous design – a daring fluorescent yellow and navy striped kit. It was an amazing outfit, quite unlike any the club had worn before. Small flashes of light blue provided the only reminder of what team you were watching, especially as the club were actually promoted in this kit!

Worn in: The remarkable play-off final vs Gillingham at Wembley when City, 2–0 down with a minute to go, fought back to win on penalties after scoring two late goals.
Worn by: Lee Crooks, who scored a super goal away to Chesterfield (final score 1–1).

H 1999–2000, 2000–01

Design: LE COQ SPORTIF
Sponsor: EIDOS

French company Le Coq Sportif signed a four-year deal to supply City's kits in 1999. The home kit retained the richer blue shade of the Kappa kit and trimmed it with broad white bands running down each side. All logos were placed centrally on the shirt, including that of the club's new sponsor – computer games manufacturers Eidos. Both the shorts and shirt featured a navy blue triangular corner design that included the club's initials. Also worn with the navy shorts from the away kit.

Worn in: A superb return to the Premiership in 00–01 – a 4–2 thrashing of Sunderland with Wanchope scoring three. Also the 5–0 win over Everton later that season.
Worn by: Andy Morrison, Jeff Whitley.

A 1999–2000

Design: LE COQ SPORTIF
Sponsor: EIDOS

The successful 99-00 season saw City achieve an incredible second consecutive promotion. The club played their away games this year in this elegant and classy white strip. Featuring an old-fashioned button-up collar and navy and light blue piping, it was a shame that it only lasted for one season as it was an excellent design. The shorts and socks were interchangeable with those of the home kit. Unusually, this away shirt featured the standard Le Coq Sportif logo, with the home shirt featuring the company's text-only version.

Worn in: A 1–0 win at Birmingham and a vital 2–2 draw with Portsmouth towards the end of the season.
Worn by: Richard Edghill, Mark Kennedy.

City bid farewell to Maine Road (sporting the Le Coq Sportif 01–03 home shirt) in May 2003 with a disappointing 1–0 defeat to Southampton.

3 1999–2000 to 2001–02

Design: LE COQ SPORTIF
Sponsor: EIDOS

It was only fitting that the most fondly regarded of all City away colour combinations was worn on the day the club finally ended their exile from the top flight in the spirited 99–00 season. It was a wonderful and popular kit – slick, simple and conventional with a straightforward red and black V-neck. So versatile was the kit that it lasted for three seasons as third choice – an almost unheard of length of time in the modern game.

Worn in: The last match of the 99–00 season – the game at Blackburn that City had to win or draw for automatic promotion. Rovers took the lead but City eventually came out winners with a final score of 4–1.

Worn by: Steve Howey, Darren Huckerby.

A 2000–01, 2001–02

Design: LE COQ SPORTIF
Sponsor: EIDOS

One of the more flashy kits issued in the modern era was this new City away strip. It was silver/grey in colour, trimmed with navy and a fluorescent yellow/green. The socks were also fluorescent – a choice that some City fans found hard to take. Even stranger were the mismatched cuffs that made the team look like they had got dressed in the dark. After last season's remarkably sedate alternative kits, the bizarre was back! Unfortunately for the club, this kit coincided with another relegation from the top flight in 00–01.

Worn in: The bitterly disappointing 2–1 defeat at Ipswich that saw the club relegated yet again at the end of the 00–01 season.

Worn by: Paulo Wanchope, George Weah.

H 2001–02, 2002–03

Design: LE COQ SPORTIF
Sponsor: EIDOS (01–02) FIRST ADVICE (02–03)

With promotion master Kevin Keegan at the helm and the club wearing this new home kit (the third to feature 'laser blue'), City returned to the Premiership in style as champions of Division 1 at the end of 01–02. This lightweight shirt marked the end of the Eidos deal and also Maine Road, with the club playing their final season at their traditional ground. As in previous seasons, 'MCFC' was included on the back of the collar.

Worn in: The wonderful 5–1 win over Barnsley that saw the club claim the 01–02 Division 1 title. Also the fine 3–1 win vs Man Utd (02–03).

Worn by: Stuart Peace, Danny Granville.

A 2002–03

Design: LE COQ SPORTIF
Sponsor: FIRST ADVICE

The final season of Le Coq Sportif's deal with City found the French company plundering the history books for inspiration. Their last away kit was this remodelling of City's late 70s Umbro design – a white shirt with red and black diagonal stripes, a simple V-neck and black piping. The shorts featured an unusual large white panel down each side and along the waistband. Finance and mortgage broking company First Advice replaced Eidos as the club's sponsor.

Worn in: A nail-biting 2–2 draw with Everton and the horrendous 5–0 mauling at Chelsea.
Worn by: Nicholas Anelka, David Sommeil, Marc Vivien Foe, Paul Ritchie.

Joey Barton was unable to make his debut for City at Middlesbrough in the 02–03 season when he realised that his Le Coq Sportif blue shirt had been stolen from the dug-out during half time.

3 2002–03

Design: LE COQ SPORTIF
Sponsor: FIRST ADVICE

For City's third strip this season, the designers once again looked to the past and produced this gorgeous-looking kit that was almost identical to the club's 1956 FA Cup final-winning outfit. It was a simple design – traditional but at the same time modern – with the light blue and amber Le Coq Sportif logo standing out well against the dark maroon of the strip. It was a good season for the club in their first season back in the top flight, which saw them finishing ninth.

Worn in: The fine 2–1 win over West Brom at The Hawthorns with goals by Anelka and Goater. Also the 1–0 defeat at Blackburn.
Worn by: Joey Barton, Robbie Fowler, Shaun Wright-Phillips.

H 2003–04

Design: REEBOK
Sponsor: FIRST ADVICE

Reebok arrived at the City of Manchester stadium and, to the surprise of many, they returned to their traditional shade of sky blue. With the addition of shadow stripes, it was very similar to the Umbro kit of the mid-80s – the club even revived sky blue socks. It was a good-looking and contemporary shirt, complete with Reebok's Play Dry moisture-management and body-cooling fabric technology.

Worn in: The FA Cup fourth round amazing 4–3 comeback at Spurs and the even better 4–1 win over Manchester Utd at home!
Worn by: Trevor Sinclair, Richard Dunne, Steve McManaman.

A 2003–04   3 2004–05

Design: REEBOK
Sponsor: FIRST ADVICE

It was like 1984 all over again! Reebok issued a new red and black striped shirt to complete what many consider to be the classic City kit range: sky blue for home, red and black for away. It was a successful updating of the old favourite with red sleeves and underarm panels of mesh fabric, and is a good example of how a traditional kit design can still be made relevant in contemporary times. 03–04 marked the departure of First Advice as shirt sponsors.

Worn in: A 3–2 vital away victory over Blackburn – the club's only away league win in this strip.
Worn by: Jonathan Macken, Sylvain Distin, Danny Tiatto.

H 2004–05, 2005–06

Design: REEBOK
Sponsor: THOMAS COOK

With the arrival of new sponsors, travel firm Thomas Cook, Reebok decided to freshen up the home strip after just one season. It was a wonderful-looking kit (launched at Manchester Airport) with a sleek continental round neck, dynamic reversed stitching for comfort and a delicate shadow pattern. The lightweight shirt also featured small epaulets of navy blue and white on each sleeve, forming quite an intimidating and confident outfit.

Worn in: The 4–0 win over Charlton and the great 7–1 Carling Cup thrashing of Barnsley.
Worn by: Paul Bosvelt, Antoine Sibierski, Stephen Jordan.

The 05–06 away kit was actually premiered at home at the end of the 04–05 season in Manchester City's 1–1 draw with Middlesbrough.

A 2004–05

Design: REEBOK
Sponsor: THOMAS COOK

After the success of their first away kit, Reebok issued a new design that was not so well received. Football fans love simplicity and tradition and, although this was not a bad-looking outfit, it just didn't hit the mark with the City faithful. It marked the return of purple to the strip, combined with a striking shoulder and neck design and horizontal navy stripes across the chest. Like the previous three Reebok kits, the shirt included the company's Play Dry fabric. 04–05 saw Keegan quit City to be replaced by Stuart Pearce.

Worn in: The 3–1 win at Portsmouth and a fine 2–1 victory over Aston Villa.
Worn by: Sylvain Distin, Danny Mills, Ben Thatcher.

A 2005–06

Design: REEBOK
Sponsor: THOMAS COOK

City's next away kit is a brave choice! One of the first of the new 05–06 Premiership kits to be unveiled, this all-navy number has again divided the opinion of the club's faithful supporters on its introduction. Following a similar template to the new West Ham home strip, the jersey features an asymmetrical design highlighted with flashes of sky blue. Diagonal shadow stripes curve down the body. Elegant and simple navy shorts and socks complete the outfit. Supporters will have to get used to seeing City playing in this rather different shade of blue during the forthcoming 05–06 season.

3 2005–06

Design: REEBOK
Sponsor: THOMAS COOK

Rather than utilising the previous season's unpopular white and purple shirt as their third choice in 05–06, City have opted for a brand-new amber and black third kit – the first time the club have worn this colour scheme since 97–98. The shirt features a different design from the other new Reebok outfits launched in the Premiership this season, with a distinctive black panel at the bottom of the jersey accompanied by black shoulder flashes. The shirt does retain Reebok's diagonal shadow pattern, however. Replica versions of the jersey will be released in a strictly limited edition.

MANCHESTER UNITED

The intimidating red, white and black of Manchester United has become world-famous over the past 15 years or so, with replica versions of the Red Devils' shirt becoming the top seller worldwide. However, the club have also – rather unjustly – also become world-famous for the amount of new strips they have introduced in recent years. Granted, the United marketing machine is certainly very powerful, but there are plenty of teams in the football league who have changed their strips on a far more regular basis than Manchester United.

Umbro took over United's kit supply in 1992, coinciding with the club's greatest ever period, which culminated in the fantastic 98–99 treble. It was also good to see United supporting local businesses, as both Umbro and long-term shirt sponsors Sharp are based in the Manchester area.

Umbro created quite a stir in 1992 when they introduced a yellow and green third kit based on the club's colours from their Newton Heath days. The first kit the club wore as Newton Heath when they formed in 1892 was in fact a red and white quartered shirt with blue shorts; the unique yellow and green halved strip did not arrive until 1894. But when the club changed their name to Manchester United in 1902, red shirts and white shorts were adopted and, apart from a brief period in the 1920s when a white shirt with a large red 'V' was worn, have been worn ever since.

Ever the trend-setters, in recent years United have set the pace not only when it comes to design aesthetics but also on the commercial side. By 1998–99 the club were selling over 1 million replica shirts worldwide, and the Nike deal that commenced in 2002 was rumoured to be worth an incredible £120 million. Fashion-wise, the club were one of the first to introduce a modern lightweight V-neck back in the 1950s, and have been at the forefront of design innovations and kit culture ever since.

For the entire 80s under German company adidas, the club sported a simple range of colour schemes: home = red; away = white; and third = blue. This cycle was broken by Umbro, whose array of exciting change designs has seen the club wear black, green and gold at various times. Also, of course, the club notoriously turned out one season in grey. The repercussions of that particular fashion statement will no doubt ensure that grey will never be seen in a Manchester United dressing room again.

DAVID BECKHAM IN THE UMBRO HOME KIT (98–00).

Sharp dropped the 'Electronics' text from their logo for the 83–84 United kits.

MANCHESTER UNITED

H 1980–81, 1981–82

Design: ADIDAS
Sponsor: NONE

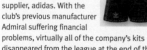

Manchester United entered the 80s with a brand new kit supplier, adidas. With the club's previous manufacturer Admiral suffering financial problems, virtually all of the company's kits disappeared from the league at the end of the 70s. This strip was a solid and dependable outfit with a large white collar and the classic adidas three-stripe trim throughout. As with all United home kits, a change pair of black shorts was also worn.

Worn in: The 1–0 home win over Norwich (80–81) – Dave Sexton's last game as manager. Plus a thrilling 2–2 draw with Man City (80–81).
Worn by: Joe Jordan, Steve Coppell.

A 1980–81, 1981–82

Design: ADIDAS
Sponsor: NONE

Adidas's first away kit for the club featured this stunning white shirt. Quite unlike any other jersey adidas produced, it was minimal in design with non-contrasting collar and cuffs. Unusually, the three-stripe trim was included under each arm and down each side rather than on the sleeve. Schoolboys across the country switched allegiance on the strength of this innovative outfit. Unlike every other adidas kit of this era, this first range of United kits included the club badge on the shorts.

Worn in: The 2–1 win at Nottingham Forest (80–81) and also a win by the same score over Liverpool at Anfield the next season.
Worn by: Sammy McIlroy, Garry Birtles, Mickey Thomas.

3 1980–81, 1981–82

Design: ADIDAS
Sponsor: NONE

For almost the whole of the 80s, the club were also armed with a blue third kit each season. Although blue can cause some unease for United fans due to their close neighbours' fondness for the colour, it also has a special place in their memories due to its appearance in the 1968 European Cup triumph. Unusually, this blue shirt was worn with the home shorts and socks. Ron Atkinson replaced Sexton as manager for the 81–82 season and guided the team to third place.

Worn in: The 5–1 win over Sunderland (81–82), which saw Steve Coppell's 206th consecutive appearance for the side – a new club record.
Worn by: Gordon McQueen, Lou Macari, Arthur Albiston, Martin Buchan.

H 1982–83, 1983–84

Design: ADIDAS
Sponsor: SHARP

This second adidas home kit was another design classic. Contemporary in every way, it included shadow pinstripes and just a hint of black on the V-neck and cuffs. Japanese hi-fi/TV manufacturers Sharp became the club's first sponsor, commencing a long relationship with the club that was to last an incredible 18 years. The shorts and socks remained the same as the previous outfit.

Worn in: The 4–0 drubbing of Brighton in the 82–83 FA Cup final replay and a great 3–0 win over Barcelona in the 83–84 European Cup Winners Cup quarter-final second leg.
Worn by: Bryan Robson, Remi Moses.

The tradition of United's black change shorts is so ingrained at the club that they look just as familiar with the home shirt as the white pair.

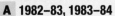

A 1982–83, 1983–84

Design: ADIDAS
Sponsor: SHARP

Rather than creating a unique design for the away kit as they had done previously, adidas launched a new white change strip that simply followed the design of the home, shadow pinstripes et al. The trim on the kit remained predominantly black. When the shirt was featured in the 83–84 Charity Shield victory over Liverpool, the Sharp logo appeared in black before returning to red for the remainder of the season.

Worn in: The 82–83 Milk Cup final 2–1 defeat to Liverpool. Also the joyous 2–1 defeat of Arsenal in the FA Cup 82–83 semi-final with a late goal. Just don't mention the shock 2–0 defeat to Bournemouth in the 83–84 FA Cup.
Worn by: Arnold Muhren, Ray Wilkins.

3 1982–83, 1983–84

Design: ADIDAS
Sponsor: SHARP

The new blue third strip again followed the design of the home and away kits. It was worn away from Old Trafford at teams whose kits were predominantly red and white (Stoke, Southampton, Sunderland etc.). However, the third shirt now had its own blue shorts and socks to match, although it was also worn with the white shorts and black socks from the home kit. The club finished in the top five of Division 1 in both seasons in which they wore this kit.

Worn in: A close 1–0 win at The Dell vs Southampton in the 82–83 season followed by a humbling 1–0 defeat to Stoke.
Worn by: Arthur Graham, Colin Gibson, Garth Crooks.

H 1984–85, 1985–86

Design: ADIDAS
Sponsor: SHARP

There was quite a change on the kit front in 84–85. Adidas remained as manufacturer, but ditched their famous three-stripe trim on the shirt, replacing it with intimidating white shoulder panels trimmed with black piping. The club badge was placed centrally below the bold V-neck and the adidas logo moved to each sleeve. The shorts now also featured fine red pinstripes.

Worn in: A tense 2–2 FA Cup semi-final in 84–85 vs Liverpool, followed by the glorious 1–0 win over Everton in the final. Also the 5–0 thrashing of Newcastle the same season with a great solo goal by Gordon Strachan.
Worn by: Norman Whiteside, Kevin Moran (the first player to be sent off in an FA Cup final).

A 1984–85, 1985–86

Design: ADIDAS
Sponsor: SHARP

Complete with exactly the same V-neck and cuffs as the home shirt, the new white away kit also featured the same shoulder panels and piping, now in black and red respectively. The rather nice pair of black shorts with red pinstripes also doubled as the home kit's change pair. A new sock design saw the adidas logo embroidered onto the turnover. Despite their FA Cup success, Utd still couldn't reach higher than fourth in Division 1.

Worn in: The incredible 2–1 FA Cup semi-final replay over Liverpool in the 84–85 season, with United triumphant after being 1–0 down at half time before Mark Hughes' fantastic goal.
Worn by: Jesper Olsen, Alan Brazil.

Despite the vast amount of Umbro shirts worn in the League at the time, 86–88 saw adidas producing kits for three of the top clubs in England: Liverpool, Manchester Utd and Arsenal.

3   1984–85, 1985–86

Design: ADIDAS
Sponsor: SHARP

One of the more popular all-blue kits with the Old Trafford faithful was the strip issued in 84–85. The jersey retained the same red, black and white V-neck and cuffs as the away shirt. The patience of the fans and directors was beginning to wear thin on the pitch, however, as the flamboyant Atkinson failed to deliver the League title.

Worn in: The tight 3–2 defeat at Sunderland and the 2–1 deficit at Stoke in the 84–85 season. Plus the 1–0 defeat the following season at Southampton. Not a lucky shirt!
Worn by: Frank Stapleton, Paul McGrath, Graeme Hogg, Gordon Strachan.

H   1986–87, 1987–88

Design: ADIDAS
Sponsor: SHARP

The three stripes were back for adidas' next outfit for the club and were now also enhanced by a fine black outline. A pretty standard adidas design, this new home outfit was worn by the side when Alex Ferguson arrived from Aberdeen as the club's new manager with the aim of rebuilding the club, who were languishing in mid-table obscurity and seemed to be in a mini crisis. A small red devil logo appeared on the shorts, replacing the traditional club badge.

Worn in: Ferguson's first match in charge: a 2–0 defeat to Oxford Utd. Also an exciting 3–3 draw with Tottenham at Old Trafford in 86–87, followed by a great 1–0 win over Liverpool.
Worn by: Viv Anderson, John Gidman.

A   1986–87, 1987–88

Design: ADIDAS
Sponsor: SHARP

Yet again the away kit replicated the design of the home in the familiar white with red and black trim. The shirt fabric for this set of kits included a new diagonal shadow stripe pattern combined with smaller horizontal bars. The black shorts and white socks (with distinctive black hoop) were also worn with the home kit when required. 86–87 saw the side finish a disappointing 11th in the table.

Worn in: The 1–0 victory over high-flying Liverpool at Anfield – incredibly the Red Devils' only away win of the season. Also worn in the classic 3–3 match at Anfield the following season. Plus the FA Cup fifth round 2–1 defeat to Arsenal in 87–88.
Worn by: Terry Gibson, Peter Davenport.

3   1986–87, 1987–88

Design: ADIDAS
Sponsor: SHARP

This all-blue third kit did not see much action – apparently, it was only worn in three away matches, all against Southampton at The Dell. The shirt retained exactly the same elegant multi-striped V-neck and cuffs as the home strip. Alex Ferguson's first full season in charge (87–88) did see a change in the club's fortunes, however, as they eventually finished second in Division 1.

Worn in: The appalling 4–1 defeat at Southampton in the 86–87 Littlewoods Cup. Also a 2–2 draw at the Dell on the opening day of the following season.
Worn by: Mike Duxbury, Billy Garton, John Sivebaek.

The 88–90 adidas home kit was infamously worn by Paul Ince before he'd even signed for the club – causing the player to become a figure of hate at the club he was with at the time, West Ham.

H 1988–89, 1989–90

Design: ADIDAS
Sponsor: SHARP

With the hope of a new era dawning at Old Trafford (perhaps inspired by the return of prodigal son Mark Hughes), adidas changed the club's kit only very slightly. The shirt now featured a vertical shadow stripe pattern interspersed with the trefoil logo, a unique wrap-over neck and white piping. The shirt was also cuffless, as were most jerseys around this time.

Worn in: A 4–1 thrashing of reigning champions Arsenal at the start of the 89–90 season, but also a humbling 5–1 defeat to rivals City at Maine Road later that season. Plus, more memorably, the 1–0 win over Crystal Palace in the 89–90 FA Cup final replay.
Worn by: Neil Webb, Lee Martin.

A 1988–89, 1989–90

Design: ADIDAS
Sponsor: SHARP

The marketing of replica football kits began to slowly increase towards the end of the 80s and reached a peak after England's exploits at Italia 90. Although the 88–90 period of United's history saw them slump yet again to mid-table, replica versions of their kits regularly featured in the football press of the time. The club's next away shirt replicated the design of the home and, like the previous away jersey, featured red more prominently than black in the trim. The shorts included an 'MUFC' monogram and shadow stripe design.

Worn in: A shock 2–0 defeat to Charlton. Also the dramatic 3–3 89–90 FA Cup final against Crystal Palace at Wembley.
Worn by: Russell Beardsmore, Mal Donaghy.

3 1988–89, 1989–90

Design: ADIDAS
Sponsor: SHARP

For the last time, United sported a blue third kit that was simply a basic replication of the home and away designs. The late 80s saw the overall fit of football shirts increase dramatically – earlier in the decade the jerseys were pretty unforgiving, whereas now a beer belly could be safely hidden away. However, the shorts were still fashionably snug.

Worn in: The great 2–0 win over a good Southampton side at the Dell in the 89–90 season, but also a 2–1 defeat at Arsenal in the 88–89 season.
Worn by: Ralph Milne, Mark Robins, Liam O'Brien.

H 1990–91, 1991–92

Design: ADIDAS
Sponsor: SHARP

Adidas' last home kit for the club was again not much of a move on from the previous. The main difference was the addition of a round neck and

a new abstract pattern on the shirt fabric. The shorts featured large red panels on either leg, on which the trademark three stripes sat. 91–92 saw the club come close to the title before being pipped at the post by Leeds.

Worn in: A revenge 1–0 defeat at the hands of Ron Atkinson's Sheffield Wednesday in the 90–91 League Cup final. Also the infamous 'battle of Old Trafford' vs Arsenal in 90–91.
Worn by: Ryan Giggs (who made his debut in a 90–91 match vs Man City).

Even though United were sporting their unique white kit in the 90–91 European Cup Winners Cup final, Barcelona strangely also adopted their change kit for the match.

A 1990–91, 1991–92

Design: ADIDAS
Sponsor: SHARP

Adidas finally broke the cycle of white away and blue third kits by combining both into this curious concoction – one of the most bizarre kits worn by the club. Although a typical garish design from the early 90s, the main problem was that the dazzling pattern used on the shirt gave an overall impression of sky blue – and sky blue in Manchester does not say United!

Worn in: The stunning 6–2 win over Arsenal in the 90–91 Rumbelows Cup and the heartbreaking 2–0 defeat to Liverpool at Anfield in 91–92 that effectively lost the title for United that season. Also the 1–0 win over Nottingham Forest in the 91–92 Rumbelows Cup final.
Worn by: Andrei Kanchelskis, Paul Parker.

3 1990–91

Design: ADIDAS
Sponsor: SHARP

With echoes of the 1968 European Cup final strip, adidas issued a one-off kit (minus Sharp's logo) for United's European Cup Winners Cup final against Barcelona. The shirt, which loosely mirrored the design of the home jersey, was worn with the home white shorts and change white socks. A limited edition replica version was also sold to commemorate the wonderful win, which saw the emergence of what was to become a formidable Manchester United side.

Worn in: The glorious 2–1 win over Barcelona in the 90–91 European Cup Winners Cup in Rotterdam with two goals from Mark Hughes.
Worn by: Mike Phelan, Clayton Blackmore, Dennis Irwin.

H 1992–93, 1993–94

Design: UMBRO
Sponsor: SHARP

Umbro's first home kit for United was one of their most important, as it was worn as the club's dominance took off. Heavily influenced by retro fashions, the shirt included a collar with a lace-up neck and an intricate 'MUFC' shadow pattern. The club won the League title in both seasons in which this kit was worn.

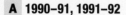

Worn in: The night at Old Trafford when the club beat Blackburn 3–1 and paraded the first ever Premier League trophy in 92–93. Also the 4–0 win over Chelsea in the following season's FA Cup final and, with it, the 93–94 double.
Worn by: Steve Bruce, Eric Cantona (in his debut – the 92–93 2–1 win over Man City).

A 1992–93

Design: UMBRO
Sponsor: SHARP

Blue was retained as Umbro's first away kit colour for the side. The shirt (which included a neat collar) and shorts incorporated a large fragmented print of the club badge combined with a black pattern resembling wood grain. It was an unusual strip that lasted for only one season. A nice touch was the smaller version of the Red Devils shield on the shorts waistband. An updated version of the Umbro diamond trim was included on the socks.

Worn in: A vital 2–1 win at Anfield vs Liverpool, along with a narrow 1–0 victory over Arsenal – both important triumphs on the way to Utd's fabulous Premier League success.
Worn by: Lee Sharpe, Dion Dublin, Ben Thornley.

Rumour has it that Umbro home jerseys only retained a large collar in the 90s due to Eric Cantona's fondness for turning them upwards during games.

3 1992–93, 1993–94

Design: UMBRO
Sponsor: SHARP

With the football world celebrating its past, Umbro's first third kit for the club was inspired by the distinctive yellow and green jersey the team first wore as Newton Heath way back in 1894. It was a radical change in United's kit policy and included the same retro lace-up collar as the home shirt. A 3D-style 'MUFC' graphic was included on the left leg of the shorts and a fine shadow pattern was featured throughout.

Worn in: A vital 2–0 win at Crystal Palace in 92–93 with goals by Paul Ince and Mark Hughes (his 100th league goal). Also worn in the 93–94 Coca-Cola Cup final defeat to Aston Villa (3–1).
Worn by: Danny Wallace, Keith Gillespie.

A 1993–94, 1994–95

Design: UMBRO
Sponsor: SHARP VIEWCAM

The formation of the Premier League saw the introduction of a new outfit for referees, replacing their infamous all-black strip. This left English teams open to play in black for the first time in the modern game, with United opting for this threatening strip trimmed with yellow and blue. Although hugely popular with fans and the team, it accompanied some black times for the club – most notably Eric Cantona's kung fu antics at Crystal Palace in 94–95.

Worn in: A real classic – the 3–3 draw at Liverpool (93–94) with United surrendering a 3–0 half-time lead. Also the 1–1 draw at West Ham that saw the club lose the title in 94–95.
Worn by: Paul Ince, Brian McClair.

H 1994–95, 1995–96

Design: UMBRO
Sponsor: SHARP

Umbro's second home kit for the club saw the white collar replaced by a unique black design. The shirt, which saw the club badge now placed within an additional shield, also featured a faint shadow print of Old Trafford – a unique idea that showed how mid-90s kit designers were constantly looking for new ways to embellish traditional home shirts. 94–95 saw the club lose 1–0 to Everton in the FA Cup final.

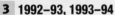

Worn in: A 9–0 demolition of Ipswich in 94–95. Also worn in Cantona's comeback – the 5–0 thrashing of City (94–95) – along with the 1–0 win over Liverpool in the 95–96 FA Cup final.
Worn by: Gary Pallister, Roy Keane.

3 1994–95, 1995–96

Design: UMBRO
Sponsor: SHARP

This blue and white striped outfit actually made appearances in three seasons. Based on a kit donned by the club in the early 1900s, it included a new design of collar and a shadow pattern of the old club crest on the front of the shirt. Of most interest was the incorporation of every past and present United player's name into the jersey fabric.

Worn in: The 3–0 win at Middlesbrough in the 95–96 season that clinched the Premiership title for the Red Devils – the first half of another double that season. Plus the second half of the 95–96 'grey kit match' at The Dell. Also worn in the 6–3 defeat at Southampton in 96–97 as an emergency kit due to a clash.
Worn by: Nicky Butt, Mark Hughes.

In the mid-90s Umbro introduced a small piece of extra type to the front of many of their shirts; the 96–98 United home jersey sported the legend 'Theatre of Dreams'.

A 1995–96

Design: UMBRO
Sponsor: SHARP VIEWCAM

Probably one of the most controversial kits in football history was this all-grey affair. It was infamous for its part in the 3–1 defeat at Southampton that saw Alex Ferguson switch shirts at half time and blame the grey kit for the defeat. Although grey goes through phases of popularity, the colour is never really a sensible kit choice due to its lack of visibility – which, according to the United players, was a major factor in the defeat at The Dell. The club did not win a single game in this strip.

Worn in: The astonishing 3–1 defeat against Southampton that saw the kit consigned to the scrapheap and also a 1–0 defeat to Arsenal and a 2–0 loss to Liverpool... grey kit anyone?!
Worn by: Paul Scholes, Steve Bruce.

A 1996–97

Design: UMBRO
Sponsor: SHARP VIEWCAM

Introduced as a replacement for the controversial grey outfit, this white kit was the complete opposite of the strip at the heart of all the problems. Plain and simple yet stylish and slick, it featured a basic collar design and a small embroidered 'Manchester United FC' monogram on the front of the shirt. Worn with the black change shorts of the home kit, it featured in some very important matches during the side's championship success of the 96–97 season.

Worn in: A superb 2–1 victory over Arsenal at Highbury followed by another glorious win at Anfield – this time 3–1 – that virtually clinched the 96–97 title for The Red Devils.
Worn by: Andy Cole, John O'Kane.

H 1996–97, 1997–98

Design: UMBRO
Sponsor: SHARP

Once the retro craze of the early 90s had died down, United took to the field in this hi-tech affair. In a slightly duller red with a large print of the club badge on each side, along with a faded black and white collar and a small Red Devil button on the neck, the shirt's first major glimpse of fame was accompanying David Beckham as he scored his wonder goal from the half-way line against Wimbledon in 96–97.

Worn in: The sublime 7–0 win over Barnsley with a hat-trick by Andy Cole. Also the 1–0 defeat to Arsenal that effectively gave the Londoners the title (both 97–98). Plus a 4–0 win vs Newcastle in the 96–97 Charity Shield.
Worn by: Karel Poborsky, Phillip Mulryne.

3 1996–97, 1997–98

Design: UMBRO
Sponsor: SHARP

Although designed to bring back memories of United's triumph in the 1968 European Cup final, this was not one of the most popular kits worn by the club and made only very few appearances in its two years of use – mainly in European games. Umbro were experimenting with new collar designs at the time and this was one of the more unusual ones: long floppy lapels and a button-up neck. Striking black and white panels completed the design.

Worn in: The shock 2–1 defeat in the 96–97 season vs Sunderland. Also the tough 3–1 victory over Feyenoord in the 97–98 Champions League in which Andy Cole scored yet another great hat-trick.
Worn by: Phil Neville, John Curtis.

MANCHESTER UNITED

A 1997–98, 1998–99

Design: UMBRO
Sponsor: SHARP VIEWCAM

Umbro pulled out all the stops for the next white away kit. This bold and uncompromising kit included shadow stripes, aggressive red and black panels on the shoulders and red and black hoops. Asymmetrical shorts (worn in both black and white versions) completed the kit.

Worn in: A win after penalties in the 97–98 Charity Shield match vs Chelsea. Also the epic 98–99 FA Cup semi-final replay vs Arsenal with Giggs' wonder goal earning a 2–1 win for United after extra time. Plus the magnificent 8–1 win at Nottingham Forest in 98–99.
Worn by: Teddy Sheringham, Ronnie Wallwork.

H 1998–99, 1999–2000

Design: UMBRO
Sponsor: SHARP

This superb kit, made from Umbro's Vapatech fabric, was typical Manchester United: trendsetting, stylish and intimidating. The collar featured a unique locking zip mechanism and fans welcomed the return of the old-school Umbro diamond trim on the sleeves and shorts. Inspired by this fine-looking outfit, United won their historic treble in 98–99 and gained Premiership success the following year.

Worn in: The 2–0 win vs Newcastle in the 98–99 FA Cup final. Plus the 2–1 victory at Spurs that sealed the title in 98–99 and the 3–1 win again vs Spurs that clinched the next season's crown.
Worn by: Henning Berg, Jaap Stam.

3 1998–99

Design: UMBRO
Sponsor: SHARP

Eager to put the grey kit debacle behind them, Umbro launched a striking new black third kit for United. Originally conceived and marketed as a 'training kit', the design incorporated the latest in fabric technology with ribbed panels down each side, combined with a neat little collar. The classic Umbro diamond trim made a comeback, although it was now fashioned in a curious white and bright green display. It was one of four kits worn by the club in the legendary treble season of 98–99.

Worn in: The 3–0 humiliation at Arsenal in the 98–99 season – a black day for United – but also a terrific win by the same score over Southampton at The Dell.
Worn by: David May, Jesper Blomqvist.

E 1997–98 to 1999–2000

Design: UMBRO
Sponsor: SHARP

Ever the innovators (and perhaps suspecting that glory was imminent), the Red Devils launched a unique new home kit designed solely for Champions League action. Featuring a simple white collar, no superfluous trim and, of course, the traditional United European white socks, it was to feature in possibly the greatest evening in the club's history.

Worn in: The stunning 3–2 victory over Juventus in the 98–99 European Champions League semi-final followed by the fantastic 2–1 victory vs Bayern Munich in the final, with two very late goals by Sheringham and Solskjaer clinching the treble for the club and catapulting this shirt into the history books.
Worn by: Ole Gunnar Solskjaer, Jordi Cruyff.

When the white and navy third kit was worn as an away strip in the 00–01 season,
a new streamlined and more dynamic version of the Umbro logo was introduced.

A 1999–2000

Design: UMBRO
Sponsor: SHARP DIGITAL

This fine strip unfortunately only saw one season of action. The kit, which marked the end of the Sharp sponsorship deal and featured a 'Sharp Digital' logo, was unlike any other United kit. It combined dark blue and black with horizontal white pinstripes. Another innovation from Umbro was the inclusion of air vents in the socks.

Worn in: The stunning 4–3 win over Middlesbrough at The Riverside Stadium. Plus the 3–1 win over Southampton at The Dell that saw United clinch their second consecutive Premiership title. A lucky shirt for the side!
Worn by: Jonathan Greening, Ronny Johnsen.

3 1999–2000   A 2000–01

Design: UMBRO
Sponsor: SHARP (99–00) VODAFONE (00–01)

The late 90s saw Umbro launch a uniform range of kits across all the clubs they supplied. They all featured an interesting reversed-stitch sleeve trim and panels of ribbed fabric. Worn in 00–01 with the logo of new sponsors Vodafone, it was also involved in the infamous incident when a hoaxer donned the shirt and cheekily joined the team photo before a European match.

Worn in: The 2–1 defeat to Arsenal in the 99–00 Charity Shield season opener and a good 1–0 win over Aston Villa in 00–01. Also that season a close 2–2 draw with West Ham.
Worn by: Dwight Yorke, Michael Clegg.

H 2000–01, 2001–02

Design: UMBRO
Sponsor: VODAFONE

This was the first Utd shirt to feature new sponsors Vodafone's logo, but the last home version to be produced by Umbro – the company who had accompanied the club through their most successful period ever. The shirt was made from Umbro's new Sportswool fabric, which was designed to minimise heat and maximise comfort. The shirt's cut was designed to appear more intimidating.

Worn in: The 6–1 win against Arsenal in 00–01 and the awe-inspiring comeback at Spurs – 3–0 down at half time, United eventually came back to win 5–3.
Worn by: David Beckham, Quinton Fortune.

3 2000–01

Design: UMBRO
Sponsor: VODAFONE

One of the smarter Utd kits from the latter days of the Umbro era was this stylish, but seldom worn, navy and red Sportswool combination. Officially marketed as a training strip, it included white reversed seams, horizontal shadow stripes and red underarm/side panels. The 00–01 season saw the club claim yet another Premiership title – their third in a row.

Worn in: A fiercely fought 1–0 defeat to Arsenal at Highbury and another 2–1 defeat, this time to Southampton. Also an exciting match vs Sunderland in the Worthington Cup, which the Red Devils eventually lost 2–1 AET.
Worn by: Gary Neville, Mikael Silvestre.

Diego Forlan famously got hot and bothered as he struggled for three minutes with Nike's Cool Motion dual layers when replacing his home shirt after celebrating his goal against Southampton.

A 2001–02

Design: UMBRO
Sponsor: VODAFONE

Umbro went out with a bang with their last kit for Utd. It was yet another groundbreaking design – the world's first reversible shirt. The double-sided jersey included the first choice white with black sleeves on one side, and the gold third design on the other, giving value for money to fans who bought replica versions. The actual match day shirts were not reversible, however. A small logo celebrating 100 years of the club playing under the name 'Manchester Utd' was also included.

Worn in: The 3–1 defeat at Liverpool and the sad 1–1 draw against Bayer Leverkusen that saw the end of the club's Champions League campaign in 01–02.
Worn by: Juan Sebastian Veron, Laurent Blanc.

3 2001–02

Design: UMBRO
Sponsor: VODAFONE

The flip side of the mesh fabric reversible shirt was this gold affair, which emerged in a season when metallic coloured shirts were back in vogue. The shorts for this revolutionary set of kits were designed to mix and match when appropriate, so the white shorts often appeared with the white shirts and the black pair with the gold. 01–02 was a disappointing season for the club, however, with speculation over Alex Ferguson's future at Old Trafford causing unrest.

Worn in: A 1–0 defeat to Arsenal – the only outing of the gold shirt in the Premiership.
Worn by: David Bellion, Bojan Djordic, Paul Scholes.

H 2002–03, 2003–04

Design: NIKE
Sponsor: VODAFONE

Nike became United's third kit manufacturer since 1980 in a massive financial deal. A typical piece of Nike design, similar to the style featured during the 2002 World Cup, the strip included their Cool Motion shirt design with dual-layer fabrics designed to keep players cool during a match. The club clinched the Premiership again in the first season this strip was worn – no doubt to the delight of Nike.

Worn in: The 2–1 win at Everton, when the 03–04 Premiership trophy was presented. Also, the 3–0 win over Millwall in the 03–04 FA Cup final. This was Beckham's last United shirt.
Worn by: John O'Shea, Kleberson.

A 2002–03

Design: NIKE
Sponsor: VODAFONE

Nike's first United away kit stuck to the tried and tested formula of white with black and red trim. Like the home shirt, it was made up of an intricate system of differing fabrics pieced together with reversed stitching and topped off with a unique collar design. More often than not the shirt was also worn with the white home shorts. The socks also set a new trend, with coloured vertical panels being favoured over the more traditional hoops.

Worn in: The poor 2–0 defeat to Liverpool in the 02–03 Worthington Cup final, but a great 3–1 win over Basel in the Champions League. Plus another 3–1 victory, this time over Charlton in the Premier League.
Worn by: Rio Ferdinand, Darren Fletcher.

Rumours around Old Trafford that the 03–05 Nike black away kit was introduced in mourning for Beckham's departure to Real Madrid are unfounded!

3 2002–03

Design: NIKE
Sponsor: VODAFONE

In a very similar shade to that worn in the club's 1968 European Cup final triumph, Nike's first third kit for United completed the standard red, white and blue range of kits favoured in the 80s. Although the shirt retained a similar stitched panelling effect to that of the home and away strips, the shorts and socks featured a new design with a fine silver and black trim.

Worn in: The 2–1 win over Bayer Leverkusen and the thrilling 3–2 win over Olympiakos Piraeus in the 02–03 Champions League. Also a 2–0 win over Southampton.

Worn by: Wes Brown, Diego Forlan, Ruud van Nistelrooy, Luke Chadwick.

A 2003–04, 2004–05

Design: NIKE
Sponsor: VODAFONE

Although perhaps not the luckiest of colours for United, black was chosen as the club's new away strip for the 03–04 season and was promoted by a stern-looking Roy Keane in pre-season publicity photos. The kit featured yet another variation in stitching and trim and included a trendy round neck, along with a very subtle shadow pattern featuring tiny crosses combined with easy-breathe material panels under the arms. The shirt was also often worn with the white shorts from the third kit.

Worn in: A 1–0 win over Liverpool followed by a 4–2 thrashing of Arsenal (both 04–05). Also that season the disappointing FA Cup final defeat against the Gunners.

Worn by: Eric Djemba-Djemba, Danny Pugh.

3 2003–04, 2004–05

Design: NIKE
Sponsor: VODAFONE

A real retro 70s collar was combined with an 80s pinstripe design and 21st century fabrics to create this great third kit. A shame, perhaps, that it was not the first choice change outfit. The shorts included horizontal trim at each leg and the socks were a straightforward reversal of the away design. The shirt was given a fresh look by the inclusion of a red Vodafone logo. Also worn with the away kit's black shorts.

Worn in: The great 2–1 win over Liverpool at Anfield and the 2–0 victory over Villa on the last day of the season (both 03–04), but best remembered for the 1–0 win over Arsenal (minus Henry) in the 03–04 FA Cup semi-final.

Worn by: Alan Smith, Cristiano Ronaldo, Kieran Richardson, Wayne Rooney, Louis Saha.

H 2004–05, 2005–06

Design: NIKE
Sponsor: VODAFONE

Nike updated the home kit with this brilliant design. Threatening and arrogant, the shirt incorporated Nike's new 'Zero Distraction' moisture-management fabric. The jersey also included a daring asymmetrical white mesh flash around the neck and left sleeve, along with a centralised badge and Vodafone logo.

Worn in: Not a good start, with Utd beaten 3–1 by Arsenal in the Community Shield. Also the epic match vs the Gunners later in the season that saw Utd end Arsenal's unbeaten run. Plus the fairytale 6–2 win over Fenerbahce that marked Rooney's debut.

Worn by: Gabriel Heinze, Liam Miller.

A 2005–06

Design: NIKE
Sponsor: VODAFONE

A new-look Manchester United side takes to the field away from Old Trafford in 05–06 in this attractive all-blue outfit – once again bringing back memories of the 1968 European Cup final. Trimmed with red, this striking kit features a standard Nike template of curved shoulder flashes along with a modern take on the old faithful V-neck. The last blue kit worn by the club (the 02–03 Nike third strip) proved popular with fans, so no doubt this vivid concoction will be well received as Alex Ferguson's United try to claw back some of the success that has eluded them in recent seasons.

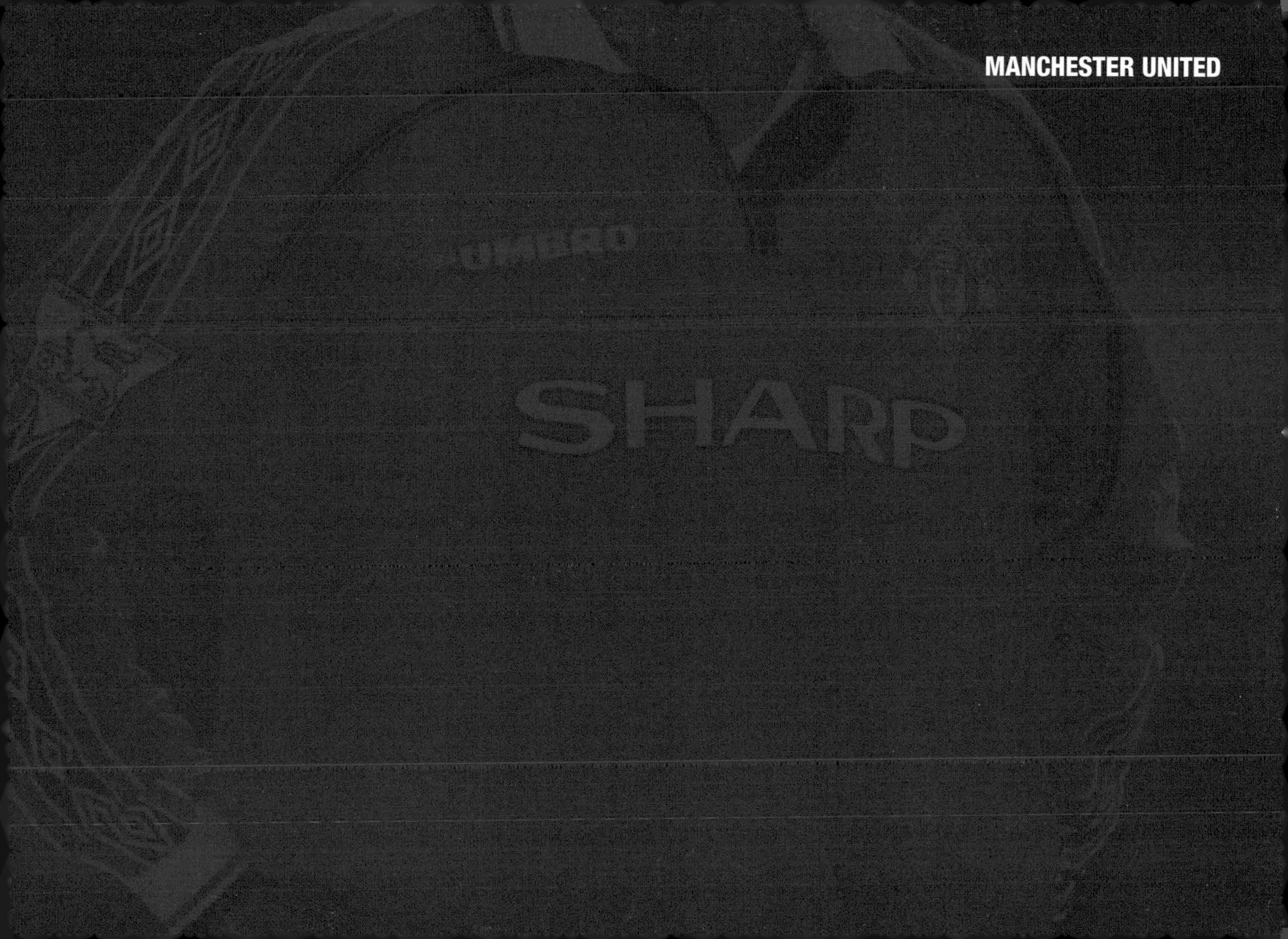
UMBRO
SHARP

MIDDLESBROUGH

It's not often that a team becomes associated with a particular style or design of kit that in truth they haven't actually worn that frequently. However, this is the situation that Middlesbrough find themselves in: to many in the football world, a red shirt with a white chest band is the club's traditional outfit, but in reality it is a style that has been worn for fewer than a dozen seasons in Boro's 129-year history. Still, that didn't stop the Riverside faithful warmly receiving the latest jersey to reinvent the white band.

Formed in 1876, the club's first strip was black and red striped, although in the 1890s they reverted to an amateur side and switched to white shirts and navy shorts. By 1900 they had resumed their professional status and adopted red shirts with a white yoke as their new kit – the expanse of white becoming a somewhat recurring theme in the club's kit design during the following years.

As the years passed, the club turned out in red shirts with white shoulders (and of course occasionally a white hoop) as well as just a plain all-red jersey. In fact, there is no one real traditional Boro shirt, shorts and socks combination, and today the selection of white or red shorts continues to vary on a regular basis. The last 25 years have also seen black (or sometimes navy blue) added to the home kit as a third colour, possibly in tribute to the first ever Boro outfit. The club's away colours are no more stable. Blue recurs often in the Boro away palette, but the side are just as well known for playing in white away from home.

Since linking up with Italian sportswear company Errea, the club have changed their home and away kits every season. The move has attracted some criticism in the past, but, as the club point out, the regular changes have become something of a Boro tradition and fans now expect and look forward to the next season's new designs. This regularity at least allows a wide and rich variety of different outfits to be worn by the Teeside club.

With their reputation as a yo-yo club well and truly put to bed after several good seasons in the Premiership, the club and their excellent Riverside stadium will no doubt hope to add to their first trophy, the 03–04 Carling Cup, with more success whether all in red, in red shirts and white shorts or even a red shirt with a white hoop.

JUNINHO IN THE 03–04 ERREA HOME SHIRT – THE JERSEY THE CLUB WORE IN THE 03–04 CARLING CUP FINAL SUCCESS.

McLean Homes included two versions of their logo on the adidas kits. The first, incorporating a key graphic, was considered hard to decipher and was replaced by a more legible text-only version.

H 1978–79 to 1981–82

Design: ADIDAS
Sponsor: DATSUN CLEVELAND (80–82)

Middlesbrough abandoned their old round neck shirt complete with the notable white horizontal panel in 1978 in favour of this glossy, up-to-date adidas kit. A simple V-neck and a white three-stripe design both featured on this all-red strip. The 78–79 season saw the adidas logos and club badge in black embroidered on the shirt.

Worn in: A brilliant 3–1 victory at Spurs on the opening day of the 79–80 season. Plus the 2–1 victory over Ipswich in 80–81 and a 1–0 win over a high-flying West Brom side in 81–82. Also in 81–82 a valiant 0–0 draw vs Liverpool – not quite enough to keep Boro in the top flight.
Worn by: Craig Johnston, Irving Nattrass, David Mills, Tony McAndrew.

A 1978–79 to 1982–83

Design: ADIDAS
Sponsor: DATSUN CLEVELAND (80–82)
McLEAN HOMES (82–83)

As with many kits of the era, the away outfit retained all the stylings of the home strip and simply replicated it in another colour, in Boro's case a rich blue. The kit was worn for an incredible five years and featured the logo of car firm Datsun Cleveland until 81–82, before being replaced by that of new sponsors McLean Homes the following season. Unfortunately, their arrival coincided with the club's relegation to Division 2.

Worn in: A hard-fought 1–1 draw vs Liverpool at Anfield (81–82). Also the thrilling 3–2 defeat to Arsenal in the 82–83 FA Cup fifth round.
Worn by: David Hodgson, Colin Ross, David Armstrong.

3 1981–82

Design: ADIDAS
Sponsor: DATSUN CLEVELAND

The club also sported this rather fetching white third shirt. Seldom worn, it simply reversed the colours of the home design and was worn with the home red shorts and change white socks, all decorated with the standard three-stripe trim. The shirt was worn against sides whose home kits contained large areas of red (or claret) and blue. The adidas logo had no fixed abode on all adidas shorts of the era, and was sometimes featured on the right leg and sometimes on the left. It was still fairly rare for clubs to feature their badge on the shorts.

Worn in: The exciting 3–2 defeat against West Ham at Upton Park.
Worn by: Billy Ashcroft, Billy Woof.

H 1982–83

Design: ADIDAS
Sponsor: McLEAN HOMES

With the club back in Division 2 and new manager Malcolm Allison at the helm, the side took to the field in a slightly different version of their previous kit. The shirt was identical, apart from the logo of new sponsors, the housing developers McLean Homes. The shorts, however, switched to white and now featured adidas' new design of contrasting panels on the legs. It was a design also worn by Norwich and the Welsh national side at the time. The socks also switched to white.

Worn in: The 2–2 draw with Bishops Stortford in the 82–83 FA Cup third round, with the non-league club coming back from 2–0 down.
Worn by: Terry Cochrane, John Craggs.

When the club had emerged from the threat of extinction, a new club badge was designed to mark the rebirth. First worn on the 87–88 kits, the crest was apparently designed in just two hours as the club reformed overnight.

DICKENS

DICKENS

H 1983–84

Design: UNKNOWN
Sponsor: McLEAN HOMES

A real mystery kit! With the adidas deal at an end, Middlesbrough took to the field in this unique-looking kit made by an unknown company who strangely didn't include their logo on the strip. The shirt was a contrast in style from previous years, with a new, rather basic-looking McLean Homes logo accompanied by snazzy shadow stripes. A small version of the club badge appeared on each sleeve, on the left leg of the shorts and, in a groundbreaking trend, on the socks.

Worn in: Impressive wins over Newcastle (3–2) and Shrewsbury (4–0). Also a last-minute winner from David Currie that earned a great 2–1 win over Chelsea.
Worn by: Heine Otto, Gary MacDonald.

A 1983–84

Design: UNKNOWN
Sponsor: McLEAN HOMES

As with the last adidas set of outfits, the next away kit followed exactly the style of the home with blue replacing red in a time-honoured Boro tradition. Blue shorts and socks completed the strip. This range of kits lasted for only one season and appear to be a real anomaly in Boro's kit history. 1984 saw the departure of Malcolm Allison as the club finished a lowly 17th in Division 2, teetering on the brink of Division 3.

Worn in: A great 2–0 win over Barnsley early in the season, but also a disappointing away defeat to Charlton Athletic by the same score.
Worn by: Andy Crawford, Gary Hamilton, Paul Ward.

H 1984–85 to 1986–87

Design: HUMMEL
Sponsor: CAMERONS (84–86) DICKENS (86–87)

At the start of the 84–85 season, Danish kit suppliers Hummel arrived at Ayresome Park with a classic 80s strip that saw the return of the Boro white chest band. Camerons Brewery became the new sponsors (some versions of their logo included the word 'Ales' beneath the brand name), before local DIY store Dickens replaced them in 1986. The strip accompanied the team through relegation, liquidation and then finally promotion in 86–87.

Worn in: A good 2–1 win over Manchester City in 84–85 and the last-day loss to Shrewsbury that relegated the club to Division 3 (85–86).
Worn by: Gary Gill, Alan Roberts.

A 1984–85 to 1986–87

Design: HUMMEL
Sponsor: HANSA (84–86) DICKENS (86–87)

Although the away kit again simply mirrored the design of the home strip (including the white chest band), the big difference came with the inclusion of a different sponsor's logo with Camerons opting to promote their Hansa brand. The shirt was also worn with blue change shorts. 1986 saw a reborn Boro emerge after being saved from closure in 85–86 by a local consortium.

Worn in: Superb away wins over Charlton (1–0) and Sheffield Utd (3–0), both in the 84–85 season. Also a fantastic 4–1 win over Rotherham in 86–87.
Worn by: Mick Buckley, Tony McAndrew.

Middlesbrough were one of the first clubs to produce their own kit in-house. Chelsea had launched their own range a season earlier, but it was to be another 10 years before more and more clubs turned their hands to sportswear production.

H 1987–88

Design: SKILL
Sponsor: DICKENS

With the club surviving their financial troubles, they faced the new season back in Division 2 with no kit deal in place. With the help of a local supplier, they decided to produce the strip themselves. The kit would later be branded under the name 'Skill', but for 87–88 a simple 'MFC' logotype was included. It was a distinctive shirt with a white chest panel and horizontal red stripes of varying width. Also worn with the red shorts of the white third kit. Two versions of the kit exist, one with a square shadow pattern and one with chevrons.

Worn in: A stunning 6–0 thrashing of Sheffield Utd and the wonderful play-off victory over Chelsea to win promotion to Division 1.
Worn by: Bernie Slaven, Dean Glover.

A 1987–88

Design: SKILL
Sponsor: DICKENS

For self-produced kits, Boro's outfits of the 87–88 season were inventive and well-considered designs. The away design opted for light and dark blue in a style that mirrored the red home kit, the only difference being the omission of the trim on the shorts. As with the home shirt, the newly designed round badge was added to the kit. The newly energised Boro gained promotion for the second season running under Bruce Rioch in 87–88 and found themselves in Division 1 once more.

Worn in: A great 2–0 win at Sheffield Utd and a 3–0 victory over Barnsley.
Worn by: Tony Mowbray, Stuart Ripley, Gary Parkinson.

3 1987–88

Design: SKILL
Sponsor: DICKENS

The remarkable 87–88 season that saw the club promoted to Division 1 via a play-off victory over Chelsea also saw them in this nice but seldom-worn third kit. It was essentially a reversal of the home kit with red shorts and white socks, therefore creating an easily interchangeable range of apparel. Another version of this shirt saw the Dickens logo in black and placed lower down the shirt.

Worn in: An unfortunate 2–1 away defeat to Bradford City in the Division 2 play-off semi-final first leg – a defeat they were eventually to overcome in the second leg by winning 2–0 at Ayresome Park.
Worn by: Trevor Senior, Paul Kerr, Gary Pallister.

H 1988–89, 1989–90

Design: SKILL
Sponsor: HERITAGE HAMPERS

With the team back in Division 1 the home shirt was changed – but only slightly. The cuffs were removed, a large 'i' logo representing the Skill brand replaced the previous season's 'MFC' logo and Heritage Hampers – a specialist food provider – became the new sponsors, their logo sitting above an additional white line. The shorts and socks remained as before.

Worn in: A cracking 1–0 win over Manchester Utd in the 88–89 season. Also the 1–0 defeat to Chelsea in the 89–90 Zenith Data Systems Cup final, in which a unique version of the shirt featuring a large all-white chest panel and wrap-over V-neck was worn.
Worn by: Gary Hamilton, Peter Davenport.

Although local newspapers have made several appearances as shirt sponsors over the years (Boro, Bolton and Portsmouth to name but three), no national newspaper has ever entered into a long-term sponsorship deal with a top flight club.

A 1988–89, 1989–90

Design: SKILL
Sponsor: HERITAGE HAMPERS

There was more of a change to the next away kit than there had been with the home, but essentially it was very similar to the previous design. A white chest panel was added to the shirt with a blue band beneath it upon which sat the logo of Heritage Hampers, who marked the end of their two-year deal in 1990 with a heartfelt and poignant ad in the match-day programme. The club struggled in the top flight in 88–89 and were eventually relegated to Division 2.

Worn in: A great 3–1 win in white shorts over Southampton at The Dell in 88–89 and a 5–3 victory at Barnsley the following season.
Worn by: Mark Procter, Alan Kernaghan, Nicky Mohan.

H 1990–91, 1991–92

Design: SKILL
Sponsor: *EVENING GAZETTE*

The second major design produced by the club via the Skill brand was this eye-catching and bold kit. A collar returned to the shirt and was now joined by a large white trim along each sleeve that continued on the cuffs. Local newspaper *The Evening Gazette* became the club's new sponsor. The shirt was often worn with the red shorts and/or white socks of the third kit when necessary.

Worn in: A stunning 6–0 win over Leicester (90–91), the 90–91 play-off semi-final defeat vs Notts County and the glorious 2–1 win over Wolves at Molineux (91–92) that clinched Boro's place in the inaugural Premiership season.
Worn by: Robbie Mustoe, Colin Walsh.

A 1990–91, 1991–92

Design: SKILL
Sponsor: *EVENING GAZETTE*

Once again, the away kit was a mirrored version of the home strip in two shades of blue, although this time the lighter blue was a slightly richer shade than that used previously. Colin Todd, who had replaced the sacked Rioch in 1990, resigned the following year and was replaced by Lennie Lawrence, who led the club to promotion in the 91–92 season.

Worn in: A great 3–1 win over Swindon in the 90–91 season followed by a 1–0 win at Charlton later in the season. Also the 91–92 Rumbelows League Cup semi-final second leg vs Manchester Utd that ended in a 2–1 defeat for Boro after extra time.
Worn by: Andy Peake, Ian Baird, Trevor Putney, Jon Gittens.

3 1990–91, 1991–92

Design: SKILL
Sponsor: *EVENING GAZETTE*

Boro also turned out in this fresh-looking third kit in the early 90s. It was another seldom-worn white reversed version of the home shirt – just like the early 80s adidas kit and the Skill outfit in the latter part of that decade. It was also worn with the shorts and socks of the home kit when appropriate. The 91–92 season marked the end of the club's series of self-produced kits, which had been the visual focus of the side's impressive renaissance from the dark days of 1986.

Worn in: The unlucky 3–2 defeat in the Rumbelows League Cup fourth round match at Villa Park vs Aston Villa (90–91).
Worn by: John Hendrie, Jimmy Phillips, Brian Marwood.

The only other side to have worn Errea kit in the Premiership is Derby County.

H 1992–93, 1993–94

Design: ADMIRAL
Sponsor: ICI

As the club prepared for their new challenge in the first ever Premier League, sportswear company Admiral became their new kit suppliers. Boro took to the field in their first home game of the season against Man City in this bold and confident strip, which included an unusual design of white shoulder panels and black piping. Chemical manufacturing giants ICI sponsored the team for the two seasons this strip was worn.

Worn in: The perfect start to the club's first Premiership campaign (a 4–1 win over reigning champions Leeds) but also the heartbreaking 3–3 draw with Norwich in the last match of the season – not quite enough to keep Boro up.
Worn by: Curtis Fleming, Willie Falconer.

A 1992–93, 1993–94

Design: ADMIRAL
Sponsor: ICI

Admiral's away kits of this era tended to border on the visually busy side, and this was no exception. It was a design also worn by Leeds at the time and featured an abstract pattern of red and black flecks across the shoulders and rising from the bottom of the shirt – typically brash early 90s fashion. The shorts were a standard Admiral design and were also worn occasionally with the home shirt.

Worn in: A well-deserved 1–1 draw away to Manchester Utd with a goal by Bernie Slaven and a difficult 4–1 defeat at Anfield vs Liverpool.
Worn by: Paul Wilkinson, Nicky Mohan.

3 1992–93, 1993–94

Design: ADMIRAL
Sponsor: ICI

In January 1993 a new third kit (mirroring the design of the away) was issued, which saw the club return to the light blue colour that had accompanied them through the uncertain times of the late 80s. Official third shirts were becoming the norm at the time, with the popularity of football at a high following Italia 90. The 92–93 season found the club once again relegated to Division 2 (now of course renamed Division 1). The end of the 93–94 season saw the appointment of Bryan Robson as manager and the start of a new era in Boro's history.

Worn in: The 1–1 draw at the City Ground vs Nottingham Forest (93–94).
Worn by: Derek Whyte, Tommy Wright.

H 1994–95

Design: ERREA
Sponsor: DICKENS

With Boro now consolidating in Division 1 under new manager Robson, they began their push back to the Premier League with this attractive new kit – their first from Italian company Errea. The shirt was trimmed with navy blue, white and red and included an interesting shadow pattern combining pinstripes and the club badge. Dickens returned for a second stint as sponsors in this last season the club were to spend at Ayresome Park.

Worn in: An opening day 2–0 win over Barnsley and the final game at Ayresome Park – the great 2–1 win over Luton. Also the 1–1 draw at Tranmere that clinched the Division 1 title.
Worn by: Uwe Fuchs, Craig Hignett.

Although the club's kits change every season, the socks are occasionally retained for two.

A 1994–95

Design: ERREA
Sponsor: DICKENS

Errea's first away kit was quite a bizarre affair, unlike anything worn before or since by the club. It was a bold decision to go with this jade and dark-green striped kit, trimmed with navy and enhanced by a fine amber pinstripe. 94–95 was the start of a long relationship between Errea and Boro, with the launch of a new home and away strip every season since. It also saw the club full of confidence as they were promoted back to the Premier League.

Worn in: The great 3–1 win over West Brom at The Hawthorns and the vital 1–1 draw at Barnsley towards the end of the season.
Worn by: Jamie Pollock, Nigel Pearson, Steve Vickers.

H 1995–96

Design: ERREA
Sponsor: CELLNET

It was an exciting time for Middlesbrough – back in the Premier League and with a new home, The Riverside Stadium. As 28,000 fans filled the ground for the first match, the side took to the field in this kit. A good move on from the previous design, the collar reverted to white and elegant white piping ran from collar to under the arm. The fabric's shadow pattern remained the same as the previous kit. Communications company Cellnet became the new sponsors. The shirt was also the first worn by new signing Juninho as he was paraded before the fans.

Worn in: The first ever game at The Riverside – a memorable 2–0 win over Chelsea.
Worn by: Nick Barmby, Neil Cox, Phil Stamp.

A 1995–96

Design: ERREA
Sponsor: CELLNET

Perhaps imagining that Boro's return to the Premier League might see some bruising encounters, Errea's second away kit for the club saw them dress the side in black and blue. A red collar and fine red trim were also added. The shorts mirrored the asymmetrical design of the home pair, but the socks were now in a striking hooped design. The shirt fabric retained the same shadow pattern as the home. This was a good season for the club, who eventually finished 12th.

Worn in: Defeats against Nottingham Forest (1–0), West Ham and Man Utd (both 2–0). Boro did not win a single league game in this strip.
Worn by: Juninho, Clayton Blackmore, Jan Fjortoft.

H 1996–97

Design: ERREA
Sponsor: CELLNET

The next Middlesbrough outfit followed the trend for large overall prints, with 'Boro' written vertically on the shirt. The shirt was only a subtle move on from the previous kit, the main difference being the unusual placing of the club badge on the left sleeve. However, the badge was moved to the centre of the shirt for the two Cup finals the team were to reach during this eventful season.

Worn in: Heartbreaking defeats in the finals of the Coca-Cola Cup (1–0 to Leicester after a replay) and the FA Cup (2–0 to Chelsea). Also the 1–1 draw with Leeds that relegated Boro.
Worn by: Emerson, Fabrizio Ravanelli (who scored a hat-trick in this strip on his debut in the thrilling 3–3 draw against Liverpool).

With the club's relegation, the 97–98 season saw the Premiership badges on each sleeve replaced by those of Nationwide Division 1.

A 1996–97

Design: ERREA
Sponsor: CELLNET

With some high-scoring results and some big signings, 96–97 was a season of promise for Boro. Unfortunately, despite their appearances in the two major Cup finals, the team were relegated to Division 1 at the end of the season. The away kit of the time was another flashy and daring design. It featured a large off-centre blue cross made up of abstract patterns, which was repeated on the right sleeve. It was another unique Errea kit and extremely eye-catching. The shorts followed the design of the home pair, with a shadow 'Boro' print included on the right leg.

Worn in: A crushing 5–1 defeat at Liverpool, but a good 3–3 draw with Manchester Utd.
Worn by: Mikkel Beck, Phil Whelan, Branco.

H 1997–98

Design: ERREA
Sponsor: CELLNET

One of the best Errea outfits worn by the club was this home kit from the 97–98 season. The shirt included a contemporary V-neck, centralised logos, diagonal shadow pinstripe fabric and a traditional white chest band with a bold black outline. It was a fine-looking strip with a small 'Boro' ID tag on the left-hand side. This kit saw the club enhance their yo-yo reputation with promotion back to the Premiership.

Worn in: A great 2–1 win over Charlton, but also more Cup final disappointment as the club again lost 2–0 to Chelsea, this time in the Coca-Cola Cup. Plus the magnificent 4–1 win over Oxford that secured promotion for Boro.
Worn by: Paul Merson, Alan Moore.

A 1997–98

Design: ERREA
Sponsor: CELLNET

It was a shame that more people did not get to feast their eyes on this wonderful set of Errea kits, due to the club not being in the Premiership this season. The away design, reminiscent of a bygone era, incorporated a large white 'Y' shape on a blue shirt, trimmed with red and a diagonal shadow pinstripe. It featured the same V-neck and design of white shorts (now trimmed with blue) as the home kit. However, the shirt was also worn with the previous away kit's blue shorts on occasion.

Worn in: A fine 2–1 win at Swindon, but an awful 4–0 defeat at Nottingham Forest – fortunately a relatively rare defeat this season.
Worn by: Gianluca Festa, Andy Townsend, Vladimir Kinder.

H 1998–99

Design: ERREA
Sponsor: CELLNET

With the club again back in the Premier League Bryan Robson signed Paul Gascoigne, who made his first appearances for the club in this kit. Black was much reduced in the overall colour scheme and two sets of fading white vertical lines were added to each side of the shirt with the badges still placed centrally. The socks remained the same as the previous strip. This Gazza-inspired side finished in the top 10 of the Premier League – a marvellous season.

Worn in: The great 3–0 win over Southampton, but also an appalling 6–1 defeat to Arsenal. Plus the controversial 1–0 defeat vs Man Utd.
Worn by: Alun Armstrong, Marco Branca, Gary Pallister.

A saucy PR stunt to launch the club's new website in April 2000 saw three young ladies adorned in body-painted versions of the Errea 00–01 home kit.

A 1998–99

Design: ERREA
Sponsor: CELLNET

This Argentina-like strip was not one of the most memorable worn by the club. The pale blue and white stripes, trimmed with a navy pinstripe and paired with navy shorts and socks, formed a rather insipid outfit that did not flatter some of the larger players! The shorts and socks were similar in design to the shorts from three years previously.

Worn in: The 2–0 win over West Ham and the superb victory by the same score over Man Utd in the FA Cup fourth round. Also worn in the 3–3 draw with Southampton at the Dell that included two red cards, a sublime Gazza free kick and a last-minute equaliser from Festa.
Worn by: Paul Gascoigne, Hamilton Ricard, Robbie Stockdale.

H 1999–2000

Design: ERREA
Sponsor: BT CELLNET

As the club prepared for their next assault on the Premiership, Errea introduced a new shirt but retained the shorts and socks from the previous design. To be honest the shirt, with a striking design of white and navy stripes running down each sleeve and the sides, jarred a little with the shorts, which were clearly designed for the previous kit. Still, the club managed to finish 12th this year so it can't have been that bad! The BT prefix was added to the Cellnet logo this year.

Worn in: The controversial 4–3 defeat at the Riverside by Man Utd with Boro so nearly equalising. Also a brilliant 2–1 win over Arsenal and a tight 2–2 draw with Newcastle.
Worn by: Alen Boksic, Mark Summerbell.

A 1999–2000

Design: ERREA
Sponsor: BT CELLNET

Errea brightened up Boro away games with this dynamic and vivid white and purple ensemble. Featuring the same collar design as the home shirt, bold purple and black panels down each arm and a large purple chest band, it was an attractive and distinctive-looking outfit. A pair of alternative purple shorts were also worn with the kit.

Worn in: A crushing 4–0 defeat in the kit's first Premiership outing at Arsenal, followed by a 2–0 defeat at Anfield. Also the amazing 1–0 win over Man Utd at Old Trafford.
Worn by: Andy Campbell, Christian Ziege, Colin Cooper.

H 2000–01

Design: ERREA
Sponsor: BT CELLNET

For a moment it seemed as if the Boro home and away kits had gone out of sync, as the new home kit followed almost exactly the style of the white and purple away strip from 99–oo! For the first time in many years the club turned out in an all-red first-choice home kit, complete of course with the familiar white chest band in a new expanded form. The season was to mark the end of Robson's spell as manager, with ex-Manchester Utd coach Steve McClaren arriving as his replacement.

Worn in: A 4–0 thrashing of Derby County, a 1–0 win over Chelsea and a hard-fought 1–0 victory against Liverpool at The Riverside.
Worn by: Paul Okon, Christian Karembeu, Carlos Marinelli.

The 01–02 home kit was actually premiered at the last match of the 00–01 season:
a 2–1 win over West Ham at The Riverside.

A 2000–01

Design: ERREA
Sponsor: BT CELLNET

Terry Venables joined the club in December 2000 as support for Robson. The Boro side took to the field in 00–01 in this mysterious all-black kit, chosen by the fans in an innovative on-line vote – the first time such a scheme had been launched. It was an intimidating outfit, highlighted only by the thin red and white stripes that contrasted well with the dark fabric. The shirt was also worn with alternative white shorts.

Worn in: The 3–1 win over Southampton at The Dell, along with an absolutely superb 3–0 hammering of Arsenal at Highbury.
Worn by: Ugo Ehiogu, Jason Gavin.

H 2001–02

Design: ERREA
Sponsor: BT CELLNET

Errea's next kit remained all red and was a very minimal and smart design. A simple round neck was accompanied by restrained white piping down each sleeve and across the chest. The shorts featured a subtle white piping trim across each leg. It was the last year of BT Cellnet's sponsorship, but the first of new manager Steve McClaren's reign with the club, who again finished well in 12th place.

Worn in: The 2–0 win over West Ham and the superb win over Man Utd by the same score in the FA Cup fourth round, followed later by the unfortunate 1–0 defeat to Arsenal in the FA Cup semi-final.
Worn by: Dean Windass, Paul Ince, Brian Deane, Mark Hudson.

A 2001–02

Design: ERREA
Sponsor: BT CELLNET

Another supporters' choice! The new away kit was unusual in that, although it featured a more conventional Boro away colour scheme of blue and black, it was the only strip the club have ever worn that included the Errea logo in a 70s-style trim along the sleeves and shorts. It was a very individual outfit that utilised the same sleek round neck design as the home, and was also worn with change white shorts.

Worn in: A 4–0 defeat in the kit's first league outing at Arsenal, the 2–0 defeat at Anfield and the 1–0 win over Man Utd at Old Trafford.
Worn by: Alen Boksic, Noel Whelan, Szilard Nemeth.

H 2002–03

Design: ERREA
Sponsor: DIAL-A-PHONE

Another stylish home kit saw the return of a collar, along with the introduction of reversed seams and breathable fabric panels under the arms and down each side of the shirt. The cuffs were replaced by a fashionable sleek white trim. The early oos had seen multi-panelled shirts become the norm, with the construction and performance of the garments more important than simple aesthetics. Dial-a-phone replaced BT Cellnet as shirt sponsors.

Worn in: The barnstorming 3–0 win over Spurs, along with a 3–1 triumph over Manchester Utd and a 1–0 victory against Newcastle.
Worn by: Massimo Maccarone, Juninho (who scored on his comeback against Everton after being injured for seven months).

The 03–04 home kit was premiered at the last home game of the 03-04 season – a cracking 5–1 win over Spurs.

A 2002–03

Design: ERREA
Sponsor: DIAL-A-PHONE

Another fans' choice saw this unfussy and good-looking all-white with navy trim outfit selected as Boro's new away kit. Again, there was a feeling of the home and away kits being out of step as this new strip mirrored the style of the previous season's home design. The Errea logos and Boro badges were nicely picked out in red on the shirts and shorts. Despite some bad results in this kit, the club managed 11th place in the final table.

Worn in: Some poor defeats away from home this season vs Arsenal (2–0), Aston Villa and Charlton (both 1–0). However, the side did gain a fine 3–1 win at Sunderland.
Worn by: Geremi, Franck Queudrue, Jonathan Greening, Gareth Southgate.

H 2003–04

Design: ERREA
Sponsor: DIAL-A-PHONE

At last, a kit that will be remembered for being worn as Boro won a major trophy for the first time – the 03–04 Carling Cup. The club's fortunes had really turned around since adopting an all-red kit, with high positions in the Premiership and now a Cup triumph. The new design was only a small move on from the previous kit and still included a collar, but also introduced breathable fabric panels.

Worn in: Without a doubt a high point for all Boro fans – the 2–1 win over Bolton in the Carling Cup final in February 2004 at The Millennium Stadium, with goals by Joseph-Desire Job and Bolo Zenden.
Worn by: Danny Mills, Gaizka Mendieta, Malcolm Christie, George Boateng.

A 2003–04

Design: ERREA
Sponsor: DIAL-A-PHONE

There was quite a change at The Riverside with the next supporters' selection. This navy and maroon strip was one of the best away kits in the Premiership this season. It featured innovative performance fabrics, a dynamic use of amber piping and breathable mesh fabric panels. It was a great outfit that inspired the side to some superb wins this season and helped the club achieve a league position of 11th for the second year running. 03–04 also saw the end of the two-year Dial-a-phone deal.

Worn in: The quite amazing 3–2 win over Man Utd at Old Trafford, plus a fine 2–0 triumph over Aston Villa at Villa Park.
Worn by: Chris Riggott, Stewart Downing, Joseph-Desire Job, Michael Ricketts.

H 2004–05

Design: ERREA
Sponsor: 888.COM

One of the best Boro kits in a long time! Heavily influenced by retro fashion, the overall feel was one of confidence, stability and style. The traditional solid white chest band was reintroduced, along with a new collar design and the logo of new sponsors 888.com, an online casino company. Simple white trim adorned the shorts. A nice touch was the addition of 'MFC' on the reverse of the collar.

Worn in: The club's first game in Europe, vs Czech side Banik Ostrava at home. Boro finished 3–0 winners, with Jimmy Floyd Hasselbaink scoring the first goal. Also worn in a great 4–0 triumph away at Blackburn.
Worn by: Mark Viduka, Ray Parlour, James Morrison.

Early versions of the 05–06 away kit featured a more basic round crew-neck before being replaced by a more intricate collar.

A 2004–05

Design: ERREA
Sponsor: 888.COM

Due to the popularity of the previous season's navy blue and maroon ensemble the two colours featured once more in the next away strip, although white was now the prominent colour. The kit saw the collar ditched in favour of a sleek continental neck. An interesting sleeve design and white reversed seams completed the design, creating a very contemporary and fashionable look for Boro, who finished the season in seventh position – earning a place in the 05–06 UEFA Cup.

Worn in: An absolute thriller at Highbury vs Arsenal, Boro eventually losing 5–3. Also a good 2–1 win over Charlton Athletic.
Worn by: Jimmy Floyd Hasselbaink, Bolo Zenden, Michael Reiziger.

H 2005–06

Design: ERREA
Sponsor: 888.COM

With Steve McLaren's side hoping to build on the previous season's success, they take to the field in 05–06 wearing a strip that retains the traditional Boro white chest band although now, as described on the club's official website, 'with a twist'. The white band, neatly outlined in black, now extends onto the right sleeve and curves down the right-hand side of the shirt in a very fashionable asymmetrical style. The old-fashioned collar has been replaced by a minimal white-trimmed V-neck. A white band has also been included on the right side of the shorts.

A 2005–06

Design: ERREA
Sponsor: 888.COM

The two-year maroon away kit experiment ends with the introduction of this fine two-tone blue strip that harks back to the classic Boro away outfits of the 80s and 90s. As usual, the design was selected by fans via the club's official website. Navy panels run under the arm and down each side, continuing on the shorts, and flashes of red throughout give the outfit a subtle lift.

NEWCASTLE UNITED

Formed in 1892 by players from the region's two local teams (Newcastle East End and Newcastle West End), Newcastle United's black and white striped kit is world famous. However, early days saw the club turn out, almost unbelievably, in red and white stripes – the main colour of Newcastle East End. Due to numerous colour clashes, though, black and white were selected for the new club's strip in August 1894. Several interesting theories exist concerning the reason behind the colour choice, ranging from the selection being a tribute to a black and white-clad monk who was an ardent early supporter of the team to inspiration coming from two magpies who were nesting in St James' Park at the time.

More often than not, the central stripe on a Newcastle shirt is black, with white appearing only very occasionally (most successfully on the first adidas kit of the mid-90s). The early 60s saw the club sporting a daring and innovative white trim on the base of the shorts, as well as striped socks.

For many fans, the Magpies are intrinsically linked with the blue star logo of Newcastle Breweries and their renowned Newcastle Brown Ale. However, from the mid-80s right up to 94–95, a large variety of logos has appeared on the prestigious black and white shirts. Sponsorship of the side from the mid to late 80s was also shared by Greenalls Beers, who chose to advertise many different versions of their brand identity. Once Newcastle Breweries returned to St James' Park they decided to promote McEwan's Lager on the away shirts and also occasionally the home.

Traditional stripes can prove problematic to kit designers as they search for new and exciting ways to alter a team's outfit. Solutions provided by Newcastle's various strip suppliers included using thick stripes, thin stripes and occasionally even both in the same design, as demonstrated in the infamous Umbro home kit of the early 90s!

The club's long relationship with adidas has seen some fine designs, with an overriding feeling of slick sophistication and just the merest hint of colour. As long as clubs such as Grimsby and Notts County remain in the lower divisions, Newcastle's feared black and white stripes will be unique in the top flight.

KEVIN KEEGAN IN THE 81–83 UMBRO HOME KIT.

WITH THANKS TO PAUL JOANNOU.

A young Paul Gascoigne made his debut for the Magpies in the V-necked Umbro home shirt vs QPR in the 84–85 season.

H 1980–81 to 1982–83

Design: UMBRO
Sponsor: NEWCASTLE BREWERIES

Newcastle's deal with Bukta ended in 79–80, so for the following season the club had a new supplier in Umbro. With the silky fabrics and minimal designs that were appearing at this time, their first home kit looked a little dated as it featured the 70s-style Umbro diamond trim and a large collar. Much to the delight of fans who enjoyed the odd glass of Newcastle Brown Ale, the club also gained its first ever shirt sponsor this season, local company Newcastle Breweries, whose famous blue star logo was worn by star signing Kevin Keegan during his first season with the club (82–83).

Worn in: Keegan's debut vs QPR in the 82–83 season – he scored the only goal in a 1–0 win.
Worn by: Terry McDermott, John Trewick.

A 1980–81, 1981–82

Design: UMBRO
Sponsor: NEWCASTLE BREWERIES

Umbro's first away kit for the club was pretty much a standard design of the time and retained all the trappings of the home in the favoured Toon away colours of yellow and green. It was a style worn by many teams in the 70s and early 80s including Everton, Manchester City and Chelsea, whose away kit of the time was actually exactly the same as Newcastle (minus the badge and sponsor's logo of course).

Worn in: The epic 80–81 FA Cup fifth round replay vs Exeter that ended in a sad 4–0 defeat for The Magpies. Also another bad defeat the following season, this time 4–1 vs Blackburn at Ewood Park.
Worn by: Imre Varadi, Mick Martin.

A 1982–83

Design: UMBRO
Sponsor: NEWCASTLE BREWERIES

This kit was a real curiosity. It was worn for only one season and was exactly the same as the previous away design, except that the yellow outfit was now trimmed with blue. It was a strange switch, although not unique – in fact the Chelsea away kit of the late 70s went through exactly the same turnabout. The early years of the new decade saw the club still stuck in Division 2, where they had been languishing since 77–78. The 82–83 season saw an improvement in their fortunes, however, and they eventually finished fifth.

Worn in: A great 2–1 win over Blackburn Rovers and a tight 2–2 draw with Grimsby.
Worn by: Kevin Keegan, George Reilly, John Anderson.

H 1983–84 to 1986–87

Design: UMBRO
Sponsor: NEWCASTLE BREWERIES (83–86)
GREENALLS (86–87)

At last the club donned a rather more modern design with new shiny fabric and a neat V-neck, trimmed with white and grey, which had been introduced as the side's away colour. The kit also featured an updated badge design and was worn for four eventful seasons with sponsorship by both Newcastle Breweries and later Greenalls Beers. It saw the birth of many modern Magpies legends under Arthur Cox and later Jack Charlton.

Worn in: Keegan's emotional last game at St James' (83–84), which saw the club promoted to Division 1. Also a 1–0 victory over Liverpool followed by a 4–1 thrashing of WBA (85–86).
Worn by: Chris Waddle, Peter Beardsley.

NEWCASTLE UNITED

Newcastle United are unusual in that they were sponsored for most of the 80s by two rival companies in the same industry: Newcastle Breweries and Greenalls Breweries.

A 1983–84, 1984–85

Design: UMBRO
Sponsor: NEWCASTLE BREWERIES

Perhaps keen to make up for their previous, rather old-fashioned away kit, Umbro went to extremes and dressed the side in this very contemporary looking and shiny silvery-grey away kit. It was a sleek, good-looking strip, complete with black pinstripes and black trim on the shorts. A little Umbro tradition still remained, however, with the famous diamond trim included on the socks turnover.

Worn in: A 1–1 draw with Grimsby and a 2–2 draw with Huddersfield (both 83–84). A 1–0 win over Stoke and an awful 3–1 away defeat at Spurs (both 84–85).
Worn by: David McCreery, Ian Stewart, Jeff Clarke, Neil McDonald.

A 1985–86 to 1987–88

Design: UMBRO
Sponsor: NEWCASTLE BREWERIES (85–86)
GREENALLS (86–88)

The 80s saw the club wear very few different kits (apart from variations in the sponsor), but after three years of the pinstripe design a new grey away kit was launched. The shirt featured a black and white chest band, a style that appeared on several other Umbro kits at the time. The shorts were updated, but the socks remained the same as the previous season. 87–88 saw the shirt sponsored exclusively by Greenalls with a variety of logos

Worn in: Another bad defeat at Spurs, this time 3–1 in the 87–88 season, followed by a good 1–0 win over Sheffield Wednesday.
Worn by: Paul Goddard, Peter Jackson, Andy Thomas, John Bailey, Glenn Roeder.

H 1987–88

Design: UMBRO
Sponsor: GREENALLS

The late 80s saw the home kit remodelled and updated with a new wrap-around neck and a diamond shadow pattern incorporated into the fabric. A chequerboard shadow pattern was also added to the shorts, and an alternative white pair with black and grey trim was also worn. After a difficult 86–87 season the club, now under manager Willie McFaul, fought their way up the table to eventually finish eighth.

Worn in: A well-earned 2–2 draw away to Man Utd followed by a wonderful 4–1 demolition of Liverpool at St James' Park.
Worn by: Paul Gascoigne (in the infamous Vinnie Jones 'nutcracker' photo), Mirandinha.

H 1988–89, 1989–90

Design: UMBRO
Sponsor: GREENALLS

In 88–89 the club issued a new-style coat-of-arms badge to replace the previous design, which had been worn for the past five years. The new crest did not bring the club much luck, however, as they were relegated in 88–89 – the first season it was in use. The only other change to the kit was again the wide variety of Greenalls logos that appeared on the shirts; early versions were either black or green, before the company finally settled for white type on a black panel in 89–90 as the club attempted to win their way out of Division 2.

Worn in: The fantastic 5–4 victory in 89–90 vs Leicester. Also the 2–0 defeat to Sunderland in the 89–90 play-off semi-final second leg.
Worn by: Mick Quinn, Kenny Wharton.

The Asics home kit also featured the Newcastle Breweries star logo on the socks – a very rare occasion of sock sponsoring.

A 1988–89, 1989–90

Design: UMBRO
Sponsor: GREENALLS

After five years in typically 80s silvery/grey strips, the club returned to a more traditional colour scheme to see out the decade. It was a vivid concoction comprising a button-up round neck coupled with green and yellow stripes with white pinstripes. To top it all off, a diagonal shadow stripe pattern was also added. Early versions of the kit saw the Greenalls logo sitting flush on the stripes before being placed within its own yellow panel for the sake of legibility. The shorts included a shadow chequerboard pattern.

Worn in: A superb 5–1 triumph over West Brom at the Hawthorns in the 89–90 season.
Worn by: Kevin Dillon, Mark McGhee, Bjorn Kristensen, Roy Aitken, Michael O'Neill.

H 1990–91 to 1992–93

Design: UMBRO
Sponsor: GREENALLS (90–91)
NEWCASTLE BREWERIES (91–93)

Umbro's answer to the problem of creating a new innovative fashion while still using the club's famous stripes was this 'barcode shirt' (official design name: 'Torino'), which combined two different stripe thicknesses and introduced a blue trim. After a poor 91–92 season the club bounced back to win the Division 1 title in 92–93. Unluckily for Umbro, the club collected the trophy while premiering the next season's new Asics kit. The shirt was also sponsored for part of 90–91 by Greenalls.

Worn in: The 6–0 win vs Barnsley in 92–93.
Worn by: Lee Clark, Kevin Scott, Brian Kilcline.

A 1990–91 to 1992–93

Design: UMBRO
Sponsor: GREENALLS (90–91)
NEWCASTLE BREWERIES (91–93)

Umbro's last away kit was to last for three seasons. It was based on Umbro's standard 'Toulon' design, with the addition of a button-up collar. Although Newcastle Breweries had returned as sponsor, they chose to promote McEwan's Lager on this shirt. Kevin Keegan returned to St James' in February 92, replacing Ossie Ardiles as manager, and saved the club from imminent relegation before inspiring them to promotion to the newly formed Premier League the following year.

Worn in: The 3–1 defeat at Blackburn in 91–92, Keegan's second game. Also the 1–1 draw at Grimsby that clinched the Magpies' 92–93 title.
Worn by: David Kelly, Scott Sellars, Robert Lee.

H 1993–94, 1994–95

Design: ASICS
Sponsor: NEWCASTLE BREWERIES

After 13 years with Umbro the club switched to Asics, a Japanese company renowned for their footwear. The change did wonders for the club. They dazzled the Premier League with some wonderful football and an elegant silky kit, with a simple collar and delicate blue trim. As with the previous home kit, the sponsors' logo varied between the familiar blue star and that of McEwan's Lager.

Worn in: A great 3–1 win over Leicester in Newcastle's first ever Premier League match. Also the 3–0 home win over Liverpool that included a hat-trick by Andy Cole.
Worn by: Steve Watson, Darren Peacock.

The alternative Newcastle Brown Ale logo was included on every away kit from 95–96 to 99–00 in place of the standard bottle label that appeared on the home version.

A 1993–94, 1994–95

Design: ASICS
Sponsor: McEWAN'S LAGER

Asics' first away kit for the club saw a radical choice – an all-blue outfit trimmed with black and white. The shirt and shorts were printed with a white paint-splattered effect, which raised eyebrows among more traditional Magpies fans who were not keen on this strange and arty pattern. Nevertheless, the club enjoyed two fine seasons in this kit. As with the last set of Umbro away kits, the McEwan's Lager logo appeared on the shirts.

Worn in: The 7–1 Coca-Cola Cup win over Notts County in 93–94 and also that season the 4–2 home win over Sheffield Wednesday, who had failed to bring a kit sufficiently different from Newcastle's black and white stripes.

Worn by: Philippe Albert, John Beresford.

3 1994–95

Design: ASICS
Sponsor: McEWAN'S LAGER

For the first time ever, an official Newcastle Utd third strip was issued. Asics selected one of their standard designs of the time and adapted it into this all-green kit trimmed with thin navy blue stripes. Scottish & Newcastle Breweries again opted to promote McEwan's Lager on the shirt. All Asics collars in this era were generous in size, as was the general cut of the strip. Gone were the days of skin-tight football kits; now baggy shirts and long shorts were the norm across the country.

Worn in: A 0–0 draw with Sheffield Wednesday, in which Keith Gillespie made his debut for the club.

Worn by: Steve Howey, Barry Venison, Ruel Fox, Keith Gillespie.

H 1995–96, 1996–97

Design: ADIDAS
Sponsor: NEWCASTLE BREWERIES

Possibly one of the best Toon kits ever! Adidas had replaced Asics as kit suppliers and introduced a shirt featuring a design reminiscent of the 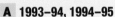 club's 1926–27 league-winning outfit, complete with button-up 'grandad' collar. The full label logo of Newcastle Brown Ale was included on the shirt for the first time. Unusually, the shorts included a version of the club badge housed within an additional shield.

Worn in: The last-gasp 4–3 defeat at Anfield in 95–96. Also the great 2–0 win over Metz in the UEFA Cup third round. Plus a 7–1 win vs Spurs and an amazing 5–0 vs Man Utd (both 96–97).

Worn by: David Ginola, Les Ferdinand.

A 1995–96

Design: ADIDAS
Sponsor: NEWCASTLE BREWERIES

The first adidas away kit resembled a hooped rugby shirt, but was inspired by a kit worn by Newcastle West End in the 1880s before they joined with Newcastle East End to form United. Appropriately, this kit featured the same 'grandad' collar as the home and was paired with ecru shorts. It was a fine kit, and a shame it was only worn for one season. In a bitter-sweet campaign for the club, they led the Premiership for much of the season before eventually losing their lead to Man Utd.

Worn in: A 3–1 win over Bolton in the first away game of the season and the 2–0 win at Sheffield Wed, with Ginola's first Premiership goal.

Worn by: Warren Barton, Peter Beardsley, Faustino Asprilla.

The famous black and white stripes stir great passions: Asprilla used his 95–97 home shirt as a flag when he scored in the UEFA Cup match vs Metz and Ketsbaia lost his 97–99 shirt in the crowd after his goal against Bolton in 97–98.

A 1996–97

Design: ADIDAS
Sponsor: NEWCASTLE BREWERIES

For their second away kit adidas produced this unusual metallic blue/silver-looking kit. The enigmatic colour was officially named 'gorge' and was accompanied by a simple shadow stripe pattern. The kit also included a neat black and white V-neck and horizontal black and white stripes across the chest. Manager Kevin Keegan shocked the football world when he quit the club in January 96 to be replaced by Kenny Dalglish.

Worn in: The 0–0 draw at Man Utd (even though there was no colour clash). Also the exciting 2–2 draw with Southampton that saw the club on the wrong end of a Le Tissier special. Plus a great 2–1 win over Sunderland.
Worn by: Robbie Elliott, Alan Shearer.

H 1997–98, 1998–99

Design: ADIDAS
Sponsor: NEWCASTLE BREWERIES

The introduction of the next adidas home kit coincided with a disappointing period for the club. Although to the neutral it looked very stylish, the kit, with its late 60s-style round neck, was not popular with the Toon fans. The shirt fabric incorporated a subtle shadow pattern and an amber trim was also introduced. The back of the shirt included a large shield in which the squad number was housed.

Worn in: The 2–0 defeat to Arsenal in the 97–98 FA Cup final. Also that season the 3–2 win over Barcelona in the Champions League. Plus a 4–0 win over Southampton in 98–99.
Worn by: Stuart Pearce, Alessandro Pistone.

A 1997–98

Design: ADIDAS
Sponsor: NEWCASTLE BREWERIES

The 97–98 Magpies away kit was definitely one of the most unusual and challenging strips to emerge in recent years. The round neck was identical to that of the home shirt, but that was where the similarity ended. This shirt was navy blue with outrageous orange and green vertical bands and trim alongside a large shadow print of the club badge that was incorporated into the fabric.

Worn in: Three matches this season that all ended in defeat: the horrendous 4–1 result at Leeds, followed later by 2–1 deficits against both Southampton and Sheffield Wednesday.
Worn by: Temuri Ketsbaia, John Barnes.

A 1998–99

Design: ADIDAS
Sponsor: NEWCASTLE BREWERIES

The start of the 98–99 season saw Dalglish out and Gullit in as Newcastle's new manager, causing a huge rush at the club shop for the Dutchman's name to be placed on the back of this new shiny-fabric away kit. It was a lively blue number trimmed with a rich yellow, and was much more conventional than the last change jersey. It was worn with adidas' 'Opio Cup' style shorts. The blue kit's introduction completed the club's Juventus-style range of outfits this season.

Worn in: The thrilling 4–3 win over Derby at Pride Park and a 1–1 draw (with amber socks) vs Sheffield Wednesday at Hillsborough.
Worn by: Nikos Dabizas, Lionel Perez, Stephane Guivarch, David Batty.

NEWCASTLE UNITED

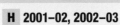

H 1999–2000, 2000–01

Design: ADIDAS
Sponsor: NEWCASTLE BREWERIES (99–00)
NTL (00–01)

New fabric technology came to Newcastle's latest kit with adidas' Climalite material, which included black mesh stripes on each side of the shirt to improve ventilation. The shirt was well received by fans when it was first worn in the last league game of 98–99, before appearing a week later at the FA Cup final defeat to Man Utd. A break with tradition saw Gullit insist the team change to white socks. NTL became the club's new sponsor in 00–01.

Worn in: Bobby Robson's first home match in charge – the superb 8–0 victory over Sheffield Wed with five goals by Shearer – along with a great 3–0 win over Man Utd (both 99–00).
Worn by: Duncan Ferguson, Gary Speed.

A 1999–2000

Design: ADIDAS
Sponsor: NEWCASTLE BREWERIES

This away kit was only actually ever worn once in a senior competitive game – the away match at Coventry. A fresh and bright looking strip, it added a new teal colour to the Newcastle Utd palette with trim on the collar and shorts and mesh panels under each arm. The 99–00 season marked the end of the club's long relationship with Newcastle Breweries, so it was farewell to the Newkie Brown logo and hello to that of telecommunications giants NTL. It was also farewell to Ruud Gullit in September 99, when he was replaced by Bobby Robson.

Worn in: The absolutely horrendous 4–1 defeat to Coventry City at Highfield Road.
Worn by: Carl Serrant, Stephen Glass.

A 2000–01

Design: ADIDAS
Sponsor: NTL

With Gullit gone, perhaps adidas wanted to mourn the death of 'sexy football' as they launched this new black kit. The strip continued the company's rather sombre approach of using just black and white for the main theme of all Newcastle kits, adding just a splash of colour. This Climalite-fabric black shirt incorporated sky blue mesh panels on each sleeve and was paired with either black or white shorts (which were also worn with the home strip).

Worn in: A thrilling 4–2 defeat at Spurs and an unlucky 2–0 defeat to Derby – a difficult spell for the club away from home.
Worn by: Kevin Gallacher, Andrew O'Brien.

H 2001–02, 2002–03

Design: ADIDAS
Sponsor: NTL

There was quite a different look for the next Magpies home kit. Lighter in weight and more technologically advanced than ever before, the unconventional shirt design featured black sleeves and only three broad black stripes on the front of the jersey. However, it featured in two great seasons for the rejuvenated club under Robson, with the team finishing fourth and third in the Premiership respectively.

Worn in: A 6–2 thrashing of Everton and the marvellous 4–3 win over Man Utd (both 01–02). In the 02–03 season, the great 3–2 win at Feyenoord with Bellamy's last-minute goal.
Worn by: Keiron Dyer, Carl Cort.

The adidas 03–04 home shirt was the fourth shirt in a row that featured a central black stripe on the front of the jersey.

A 2001–02

Design: ADIDAS
Sponsor: NTL

Newcastle's fine 01–02 season saw them wear this curious shade of muted blue for their new away kit. With dark grey panels under each arm and a new style of adidas three-stripe trim, it was another good-looking outfit that was often worn during the season. In fact, the club lost only two Premiership games while wearing it – a crushing 3–1 loss to new boys Fulham and a defeat on the last day of the season to Southampton.

Worn in: Splendid wins over Spurs (3–1) and Bolton (4–0), as well as the 3–2 comeback against Derby (who were 2–0 up at one point).
Worn by: Laurent Robert, Jermaine Jenas, Craig Bellamy, Lomana LuaLua (who scored the injury-time winner over Derby).

A 2002–03

Design: ADIDAS
Sponsor: NTL:HOME

Another interesting colour choice found the club sporting a navy and grey away kit. It was a really minimal, stylish design with a new continental neck and breathable fabric panels under each arm. It also saw NTL, in the last year of their deal with the Magpies, promoting their NTL: Home internet service.

Worn in: A superb 1–0 home win over Juventus in the Champions League – a rare case of the club not playing in their home kit at St James' Park. The only Premiership match in which this shirt was worn was the 2–2 draw at West Brom in the last match of the season.
Worn by: Jonathan Woodgate, Hugo Viana.

H 2003–04, 2004–05

Design: ADIDAS
Sponsor: NORTHERN ROCK

In 04–05 a new home kit was worn that reverted to a more recognised display of black and white stripes. Although reasonably traditional in appearance, the shirt was actually an ingenious combination of Climalite fabric along with black mesh stripes for added ventilation and moisture control. Blue was reintroduced with subtle trim on the cuffs and shorts.

Worn in: The home 3–1 win vs Fulham featuring a stunning mid-air goal from Robert. Also the fine 2–1 home win over PSV in the UEFA Cup quarter final 1st leg and a great 3–0 home win over Portsmouth (all 03–04 season).
Worn by: Lee Bowyer, Titus Bramble.

A 2003–04

Design: ADIDAS
Sponsor: NORTHERN ROCK

The club were back in black with this intimidating and rather swish-looking Climalite strip. The shirt featured a sleek minimal neck design and grey mesh panels down each side. It was not a lucky shirt for the side, however, as they failed to win a single league game wearing it. NTL were replaced by Newcastle-based bank Northern Rock as shirt sponsor.

Worn in: Two thrilling away draws: 2–2 at Leeds on the opening day of the season and 3–3 at St Mary's vs Southampton. Also, the sad 2–0 defeat to Marseilles in the UEFA Cup semi-final second leg.
Worn by: Brian Kerr, Nolberto Solano, Stephen Caldwell.

NEWCASTLE UNITED

There was some confusion at the 03–04 away game at Fulham, in which Newcastle sported their grey third strip and the Londoners also turned out in an away kit.

3 2003–04

Design: ADIDAS
Sponsor: NORTHERN ROCK

For the first time since the green Asics design of 94–95, a unique third kit was launched. Made of adidas' Climalite fabric and primarily intended for European games, it simply reversed the design of the standard black away kit. Unlike that kit, this grey outfit proved very lucky for the side as the team did not lose a single competitive match in which it was worn.

Worn in: The nail-biting 3–2 away win at Fulham in the Premiership, along with the impressive 3–0 away win over Real Mallorca in the UEFA Cup fourth round second leg.
Worn by: Hugo Viana, Shola Ameobi.

A 2004–05

Design: ADIDAS
Sponsor: NORTHERN ROCK

Adidas continued their trend for stunning and innovative Toon away kits. This curious combination of fading dark blue and black created a subtle striped effect on the front of the shirt highlighted with white, forming a daring-looking outfit that went down well with the fans. The feel of the shirt was also enhanced with Climacool, adidas' latest improved lightweight material. The season saw the club struggle in the Premiership, eventually leading to Robson's departure and the appointment of Graeme Souness as manager.

Worn in: A 2–1 win over Southampton at St Mary's early in the season.
Worn by: Patrick Kluivert, James Milner, Steven Taylor.

3 2004–05

Design: ADIDAS
Sponsor: NORTHERN ROCK

After five years of relatively sombre kits the club introduced a welcome zest of colour with their new yellow third strip, which was earmarked mainly for European action. Featuring a similar collar to that of the away strip and the latest hi-tech lightweight fabric from adidas for effective moisture management and ventilation, it was a great-looking outfit that was involved in some vital European wins away from home.

Worn in: A superb 5–1 win away vs Bnei Yehuda in Tel-Aviv, followed by a vital 1–0 win at Panionios Athens (with a winning goal by Alan Shearer) in the UEFA Cup group matches.
Worn by: Nicky Butt, Jamie McClen, Michael Chopra.

H 2005–06, 2006–07

Design: ADIDAS
Sponsor: NORTHERN ROCK

Newcastle and adidas continue their penchant for inventive new ways to re-style the famous black and white stripes with this

astounding shirt. With curved trim throughout, and a brave new design of the famous adidas three stripes stretching from the front of the shirt to the back, the jersey has a very organic feel. A new invention of trim on the shorts and tiny versions of the club badge attached to the back of the socks complete this fine-looking outfit. The Northern Rock logo is also now refreshed and rendered in gold. The kit was premiered in the last game of the 04–05 season – a 1–1 draw with champions Chelsea.

The majority of squad numbers and names on the backs of Premiership shirts are rendered either in black or white. The 05–07 Magpies home shirt sees them printed in a rich gold.

A 2005–06

Design: ADIDAS
Sponsor: NORTHERN ROCK

Graeme Souness' side sport yet another impressive and highly stylish adidas design on their travels in 05–06. This Climacool shirt is an enigmatic array of two shades of 'cypress green' combined with white three-stripe trim and breathable fabric panels (officially entitled 'APV' or 'Anatomically Placed Ventilation') on each shoulder and side. As with the home shirt, arched panels on each lower side help to emphasise body shape and definition. These panels are also mirrored in cypress green on the white shorts.

3 2005–06

Design: ADIDAS
Sponsor: NORTHERN ROCK

Worn for the first time in the Intertoto Cup third round first leg 3–1 win at FK ZTS Dubnica, this all-blue strip is Newcastle's third choice outfit in 05–06 and will be sported primarily in cup games. The kit features a similar template to the green away strip and is one of the most vivid shades of blue worn by the club in recent years. As with the away shorts, the adidas logo is tucked away on the left leg under the three-stripe trim, leaving plenty of space for the squad number.

PORTSMOUTH

When Portsmouth were formed in 1898 they sported an unusual strip of salmon pink jerseys trimmed with claret – a strip that no doubt would have gone well with Pompey's sponsor from 02–05, Ty! However, it is the side's blue shirts, white shorts and red socks that are more commonly associated with the club. The colour scheme has been worn since 1910 and is thought to have been influenced by the large presence of the armed forces in the town.

In fact, the club have been remarkably loyal to the colour scheme, the only real changes coming with the design of club crest worn on the shirts. Three different designs have been featured in recent years: the anchor and football combination of the 70s and 80s, the Portsmouth city crest worn as the 90s kicked off and today's more traditional moon and stars shield design, which was worn in the club's FA Cup final success of 1939.

It is perhaps fitting, given Pompey's connections to the navy, that Admiral have returned to Fratton Park three times in the last 25 years to supply the team kit. The club are also notable for being one of the relatively few professional clubs whose kit has been produced by Gola, a firm more noted for their footwear and other sporting accessories. Since 1999 the club have taken charge of their apparel with the creation of the Pompey Sport brand and the introduction of some fine kits.

White always seems to be an away colour that suits Portsmouth, although red also makes a regular reappearance on the club's travels, normally paired with black. Over the years, yellow, orange and gold have also been worn away from home. The club's first season back in the top flight (03–04) also saw the strange decision to issue a navy blue away kit that was virtually identical to the home strip. The subtle difference of shade was decided to be sufficient and the club chose to sport the outfit at every away game possible, saving the favourite royal blue shirt for home games only. Such a radical decision meant that the side had to rely pretty heavily on a third kit to cope when playing away at a team sporting blue.

Despite the unsettling events of the 03–04 season, Portsmouth are renowned for their excellent support and it is these loyal supporters who will be hoping that the blue, white and red of Portsmouth – serenaded by the Pompey Chimes – will grace the Premiership for some time yet.

WITH THANKS TO SAMUEL HILL.

PAUL MERSON IN THE 02–03 POMPEY SPORT PROMOTION WINNING HOME KIT.

Another major team whose kit was supplied by Gola in the 80s was the fictional Melchester Rovers – captained by a certain Roy of the Rovers.

H 1980–81, 1981–82

Design: GOLA
Sponsor: NONE

Portsmouth started the decade in a new division, the third, and with a new kit from sportswear company Gola in one of the company's rare professional football contracts. It was a very individual and stylish kit for the time, with unique shoulder flashes that continued across the back, trimmed with red bands. The late 70s had not been a good time for the club, but with the previous season's promotion there was a new sense of optimism at Fratton Park.

Worn in: The tremendous 80–81 League Cup fourth round tie at Anfield vs the mighty Liverpool, where Pompey unluckily lost 4–1.
Worn by: David Gregory, Mick Tait, Steve Aizlewood.

A 1980–81, 1981–82

Design: GOLA
Sponsor: NONE

As with many Pompey kits at the time, the away strip was just a straight copy of the home but in red (including the red socks from the home outfit). The shirt also replicated the same shoulder flash design. The shorts included a single white band on each leg. The momentum from 79–80 carried through to the early 80s as the club tried to recapture past glories. Bobby Campbell took over from Frank Burrows as manager in 81–82.

Worn in: A good 1–0 win over Gillingham (courtesy of a David Gregory goal) in the 80–81 season.
Worn by: Alan Garner, Leigh Barnard, Keith Viney.

H 1982–83

Design: GOLA
Sponsor: NONE

Gola modernised the club's kit for the 82–83 season, giving it matching V-neck and cuffs and elegant pinstripes to create a very nice-looking,

minimalist outfit, similar to that worn by high-flying Ipswich Town at the time. The Gola logo was also updated and now provided the only flash of red on the home shirt. This great kit accompanied a rampant Pompey to the Division 3 title this year.

Worn in: A barnstorming 4–1 win over Sheffield Utd on the opening day of the season, plus a solid 4–1 win over Hereford in the first round of the FA Cup.
Worn by: Alan Biley, John McLaughlin.

A 1982–83

Design: GOLA
Sponsor: NONE

As with the previous range, the new red away kit mirrored the design of the home and formed a formidable, almost Liverpool-like strip – clearly the club were aspiring to the top teams in Division 1 with both kits this year! Curiously, the club badge was rotated on this second batch of Gola kits, with the anchor now sitting vertically – the only time in recent years that this has occurred. These outfits marked the end of the three-year Gola deal.

Worn in: A vital 2–1 win at Reading, but also some grim away defeats (4–0 to Southend and 5–1 to Bristol Rovers) in an otherwise superb 82–83 season.
Worn by: Bill Rafferty, Neil Webb, Colin Sullivan.

The Le Coq Sportif home shirt was identical to that worn by Oldham Athletic at about the same time.

H 1983–84, 1984–85

Design: LE COQ SPORTIF
Sponsor: NONE

French kit designers Le Coq Sportif arrived at Fratton Park in 83–84, bringing with them this brilliant kit. Plain and simple with matching V-neck and cuffs, minimal white and red trim and the company's standard double shadow stripes that continued on the shorts, it was a fitting outfit for a classy Pompey side who, now managed by Alan Ball, finished 84–85 in fourth place in Division 2 – narrowly missing out on promotion on goal difference.

Worn in: A great 2–1 win over Nottingham Forest in the 84–85 Milk Cup second round first leg. Also a dramatic 4–4 draw with Fulham and a 3–2 home win against Grimsby.
Worn by: Noel Blake, Billy Gilbert, Mark Hateley (in his superb 83–84 season).

A 1983–84, 1984–85

Design: LE COQ SPORTIF
Sponsor: NONE

Le Coq Sportif's main away kit for the club switched to white with a delicate blue and red horizontal pinstripe. The shirt, which like most strips of the time was pretty snug, also featured the infamous Le Coq Sportif high-fitting round neck and inset combination worn by clubs such as Chelsea and Everton. The blue shorts were also worn with the home kit when necessary and vice versa.

Worn in: An important 2–0 win vs Oldham at Boundary Park and the bizarre 84–85 3–2 defeat vs Wimbledon, when the Dons scored without even touching the ball after a centre kick courtesy of a Noel Blake own goal.
Worn by: Vince Hilaire, Ivan Golac.

3 1983–84, 1984–85

Design: LE COQ SPORTIF
Sponsor: NONE

Although the main away kit was now white, the team also sported this seldom-worn all-red outfit against those teams whose jerseys were predominantly blue or white. It followed the design of the home shirt, complete with matching V-neck and classy shadow stripes. The shorts, like those of the home and away, included white trim along the bottom of each leg. Worn with the home kit's red socks.

Worn in: The 2–1 defeat vs Blackburn Rovers at Ewood Park in 83–84 and a fine 1–0 win over the same club the following season.
Worn by: Mick Kennedy, Kevin Dillon, Dave Bamber, Bobby Doyle.

H 1985–86, 1986–87

Design: UMBRO
Sponsor: NONE

Another good strip was this outfit by English sportswear giants Umbro. It followed pretty much the same style as the previous design, with delicate white and red trim on the non-contrasting V-neck and cuffs, which were becoming something of a Pompey trademark. The shirt also featured a rare example of the Umbro logo included as part of a shadow stripe pattern. This marvellous kit graced the backs of the team as they finally gained promotion to Division 1 in 86–87. Also worn with the blue shorts from the away kit.

Worn in: Convincing home wins over Stoke (3–0) and Carlisle (4–0) – part of a run of 14 consecutive home wins.
Worn by: Mick Channon, Paul Wood.

Umbro's white away kit also made an appearance in the Admiral era of 87–89 in the 2–0 away game at Crystal Palace, when both the club's kits clashed with the red and blue of the Selhurst Park club.

A 1985–86, 1986–87

Design: UMBRO
Sponsor: NONE

The club's next away kit was a rare and unique Umbro design that saw the company's logo appearing on each sleeve rather than on the front right-hand side of the shirt, which was now filled with dashing blue panels trimmed with red. Two examples of the jersey exist: the match-day version with the badge placed centrally as shown here, but also the replica version with the badge placed on the left-hand side. A new style of Umbro socks, with a single logo embroidered onto the turnover, was also introduced.

Worn in: An unlucky 3–2 defeat away to Aston Villa in the 85–86 FA Cup third round replay.
Worn by: Kenny Swain, Lee Sandford, Eamon Collins.

3 1985–86, 1986–87

Design: UMBRO
Sponsor: NONE

Although officially a third strip, this all-red Umbro outfit (named in an Umbro catalogue of the time as the 'World Cup' design) must have been as popular as the standard white away kit as it was worn by manager Alan Ball and the training staff in the club's team photo at the time. Like the home kit it featured white piping to the sleeve, but combined this with a shiny shadow pinstripe throughout the shirt fabric.

Worn in: The 1–0 win over Division 1 Sheffield Wednesday in the 86–87 Full Members Cup.
Worn by: Paul Mariner, Paul Hardyman, Kevin O'Callaghan.

H 1987–88, 1988–89

Design: ADMIRAL
Sponsor: SOUTH COAST FIAT (87–88)

With the club now back in Division 1 after 28 long seasons away, they took to the field in this lively Admiral outfit. It included bold red and white pinstripes and contrasting white wrap-over V-neck and cuffs, along with a shadow chequerboard pattern on the shorts. The Admiral logo also appeared on the socks. The South Coast Fiat car dealership became the club's first ever shirt sponsor in 87–88.

Worn in: The club's first win of the 87–88 season – a 2–1 home win over West Ham. Also the wonderful 2–0 victory over arch rivals Southampton at the Dell the same season.
Worn by: Mick Quinn, Clive Whitehead.

A 1987–88, 1988–89

Design: ADMIRAL
Sponsor: SOUTH COAST FIAT (87–88)

The Admiral away kit was just as bold and brash as the home – quite a change from the subtle elegance of Le Coq Sportif and Umbro. The shirt was actually one of the few examples of those two stalwarts of 80s kit design – pinstripes and shadow stripes – merging together. It also set the trend for future Pompey away kits by pairing red with black. Unfortunately, Alan Ball's men struggled in their first season back in the top division and were relegated back to Division 2.

Worn in: The 2–1 FA Cup third round victory over Blackburn Rovers in the 87–88 season. Also a brilliant 3–3 draw away to Chelsea the following year.
Worn by: Mike Fillery, Barry Horne, Ian Baird.

The 92–93 season saw an abrupt end to the Influence kit's life due to a financial crisis at the company. Asics stepped in with a replacement in this highly unusual state of affairs.

H 1989–90, 1990–91

Design: SCORELINE
Sponsor: GOODMANS

A more subtle and uncluttered strip arrived at Fratton at the end of the 80s courtesy of Scoreline, who had replaced Admiral. The shirt featured a chequerboard shadow pattern throughout and a neat button-down collar. Hampshire-based hi-fi and electrical goods manufacturers Goodmans became the club's first long-term sponsor. A revived design of club badge was also introduced.

Worn in: Two close results vs Man Utd in the 89–90 League Cup second round: a 3–2 defeat at home and a creditable 0–0 draw at Old Trafford. Also a 5–1 win over Hull (90–91).
Worn by: Steve Wigley, Mark Chamberlain.

A 1989–90, 1990–91

Design: SCORELINE
Sponsor: GOODMANS

This was not the first away kit in the English League over the years that attempted to emulate the mighty Brazil, and it won't be the last. The blatant Brazilian connection was later played down by the club, as the shirt was also worn with royal blue shorts, yellow shorts and also yellow socks at various times. The Scoreline kits were worn under three managers: John Gregory, Frank Burrows and Tony Barton. The club badge was also included on the socks.

Worn in: An exciting 3–3 draw vs Oldham and a vital 1–0 win over Ipswich (both 89–90).
Worn by: Graeme Hogg, John Beresford, Gary Stevens, Jimmy Gilligan.

H 1991–92, 1992–93

Design: INFLUENCE
Sponsor: GOODMANS

New manager Jim Smith led Portsmouth through two good seasons in this confident new Influence kit. It followed on from the previous Scoreline outfit by including a button-up collar, no cuffs and an intricate two-tone shadow pattern. Early versions of the shirt featured a slightly different Influence logo, outlined in yellow. Often worn with blue shorts, even when there was no colour clash.

Worn in: The 4–2 win vs Middlesbrough in the 91–92 FA Cup fifth round replay, plus the two games vs Liverpool in the semi-final that ended in an unlucky penalties defeat for Pompey.
Worn by: Andy Awford, Guy Whittingham.

A 1991–92, 1992–93

Design: INFLUENCE
Sponsor: GOODMANS

This red and black Influence away kit followed the design of the home, including the collar and the zigzag shadow pattern. Like the home shirt, it was also much baggier than those worn in recent years. 92–93 was a wonderful season for Portsmouth as well as for 47-goal hero Guy Whittingham, with the club so nearly clinching promotion to the newly formed Premier League, finishing third but missing out in the play-offs. Like the home outfit, this strip was replaced mid-92–93 by the new Asics kit.

Worn in: The brilliant 3–2 away win against Birmingham City with a goal by Alan McLoughlin and two from Guy Whittingham.
Worn by: Martin Kuhl, Darren Anderton, Kit Symons, Alan McLoughlin.

When the club played Man Utd in 93–94, the word 'Pompey' was included on the back of the Portsmouth shirts.

H 1993–94, 1994–95

Design: ASICS
Sponsor: GOODMANS

The new Asics kit for the 93–94 season actually made some early appearances towards the end of the previous season. It was a typically loud, but stylish, early 90s kit with a large button-up collar and flashy printed fabric. The kit also introduced a new larger club badge based around the Portsmouth city crest rather than the previous shield. The socks featured a nice white turnover with blue trim.

Worn in: The heartbreaking and highly controversial 2–2 draw in the 92–93 play-off semi-final second leg vs Leicester. Also the tense 2–2 draw at Man Utd in the 93–94 Coca-Cola Cup fifth round, where Pompey came from behind twice to earn a replay.
Worn by: Paul Walsh, Guy Butters, John Durnin.

A 1993–94, 1994–95

Design: ASICS
Sponsor: GOODMANS

Like the home equivalent, this distinctive red and black halved shirt also made an early appearance in 92–93. The early 90s saw all shirts become baggier and shorts much longer, and this strip was no exception. After the excitement of the last two years, the lifespan of this first set of Asics kits coincided with some disappointing times for the club as they languished in the lower reaches of Division 2 under manager Terry Fenwick.

Worn in: The unfortunate 1–0 defeat in the 92–93 play-off match against Leicester. Also worn in a 3–3 draw vs Blackburn in the 93–94 FA Cup. Plus the superb 3–2 win over Everton in the 94–95 Coca-Cola Cup second round.
Worn by: Gerry Creaney, Warren Neill, Preki.

3 1994–95, 1995–96

Design: ASICS
Sponsor: GOODMANS HI FI (94–95)
THE NEWS (95–96)

The second season of Asics' deal with the club also saw the introduction of this strong white third kit, which completed a fine set of strips for 94–95. It was a standard Asics design of the time and featured navy blue stripes and shorts. The sponsors' logo changed slightly to Goodmans Hi Fi in the first year of use, before being replaced altogether the following season by local paper The News. A nice touch was the addition of 'Pompey' text to each cuff.

Worn in: The fine 2–0 victory over Swindon with goals by Deon Burton and Preki in the difficult 95–96 season. Also worn in that season's 1–0 defeat to Charlton in the FA Cup.
Worn by: Robbie Pethick, Bjorn Kristensen.

H 1995–96, 1996–97

Design: ASICS
Sponsor: THE NEWS

Asics' next home kit was a bit of a strange outfit. Minimal in design, its main features were a high-fitting chunky wrap-over round neck combined with an innovative stitched panel that contained the club's monogram, 'PFC'. The club badge was now contained within a large white shield. Also, a small graphic on each sleeve commemorated 1898, the club's founding year.

Worn in: A 4–1 thrashing of Southend in the opening game of the 95–96 season, along with the 3–0 defeat to Southampton in the 95–96 FA Cup third round. Also worn in the club's great 3–2 win over Leeds in the 96–97 FA Cup fifth round battle at Elland Road.
Worn by: Jimmy Carter, Deon Burton.

When Admiral arrived in 97–98 it was the third time they had been Portsmouth's kit suppliers.

A 1995–96, 1996–97

Design: ASICS
Sponsor: *THE NEWS*

The club's next away strip was a real gem. Sticking with red and black, the shirt now featured stripes combined with a subtle two-tone red trim and a unique collar design. It was a strong Asics design – distinctive yet also basic and functional. After escaping relegation by the skin of their teeth in 95–96, the club's form improved the following season and they eventually finished seventh in Division 2.

Worn in: A good 1–0 win at Reading in the 95–96 season, plus the dramatic last match of that campaign at Huddersfield with Deon Burton's goal earning a win for Pompey and saving them from relegation.
Worn by: Fitzroy Simpson, Paul Hall, Lloyd McGrath, Andy Thomson.

3 1996–97

Design: ASICS
Sponsor: *THE NEWS*

96–97 brought a new third kit to Fratton Park – the last to be made by Asics and the last to be sponsored by *The News*. It was another great-looking shirt – uncluttered and distinguished. The collar was an interesting red and navy striped design with broad red and navy bands adorning each sleeve. Another new arrival this season was that of Terry Venables as new Chairman of the club.

Worn in: The 0–0 draw vs Oldham at Boundary Park and the fine 2–1 win over Crystal Palace (both 96–97).
Worn by: Sammy Igoe, Martin Allen, Russell Perrett.

H 1997–98, 1998–99

Design: ADMIRAL
Sponsor: KJC MOBILE PHONES

Admiral returned after eight years to once again produce Pompey's kit. It was a bold and confident strip with a large white collar and cuffs matched with centralised badges. The fabric featured an attractive shadow pattern based around the club badge, which this season returned to the classic moon and star shield design. KJC Mobile Phones became the new shirt sponsor.

Worn in: Another last game relegation battle – a 3–1 win vs Bradford keeping Pompey up (97–98). Also that season the unlucky 2–2 draw with Aston Villa in the FA Cup third round. The following year it was worn as Leeds thrashed Pompey 5–1 in the FA Cup fifth round.
Worn by: Adrian Whitbread, John Aloisi.

A 1997–98, 1998–99

Design: ADMIRAL
Sponsor: KJC MOBILE PHONES

After a poor start Alan Ball returned to manage the cash-strapped club, replacing Terry Fenwick. The away kit saw the club wearing yellow for the first time since the 90–91 season. The shirt pretty much followed the design of the home, with the exception of a large star and moon graphic on each sleeve. Worn with both blue and yellow shorts and socks.

Worn in: A 1–0 win at Reading followed by a great 3–0 triumph at West Brom (97–98). Plus the unlucky 1–0 defeat at Villa Park vs Aston Villa in the 97–98 FA Cup third round replay.
Worn by: Mathias Svensson, Jeff Peron, Thomas Thogersen, Matt Robinson.

99–00 saw squad names and numbers included on the back of the Pompey shirts for the first time.

PORTSMOUTH

3 1998–99

Design: ADMIRAL
Sponsor: KJC MOBILE PHONES

Admiral's new third kit for the club was another smart affair. The shirt returned to white and was now coupled with a broad navy sleeve stripe and neat V-neck, all trimmed with yellow. The fabric also featured a fresh shadow stripe design. The club badge and logo once again appeared on either side of the shirt. Standard Admiral white and navy socks and navy shorts completed the outfit.

Worn in: Another FA Cup shock – a great third round win over Nottingham Forest at the City Ground. Plus the 2–2 draw vs Bristol City in the same season.

Worn by: Michalis Vlachos, David Waterman, Steve Claridge, Stefani Miglioranzi.

H 1999–2000

Design: POMPEY SPORT
Sponsor: THE POMPEY CENTRE

There were big changes at Fratton Park this season with Milan Mandaric saving the club from closure, Alan Ball departing once more and the club taking over the production of their own kit under the brand name Pompey Sport. Several other clubs (including Southampton) were just starting to produce their own kit at this time. However, the first home-produced design was a bit of an anti-climax as it was rather plain and seemed a little dated.

Worn in: A 2–0 win over Sheffield United on the opening day of the season. Also a good 2–1 win over Norwich later in the campaign and an impressive 3–0 win over Barnsley courtesy of a Claridge hat-trick.

Worn by: Jason Cundy, Kevin Harper.

A 1999–2000

Design: POMPEY SPORT
Sponsor: NONE

The first Pompey Sports away kit mirrored the design of the home, apart from the addition of a collar. Although the local business/retail development 'The Pompey Centre' became the new home shirt sponsor in November 99, this away shirt remained unsponsored. This kit's blue shorts were also worn with the home kit when necessary. It was another difficult season for the club, who only just avoided relegation under new manager Tony Pulis.

Worn in: A 1–0 win at Portman Road vs Ipswich and a 1–1 draw with Blackburn later in the season. Also worn in the 4–2 defeat at Manchester City.

Worn by: David Hillier, Matt Robinson.

H 2000–01, 2001–02

Design: POMPEY SPORT
Sponsor: BISHOPS PRINTERS

The next Pompey Sport strip was a vast improvement over the previous season. Gone were the old-fashioned neck and red trim, and in came a slick wrap-over neck and, for the first time, yellow piping. The shirt was also worn with blue shorts and socks. Local printing company Bishops Printers became the new shirt sponsor. The club survived relegation on the last day of the season yet again, following a home match vs Barnsley.

Worn in: A 4–4 thriller vs Barnsley (01–02). Also that season a 4–2 win over Crystal Palace – one of the few highlights of that campaign.

Worn by: Robert Prosinecki, Peter Crouch.

For the home game vs Coventry in 01–02, a kit mix-up led to Pompey lending the Midlanders their away strip in order to complete the match without a colour clash.

A 2000–01, 2001–02

Design: POMPEY SPORT
Sponsor: BISHOPS PRINTERS

This fresh white kit trimmed with just the merest hint of blue was the next Pompey Sport away outfit. Although it featured the same piping design as the home shirt, it included a more traditional collar. It was worn with a unique pair of blue-trimmed white shorts. As with all of this last batch of self-produced kits, a gothic-script 'PFC' was included on the socks. More managerial unrest occurred at the club with first Steve Claridge being made player-manager before Graham Rix replaced him.

Worn in: A great 3–2 win at Crystal Palace with a late winner from Michael Panopoulos after Pompey were 2–0 down after 10 minutes.
Worn by: Darren Moore, Lee Mills, Rory Allen, Luke Nightingale, Lewis Buxton.

3 2000–01, 2001–02

Design: POMPEY SPORT
Sponsor: BISHOPS PRINTERS

To cope with frequent colour clash problems caused by the blue home and white away strips, a bold and bright orange outfit was also worn. Complete with a V-neck and a horizontal black band trimmed with white, it was an unorthodox but exciting kit. Harry Redknapp joined the club in 01–02 as director of football, but eventually replaced the sacked Rix as manager. The 01–02 season was also marked by sadness as Pompey goalkeeper Aaron Flahavan died in a car crash in August 01.

Worn in: The lucky 1–0 win at Stockport (01–02) and two awful defeats to Blackburn that same season: a 4–0 hammering in the Carling Cup and 3–1 in the league.
Worn by: Mark Burchill, Lee Bradbury.

H 2002–03

Design: POMPEY SPORT
Sponsor: TY

With Redknapp now in charge and Milan Mandaric funding some inspirational new signings, Pompey made another assault on Division 1 in this eye-opening strip that was worn for just one season. With its dynamic white and red flashes down each side and the bold logo of new sponsors, toy manufacturers Ty, it was a design that initially divided Pompey fans. However, by the end of the season – with promotion in the bag – they loved it!

Worn in: A 2–0 win over Forest in the first home game of the season. Also a 6–2 victory over Derby and the 3–2 win at home vs Rotherham that sealed the Division 1 crown.
Worn by: Linvoy Primus, Paul Merson, Tim Sherwood, Gianluca Festa.

A 2002–03

Design: POMPEY SPORT
Sponsor: TY

A truly treasured shirt in the Portsmouth wardrobe was this all-gold affair that accompanied the club on their travels in their promotion-winning season of 02–03. It was a lucky kit – the team lost just one match in it, 2–1 at Wimbledon. The shirt featured a trendy new minimal V-neck, navy reversed seams and unusual oval side panels, which were also featured on the shorts. A new format of the Pompey Sport logo was featured on both this and the home kit.

Worn in: The astonishing 5–0 win over Milwall at The New Den and another 3–2 win at Crystal Palace – again with a late winner after being 2–0 down!
Worn by: Yakubu, Nigel Quashie, Gary O'Neil.

In 02–03, for the first time in many years, an alternative pair of blue shorts were not worn with the home kit. Instead, the club preferred to don the gold kit if there was a shorts clash.

3 2002–03, 2003–04

Design: POMPEY SPORT
Sponsor: TY

Another all-white kit made an appearance in the 02–03 season, this time as third choice. White always suits Pompey and this kit was retained for the club's 03–04 arrival in the Premiership, where it saw a lot of action. The design was essentially based on that of the home kit minus the red trim.

Worn in: A 1–1 draw with Leicester in 02–03 followed by a storming 4–0 thrashing of Coventry. Plus a disappointing 3–1 defeat to an already relegated Leicester and an unlucky 1–0 defeat to Everton (both 03–04).
Worn by: Svetoslav Todorov, Steve Stone, Vincent Pericard, Jason Crowe.

H 2003–04, 2004–05

Design: POMPEY SPORT
Sponsor: TY

Redknapp's Pompey were in the Premiership for the first time and had a brilliant first season in the top flight, finishing 13th. To accompany them was this fine kit. The shirt incorporated a simple yet elegant slick round neck with a dynamic white flash on each shoulder. Hampshire-based Ty remained as sponsors, providing one of the most unique shirt sponsor's logos in football.

Worn in: The stunning wins in 03–04 over Leeds (6–1) and Liverpool (twice, both 1–0). Plus a great 2–0 triumph over Man Utd and a sublime 4–1 thrashing of Southampton in the 04–05 season.
Worn by: Hayden Foxe, Patrick Berger, Teddy Sheringham, Arjan de Zeeuw.

A 2003–04, 2004–05

Design: POMPEY SPORT
Sponsor: TY

The club's first season in the Premiership saw them adopt a rather curious kit philosophy. The home kit, as usual, was blue, and the away kit was… also blue. Granted, it was a much darker shade, but it was still blue! The kit, which followed exactly the style of the home but trimmed in red, was designed to be worn in every away game whether there was a clash or not. Against teams in blue the team donned their white third kit. Although some clubs do don their away kit at the drop of a hat, it was still a distinctly unusual move.

Worn in: Some great results back in the top flight: a 1–1 draw at Highbury vs Arsenal, a 2–1 win vs Blackburn and a 2–1 victory over Leeds.
Worn by: Matt Taylor, Aliou Cisse.

3 2004–05

Design: POMPEY SPORT
Sponsor: TY

With the previous white third kit having run its course, a new design was launched to cope with the awkward 'two blue kits' scenario. It was

another flash and slightly retro-looking design, with simple blue and yellow vertical stripes and an elegant V-neck. The 04–05 season saw Redknapp depart as manager after a rift with Mandaric. Velimir Zajec took control of the team, before being replaced by Alain Perrin.

Worn in: A 2–2 draw with Norwich in this fine kit's Premiership debut. Plus defeats to Everton (1–0) and Chelsea (3–0), but a good 2–0 win over Cardiff in the Carling Cup fourth round.
Worn by: David Unsworth, Lomana Lua Lua.

PORTSMOUTH

The first versions of the 05–06 kits, unveiled at the press conference to launch the OKI sponsorship deal, omitted the Jako logo.

H 2005–06

Design: JAKO
Sponsor: OKI PRINTING SOLUTIONS

After three eventful years that saw Portsmouth gain promotion to the Premiership and then more than hold their own with the big boys, Ty departed from the club's shirts. They have been replaced, with great fanfare, by OKI Printing Solutions – a Japanese company that specialises in computer printers and who previously sponsored Scottish club Clyde in the early 90s. Another departure is that of the club's own Pompey Sport brand. Instead, Portsmouth's kits in 05–06 are supplied by Jako. Their first outfit is this highly contemporary affair, oozing sophistication and style, with an asymmetrical white band trimmed with yellow.

A 2005–06

Design: JAKO
Sponsor: OKI PRINTING SOLUTIONS

With Southampton (with, of course, ex-Portsmouth boss Harry Redknapp) relegated at the end of 04–05, perhaps Alain Perrin and Pompey feel it is safe to wear red again! The 05–06 Jako away design follows the style of the home kit, replicated in a flamboyant red and gold ensemble. Although the new home design has been warmly received by the Fratton Park faithful, there have been mixed opinions about this away version. A new Portsmouth third kit is due to be released before Christmas 2005.

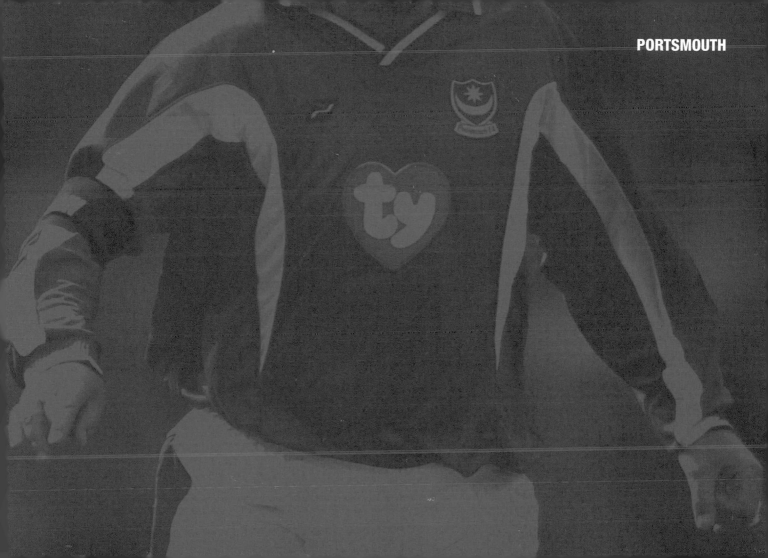

SUNDERLAND

Sunderland are fiercely proud of their heritage and history, a fact that is evident in their choice of change colours. The combination of light and navy blue that the Black Cats have often worn away from home over the past 25 years were actually the colours sported by the club when they first played way back in 1879, when they formed as Sunderland and District Teachers' Association FC. Early kits included light blue shirts and navy shorts and later a halved jersey. Eventually, the club switched to red and white halved shirts in the hope that the red would inspire success, and in 1890 they finally adopted the stripes that have accompanied them through to the present day.

The early 1900s saw the club become a driving force in English football with the red and white stripes paired with black shorts and socks. The late 50s saw a switch to white shorts, as well as a disastrous relegation to Division 2. A decade of under-achievement followed, before manager Bob Stokoe brought back the black shorts of the glory days and the Sunderland renaissance began.

The 80s saw the club ditch the traditional attire of old faithful Umbro for sleek new continental style courtesy of Le Coq Sportif, who produced one of the club's more controversial home kits that abandoned the traditional broad stripes, replacing them with a white shirt and thin red stripes outlined in black. In the mid-80s, American sportswear company Nike made their first foray into English football apparel with Sunderland, but it was not until the dawning of the new millennium that the company really revitalised and dominated the English market. The year 2000 saw Nike return to Sunderland once more as kit supplier.

For a long period, local brewery Vaux supported the Mackems and over the years promoted various individual Vaux brands such as Tuborg Lager, Samson and Scorpion. As the company were so intertwined with Sunderland AFC, it was a sad day when the brewery closed and the Vaux name disappeared from the red and white shirts forever.

With the club's arrival at new home The Stadium of Light in 97–98, a new club crest was introduced, carefully designed to symbolise local landmarks and heritage. With Sunderland successfully battling to regain their position in the top flight for the 05–06 season, their excellent approach to the game and the loyalty of their fans has been suitably rewarded.

KEVIN PHILLIPS IN THE 97–99 ASICS HOME KIT.

The 80–81 season saw both the home and away shirts produced in a new silkier fabric.

H 1977–78 to 1980–81

Design: UMBRO
Sponsor: NONE

Sunderland's first kit of the 80s was the outfit that had guided them through three seasons in Division 2 after suffering relegation in the 76–77 season. Plain and simple, the only concession to fashion was the typically 70s wing collar. Early seasons saw the Umbro logo on the shirt embroidered in white and slightly narrower red stripes. The 79–80 season culminated in a magnificent promotion back to the top flight under the managerial control of Ken Knighton.

Worn in: The 79–80 home 2–0 win vs West Ham that clinched promotion for the club. Also a superb 4–0 away win at Manchester City the following season.

Worn by: Shaun Elliott, Stan Cummins.

A 1977–78 to 1980–81

Design: UMBRO
Sponsor: NONE

Throughout the lifespan of this last range of Umbro kits, the club seemed to alternate between this blue away kit and the white third version. The combination of blue shirt, red and white Umbro diamond trim and red and white striped collar made this a very unique and distinctive kit. Unusually, none of these late 70s/early 80s kits were updated to include the Umbro text beneath the famous diamond logo on the front of the shirt.

Worn in: The 1–0 win over Crystal Palace in the 80–81 season. Also the amazing 1–0 win at high-flying Liverpool later that season that kept the Mackems in Division 1.

Worn by: Gordon Chisholm, Jeff Clarke, Bryan "Pop" Robson, Kevin Arnott.

3 1977–78 to 1980–81

Design: UMBRO
Sponsor: NONE

The club also sported this nice white third kit in the late 70s and early 80s. Featuring a slightly tweaked collar design and the standard Umbro diamond trim, it was worn with either the black shorts of the home kit or the white shorts of the away. The home kit's white change socks completed the outfit. After two top 10 finishes in 77–78 and 78–79, the club were promoted at last to Division 1 at the end of the 79–80 season.

Worn in: The 3–1 defeat to Nottingham Forest at the City Ground in the 80–81 season.

Worn by: Gary Rowell, Joe Hinnigan.

H 1981–82, 1982–83

Design: LE COQ SPORTIF
Sponsor: NONE

With silky, shiny shirts rapidly replacing the cotton jerseys of the 70s, there was a radical rethinking of kit design within football clubs. Sunderland's response was this outfit from French designers Le Coq Sportif. It followed a standard 80s trend of twisting tradition and bringing a dramatic modern approach to the team's kit design. Unfortunately, for many fans the new predominantly white shirt with thin red stripes was too far away from the heritage of the club. Worn with red shorts rather than black.

Worn in: The great 1–0 win over Manchester City in the last game of 81–82 that assured the club's top flight status for another season.

Worn by: Ally McCoist, Colin West.

Cowies arrived at the club as shirt sponsors just in time to benefit from the lifting of the ban on sponsored kits during televised matches.

VAUX

TUBORG

A 1981–82, 1982–83

Design: LE COQ SPORTIF
Sponsor: NONE

Blue remained the prominent away colour for Le Coq Sportif's change kit, although now it was a lighter shade trimmed with royal blue and red. Like the home shirt, the Le Coq Sportif logo was placed on each sleeve and the club badge centrally. Widely spaced red pinstripes completed the look. In the two years these kits were worn, the club maintained their top flight status under manager Alan Durban.

Worn in: The 0–0 draw with Manchester Utd in 81–82 and a tight 1–0 win over Stoke the following season. Just don't mention the horrifying 8–0 defeat at Watford, also in the 82–83 season.

Worn by: Nick Pickering, Tom Ritchie.

3 1981–82, 1982–83

Design: LE COQ SPORTIF
Sponsor: NONE

This smart all-red strip was also worn during the early 8os. Like the home and away kits, the V-neck and cuffs included a neat trim. White pinstripes adorned the shirt in a much more standard spacing than the away. The shirt was worn with the red shorts and socks from the home kit. A modern replica version of this shirt has also been produced in recent years.

Worn in: The 0–0 draw vs Coventry in 81–82. Also a shocking 3–0 defeat against West Brom in 82–83, followed by a good 1–0 win over Notts County later in the season.

Worn by: Rob Hindmarch, Jimmy Nicholl.

H 1983–84 to 1985–86

Design: NIKE
Sponsor: COWIES (83–85) VAUX (85–86)

The new Sunderland kit of 83–84 was quite a milestone in football kit design as it marked the design debut in English football of US firm Nike, whose UK office was based at the time in Tyne and Wear. The shirt saw a return to traditional stripes, now restyled with white sleeves and shoulders. Another difference was the inclusion of the manufacturer's logo on the left-hand side of the shirt and the club badge on the right, rather than vice versa.

Worn in: The unlucky 84–85 Milk Cup final vs Norwich that ended in a 1–0 defeat for the club, with Clive Walker missing a penalty. A great 3–1 win over Southampton on the opening day of the 84–85 season.

Worn by: Ian Wallace, Barry Venison.

A 1983–84 to 1985–86

Design: NIKE
Sponsor: COWIES (83–85) TUBORG (85–86)

Nike persevered with two shades of blue for the new away kit. Motor vehicle dealers Cowies became the club's first ever shirt sponsor 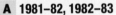 in 83–84, although their logo was replaced by that of Tuborg lager two years later. The shirt was also worn with navy blue shorts. 84–85 was a mixed season for the club, as they were relegated to Division 2 despite reaching the Milk Cup final that year.

Worn in: A creditable 0–0 draw with Man Utd in the 85–86 FA Cup fourth round. Plus a 2–2 draw at Stoke City in 84–85.

Worn by: Clive Walker, Shaun Elliott, Alan Kennedy, Steve Berry, Lee Chapman.

The club's Patrick kit had a short but eventful life, accompanying the
club through relegation and promotion in the two years it was worn.

3 1983–84 to 1985–86

Design: NIKE
Sponsor: COWIES (83–85) TUBORG (85–86)

A third kit was also issued by Nike, and it was
arguably the weakest of the three designs they
produced. The strip was a rather insipid yellow
colour trimmed with blue piping. As with the
standard away kit, it was sponsored by Cowies
in the first two seasons of use before bearing
the logo of Tuborg lager, a brand produced by
the club's new sponsors, local brewers Vaux.
After slipping into Division 2 in 84–85, the club
struggled again in 85–86, finishing only 18th in
the table.

Worn in: The 2–2 draw at Sheffield Wed in the
84–85 season and a dismal 2–0 away defeat to
Blackburn Rovers the following year.

Worn by: Reuben Agboola, David Hodgson,
Iain Munro.

H 1986–87, 1987–88

Design: PATRICK
Sponsor: VAUX

Another French sportswear firm, Patrick,
became the club's new kit manufacturers in
86–87. Unfortunately, their arrival coincided
with a bleak period for the club (now managed
by Lawrie McMenemy) as they were relegated
to Division 3 via the play-offs at the end of an
awful 86–87 season. The kit itself followed a
similar path to that of the last Nike outfit,
although now the sleeves and shoulders were
red. This kit was now worn with white socks.

Worn in: An awful 6–1 defeat at Blackburn in
86–87, but some great wins in 87–88: 7–0 vs
Southend (with Gates scoring four) and 4–1
results against Wigan and Mansfield.

Worn by: Frank Gray, George Burley,
Gordon Armstrong.

A 1986–87, 1987–88

Design: PATRICK
Sponsor: TUBORG

Accompanying the club as they were relegated
to Division 3 was this blue away kit. It mirrored
the design of the home, but in the traditional
two blue shades. Vaux continued to promote
Tuborg Lager on the shadow-striped shirts.
After just one season in Division 3, the club
bounced back in 87–88, finishing top of the
table and gaining promotion back to Division 2
under Denis Smith.

Worn in: Some poor away defeats in the
relegation season of 86–87: 3–0 against Stoke
and 2–1 vs Sheffield Utd. Also the encouraging
1–0 win away at Brentford in the first game of
the 87–88 season.

Worn by: Dave Swindlehurst, Mark Proctor,
Eric Gates, Paul Lemon, Gary Owers.

H 1988–89 to 1990–91

Design: HUMMEL
Sponsor: VAUX

A revitalised Sunderland were back in Division
2 and were soon to be in Division 1 with this
marvellous new Hummel kit. The shirt featured
the first traditional usage of stripes since the
Umbro days. A modern wrap-over round neck
was introduced, along with Hummel's chevron
trim. After losing to Swindon in the 89–90 play-
off final, Sunderland were amazingly promoted
to Division 1 following a scandal concerning
Swindon's financial irregularities.

Worn in: A superb 4–0 win over Portsmouth in
88–89. Also a 2–0 win over Newcastle in the
89–90 play-off semi-final and a 0–0 at Roker
Park in 90–91 that postponed Arsenal's title
celebrations until their following game.

Worn by: John MacPhail, Marco Gabbiadini.

An alternative version of the 88–91 third shirt was also worn, which featured a wrap-over V-neck from which piping ran to under the arms.

A 1988–89 to 1990–91

Design: HUMMEL
Sponsor: VAUX

Hummel attempted to rejuvenate the by now de rigueur blue Sunderland away kit. Gone were the two shades of blue, replaced by a plain and simple royal blue trimmed with white chevrons and red piping. The shirt fabric also featured a Hummel shadow pattern and was worn with both white and blue shorts. The 90–91 season surprisingly saw the side struggle in Division 1, and they were eventually relegated once again.

Worn in: The 89–90 play-off final vs Swindon. Plus a thrilling 3–3 draw vs Spurs (90–91).
Worn by: Thomas Hauser, Steve Doyle, Richard Ord.

3 1988–89 to 1990–91

Design: HUMMEL
Sponsor: VAUX

Another fresh-looking kit was Hummel's yellow third kit, which was introduced in 88–89 and completed a fine range of strips. It mirrored the design of the away strip and was a bright addition to the Sunderland away palette, which had grown just a little stale after eight years of blue kits. It must have been popular within the club as it was worn by the management and coaches in the official team photos at the time.

Worn in: A dramatic 2–2 draw with Blackburn at Ewood Park in the 88–89 season with two goals by hero Marco Gabbiadini.
Worn by: Michael Heathcote, Colin Pascoe.

H 1991–92 to 1993–94

Design: HUMMEL
Sponsor: VAUX

One of the best shirts worn by the club was the second home jersey produced by Hummel as the club faced life back in Division 2. With its elegant collar and new restrained Hummel trim, it exuded class and really should have been seen in the top division. The shorts featured a nice trim of red and white and the club badge appeared on the socks for the first time. Also worn with change red shorts.

Worn in: The 91–92 FA Cup semi-final 1–0 win over Norwich with a goal by John Byrne. Also worn in the brilliant 6–2 victory over Millwall in the League that season.
Worn by: Peter Davenport, Paul Bracewell.

A 1991–92 to 1993–94

Design: HUMMEL
Sponsor: VAUX

This white, purple and green strip was completely different from any other worn by the club as Hummel abandoned all tradition for a contemporary and radical design. It is forever ingrained in the memory of the club due to the FA Cup final defeat to Liverpool. The kit was worn under three managers (Malcolm Crosby, Terry Butcher and Mick Buxton), with the Mackems only just avoiding relegation once again to the old Division 3 (now renamed Division 2 post-Premier League) in 92–93.

Worn in: The disappointing 2–0 defeat to Liverpool in the 91–92 FA Cup final. Also a 5–3 goal extravaganza vs Swindon (91–92)
Worn by: Kevin Ball, Don Goodman, John Kay, Mick Harford, Phil Gray.

The 94–95 home and away shirts both also included the Avec logo on the left lapel of the collar.

3 1993–94

Design: HUMMEL
Sponsor: VAUX

Hummel introduced this seldom-worn vibrant yellow third kit – their last for the club – in the 93–94 season. It was a flashy and confident shirt with an intricate black sleeve pattern similar to the style worn by Watford at about the same time. Oddly, the Hummel logo ran at a 45-degree angle alongside the sleeve pattern. The kit marked the end of an interesting six years with the Danish firm, although sadly their fine second set of kits was never worn in the top division. 93–94 saw the club finishing 12th.

Worn in: The disappointing 2–1 defeat to Wimbledon in the 93–94 FA Cup fifth round.
Worn by: Andy Melville, Brian Atkinson, Derek Ferguson.

H 1994–95, 1995–96

Design: AVEC
Sponsor: VAUX SAMSON

Little-known sportswear firm Avec took over the Mackems' kit production in 94–95 with the club at the time nothing more than an average Division 1 side, but within two years they were champions. The first Avec kit was an unusual affair, featuring traditional enough elements such as a proper collar but topped with a curious flash design on each shoulder. A continuation of the stripes on the shorts finished off the design. Also worn with both red and white change shorts.

Worn in: Another six-goal thrashing of Millwall and the 0–0 draw with Stoke that finally sealed the Division 1 title for the Mackems (95–96).
Worn by: Lee Howey, Michael Gray, Shaun Cunnington, Brett Angell.

A 1994–95

Design: AVEC
Sponsor: VAUX SAMSON

The Black Cats' next away kit was an unorthodox and garish teal outfit that lasted for only one season. As with the home kit, the fit of the shirt and shorts was much larger than in previous years, but it was the shorts design that really divided opinion – they featured a strange red pattern based on the elements of the Avec logo and were quite unlike any other pair around! Vaux began promoting their Samson brand on all the Sunderland shirts at this time. Peter Reid arrived as manager.

Worn in: Two hard-fought draws early in the season: 2–2 vs Middlesbrough with two goals from Russell and a 0–0 against Sheffield Utd.
Worn by: Ian Rodgerson, Stephen Brodie, Martin Gray.

A 1995–96 3 1996–97

Design: AVEC
Sponsor: VAUX SAMSON

Another challenging design was introduced in 95–96 (Reid's first full season as manager) to replace the previous teal outfit. It saw a return of yellow, now trimmed with blue, and featured a long floppy collar and faded bands reaching down the shoulders and sleeves. This very distinctive kit, which included the squad number and name in red, also featured the same Avec logo shadow pattern that graced the fabric of the standard home and away strips. Worn as a third kit in the 96–97 season.

Worn in: The brilliant 2–2 draw with Man Utd at Old Trafford in the 95–96 FA Cup third round. Also vital wins over West Brom and Crystal Palace in the 95–96 season.
Worn by: Dariusz Kubicki, Martin Scott.

Sunderland were the only side ever to wear an Avec kit in the top English division.

H 1996–97

Design: AVEC
Sponsor: VAUX SAMSON

With the club celebrating their magnificent promotion back to the Premiership and looking forward to their new stadium, a new home kit was launched by Avec – the last to be worn at Sunderland's traditional home, Roker Park. It was a real back to basics design with a simple V-neck and cuffs, plain black shorts and retro-styled socks. The club badge was contained within an additional shield. Also worn with the white shorts and socks of the away kit.

Worn in: A great 3–0 win over Chelsea followed later in the season by the absolutely wonderful 2–1 triumph over Manchester Utd. Also, of course, the last match at Roker Park: a 3–0 whitewash of Everton.

Worn by: Craig Russell, David Kelly.

A 1996–97

Design: AVEC
Sponsor: SCORPION LAGER

The final kit of the three-year Avec deal was another fresh design. Like the home outfit, it was plain and straightforward and was essentially the home shirt minus the red stripes. Vaux chose to promote their Scorpion Lager on this shirt. The shorts and socks at this time were interchangeable with the home and were often mixed and matched throughout the season, which unfortunately saw the club once again relegated to Division 1.

Worn in: An astonishing 4–1 over Nottingham Forest in the club's first away game of the season. Also the 1–0 defeat to Wimbledon that relegated the Mackems at the end of 96–97.

Worn by: Gareth Hall, Chris Waddle, Paul Stewart.

H 1997–98, 1998–99

Design: ASICS
Sponsor: LAMBTONS BEER

Everything was new at Sunderland in 97–98: a new stadium, The Stadium of Light; a new kit supplier, Asics; a new sponsor, Lambtons Beer; and a new club crest! In fact, the only old thing was the inspiration behind this marvellous new kit, which was clearly influenced by the strip worn by the club at Roker Park in the 1920s. The Asics logo was neatly tucked away on the collar.

Worn in: The 5–2 win over Bury, with four goals from Phillips securing promotion back to the Premiership. Plus the 2–1 win over Birmingham that won the Division 1 title for the club (98–99). Also that season the 2–1 Worthington Cup semi-final defeat to Leicester.

Worn by: Alex Rae, Allan Johnston.

A 1997–98   3 1998–99

Design: ASICS
Sponsor: LAMBTONS BEER

Asics introduced another very striking kit for their first away outfit for the club. The shirt had a shimmering metallic gold effect, trimmed with a simple collar. Matched with plain navy (or gold) shorts and gold socks, it was another highly individual strip. The design lasted for only one season as the standard away kit before becoming a third choice in 98–99.

Worn in: An unfortunate 2–0 defeat to Sheffield Utd on the opening day of the 97–98 season, followed by the heartbreaking defeat to Charlton in the Division 1 play-off final.

Worn by: Steve Agnew, Jan Eriksson, Lee Clark, Michael Bridges.

Although many sides started sporting squad numbers on the front of players' shorts in 99–00, Sunderland did not include them until the 00–01 season.

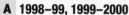

A 1998–99, 1999–2000

Design: ASICS
Sponsor: LAMBTONS (98–99)
REG VARDY (99–00)

This inspired navy blue design accompanied Peter Reid's men as they took Division 1 by storm in 98–99 before enjoying a great Premiership season the following year. It was another distinguished outfit with a large white and red horizontal band and simple red and white collar and cuffs. Lambtons ceased being shirt sponsor after two years with the club and 99–00 saw the new Reg Vardy logo fit neatly on the shirt.

Worn in: A classic 4–0 win over Sheffield United and a 5–2 thrashing of Bury (both 98–99) and a great 2–1 win over Southampton in the 99–00 season.
Worn by: Darren Williams, Nicky Summerbee.

H 1999–2000

Design: ASICS
Sponsor: REG VARDY

Asics' last home strip for the club lasted for only one season, but coincided with the Mackems' return to Premiership action. A fairly pedestrian design, the only outstanding element was the unusual and slightly retro-feeling button-up round neck. Car dealers Reg Vardy became the club's new sponsor in the first year of a long association with the club. Also worn with white change shorts.

Worn in: A great 2–0 win over Watford early in the season followed by a great 5–0 away win at Derby with a Phillips hat-trick. Also a sweet 2–1 victory over Newcastle at St James' Park.
Worn by: Niall Quinn, Paul Butler, Steve Bould.

H 2000–01, 2001–02

Design: NIKE
Sponsor: REG VARDY

Sunderland's second consecutive season in the Premiership was accompanied by a new kit supplier, Nike. Reg Vardy remained as sponsor. A no-frills V-neck was introduced, along with neat curved piping on the shorts. Often worn with the white shorts from the matching away kit when necessary. In one of the best-looking Black Cats kits for a while, the club reached seventh in the league in the first season it was worn, although they found the going harder the following year and finished a lowly 17th.

Worn in: A horrendous 5–0 thrashing at Ipswich, an important 2–0 victory over Leeds and the 1–1 draw against Derby that ensured the club's place in the top flight (01–02).
Worn by: Kevin Phillips, Stefan Schwarz.

A 2000–01 3 2001–02

Design: NIKE
Sponsor: REG VARDY

Nike's first away kit for Sunderland in their second spell at the club was a real classic. It not only looked good, it felt good too, with lightweight fabric and breathable mesh panels made of Nike's hi-tech Dri-Fit material designed for optimum comfort and performance. Although officially maintained as a third shirt in the 01–02 season, it seems the kit was not worn in that year's disappointing Premiership campaign.

Worn in: A good 1–0 win at Charlton and an impressive 2–2 draw at Arsenal later in the season (both 00–01). Plus the exciting 4–2 win over Crystal Palace after extra time in the FA Cup third round of that year.
Worn by: Don Hutchison, Danny Dichio.

Nike's innovative dual-layered Cool Motion shirts were originally introduced in the 2002 Japan World Cup, where they were worn in many matches.

3 2000–01

Design: NIKE
Sponsor: REG VARDY

This all-navy shirt was only worn once by the club in a game at Southampton. Essentially the same design as the club's white away kit, and almost identical to Arsenal's third strip at the time, it was a standard Dri-Fit Nike style with lightweight mesh fabric panels and reversed seams. A minimal white and red trim adorned the collar. The shirt was paired with the standard white shorts and socks from the away kit.

Worn in: The 1–0 win over Southampton at The Dell towards the end of the 00–01 season – the only time the shirt was worn.
Worn by: Chris Makin, Paul Thirlwell, Michael Reddy.

A 2001–02

Design: NIKE
Sponsor: REG VARDY

Hoping to improve on the previous two seasons' seventh place, and inspired by an early colour scheme worn by the club in the 1800s, the Black Cats wore this impressive two-tone blue shirt for their away kit. One of the first shirts to include the radical, minimal round neck that was to become popular in kit design in forthcoming seasons, it was nicely trimmed with red and was worn many times this season. It was a difficult campaign for Peter Reid's club and they only just escaped relegation to Division 1.

Worn in: The kit's Premiership debut – a 2–0 defeat at Fulham – plus a painful 4–1 defeat at Old Trafford. Also a good 2–0 win at Bolton.
Worn by: Jason McAteer, Kevin Kyle.

H 2002–03, 2003–04

Design: NIKE
Sponsor: REG VARDY

By 2002 Nike were one of the leading forces in football kit design, with their revolutionary dual-layered Cool Motion shirts created to draw excess moisture from the body and maintain an even temperature. This flashy outfit combined traditional red strips with dynamic mesh panelling and reversed seams.

Worn in: A good 2–0 win over Spurs and the 2–0 defeat to Birmingham that relegated the Mackems to Division 1 (both 02–03). Also the 1–0 defeat to Millwall in the FA Cup semi-final and the epic Division 1 play-off semi-final defeat vs Crystal Palace (both 03–04).
Worn by: John Oster, Emerson Thome.

A 2002–03

Design: NIKE
Sponsor: REG VARDY

A bold change occurred with the club's new away kit. The shirt featured all the Cool Motion benefits of the home with slick white mesh panels down each side, but was now a highly unusual powder blue colour unlike anything the club had worn previously. 02–03 started poorly for Sunderland, leading to the sad departure of Peter Reid after seven years who was superseded by what turned out to be a short-term replacement in Howard Wilkinson.

Worn in: The amazing 7–0 thrashing of Cambridge in the second round of the 02–03 Worthington Cup, and consecutive 2–1 defeats to Southampton and Manchester United in the Premiership later that season.
Worn by: Jody Craddock, Gavin McCann.

A white panel was included on the back of the 04–05 Diadora home shirt in order that the players' names could be read more easily by referees.

A 2003–04

Design: NIKE
Sponsor: REG VARDY

Although the club were back down in Division 1, they looked forward to the 03–04 season with new manager Mick McCarthy and another great Nike design – their last for the club. This all-navy lightweight outfit was elegantly trimmed with red mesh panels designed for effective breathability and comfort along with a sleek new neck. Also worn with the change white shorts and socks from the home kit.

Worn in: An awful 2–0 defeat to Nottingham Forest in the first game back in Division 1. Performances improved later in the season, however, with a solid 3–0 win over Walsall.
Worn by: Marcus Stewart, Julio Arca, Kevin Kilbane.

H 2004–05

Design: DIADORA
Sponsor: REG VARDY

After four fruitful years fashion-wise with Nike as kit supplier, Sunderland switched to Diadora, who introduced a new kit complete with a 'lucky' central white stripe which indeed did prove fortunate for the club as they gained promotion back to the Premiership in 04–05. Plain and inoffensive, the design included a neat collar with a simple white band on one lapel and hi-tech moisture-repelling mesh panels under each arm.

Worn in: A vital 2–0 win vs Ipswich and the 1–0 win over Stoke that clinched the Coca-Cola Championship title for The Black Cats (04–05).
Worn by: Mark Lynch, Stephen Caldwell.

A 2004–05

Design: DIADORA
Sponsor: REG VARDY

With the club attempting another push at Division 1 (now renamed the Coca-Cola Championship), they took to the field in this attractive all-white away kit. With a continental-style minimal blue neck and red and blue trim, it was a great-looking outfit. Diadora's unique curved embellishments, introduced throughout most of the Italian company's kits this season, were also included. Also worn with alternative blue change shorts.

Worn in: A 1–0 win at Stoke and a sweet 2–1 triumph over Nottingham Forest.
Worn by: Dean Whitehead, George McCartney, Gary Breen.

H 2005–06

Design: LONSDALE
Sponsor: REG VARDY

As Sunderland and Mick McCarthy prepared for their return to the top flight, the premature departure of kit suppliers Diadora saw Lonsdale, who had recently supplied some classy strips for Blackburn Rovers, step in. With the season just weeks away, new designs were drawn up and soon the club's 05–06 kits were premiered on the official website. The home shirt, with its red band across the back, is inspired by the famous Thomas Hemy painting of the Sunderland team of the 1890s that hangs in the Stadium of Light.

A **2005–06**

Design: LONSDALE
Sponsor: REG VARDY

In an official club poll towards the end of the 04–05 season, Sunderland fans had voted for an all-black outfit for the team's next away strip. Despite Diadora's departure and with deadlines looming, new kit suppliers Lonsdale have pulled out all the stops to produce this fine-looking kit that remains true to the overall feel of the menacing black design that had proved popular with supporters. The strip includes a tidy V-neck and red and silver flashes on each shoulder, carefully positioned to imply an intimidating and impressive physique. Although very similar in design to the home shorts, the away kit's black shorts feature red and silver trim.

SUNDERLAND

TOTTENHAM HOTSPUR

It is entirely appropriate that white, the most pure and chivalrous of all football colours, is the hue that came to be associated with Tottenham Hotspur – after all, the club were named after 15th century hero Sir Henry Percy, known to adventure-seeking school boys as Harry Hotspur. However, the famous lilywhite shirts and navy blue shorts did not comprise the first outfit the club wore when they were formed as The Hotspur Football Club back in 1882; their first kit was in fact all navy blue, and early years saw the team take to the field in light blue and white halved shirts, red shirts with navy shorts and even chocolate and gold striped jerseys. The turn of the century saw the club gain professional status, and in 1898 white shirts, inspired by the great Preston North End team of the time, were introduced – and were here to stay.

Apart from one season in the mid-80s navy blue shorts have always complemented the white shirts at home in recent years, although the club have no qualms about donning white change shorts if a clash necessitates. In fact, every home outfit produced in recent years has always included alternative white shorts that follow the design of the navy blue home pair. In Europe, however, it has been a different story, with some of the club's greatest successes coming while sporting an all-white strip. Preferred away colours are navy blue (in tribute to the club's first-ever kit) and yellow, although pale blue has also been popular at times.

The club have embraced the recent commercial rise of football and the last 30 years have seen the side wearing kits by almost all of the major sportswear firms. The 80s saw Spurs go one step further at one stage, with the club buying shares in Danish company Hummel, known at the time for their dashingly European outfits.

Spurs have never been afraid of embracing new fashions on the field: they were one of the first British clubs to wear a shadow striped kit, the first to reintroduce longer shorts (in conjunction with Umbro at the 1991 FA Cup final) and, very recently, one of the few Premiership sides to turn out in Kappa's skin-tight stretchable jerseys – a new innovation in sportswear designed to form the most comfortable and practical apparel. No doubt, whatever the next revolutionary development in football wear may be, Spurs' involvement will not be far behind.

WITH THANKS TO ANDY PORTER.

NAYIM IN THE CLASSIC UMBRO HOME KIT OF 91-93.

The 81–82 FA Cup final (and replay) saw both Spurs and Queens Park Rangers playing in their away kits.

H 1980–81, 1981–82

Design: LE COQ SPORTIF
Sponsor: NONE

Spurs dived into the 80s under manager Keith Burkinshaw with the very latest in kit design. Gone were the scratchy cotton, wing-collared jerseys – in came new sleek, shiny, polyester shirts. Le Coq Sportif led the way in kit design in this period and this Spurs strip is a typical example.

Worn in: The 100th FA Cup final against Man City – 1–1 in the first match and 3–2 in the replay. Also that year's classic FA Cup semi-final vs Wolves. In 81–82 it saw action in the 2–1 defeat to Liverpool in the Milk Cup final.
Worn by: Paul Miller, Ricky Villa (scoring his wonder goal in the 80–81 FA Cup final).

A 1980–81, 1981–82
3 1982–83, 1983–84

Design: LE COQ SPORTIF
Sponsor: NONE

The first away kit of the 80s was just as good as the home. A little snug-fitting, it has to be said, it was nonetheless a shirt of classic simplicity with just a small navy panel on each shoulder. As with the home shirt, it featured a central badge and the Le Coq Sportif logo on each sleeve – the height of fashion! Spurs reached the FA Cup final again in 81–82 after beating both Arsenal and Chelsea en route.

Worn in: Not a classic match by any means, but the kit was worn in the 81–82 FA Cup final replay 1–0 victory over QPR.
Worn by: Steve Perryman, Garth Crooks, Tony Galvin, Osvaldo Ardiles.

H 1982–83

Design: LE COQ SPORTIF
Sponsor: NONE

This classic outfit – regarded by many Spurs fans as one of the best the club have worn – was simple and elegant with a shadow stripe design on

the shirt, continued on the shorts. The 82–83 season was the club's centenary and this special kit was worn for just that one season to mark the occasion, although it was revived in 83–84 for the club's UEFA Cup campaign.

Worn in: A great 5–0 massacre of Arsenal in 82–83 and the 83–84 UEFA Cup 4–2 victory over Feyenoord in the second round, along with the dramatic 4–3 penalty shoot-out win over Anderlecht in the final.
Worn by: Steve Archibald, Graham Roberts.

A 1982–83

Design: LE COQ SPORTIF
Sponsor: NONE

The club switched to light blue, a colour used early in the club's life within their 1885 kit, for their next away kit. It followed the silky and shiny design of the home, complete with shadow stripes and non-contrasting V-neck and cuffs. As with the home shirt, a special commemorative badge marked the club's centenary. This was a great season for the club, who eventually finished fourth in the league.

Worn in: Good 1–0 wins over Sunderland and West Bromwich Albion – rare victories in the shirt this season.
Worn by: Mickey Hazard, Gary Mabbutt, Chris Hughton, Alan Brazil.

A Holsten-sponsored version of the revived 82–83 centenary home shirt was worn in the 83–84 UEFA Cup final triumph over Anderlecht.

H 1983–84, 1984–85

Design: LE COQ SPORTIF
Sponsor: HOLSTEN

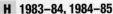

Once the celebrations marking the club's centenary had ended, the side reverted to an amended version of the previous kit. The badge (a more traditional version now without any special text) was placed back in the centre of the shirt, with the Le Coq Sportif logo once again moved to the sleeves. The kit was stylish and glamorous – just like the early 80s Spurs squad, who came close to the title in 84–85.

Worn in: The 2–1 win over Forest at White Hart Lane in 83–84 – the first league match to be screened live. Plus a thrilling 1–1 game with Man Utd in the last game of the 83–84 season.
Worn by: Gary Stevens, Tony Galvin.

A 1983–84, 1984–85

Design: LE COQ SPORTIF
Sponsor: HOLSTEN

As with the home version, the away kit copied the minor tweaks to the positioning of the club badge and the Le Coq Sportif logo. The other important addition to both the home and away shirts came in 1983 with the arrival of brewers Holsten, who became the club's first-ever sponsor. Despite some managerial changes with Peter Shreeves replacing Burkinshaw, it was a good period for Spurs. In 1983 the club was floated on the stock market instigating a focus on the more commercial side of the football world, including the sale of replica shirts.

Worn in: A great 4–2 win over Luton in the 83–84 season.
Worn by: Mark Falco, John Chiedozie.

H 1985–86, 1986–87

Design: HUMMEL
Sponsor: HOLSTEN

It's almost impossible to look at this glamorous kit without seeing the long flowing hair of Hoddle and Waddle as they mesmerised defences.

The shirt featured an intricate design on the chest, topped with piping to the V-neck and Hummel chevron trim. Paired in the 85–86 season with white shorts to create a stylish all-white kit for the club, it was worn with a more traditional navy pair the following season.

Worn in: The 86–87 League Cup semi-final vs Arsenal that ended in a Spurs defeat, plus a 5–1 win over Oxford the previous year.
Worn by: Richard Gough, Clive Allen (who scored an incredible 49 goals in 86–87).

A 1985–86, 1986–87

Design: HUMMEL
Sponsor: HOLSTEN

The mid-80s saw the first dawning of some of the more flamboyant kit designs of recent years. With new kit supplier Hummel on board (in whom the club had recently purchased shares), this blue away kit was just as daring as the home. The shirt combined diagonal shadow stripes with alternate blue and white pinstripes. In the 85–86 season the light blue shorts were occasionally worn with the home kit when a clash occurred.

Worn in: The 5–2 win over QPR in the 85–86 season. Also a 3–1 defeat to Luton Town the following year and an emergency appearance due to a colour clash in the shock 2–1 defeat to Port Vale (87–88 FA Cup fourth round).
Worn by: Chris Waddle, Mitchell Thomas.

The 86–87 FA Cup final saw Spurs premiering their brand new Hummel kit with at least half the team's jerseys rather embarrassingly missing the Holsten logo.

3 1986–87   A 1987–88

Design: HUMMEL
Sponsor: HOLSTEN

For the first time ever, the club sported an officially marketed third kit. Similar to the away strip (minus the chevron trim), this dark blue affair included a contrasting V-neck and cuffs and pale blue and white diagonal pinstripes. It was strange to see two separate kits from the same range in the same colour (albeit a different shade) worn in the same season. The kit was retained as the club's main away choice for 87–88, although it did cause some problems with the referees' black kit.

Worn in: A 2–1 win over Derby in 87–88, but also two poor defeats to QPR and Luton that season (both 2–0).
Worn by: Steve Hodge, Johnny Metgod.

H 1987–88, 1988–89

Design: HUMMEL
Sponsor: HOLSTEN

Hummel were clearly ahead of their time with their introduction of a collar on the next Spurs home kit (although an early version was produced with just a simple V-neck). This latest kit, which launched the Terry Venables era, was far more restrained than the previous design. It featured piping from collar to arm and a small chevron shadow pattern. 'THFC' was included on the left leg of the shorts.

Worn in: The 86–87 FA Cup final 3–2 defeat to Coventry (with white shorts) and a good 3–1 win over Newcastle in the following year.
Worn by: Nico Claesen, Paul Gascoigne (who joined the club for £2 million in 1988).

A 1988–89 to 1990–91

Design: HUMMEL
Sponsor: HOLSTEN

After five years of playing away in various shades of blue, the club returned to yellow as their change colour. It was a good, functional kit, popular with the fans and the team. It lasted for three seasons until the end of the Hummel deal. The shirt featured a minimal chevron trim on each sleeve and on the right leg of the shorts – a design that was to continue with the next home kit. A new version of the Holsten logo was also included.

Worn in: A 3–1 win over Luton in 88–89 and a superb 4–2 win over Sheffield Wednesday in the 89–90 season. Also a 2–0 win over Leeds the following campaign.
Worn by: Vinny Samways, Guy Butters, David Howells, Pat Van den Hauwe.

H 1989–90, 1990–91

Design: HUMMEL
Sponsor: HOLSTEN

The club ended the decade in a perilous financial state, but in another nice strip – the last to be produced by Hummel and almost identical to the one worn by Real Madrid at the time. It borrowed some of the stylings from the previous year's away outfit, including the shadow pattern. As with the away kit, the club badge was also included on the socks. Another nice touch was the inclusion of the club's monogram within the V-neck design.

Worn in: A 2–1 win over Man Utd in 89–90 plus the 90–91 FA Cup semi-final 3–1 win vs Arsenal, which included the great Gazza free kick.
Worn by: Gary Lineker, Paul Stewart.

Tottenham have often worn an all-white strip in European ties and important Cup games.

H 1991–92, 1992–93

Design: UMBRO
Sponsor: HOLSTEN

A great kit – the first by new suppliers Umbro. It was another trendsetting outfit, as it was one of the first in the country to include longer, baggier shorts than those favoured in the 80s – something that drew a lot of attention when worn for the first time in the 90–91 FA Cup final. A large collar returned to the shirt. Navy socks were worn instead of white.

Worn in: The dramatic 90–91 FA Cup 2–1 final victory over Forest – with Gazza's infamous tackle that marred his last match for Spurs. Plus the 4–1 defeat to West Ham in 92–93.
Worn by: Paul Allen, Jason Cundy (who scored a wonder goal vs Ipswich in 92–93).

A 1991–92 to 1993–94

3 1994–95

Design: UMBRO
Sponsor: HOLSTEN

Umbro stuck with yellow as Spurs' change colour and created another popular kit that lasted for an incredible four seasons. Like the home version, it featured a shadow pattern comprising the Umbro logo and club initials, but was topped with an asymmetrical navy and sky blue graphic pattern on the right sleeve and left leg of the shorts.

Worn in: The 4–2 win at Man City in the FA Cup sixth round (92–93). Also the astonishing 6–2 win over Southampton in 94–95, with a great hat-trick by Ronny Rosenthal.
Worn by: Gordon Durie, Nick Barmby, Nayim, Neil Ruddock, Terry Fenwick.

3 1991–92 to 1993–94

Design: UMBRO
Sponsor: HOLSTEN

One of the most interesting kits worn by the club was this third strip introduced by Umbro in Spring 1992. The marketing of third kits increased dramatically post-Italia 90, with three different outfits becoming the norm. This shirt featured a subtle rendering of 'Spurs' within fine vertical lines on the top half of the shirt, which continued on the shorts. 92–93 ended in confusion at the club, with Terry Venables sacked by Alan Sugar.

Worn in: A 1–0 win over Newcastle in the opening day of the 93–94 season. Also a 0–0 draw with Feyenoord in the 91–92 Cup Winners Cup quarter-final second leg, which marked the end of Spurs in Europe for that season.
Worn by: Andy Gray, Dean Austin.

H 1993–94, 1994–95

Design: UMBRO
Sponsor: HOLSTEN

Umbro's second home kit was a more pedestrian affair than the previous design, but is remembered for launching new manager Ossie Ardiles' attack-minded team. The mid-90s saw kit companies experimenting with different collar designs, and this one saw an almost double-layered effect with two folds of material. An intricate shadow pattern and small 'Spurs' ID tags on each cuff completed the design. Yellow was also added to the trim for the first time.

Worn in: The 2–1 win at Liverpool (FA Cup 94–95) with Klinsmann scoring a last-minute winner. Plus a 5–0 win over Oldham in 93–94.
Worn by: Darren Anderton, Jurgen Klinsmann.

Navy was the preferred away colour for Spurs throughout the 40s, 50s and 60s.

TOTTENHAM HOTSPUR

A 1994–95

Design: UMBRO
Sponsor: HOLSTEN

With Gerry Francis replacing Ardiles as club manager, Spurs were obviously hoping for a purple patch with this unorthodox new away kit, and in fact the club had a better season than expected. The club played in navy blue with an abstract purple design down one half of the shirt and on the left sleeve. Worn for only one season, it was a controversial and sombre design and the last to feature the logo of long-term sponsors Holsten – at least for the time being.

Worn in: The 4–3 victory over Sheffield Wed – Jurgen Klinsmann's goal-scoring debut and his famous dive celebration afterwards.
Worn by: Ronny Rosenthal, Sol Campbell, Justin Edinburgh, Teddy Sheringham.

H 1995–96, 1996–97

Design: PONY
Sponsor: HEWLETT PACKARD

American apparel company Pony began supplying Spurs' kit in 95–96. At the time, Pony's kits were all over the English league – Coventry, Southampton and West Ham to name but three. The home shirt featured a large collar with big silver buttons on the neck and the club's motto in navy. The shirt also incorporated a shadow pattern of the club badge, which was now in a classic 60s design and housed in a shield. Also worn with white shorts.

Worn in: The stunning 4–1 demolition of Man Utd at White Hart Lane (95–96) – a famous victory for the club with two Armstrong goals.
Worn by: Ruel Fox, John Scales.

A 1995–96   3 1996–97

Design: PONY
Sponsor: HEWLETT PACKARD

Pony's first away kit for Spurs remained purple and navy, although now combined in stripes and trimmed very prominently with white. Stylish white and navy trimmed each leg of the shorts. It was, however, another very dark-looking kit and was seldom worn. Computer manufacturers Hewlett Packard became the club's new sponsor, replacing long-term partners Holsten.

Worn in: A rare outing for this strip vs Blackburn Rovers and the away win at Coventry during 95–96 (although Spurs chose to wear the yellow kit to play the club again in the Coca-Cola Cup later the same month).
Worn by: Colin Calderwood, Jason Dozzell, Gheorghe Popescu, Ilie Dumitrescu.

3 1995–96   A 1996–97

Design: PONY
Sponsor: HEWLETT PACKARD

95–96 saw a return to bright yellow for the club's away colours. It was a popular design that was worn often during its two years of service. The shirt featured a fashionable 70s-style inset collar and navy sleeves. A complex shadow pattern comprising the club badge, similar to the version featured on the home shirt, ran through the material of the shirt and shorts, which also included a navy waistband.

Worn in: The 3–1 victory over Leeds at Elland Road (95–96) and the amazing 4–0 victory at Sunderland. Also the humiliating 6–1 defeat at Bolton in the 96–97 Coca-Cola Cup.
Worn by: David Howells, Steffen Iversen (who scored a superb hat-trick in the 4–0 win over Sunderland).

The first adidas home kit to include hi-tech mesh panels under each arm for breathability was launched in 1999 with the aid of a huge painted mural of the Spurs team.

H 1997–98, 1998–99

Design: PONY
Sponsor: HEWLETT PACKARD

The last home shirt to be made by Pony was this nice blend of retro styling and modern materials. The shirt had a simple wrap-over V-neck and navy piping, combined with a vertically ribbed fabric. Hewlett Packard remained as sponsor, but the club crest was in a new heraldic shield design – quite a change from the minimal style of the previous badge.

Worn in: The 98–99 Worthington Cup final 1–0 win over Leicester at Wembley – the club's first major trophy in seven years. Also, a 1–0 win over Barnsley in the 98–99 FA Cup sixth round with a wonderful solo goal from Ginola.
Worn by: Jose Dominguez, Clive Wilson.

A 1997–98

Design: PONY
Sponsor: HEWLETT PACKARD

With Christian Gross installed as manager to replace Gerry Francis, the club sported one of the nicest kits produced by Pony during their relegation fight. This classy navy and ecru design maintained the same collar and cuff design as the home and added underarm panels trimmed with amber piping, which worked well with the navy and ecru shades. Although the shirt and shorts featured a more heraldic Spurs badge, the socks, as with the home kit, included the earlier, more traditional variant of the team's badge.

Worn in: The superb 3–0 win at Ewood Park vs Blackburn in the 97–98 season.
Worn by: David Ginola, Stuart Nethercott.

A 1998–99

Design: PONY
Sponsor: HEWLETT PACKARD

The last kit to be produced by Pony for Spurs (now managed by George Graham who took over in October 1998) was this stylish all-purple outfit. Minimal in design with a simple wrap-over V-neck and restrained white piping, it saw a return to a more 80s style of kit – a million miles away from the busy design of the first Pony home kit! The four-year deal with Pony was said to be worth £10 million, but although the club sported some nice Pony designs, the kits of this era are not the most fondly remembered by fans.

Worn in: The 2–0 defeat to Leeds Utd at Elland Road – Spurs' first loss in 17 games. Also worn in a 1–0 win over Derby at Pride Park.
Worn by: Ramon Vega, Andy Sinton, Rory Allen.

H 1999–2000, 2000–01

Design: ADIDAS
Sponsor: HOLSTEN

Old favourites Holsten returned in the 99–00 season as shirt sponsors. In fact, to the neutral observer the brand was so linked with the club that it seemed like they had never been away! Adidas became the new kit supplier in a three-year deal and produced this fine home kit, which was premiered to great excitement in the last home game of 98–99 against Chelsea. The more traditional club badge also returned this season in preference to the shield design.

Worn in: A thrilling 3–2 result over Everton with two late Spurs goals clinching the win, and a glorious 2–1 triumph over North London rivals Arsenal (both 99–00 season).
Worn by: Stephen Clemence, Allan Nielsen, Chris Armstrong.

Roy Reyland, the Tottenham kit man, revealed in an interview during the 00–01 season that most of the Spurs first team, in common with many clubs, change their shirts at half-time during a match.

A 1999–2000

Design: ADIDAS
Sponsor: HOLSTEN

Yellow also made a welcome comeback as the first choice change colour in 1999, albeit in a slightly truncated form, topped with navy shoulders, sleeves and side panels. The shirt also featured a slightly different collar from that of the home. The white adidas 'Champion'-style shorts and socks were interchangeable with the navy equivalents worn with the home kit at the time.

Worn in: A rare win at Southampton – this time 1–0 – and a good victory by the same score over Derby County at Pride Park.
Worn by: Mauricio Tarrico, Stephen Carr, Matthew Etherington.

A 2000–01

Design: ADIDAS
Sponsor: HOLSTEN

For the first time since the mid-80s, the club turned out in a plain navy blue shirt, now trimmed simply with white. It was a good-looking although perhaps slightly pedestrian design, similar to that worn by Newcastle at the same time. The shirt featured white mesh panels down both sides. This new kit was actually premiered in the last home match of the 99–00 season vs Sunderland, which Spurs won 3–1. March 01 saw prodigal son Glenn Hoddle return to the club as manager – surely the glory days were just around the corner.

Worn in: A brilliant match at Leeds that unfortunately ended in a 4–3 defeat for Spurs, plus a dismal 2–1 defeat to Derby.
Worn by: Ben Thatcher, Luke Young.

H 2001–02

Design: ADIDAS
Sponsor: HOLSTEN

The final year of adidas' three-year deal with Spurs saw them introduce three new kits. The home shirt was a much more restrained design than the previous one and reintroduced a simple V-neck, as well as underarm and side mesh panels. Pale blue was used as a trim colour. The kit was worn during the club's good run in the League Cup this season. Also worn with the white shorts of the away kit.

Worn in: The incredible 5–3 defeat to Man Utd at home, with Spurs surrendering a three-goal lead. Also a great 5–1 win over Chelsea in the Worthington Cup semi-final.
Worn by: Les Ferdinand (who scored the 10,000th goal in the Premiership in the 4–0 drubbing of Fulham).

A 2001–02

Design: ADIDAS
Sponsor: HOLSTEN

It had been many years since Tottenham had worn pale blue, but adidas revived it for their last away kit at the club. The actual design was almost identical to that of the home, the only difference (apart from the colour of course) being the new curved style of the adidas three-stripe trademark on the sleeves. 01–02 also saw the end of Holsten's short second period of shirt sponsorship at the club.

Worn in: An early season 2–1 defeat at Leeds, plus a hard-fought 2–0 win over Fulham at Craven Cottage.
Worn by: Gus Poyet, Christian Ziege, Gary Doherty.

Some Spurs fans expressed horror at the presence of red on the first Kappa home shirt – a colour, of course, rather too closely connected to their North London rivals.

3 2001–02

Design: ADIDAS
Sponsor: HOLSTEN

With Hoddle's Spurs due to meet Blackburn in the final of the Worthington Cup, adidas produced this one-off yellow and blue third kit as both the club's kits would have clashed with Blackburn's blue and white halved shirts. Very similar to adidas' first away kit for the club, the shirt featured an identical V-neck design to both the home and away jerseys. Worn with the blue shorts and socks from the home kit. A replica version was never issued.

Worn in: The disappointing 2–1 defeat against Blackburn in the Worthington Cup final at Cardiff's Millennium Stadium.
Worn by: Tim Sherwood, Sergei Rebrov, Steffen Freund.

H 2002–03, 2003–04

Design: KAPPA
Sponsor: THOMSON

The brand-new Kappa-produced kit was another groundbreaking design and the first of their new skin-tight range of kits – entitled Kombat 2002 – to be worn in the Premiership. The design itself was minimal, lightweight and undoubtedly cool. The new shirt featured a slick continental round neck and visible seams, which were reversed for comfort.

Worn in: The 1–1 draw with Arsenal at White Hart Lane in 02–03 plus the 4–3 win vs Everton that season, which included a Keane hat-trick. Also the 4–4 goal-fest vs Leicester in 03–04.
Worn by: Jamie Redknapp, Milenko Acimovic, Jonathan Blondel.

A 2002–03

Design: KAPPA
Sponsor: THOMSON

The new skin-tight and stretchable shirts designed by Kappa were first worn by the Italian national side in 2000. For a long time, club kits had been very baggy to make the players seem larger and more fearsome, but the new style was introduced to thwart shirt-pulling and to create a more lightweight design. Kappa's first away kit for Spurs was a dark combination of navy and black – a sombre-looking outfit that was almost identical in design to the home kit. Like the home and third shirt, the back of the collar incorporated a neat 'THFC' monogram.

Worn in: The great 3–2 win vs Manchester City – the club's only league win in this strip.
Worn by: Robbie Keane, Anthony Gardner.

3 2002–03

Design: KAPPA
Sponsor: THOMSON

Spurs' new yellow third shirt was definitely not one for the more fuller-figured Tottenham fan – the last thing you would want when wearing a tight, clinging strip that shows up every curve is for it to be in the most vibrant colour imaginable, thus drawing even more attention to yourself! Having said that, this flash of bright yellow was very welcome in the minimal two-tone palette Kappa initially introduced for the club. The shirt mirrored the design of the home and away jerseys, with the simple addition of navy panels under each arm and down the sides.

Worn in: A good 2–1 win at Blackburn Rovers and a 3–2 triumph over West Brom.
Worn by: Oyvind Leonhardsen, Dean Richards.

Unusually, the new 03–04 blue away shirt was actually premiered in the last match of the 02–03 season – at home! Spurs also previewed the navy blue adidas away kit of 00–01 in the last home match of 99–00.

A 2003–04

Design: KAPPA
Sponsor: THOMSON

Kappa launched two new strips in the 03–04 season, both in incredibly rich colours. The new away strip was a vivid light blue and featured a slightly different reversed seam design from the previous range of kits, along with mesh panels to aid breathability. It also included no contrasting trim of any kind, creating a sumptuous solid blue colour. A new version of the Thomson logo was included on this shirt.

Worn in: The 4–0 thrashing by Blackburn in the last home game of 02–03 – not a good start for the shirt. In fact, the club won only one game in this kit the following season – 1–0 vs Leeds.
Worn by: Chris Perry, Ledley King.

3 2003–04

Design: KAPPA
Sponsor: THOMSON

Following the design of the away strip, the new third kit saw the club sporting purple for the first time since 98–99. However, like the away shirt, it was now an interesting and startling new shade. The Kappa kits at this time focused mainly on comfort, lightweight wearability and a minimalist style, rather than on flashy details and trim.

Worn in: The superb 3–0 win over Coventry in the Carling Cup second round game at Highfield Road and the unlucky 1–0 defeat by Blackburn.
Worn by: Helder Postiga, Bobby Zamora, Goran Bunjevcevic.

H 2004–05

Design: KAPPA
Sponsor: THOMSON

Kappa replaced the 'Kombat 2002' with the 'Kombat 2004'. Like the previous home kit, it was produced in a highly stretchable, lightweight Lycra fabric. A much plainer design than in previous years, there was no navy trim on the home shirt at all – just breathable fabric underarm panels and reversed seams. Another update was the anatomical cut of the shirt (much more fitted than other baggier shirts) for additional comfort. The new shirt also featured a nice little 'Spurs' ID on the back of the minimalist round neck.

Worn in: The sublime 5–2 thrashing of Everton on New Year's Day 2005 and the nail-biting 5–4 defeat to Arsenal at White Hart Lane.
Worn by: Sean Davis, Jermain Defoe.

A 2004–05

Design: KAPPA
Sponsor: THOMSON

The club's new away kit reverted to navy blue in a simple reversal of the home design, which meant of course no white trim. Paired with white shorts and navy socks, the whole set of outfits was completely interchangeable for easy colour-clash problem solving. The club suffered turmoil in the managerial hot seat when new boss Jacques Santini quit after just 13 games, to be replaced by Martin Jol.

Worn in: The exciting extra time 4–3 victory over Bolton in the Carling Cup, after the game was level at 2–2 at 90 minutes.
Worn by: Pedro Mendes, Frederic Kanoute, Michael Brown, Simon Davies.

TOTTENHAM HOTSPUR

3 2004–05

Design: KAPPA
Sponsor: THOMSON

As had become the norm with the club, a new third strip was launched with the latest range of outfits. Like the previous efforts, it followed exactly the design of the home and away, although the colour reverted to the old favourite yellow. A nice touch present on all this series of kits was the addition of a large bold 'SPURS' down each sock.

Worn in: A great early 04–05 season 1–0 win away at Newcastle with Atouba scoring the winner, followed by another good 1–0 win, this time at Blackburn Rovers.

Worn by: Johnnie Jackson, Dean Marney, Pedro Da Silva Mendes.

H 2005–06

Design: KAPPA
Sponsor: THOMSON

Despite much speculation from some Spurs fans, Kappa continue to supply the club's kit for the 05–06 season. The home design features navy sleeves and side panels framing the white body of the shirt to create a design quite unlike any previously worn by the club. Whereas the 04–05 all-white jersey was intended to reflect Spurs' heritage, it was decided that the new shirt should be far more contemporary and radical. The general opinion among the club's supporters is positive about the design. Kappa have included a new type-only version of their logo to replace the more familiar marque.

A 2005–06

Design: KAPPA
Sponsor: THOMSON

If supporters feel the new home design is radical, it is nothing compared to the away! Featuring a shade of royal blue not generally associated with the club, and trimmed with yellow, the shirt borrows elements of the home to create this vivid concoction. It is certainly a big departure from the tradition of the club and one senses it may be some time before the White Hart Lane faithful get used to seeing their team in this outfit away from home as Martin Jol's side aim to continue the progress made during the previous season.

3 2005–06

Design: KAPPA
Sponsor: THOMSON

Since Kappa came on board as the club's kit suppliers a new away and third jersey have been launched every season. For 05–06, a more familiar Spurs kit design has been used for the new third outfit. Like the away strip, only certain features of the home kit (such as the contrasting sleeves) are included. The simply designed white shorts are able to be worn with the home kit when necessary.

TOTTENHAM HOTSPUR

WEST BROMWICH ALBION

Formed by local Sandwell cricketers in 1879 as West Bromwich Strollers, West Bromwich Albion have sported the same colours of navy blue and white stripes for over a hundred years. Early days though saw a vast array of colours and styles tried, including red and blue quarters, yellow and white quarters, red and white hoops and chocolate and blue halves before the club switched to navy and white. Since then, as with all clubs, the strips were moulded into whatever fashion dictated at the time. From the heavy cotton jerseys of the 1930s and 40s to the ultra-lightweight synthetic fabrics of today.

The famous navy stripes have also varied considerably in width over the years and for a short period in the early 90s the side sported a curious combination of thick and thin stripes printed in a vibrant zig-zag design that resembled rippled fabric.

White shorts are the norm for a Baggies home outfit although for several seasons in the 80s and 90s a navy pair was preferred. White sleeves are also a recurring theme in the club's wardrobe. Most of the 60s saw the side in this particular outfit and it is a style that has seen a resurgence under recent kit designers Diadora and Patrick.

The change kit most people instantly associate with the club is of course yellow and green stripes – made famous during the Umbro-supplied Ron Atkinson era of the late 70s and early 80s. Since then various combinations of red, yellow and even occasionally white crop up in Albion away strips producing a rich variety of fine designs.

When it comes to shirt sponsors, for the most part the club have stuck loyally to local companies. Kitchen appliance manufacturers BSR (later Swan) and the electrical goods chain Apollo 2000 were both based in the Midlands. Plus of course Sandwell Borough Council and The West Bromwich Building Society have both sponsored the club shirt.

Despite the boom in replica shirt sales the club are not known for issuing a plethora of different kits and designs. In fact, examining their kit history shows that strips often mutated slowly from one into another without drastic change. Over the years stripes have been narrowed, trim added to collars and most mysteriously of all different kit suppliers' logos appeared on shirts from previous seasons! The club's superb 'Great Escape' of the 04–05 season has ensured, however, that one of the oldest kit designs in English football will appear in the top flight for another season.

CHRIS WHYTE IN THE SCORELINE HOME KIT WORN IN 89–91.

With the arrival of new 80s silky fabrics, Albion's kits were updated with the stripes on both the club's home and away shirts becoming distinctly narrower in the 81–82 season in comparison to the previous few years.

H 1977–78 to 1981–82

Design: UMBRO
Sponsor: BSR (81–82)

English sportswear giants Umbro had supplied West Brom's kit since 72–73 and produced a series of kits that evolved gradually over the years. First an Umbro logo appeared on the shirt in the mid-70s. The WBA script logo then replaced the previous throstle design and finally the famous Umbro diamond trim arrived in time for the 77–78 season. As with all West Brom kits the shirt was often worn with either navy blue or white shorts.

Worn in: The superb 2–0 win over Liverpool in 80–81. Plus a disappointing 1–0 FA Cup semi-final defeat to QPR in 81–82.
Worn by: Cyrille Regis, Laurie Cunningham.

A 1977–78 to 1981–82

Design: UMBRO
Sponsor: BSR (81–82)

The club had turned out primarily in either yellow or white away from home during the 60s and 70s, but Umbro's arrival introduced the now familiar yellow and green striped away kit. Complete with sturdy button-up collar and diamond trim, it followed exactly the design of the home outfit. 1978 saw the appointment of Ron Atkinson as manager, who guided the side through a good period. In 1981 electronics company BSR (Birmingham Sound Reproducers) became the club's first sponsor.

Worn in: The 77–78 FA Cup semi-final 3–1 defeat to Ipswich (who unusually also sported their away kit in the match). Also another semi-final loss, this time 1–0 vs Spurs in 81–82.
Worn by: A permed Bryan Robson, Tony Brown.

H 1982–83

Design: UMBRO
Sponsor: SWAN

A long overdue radical modernisation occurred with The Baggies' kit in 1982. Gone were the old-fashioned wing collars, replaced by minimal V-necks. Also, each broad navy stripe was now accompanied by a fine pinstripe on either side. BSR opted to promote their kitchen appliance brand, Swan, on the new kits. The shorts dropped the Umbro diamond trim.

Worn in: Three great wins in the 82–83 season: 5–0 over Brighton, 3–1 vs ex-manager Ron Atkinson's Manchester Utd and 4–1 against Ipswich Town.
Worn by: Derek Statham, Peter Eastoe, John Wylie, Alan Webb.

A 1982–83, 1983–84

Design: UMBRO
Sponsor: SWAN

The familiar yellow and green was replaced during Umbro's kit overhaul by this trendy yellow and navy ensemble. Featuring the same basic V-neck and trim design as the home, the only embellishment was the double horizontal pinstripes across the shirt. Atkinson's departure in 1981 along with Bryan Robson and Remi Moses sent the side into decline and by 83–84 they had begun to hover close to the Division 1 relegation zone.

Worn in: An awful 6–1 defeat at Ipswich Town in 82–83. A 1–0 win over Chelsea in the 83–84 Milk Cup.
Worn by: Romeo Zondervan, Martin Jol.

Up until the 80s, TV regulations banned the use of sponsored shirts in televised games. The ban was not lifted until the 83–84 season, but even then restrictions on logo size still applied.

SWAN

Apollo 2000

Apollo 2000

H 1983–84 to 1985–86

Design: UMBRO
Sponsor: SWAN (83–84)
WEST MIDLANDS HEALTH AUTHORITY (84–86)

After just one season the West Brom home kit was slightly tweaked. The V-neck now sported a complex multi-striped design, the shorts included two narrow navy stripes and the Umbro diamond trim appeared on the socks. Football-wise It was a difficult time for the club as they finished in the bottom half of the table in all three seasons this kit was worn.

Worn in: A 4–1 win over Nottingham Forest (84–85) and a 3–1 victory over Birmingham in that season's Milk Cup third round replay.
Worn by: David Cross, Tony Grealish, Steve MacKenzie, Tony Morley.

A 1984–85, 1985–86

Design: UMBRO
Sponsor: WEST MIDLANDS HEALTH AUTHORITY

A smart new pinstriped yellow shirt appeared in 84–85. The West Midlands Regional Health Authority took over shirt sponsorship in 1984 and promoted a 'no smoking' campaign on the front of the jerseys. There's no smoke without fire and there was definitely little fire at The Hawthorns in the mid-80s with the club sadly relegated at the end of a dreadful 85–86 season – the worst in West Brom's history.

Worn in: A good 2–1 win over Luton Town and a thrilling 4–3 defeat to Southampton (both 84–85 season).
Worn by: Martyn Bennett, Garry Thompson.

H 1986–87 to 1988–89

Design: UMBRO
Sponsor: APOLLO

As the club prepared for life in the Second Division under manager Ron Saunders, a new range of kits was introduced. In an unfashionable move a collar was re-introduced to the shirt, which now featured broader stripes similar in width to those worn by the club in the mid-70s. White shorts were abandoned and replaced by a navy pair.

Worn in: Three good 86–87 home wins: 3–2 vs Birmingham, 3–0 against Leeds and 4–1 vs Stoke. Also a stunning 5–3 win over Crystal Palace at The Hawthorns in 88–89.
Worn by: Carlton Palmer, Darren Bradley, David Burrows.

A 1986–87, 1987–88

Design: UMBRO
Sponsor: APOLLO

It was time for a change on the away kit front and in an attempt to invigorate West Brom's performances away from home this bold all-red kit was introduced. The kit featured a multi-striped V-neck and navy piping along with a new design of club badge based around the Albion throstle that was introduced in 1986 and which replaced the script logo that the club had been sporting for over 10 years. Gas and electrical superstore chain Apollo became the club's new sponsor and in 88–89 updated their logo to the new 'Apollo 2000' brand.

Worn in: A superb 4–1 win at Birmingham in the 88–89 season.
Worn by: Paul Dyson, Kevin Steggles, George Reilly, Gary Robson.

A 1988–89

Design: UMBRO
Sponsor: APOLLO

Yellow and green made a welcome return to the West Brom wardrobe after a gap of six years. Now updated into a contemporary Umbro design, the shirt featured a neat button-up round neck and diagonal shadow stripes. The shadow patterned shorts featured an Umbro 'spear' trim on each leg. As with the home and away strips, the Apollo logo was updated in the 88–89 campaign. After the departure of Ron Saunders, Ron Atkinson returned to the club for a brief spell in the 87–88 season.

Worn in: A solid 3–0 win at Sunderland in the 86–87 season followed by an awful 4–1 drubbing at Crystal Palace the following year.
Worn by: Garth Crooks, Robert Hopkins.

H 1989–90, 1990–91

Design: SCORELINE
Sponsor: APOLLO (89–90)
          SANDWELL COUNCIL (90–91)

After 17 years Umbro departed The Hawthorns and Scoreline took over kit production duties. They retained the navy shorts and broad stripes of the previous shirt, but also introduced a button-up round neck. This strip accompanied some very bleak times for the club in the two seasons in which it was worn, culminating in a devastating relegation to the Third Division at the end of 90–91 under manager Bobby Gould.

Worn in: A humiliating 4–2 FA Cup defeat to non-league Woking and four 1–1 draws at the end of the season as The Baggies fought to avoid the drop (90–91).
Worn by: Chris Whyte, Bernard McNally.

A 1989–90, 1990–91

Design: SCORELINE
Sponsor: SANDWELL COUNCIL

Scoreline persevered with a yellow and green kit in a design that mirrored that of the home outfit. While Apollo 2000 continued their sponsorship of the home jersey, WBA's local council, Sandwell, featured their logo on the away shirt. Eventually, in the 90–91 season the Borough Council, complete with new logo design, took over sponsorship of both the home and away kits. The Scoreline West Brom kits saw the club badge included on the socks.

Worn in: An impressive 89–90 3–1 win over Leicester City. The 1–1 draw at Bristol Rovers in the last game of the 90–91 season that sadly finally relegated the club to Division 3.
Worn by: Colin Anderson, Steve Parkin, Brian Talbot, John Thomas.

H 1991–92

Design: INFLUENCE
Sponsor: SANDWELL COUNCIL

With Gould attempting to inspire a demoralised West Brom side to lift themselves out of Division 3, Influence Sportswear arrived at The Hawthorns as kit supplier. Theirs was a fine kit influenced by the white-sleeved West Brom kit of the 60s and early 70s. The shorts reverted to white (although a navy pair was also worn) and a good old-fashioned collar was reintroduced to the shirt.

Worn in: A fantastic 6–3 win over Exeter in the first home match of the season. Also impressive results over Preston (3–0), Bournemouth (4–0) and Brentford (2–0).
Worn by: Colin West, Don Goodman.

Football League sponsors over the years have included Canon, Today, Barclays, Endsleigh and Nationwide.

A 1991–92

Design: INFLUENCE
Sponsor: SANDWELL COUNCIL

Influence introduced this dazzling new red and yellow away kit that followed the design of the home. It was a good-looking outfit, much baggier in size than the rest of the club's outfits during the 80s, and quite unlike anything The Baggies had worn colour-wise up to that point. Although many people's favourites to go up from Division 3, West Brom could only manage seventh place at the end of the 91–92 season, a disappointment that eventually led to Bobby Gould's departure from the club.

Worn in: A great 3–0 win over local rivals Birmingham City, but also poor defeats to Bolton (3–0) and Preston (2–0).
Worn by: Daryl Burgess, Paul Raven.

H 1992–93

Design: THE ALBION COLLECTION
Sponsor: SANDWELL COUNCIL

Ex-Spurs legend Ossie Ardiles took over the managerial role at the beginning of 92–93, which saw West Brom sporting this curious new variation on the famous old navy and white stripes. Produced by the club themselves and branded 'The Albion Collection', the shirt featured outrageous wavy stripes of varying width that gave the odd impression of crumpled fabric.

Worn in: A great 4–0 win over Fulham and the 2–0 win over Swansea in the Division 2 play-off semi-final second leg that took the club through to the final.
Worn by: Kevin Donovan, Ian Hamilton.

A 1992–93

Design: THE ALBION COLLECTION
Sponsor: SANDWELL COUNCIL

The Albion Collection continued the red and yellow colour scheme, introduced by Influence the previous season, in this strip that again followed exactly the design of the home – wavy lines and all. Like the equivalent home (and third) jerseys, the collar included a neat 'WBA' monogram. The 92–93 season was the last to feature Sandwell Council as shirt sponsor. Under the guidance of Ardiles, West Brom climbed the table, eventually finishing in fourth place and into the play-offs

Worn in: Away wins at Huddersfield (1–0) and Chester (3–1). Also the 2–1 defeat to Swansea in the first leg of the play-off semi-final.
Worn by: Steve Lilwall, Bob Taylor (who finished top scorer for the club this season).

3 1992–93

Design: THE ALBION COLLECTION
Sponsor: SANDWELL COUNCIL

Albion also donned a version of their 'wavy-line' kit in the more familiar yellow and green colour combination in 92–93. It seemed to bring them luck as they eventually crawled their way out of Division 3 (now renamed 'Division 2' due to the advent of The Premier League) courtesy of a stunning performance at Wembley in the play-off final. It was the first time in 22 years that the club had played at the famous old stadium.

Worn in: A close 4–3 defeat at Stoke City, but also the marvellous 3–0 victory over Port Vale at Wembley in the Division 2 play-off final.
Worn by: Kevin Donovan, Gary Robson, Andy Hunt.

The 92–94 West Brom home shirt was similar to a design worn by Newcastle United a few seasons earlier – a design nicknamed 'The Barcode Shirt' by fans unhappy at the controversial design.

H 1993–94

Design: PELADA
Sponsor: COUCHER & SHAW

There were a few changes around The Hawthorns at the start of the 93–94 season. The club were now playing Division 1 football, Ardiles had left to manage Spurs, Coucher & Shaw replaced Sandwell Council as shirt sponsors and more unusually a new manufacturer's logo, Pelada, appeared on the Albion Collection club strip from the previous season. The actual design remained pretty much the same. Keith Burkenshaw took over as manager.

Worn in: A double victory over arch-rivals Wolves – a thrilling 3–2 win at The Hawthorns and a solid 2–1 at Molineux.
Worn by: Wayne Fereday, Simon Garner.

A 1993–94

Design: PELADA
Sponsor: COUCHER & SHAW

For the first time since 1989 West Brom took to the field away from home in a change kit that did not just simply replicate the striped design of the home. Pelada introduced a suave new outfit comprising very narrow yellow and green stripes. Unfortunately, the red Coucher & Shaw logo clashed violently with the colour schemes, making it difficult to decipher at a distance. The club found it hard to adjust to First Division football and battled relegation for much of the season.

Worn in: The 1–0 win at Fratton Park vs Portsmouth in the last match of the season that enabled The Baggies to escape relegation on goal difference.
Worn by: Ian Hamilton, Paul Mardon.

H 1994–95

Design: PELADA
Sponsor: GUESTS WEST BROMWICH

Pelada revamped the home shirt into this more sophisticated affair. The collar remained and more conventional stripes

(although slightly narrower than those sported in recent years) were reintroduced. Yellow was also added as an additional trim. Car dealers Guests became the new shirt sponsor and a new badge, the Sandwell coat of arms, was also included for the first time. Pelada also updated their logo.

Worn in: The extraordinary 5–2 defeat to Swindon – a match that West Brom had led 2–1 with only 16 minutes left.
Worn by: Craig Herbert, Mike Phelan.

A 1994–95

Design: PELADA
Sponsor: GUESTS WEST BROMWICH

The 94–95 away kit remained the same as before except for the arrival of Guests as sponsor (whose 'cut and paste' logo application at least gave their brand some clarity against the yellow and green stripes) and the new Pelada and club logos. Piping was added to the shirt and, as with the home kit, the more traditional throstle motif that The Baggies had favoured for almost ten years was now also included on the shirt collar and shorts. With the club struggling, Alan Buckley replaced Burkenshaw and the club managed to escape the drop.

Worn in: The 2–1 win at Portsmouth and a 2–0 victory at Reading – rare away wins this year.
Worn by: Tony Rees, Paul Agnew

Another team that included two versions of their club badge on the same shirt in the same season was Leeds Utd on their mid-90s Asics home kit.

H 1995–96

Design: PATRICK
Sponsor: GUESTS WEST BROMWICH

For the second time in recent seasons a new manufacturer's logo mysteriously appeared on a Baggies shirt that otherwise remained pretty much identical to the previous. This time, it was French sportswear company Patrick who took over the club's kit. Another tweak was the additional shield that now housed the coat of arms badge on the shirt. After a dreadful run of 11 defeats, the club rallied to finish well in the league.

Worn in: A superb 3–1 win over Southend Utd and an exciting 3–2 victory over Derby in the last match of the season.
Worn by: Peter Butler, Richard Sneekes.

A 1995–96, 1996–97

Design: PATRICK
Sponsor: GUESTS WEST BROMWICH

In their first season at The Hawthorns, Patrick launched this marvellous yellow and sky blue away kit. Far less harsh than many of the change outfits the side had worn over the past 20 years, with its contemporary collar and sky blue sleeves, it was an elegant and restrained design. The throstle badge still appeared on the long shorts and now also on the rather dashing hooped socks. 96–97 saw Buckley sacked to be replaced by Ray Harford

Worn in: Excellent away wins at Leicester and Luton in the 95–96 season (both 2–1). Plus a solid 3–2 victory at Birmingham City in the following campaign.
Worn by: Paul Edwards, Stacy Coldicott, David Gilbert, Phil King.

H 1996–97, 1997–98

Design: PATRICK
**Sponsor: GUESTS WEST BROMWICH (96–97)
WEST BROMWICH BUILDING SOCIETY (97–98)**

As retro fashions heavily influenced the Football League, West Brom took to the field in this brilliant new kit. Almost identical in style to the Newcastle United design of the time, it featured a very basic and workmanlike 'grandad' collar and narrow navy and white stripes. It was a great example of simple football kit fashion. This baggy Baggies shirt was also worn with the navy shorts from the away kit when necessary.

Worn in: The dismal 4–2 home defeat to Wolves, but also the stunning 5–1 victory over a high-flying Norwich City side (both 96–97).
Worn by: Lee Ashcroft, Paul Groves, Shawn Cunnington, Paul Peschisolido.

A 1997–98, 1998–99

Design: PATRICK
Sponsor: WEST BROMWICH BUILDING SOC.

Guests drove out of The Hawthorns at the end of 96–97 to be replaced by The West Bromwich Building Society as shirt sponsors. Patrick continued their range of classy kits with this rich and attractive red and navy ensemble. After briefly leading Division 1 at one point in 97–98, Harford mysteriously left the club and, after a dip in form, new manager Denis Smith took the side to an eventual tenth place. However, behind-the-scenes financial wranglings at the Albion were creating turmoil.

Worn in: Away defeats in the 97–98 season against Birmingham, Manchester City and Huddersfield (all 1–0).
Worn by: Kevin Kilbane (WBA's record signing at the time), Matt Carbon, Sean Flynn.

In its first season of use, the 98–00 home shirt was also worn with the navy shorts from the 97–99 away kit and a unique pair of navy shorts that mirrored the design of the white pair in the second year.

H 1998–99, 1999–2000

Design: PATRICK
Sponsor: WEST BROMWICH BUILDING SOC.

As West Brom attempted their next assault on Division 1, Patrick introduced another good home kit. White sleeves returned and were now adorned with 70s-style trim. New boss Brian Little replaced the sacked Smith in 1999 and then was eventually superseded by Gary Megson, who just managed to save the club from another relegation.

Worn in: An impressive 4–1 win over promotion-chasing Watford in 98–99. Also the glorious 2–0 win over champions Charlton in the last game of 99–00 that saved The Baggies from dropping down to Division 2.
Worn by: James Quinn, Jason Van Blerk.

3 1998–99

Design: PATRICK
Sponsor: WEST BROMWICH BUILDING SOC.

The Baggies' home kit and red away was causing some colour clash problems against teams playing in red and white stripes, so for the 98–99 season Patrick issued this seldom-worn all-navy third shirt. The design adopted most of the trappings of the equivalent home jersey with just a little additional red trim. The shirt was worn with the white shorts from the home kit, which interestingly featured the club badge and Patrick logo incorporated into the trim on the side of each leg.

Worn in: A dreadful 3–0 defeat vs Brentford at Griffin Park in the Worthington Cup.
Worn by: Lee Hughes, Micky Evans, Fabian De Freitas, Mario Bortolazzi.

A 1999–2000, 2000–01

Design: PATRICK
Sponsor: WEST BROMWICH BUILDING SOC.

Patrick introduced a new yellow away kit in 1999 that featured broad navy bands down each sleeve, a simple wrapover collar and navy chest panel on which the sponsors' logo sat. It was the first time since the Umbro away kit of 84–86 that the club had worn yellow and navy.

Worn in: An unfortunate 2–1 defeat at Blackburn Rovers in 99–00 and a Baggies win by the same score that season against Port Vale – the only league victory for the club in this strip that campaign. Also the poor 3–0 defeat to Bolton in the second leg of the 00–01 play-offs semi-final.
Worn by: Jordao, Jason Roberts, Phil Gilchrist.

H 2000–01, 2001–02

Design: PATRICK
Sponsor: WEST BROMWICH BUILDING SOC.

Megson's revolution began to take hold as the club, now wearing this navy-sleeved home strip, finished sixth in 00–01 before at last sealing promotion to the top flight for the first time since 1986. The shirt featured a baseball-style round neck and elegant red piping. The club badge reverted to a more traditional throstle and shield design and was accompanied by extra text marking 100 years at The Hawthorns.

Worn in: The disappointing 2–2 draw with Bolton in the 00–01 play-offs semi-final. Plus the joyous 2–0 win over Crystal Palace that clinched promotion at the expense of Wolves!
Worn by: Derek McInnes, Scott Dobie.

As many clubs in the league began to fully embrace modern technology and contemporary aesthetics within their kit design, it was a little unusual to see West Brom taking to the field in a large old-fashioned collar in 01–03.

A 2001–02, 2002–03

Design: THE BAGGIES
Sponsor: WEST BROMWICH BUILDING SOC.

The strange trend for switching kit suppliers mid-design occurred again in the club's promotion-winning 01–02 season. At home they wore the Patrick navy and white strip – away they wore a very baggy retro-looking outfit in traditional yellow and green that contained no mention of Patrick and was seemingly produced by a company named 'The Baggies'. Nevertheless, it was a good-looking outfit and graced the backs of the West Brom players in their first venture into the Premiership during the 02–03 season.

Worn in: The 2–1 win at Sunderland at the end of 02–03 that sadly was not enough to prevent WBA being relegated to Division 1.
Worn by: Darren Moore, Andy Johnson.

H 2002–03

Design: THE BAGGIES
Sponsor: WEST BROMWICH BUILDING SOC.

To mark the club's long-awaited return to top flight football a new home kit was launched that bore a startling resemblance to the 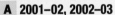 kit worn by Jeff Astle and the classic West Brom side of the late 60s and early 70s. Narrow stripes were combined with a wrap-over neck and white sleeves to form a nice outfit. Unfortunately, it accompanied an unfortunate Baggies side that found themselves struggling in The Premiership.

Worn in: 1–0 wins over Fulham, Southampton and Middlesbrough – rare highlights of an eventful season in the top flight.
Worn by: Danny Dichio, Jason Koumas.

H 2003–04

Design: DIADORA
Sponsor: WEST BROMWICH BUILDING SOC.

After just one season the club were back in Division 1 and Italian sportswear firm Diadora became the team's new kit supplier. Their first strip for The Baggies blended white sleeves and broad stripes together with large red panels under each arm and a trendy red minimal round neck design. The white shorts also included an unusual red and navy trim. Gary Megson led the side through a fantastic season, gaining promotion once again.

Worn in: A 2–0 win over Man Utd in the Carling Cup and the 2–0 win vs Bradford that meant West Brom were back in the Premiership.
Worn by: A re-signed Lee Hughes, Bernt Haas.

A 2003–04

Design: DIADORA
Sponsor: WEST BROMWICH BUILDING SOC.

Diadora retained the familiar yellow and green in this fine strip based loosely on the home design, including the slick round neck and broad stripes but with additional yellow panels on each sleeve. It was a kit that saw a lot of action in an exciting campaign for the club. 03–04 also marked the last year of sponsorship from long-term partners The West Bromwich Building Society.

Worn in: A good 1–0 win over Derby and an impressive 2–1 triumph over Newcastle Utd in the Carling Cup. Plus the vital 3–2 victory vs high-flying Ipswich at Portman Road towards the end of the season.
Worn by: Geoff Horsfield, Thomas Gardsoe, Sean Gregan, Paul Robinson, Mark Kinsella.

West Brom wore a white kit in one of the most memorable matches in their history – the 1968 FA Cup final vs Everton with Jeff Astle scoring the winning goal in extra time.

H 2004–05

Design: DIADORA
Sponsor: T-MOBILE

The Baggies celebrated their welcome return to Premiership action with a smart new set of kits from Diadora. The shirt continued the white sleeves from the previous few designs, although the navy stripes on the body of the shirt were now narrower. Blue panels were also introduced under each arm. This home kit will forever be remembered by West Brom fans for its part in the Great Escape of 04–05 when the club defied all the odds to avoid relegation.

Worn in: A fine 1–1 draw at Old Trafford earning The Baggies a precious point towards the end of the campaign and, of course, the crucial 2–0 win over Portsmouth on the last day of the season that saved the club from going down.
Worn by: Jonathan Greening, Robert Earnshaw.

A 2004–05

Design: DIADORA
Sponsor: T-MOBILE

For the first time since the 98–99 season West Brom took to the field in a red and navy away outfit. Slightly retro in feel, the kit featured the same collar and trim design of the home strip but also introduced centralised club badge and logos. The kit included navy blue shorts and socks that were easily interchangeable with the white equivalents from the home outfit. The mobile phone company T-Mobile became the new shirt sponsors.

Worn in: The 1–1 draw with Blackburn Rovers on the opening day of the season. Also an exciting 3–2 defeat at Fratton Park vs Portsmouth.
Worn by: Paul Robinson, Kieran Richardson, Zoltan Gera, Martin Albrechtsen.

3 2004–05, 2005–06

Design: DIADORA
Sponsor: T-MOBILE

To complete a fine array of outfits, Diadora also launched this classy third shirt. Worn with the white shorts and socks of the home strip, the shirt followed the simple design of the away – complete with two vertical navy lines. 04–05 proved an eventful season for The Baggies. Manager Gary Megson was sacked in October 2004 after announcing his intention to leave The Hawthorns at the end of the season and club legend Bryan Robson took over the side, who spent much of the campaign firmly rooted in the relegation zone.

Worn in: A 2–2 draw at fellow strugglers Southampton in the 04–05 season – the kit's only outing in the Premiership that year.
Worn by: Andy Johnson, Darren Purse, Kanu.

H 2005–06

Design: DIADORA
Sponsor: T-MOBILE

With the Baggies breathing a sigh of relief at their prolonged stay in the Premiership, Diadora have breathed new life into the famous navy and white stripes with a creation clearly influenced by the Umbro design worn during the late 70s playing career of the club's current manager Bryan Robson. With many clubs commemorating their centenaries at around this time, 2005 sees a plethora of anniversary kits that revive bygone colour schemes and fashions. With its large collar and broad stripes, the club's 05–06 home strip abandons futuristic style with a simple, elegant outfit that pays tribute to arguably the last great West Brom side.

A 2005–06

Design: DIADORA
Sponsor: T-MOBILE

Continuing the fine-looking outfits paraded the previous season by the Baggies, 05–06 also sees the team wear this dashing all-navy strip complete with a 70s-style red and white diagonal band. Quite unlike anything worn by the club before, it will give the club a highly distinctive look as they aim to stay in the top flight once again. With Crystal Palace relegated and Birmingham and Sunderland switching to Lonsdale, West Brom are the only Premiership side to wear a Diadora kit in the 05–06 campaign.

WEST HAM UNITED

Known throughout the English game for their stylish and attractive football, West Ham are also renowned for their smart kits. The majority of fans prefer to see the side in simple claret shirts with light blue sleeves, white shorts and white socks. Fortunately for the Hammers faithful, most kit suppliers are keen to uphold the preferred look, with many in recent years also opting to revive what is regarded as the classic West Ham away kit: a light blue shirt with two claret hoops.

The club were founded in 1900 and early kits saw the side sporting red, white and blue and an all-navy ensemble. However, it was not long before the famous claret and blue was selected as the club strip. Since then the kit has simply been revised with the fashions of the age, from round lace-up necks in the 20s, hefty button-up collars in the 30s and 40s (revived successfully by Pony in the mid-90s) to the classic crew neck of the 60s and 70s – possibly the club's most famous era.

One of the most distinctive kits worn by the club was donned in the mid-70s and produced by Admiral. The shirt remained claret but was now accompanied by a large light blue 'yoke' across the sleeves and chest. Together with the minimalist and stylish white away kit, it created a very attractive set of outfits. Recent years have seen several manufacturers such as Fila, Scoreline and adidas all experiment with various ways to match the claret and blue, but at one time or another they all seem to have reverted to the traditional blue sleeve design so beloved of the Upton Park crowd.

After the light blue away kit was ditched in the 70s, white became the preferred change colour choice in the 80s. However, when US-based company Pony arrived at the club in 1993, they were inspired by the nostalgic retro trend running through football at the time to recreate some of the more traditional designs the club have worn. Since then, navy blue has also made several appearances as the change colour, no doubt influenced by the side's earliest incarnation at the East London Thames Ironworks company – a kit that in turn was inspired by the company owner's old school colours.

Although recent years have seen the club lose its 'yo-yo' reputation, 03–04 found them out of the top flight for the first time in 10 years. But the club's team spirit, fervent support and inspirational colour scheme have helped the side achieve promotion back to the Premiership once again.

FRANK McAVENNIE IN THE ADIDAS HOME KIT OF 85–87

Early versions of the Avco Trust logo featured the company's full name, while later versions just included 'Avco'.

WEST HAM UNITED

H 1980–81 to 1982–83

Design: ADIDAS
Sponsor: NONE

Adidas had quite a tough act to follow when they took over the kit production for John Lyall's men in 1980. The previous Admiral outfits were highly regarded by Hammers fans, especially the white away kit worn in the 79–80 FA Cup win over Arsenal. Still, adidas managed to win over the doubters with a marvellous home and away kit. Very contemporary in feel, they upheld all the traditions of the club and merged them with a touch of continental flair.

Worn in: The unlucky 2–1 defeat to Liverpool in the 80–81 Milk Cup final replay. Also a 2–1 win over a high-flying West Brom in 82–83.
Worn by: David Cross, Paul Goddard, Tony Cottee (who scored on his debut in the 3–0 win vs Spurs in 82–83).

A 1980–81 to 1982–83

Design: ADIDAS
Sponsor: NONE

The club's first away kit of the decade was a piece of classic adidas design – clean and simple with a claret and blue three-stripe trim on the sleeves. The shorts and socks of both this and the home kit were interchangeable between the outfits. These great new adidas kits must have brought the club some luck as they stormed to the Division 2 top spot in 80–81 and gained promotion to the top flight.

Worn in: The 1–0 defeat to Liverpool in the 80–81 Charity Shield and the 1–1 draw with the Reds in the 80–81 League Cup final. Plus the bizarre European match vs Castilla that was played behind closed doors.
Worn by: Alan Devonshire, Ray Stewart.

H 1983–84, 1984–85

Design: ADIDAS
Sponsor: AVCO TRUST

Another good kit from adidas. The shirt still featured light blue sleeves, but now combined them with a broad light blue horizontal panel trimmed with white piping, upon which sat the logo of the club's first ever shirt sponsor – Avco Trust, a financial investment company. The shorts and socks from the previous home kit were retained for this kit – a turn of events that would not occur today!

Worn in: A cracking 4–0 win over Birmingham in the opening game of the 83–84 season, followed by the amazing 10–0 thrashing of Bury in the Milk Cup that season.
Worn by: Geoff Pike, Trevor Brooking (who made his last ever appearance for the club in this shirt vs Everton in the 83–84 season).

A 1983–84, 1984–85

Design: ADIDAS
Sponsor: AVCO TRUST

This was essentially the same away kit as before, now just slightly remodelled and restyled to include pinstripes – the essential fashion trend of the 80s. As with the home kit, a new club badge was included; it was a much simpler design than before, consisting of two crossed hammers and the club's initials. It was a badge design that was only to last for the lifespan of this kit and was not carried over on to further outfits. As with the home kit, the shorts and socks remained as before.

Worn in: The important 1–0 win over Ipswich in 84–85 that saved the club from relegation. Plus the exciting 4–2 defeat to Man Utd in the 84–85 FA Cup quarter-final.
Worn by: David Swindlehurst, Paul Allen.

'I suppose it'll be back to baggy shorts one day': prophetic West Ham captain Billy Bonds speaking in 1987 when shorts were at their tightest!

H 1985–86, 1986–87

Design: ADIDAS
Sponsor: AVCO TRUST

Depending on your point of view, this was either an example of a sleek and stylish 80s revamp of a club's heritage, or a travesty that dishonoured tradition. Either way, it was certainly a smart affair, with a striped V-neck and cuffs and fine light blue horizontal pinstripes, although there was some disapproval among the older Hammers fans. However, they couldn't complain about events on the pitch – in 85–86 the club finished third in Division 1, their highest ever place.

Worn by: A fine 2–1 win over Man Utd and an 8–1 triumph over Newcastle (both 85–86). Also, a great 3–2 result vs QPR with Tony Cottee scoring a hat-trick (86–87).
Worn by: Frank McAvennie, Alvin Martin.

A 1985–86, 1986–87

Design: ADIDAS
Sponsor: AVCO TRUST

After seven years as West Ham's kit suppliers, adidas ended their partnership with this away kit. It followed the same sophisticated design as the home, but of course in white with blue shorts and socks. The shirt included claret piping and trim. As with the home kit, the club's initials 'WHUFC' were included on the shorts (which seemed to be even skimpier than ever) and the adidas logo appeared on the socks for the first time.

Worn by: The 2–1 win at Ipswich at the end of the 85–86 season that helped the Hammers achieve third place in Division 1. Plus a sublime 4–0 win at Chelsea in 85–86.
Worn by: Mark Ward, Stewart Robson, Alan Dickens, Gary Strodder.

H 1987–88, 1988–89

Design: SCORELINE
Sponsor: AVCO TRUST

With the adidas deal at an end, smaller sportswear company Scoreline became the club's new kit supplier. It was a typically dependable kit from the company – simple, fresh and functional. The badge was placed centrally and the Scoreline logo was included on each sleeve. A large light blue panel ran down each side of the shirt and a smart shadow pinstripe ran through the shirt fabric. It was the last home kit worn under manager Lyall, who resigned at the end of the 88–89 season with the club relegated to Division 2.

Worn in: A 3–2 defeat of Forest in the 87–88 season and the 88–89 Littlewoods Cup semi-final defeat, 5–0 on aggregate to Luton.
Worn by: Leroy Rosenior, Liam Brady.

A 1987–88, 1988–89

Design: SCORELINE
Sponsor: AVCO TRUST

The Scoreline away kit replicated the design of the home with white replacing claret as the primary shirt colour, as had become the West Ham tradition. The shorts and socks of the two kits, like all Hammers outfits from the 80s, were designed to be worn with either the home or away shirt when required.

Worn in: A 3–0 defeat to fellow Londoners Charlton in 87–88. Also an important 1–0 win over Aston Villa at Villa Park (88–89), plus the sad 5–1 defeat to Liverpool at Anfield that same season that confirmed the club's relegation to Division 2.
Worn by: Tony Gale, Frank McAvennie (who returned to the club from Celtic), Eamonn Dolan.

West Ham have played in blue and white stripes before, in a match away at Burnley in 1925 when their normal away colours at the time (blue shirt with claret sleeves) still caused a clash problem with Burnley's jersey.

H 1989–90, 1990–91

Design: BUKTA
Sponsor: BAC WINDOWS

Bukta, who had in fact produced the Hammers strip in the mid-70s, arrived as kit supplier in 1989 and their designs were worn under short-lived manager Lou Macari as the side battled to escape Division 2. The shirt had quite a retro feel, combined with modern flair, and saw a return of the favourite blue sleeves, now trimmed with white piping. The 89–90 season saw an earlier Bukta logo included on the kit before it was updated in 90–91. BAC Windows replaced Avco Trust as sponsors after six years.

Worn in: A 5–0 thrashing of Sunderland in 89–90 plus the amazing 5–4 defeat to Blackburn later in the season. Plus the great 3–1 win over local rivals Millwall (90–91).
Worn by: Martin Allen, Jimmy Quinn.

A 1989–90, 1990–91

Design: BUKTA
Sponsor: BAC WINDOWS

The new white away shirt again mirrored the design of the home, with claret piping and a neat claret and blue button-up round neck. As with the home shirt, the fabric featured a small chequerboard shadow pattern comprising a crossed hammers logo. Unusually, claret shorts were worn instead of blue. After finishing seventh in Division 2 in 89–90 the club, under the managerial reign of Billy Bonds, achieved first place the following season and once more gained promotion to the top flight.

Worn in: The devastating 6–0 defeat to Oldham in the 89–90 Littlewoods Cup semi-final first leg. Also the dismal 4–0 defeat to Forest in the 90–91 FA Cup semi-final.
Worn by: Stuart Slater, Trevor Morley.

H 1991–92, 1992–93

Design: BUKTA
Sponsor: BAC WINDOWS (91–92)
DAGENHAM MOTORS (92–93)

Bukta's second home kit for the club was an intimidating design with white and light blue shoulder flashes, repeated on the sleeves and combined with light blue piping. The baggy-fitting shirt also saw the return of a button-down collar (complete with a neat 'WHUFC' motif) and the introduction of the club badge repeated in a shadow pattern. 91–92 found the club bottom of the table and back in Division 2 the following season.

Worn in: A good 1–0 win over high-flying Manchester Utd followed by a 3–0 triumph over Nottingham Forest in the 91–92 season. Plus a great 6–0 win vs Sunderland in 92–93.
Worn by: Julian Dicks, Ian Bishop.

A 1991–92, 1992–93

Design: BUKTA
Sponsor: BAC WINDOWS (91–92)
DAGENHAM MOTORS (92–93)

As the club struggled for survival in their first season back in Division 1, they wore this unorthodox new blue and white striped away kit. For the first time in over 15 years the club took to the field in an away kit that wasn't plain white. The restyled 'Argentina' look was popular with fans and replica versions sold well. With the club back in Division 2 in 92–93, local car dealers Dagenham Motors became the new shirt sponsors in a season that saw the club promoted to the Premier League.

Worn in: A 3–2 triumph vs Crystal Palace and a superb 1–0 win at Arsenal (both 91–92).
Worn by: Peter Butler, Tim Breacker.

Pony were taking the top flight by storm in the early 90s, supplying kits for Southampton, Coventry and Tottenham as well as West Ham.

3 1991–92

Design: BUKTA
Sponsor: BAC WINDOWS

In 91–92, an official Hammers third strip was launched for the first time. A new collar design was introduced, along with a bright pattern of diagonal claret and blue bars topped with an identical shadow pattern to that of the home and away kits. Blue piping ran from the collar to under the arms. Worn with the shorts and socks of the home outfit, it was a bold and brash design that exuded confidence – unlike the team, who were eventually relegated in 91–92 after finishing in last place in Division 1.

Worn in: An exciting 2–2 draw with Oldham in the 91–92 season.
Worn by: Steve Potts, George Parris, Mike Small.

H 1993–94, 1994–95

Design: PONY
Sponsor: DAGENHAM MOTORS

After four years Bukta were replaced by American sportswear company Pony. Football's rise in popularity post-Italia 90 had also seen a rebirth of retro fashions, which strongly influenced kits of this time. The first Pony home kit attempted to mirror the classic West Ham kit of the 60s and 70s with a striped crew neck, light blue sleeves and the Pony 'tick' trademark on the chest – recreating the famous light blue 'yoke'. It was an adventurous design that accompanied the club back in the top flight.

Worn in: The 3–0 win at Liverpool and the brilliant 2–0 triumph over top-of-the-table Blackburn (both 94–95).
Worn by: Matt Holmes, Michael Hughes.

A 1993–94, 1994–95

Design: PONY
Sponsor: DAGENHAM MOTORS

Pony's retro influence was plain for all to see with their first away kit for the club. It saw a return of the classic Hammers change strip for the first time in almost 20 years. The shirt was completed by a simple claret crew neck and cuffs to create a brilliant modern restyling of Hammers fans' favourite away jersey. Only the baggier fit of the strip, the Pony shadow pattern and sponsors' logos dated it to the early 90s. January 94 saw the arrival of Harry Redknapp as manager.

Worn in: The amazing 1–0 win at Highbury against Arsenal in the 94–95 season, courtesy of a Don Hutchison goal.
Worn by: David Burrows, Paulo Futre, Jeroen Boere.

3 1994–95, 1995–96

Design: PONY
Sponsor: DAGENHAM MOTORS

With the club consolidating their position in the top flight, a new third strip was launched. It was quite a development design-wise from any previous Hammers kits – white with claret sleeves and V-neck, trimmed with navy blue. The shirt featured an identical Pony shadow trim to the home and away. The logos were placed centrally on the shirt and a navy blue trim that included the Pony logo adorned the shorts. 94–95 saw the side finish 14th under Redknapp.

Worn in: A vital 2–0 win over Aston Villa at Villa Park in the 94–95 season.
Worn by: Mike Marsh, John Moncur, Kenny Brown, Don Hutchison.

The 95–96 match against Arsenal at Upton Park saw the Gunners sporting red, which along with their white sleeves and shorts clashed horribly with the Hammers' home kit.

H 1995–96, 1996–97

Design: PONY
Sponsor: DAGENHAM MOTORS

Pony delved further into the club's archives to produce their next home kit. If the last home outfit was influenced by the 70s, this new one, with its large old-fashioned collar, was inspired by the Hammers side of the 30s and 40s. To celebrate the club's centenary, a shadow pattern of bubbles and the number '100' was incorporated throughout the fabric of the shirt and shorts. Following the mid-90s trend, the club badge was now housed within an additional shield. Claret and blue hooped socks were worn rather than traditional white.

Worn in: A 2–1 win over Southampton with both goals by Dowie in 95–96. Also the 5–1 victory over Sheffield Wed the following year.
Worn by: Danny Williamson, Marc Rieper.

A 1995–96 3 1996–97

Design: PONY
Sponsor: DAGENHAM MOTORS

The next away kit took all the stylings of the home strip – baggier fit, shadow pattern and all – and converted it once again into the classic West Ham away style, albeit in a now slightly deeper shade of blue. As with the home kit, a small version of the hammers motif was added within the collar. The blue shorts were often worn with the home shirt. This new kit did not capture the imagination of the fans as much as the previous version, and it was replaced as first choice change strip after just one season.

Worn in: Many defeats in 95–96: 1–0 at Arsenal, 2–0 to Liverpool and 4–2 to Middlesbrough.
Worn by: Tony Cottee (in his second stint at the club), Slaven Bilic, Marco Boogers, Dani.

A 1996–97

Design: PONY
Sponsor: DAGENHAM MOTORS

The mid-90s saw a strange trend for ecru kits emerge throughout the football world. West Ham were no exception and introduced this new away kit in the curious colour. The shirt was topped with a navy and claret inset collar and navy side panels, which worked well with the amber of the one-off badge design. The move away from traditional bright colours at this time was due to clubs producing kits with replica shirts for fans in mind.

Worn in: A 3–1 defeat away at Chelsea and a 2–0 win over Nottingham Forest.
Worn by: Robbie Slater, John Hartson, Iain Dowie.

H 1997–98, 1998–99

Design: PONY
Sponsor: DR MARTENS

Retro influences were left firmly behind with the next home kit, which featured a new variation on the traditional colours. White was added as trim to the collar and cuffs and a fine shadow stripe was included. The socks were now claret, and a change pair of claret shorts was also worn. After five years, the club's deal with Dagenham Motors ended and for the majority of the season the shirt was without a sponsor, until footwear giants Dr Martens stepped in towards the end of 97–98.

Worn in: A good 2–1 home win over Liverpool and the nightmare 4–3 defeat by Wimbledon.
Worn by: Stan Lazaridis, Paul Kitson.

The first Fila home kit was premiered at the last game of the 98–99 season – a resounding 4–0 win over Middlesbrough.

A 1997–98   3 1998–99

Design: PONY
Sponsor: DR MARTENS

A radical revamp of the club's away kit occurred in 1997. The shirt remained light blue (including new shadow stripes) but was now trimmed with navy blue and just a hint of claret. Paired with the navy shorts and navy socks, it made a very distinctive outfit. As with the home kit, the majority of the 97–98 season saw the kit unsponsored – quite a rare occurrence for a Premiership club at the time.

Worn in: The great 2–1 away win at Barnsley in the first game of the 97–98 Premiership campaign. Also worn in the 5–0 drubbing received at the hands of Liverpool at Anfield.
Worn by: Rio Ferdinand, Andy Impey, Richard Hall, Marc Keller, Javier Margas.

A 1998–99

Design: PONY
Sponsor: DR MARTENS

This all-white outfit, which was worn for one season only, marked the end of the club's fruitful relationship with Pony. The shirt was really ahead of its time with its use of piping combined with underarm and side panels. The shirt also included a neat shadow pinstripe and a small crossed hammers motif below the inset V-neck design. Also worn, for some curious reason, with the standard white shorts. Although the club finished fifth in the Premiership this season, they did not win a single league game in this white kit.

Worn in: A 2–2 draw with Liverpool at Anfield (the club had not scored there in 10 years).
Worn by: Trevor Sinclair, Ian Wright, Eyal Berkovic, Neil Ruddock.

H 1999–2000, 2000–01

Design: FILA
Sponsor: DR MARTENS

With the deal with Pony completed, Italian company Fila became the club's new kit supplier in a four-year deal. Their first home kit

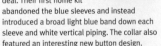

abandoned the blue sleeves and instead introduced a broad light blue band down each sleeve and white vertical piping. The collar also featured an interesting new button design.

Worn in: A 2–1 win over Wimbledon in 99–00, which included a superb Paolo Di Canio goal. Also the 1–1 draw with Everton the following year when the Italian stopped play after an injury to the Everton goalkeeper. Plus the 2–2 draw with Man Utd in 00–01.
Worn by: Frank Lampard, Frederic Kanoute.

A 1999–2000   3 2000–01

Design: FILA
Sponsor: DR MARTENS

Fila's first away kit was a really unusual design. The shirt was white with navy blue sleeves and sides and incorporated claret panels under each arm – all trimmed with elegant white piping. The collar featured a small inset neck that included a small version of the crossed hammers – a recurring theme in the club's kits. Like the home outfit, the shirt fabric featured Fila's F-Tec fabric, designed to manage perspiration effectively and keep players dry.

Worn in: The not fondly remembered 7–1 humiliation by Manchester United at Old Trafford and an exciting 2–2 draw with Aston Villa (both 99–00).
Worn by: Scott Minto, Marc-Vivien Foe, Paolo Di Canio.

Fila's new pinstripe shirt as worn by the Hammers in 02–03 was also produced in navy blue for the Scottish national side.

A 2000–01

Design: FILA
Sponsor: DR MARTENS

For the first time since their very early days, the club sported an all-navy blue outfit. The minimalist design featured white and light blue trim, with the only inclusion of claret being on the club badge. As with both the home and away kits, a graphic of the crossed hammers was included on the socks. Redknapp left the club at the end of the season, much to the dismay of the fans. After three seasons in the top 10, the club slumped to 15th place.

Worn in: The unforgettable 1–0 win over Manchester Utd at Old Trafford in the FA Cup fourth round, with Di Canio's cheeky winning goal. Also, the 2–1 defeat at Middlesbrough – the first game after Redknapp's departure.
Worn by: Nigel Winterburn, Svetoslav Todorov.

H 2001–02, 2002–03

Design: FILA
Sponsor: DR MARTENS

Glenn Roeder's first full season in charge at Upton Park saw the introduction of two new kits that brought a back-to-basics approach to the club's on-the-field fashion. The new home kit saw the appearance of a wrap-over neck and the return of traditional blue sleeves. A small Fila logo was included on the left sleeve to indicate the shirt's light and breathable F-Tec fabric. The previous home kit's change white socks were the new first choice.

Worn in: Three consecutive home wins early on in the 01–02 season, against Newcastle (3–0), Southampton (2–0) and Chelsea (2–1). Also a 5–1 thrashing at Chelsea that season.
Worn by: Joe Cole, Michael Carrick, Ian Pearce (who scored a great goal to beat Spurs).

A 2001–02 3 2002–03

Design: FILA
Sponsor: DR MARTENS

Fila revived the classic West Ham away kit – blue shirts with two horizontal claret stripes – for the 01–02 season, much to the delight of the fans. As usual, the minimally trimmed blue shorts were also occasionally worn with the home shirt where necessary. 01–02 was a fine season for the club, who eventually finished seventh in the Premiership.

Worn in: A thrilling 4–4 draw with Charlton at the Valley and the dismal 2–0 defeat at Middlesbrough that saw Thomas Repka sent off on his debut.
Worn by: Steve Lomas, Don Hutchison, Jermaine Defoe.

A 2002–03

Design: FILA
Sponsor: DR MARTENS

The early 00s saw the return of some elements from 80s football fashions, and this pinstriped Hammers shirt was a perfect example. It was the last kit to be produced for the club by Fila, who decided to pull out of football kit design at this time despite having produced some brilliant and highly individual outfits. Unfortunately for the club, they were relegated at the end of the season after ten eventful years in the top division.

Worn in: The battling 2–2 draw with Birmingham – just not good enough to keep the club in the Premiership – and the 4–2 defeat to Charlton at The Valley.
Worn by: Thomas Repka, Christian Dailly, Sebastien Schemmel.

Asymmetrical designs became all the rage in the early 2000s. Apart from the West Ham home kit in 2005, Reebok also introduced similarly 'unbalanced-looking' outfits for Bolton and Manchester City.

H 2003–04, 2004–05

Design: REEBOK
Sponsor: JOBSERVE.COM

Reebok arrived at Upton Park as the new kit supplier in 03–04 and their first home design was a very hi-tech affair including Reebok's Play Dry fabric, designed to keep players drier and more comfortable. Instead of being all blue, the sleeves featured sleek triangular blue panels. Recruitment agency Jobserve.com replaced Dr Martens as club sponsor.

Worn in: The amazing 2–0 win over Ipswich in the 03–04 play-off semi-final 2nd leg that overcame the 1–0 deficit from the first leg and booked the Hammers' place in the final. Also a 1–0 win over Norwich in the 04–05 FA Cup.
Worn by: Teddy Sheringham, Sergei Rebrov.

A 2003–04

Design: REEBOK
Sponsor: JOBSERVE.COM

Obviously keen to make an impact with the club in Division 1, Reebok ditched tradition to create an innovative and intimidating all-navy blue away kit. Unlike the previous navy design, the Play Dry fabric was trimmed with amber and included reversed seams and a minimal contemporary neck. It was worn as West Ham battled in vain to return to the Premiership under new manager Alan Pardew, who arrived at the club in March 2004.

Worn in: A solid 2–0 win at Nottingham Forest at The City Ground and a 2–1 triumph over Bradford (both 03–04).
Worn by: Brian Deane, Jobi McAnuff, Matthew Etherington.

A 2004–05   3 2005–06

Design: REEBOK
Sponsor: JOBSERVE.COM

The old favourite West Ham shirt returned in 04–05, although now dramatically updated with Reebok's latest house style. The jersey included breathable claret fabric panels on the shoulders and under the arms and, instead of the traditional two claret hoops, a modern design was preferred. Dynamic claret panels adorned the shorts and a complex claret trim was included on the sock turnovers.

Worn in: Vital away wins at Crewe (3–2) and Sheffield United (2–1) and an unlucky 2–1 defeat to lowly Nottingham Forest.
Worn by: Marlon Harewood, Malky Mackay, Carl Fletcher, Nigel Reo-Coker.

H 2005–06

Design: REEBOK
Sponsor: JOBSERVE.COM

The Hammers' home kit for 05–06 was premiered in the 04–05 season play-offs and was proudly worn as the club overcame Ipswich and then Preston North End to reclaim their place in the Premiership. Alan Pardew's men face the cream of English football in this extraordinary Reebok outfit. At first glance the asymmetric sleeves and trim look unusual, but the design has been cunningly crafted to accentuate body size and performance, creating a very contemporary and challenging outfit.

A 2005–06

Design: REEBOK
Sponsor: JOBSERVE.COM

In a colour scheme reminiscent of the Fila
away kit of 99–00, Reebok have introduced
this navy and white affair for West Ham's
return to the Premiership. Neat navy underarm
sleeve panels are combined with intricate
stitching, a typical Reebok neck and claret
panels running along the seam. With more
challenging kit designs appearing in 05–06,
Reebok have tended to stick with more sedate
and symmetrical away designs.

WIGAN ATHLETIC

Wigan's recent success, culminating in their promotion to the Premiership at the end of the 04–05 season, is proof of the power and importance of commercial factors in the modern football world. Owner Dave Whelan, the man behind JJB Sports, has rejuvenated the club, who currently proudly display his company's name on their shirts, play their home games in the wonderful JJB stadium and now, for the 05–06 season, also have their kits produced by his company.

The club have only actually been members of the Football League since 1978. Since then their character and spirit have taken them from near-bankruptcy, through several play-offs and finally now to the top flight.

Along the way the players have worn a vast array of exiting and colourful kits – always featuring a healthy dose of blue. For a short while in the late 80s the side dabbled with some dynamic white shirts – possibly to cope with the logo of then sponsors, Heinz. In fact, the only time the side have not worn blue in some form or other was at the club's foundation in 1932 after the demise of Wigan Borough. Way back then, the side took to the field in the rugby-dominated town wearing red and white halved jerseys paired with black shorts. After the end of World War II, the side switched to blue shirts, as apparently the local sportswear supplier had only that colour in stock. Blue has remained ever since at the club.

Once they had joined the league, the club donned a blue and white striped shirt – a style making a comeback as the Latics prepare for life in the Premiership in 05–06. Since that time pinstripes, shadow stripes, black and blue stripes and even a blue and white diagonal design have all made appearances, with different degrees of success, at Springfield Park and later the JJB Stadium.

Wigan have also enjoyed a wide palette of away colours. Yellow makes many reappearances in their wardrobe, but red, white, maroon and even green have been worn away from home over the last 25 years.

The club have been supported over the years by major local companies via shirt sponsorship. Food giants Heinz were the first to enter into a long-term deal with the club in 1984, but it is JJB Sports who have become associated with the side and it is JJB who will be firmly behind the Latics as they play in the top English division for the first time.

WITH THANKS TO BERNARD RAMSDALE & ANDY WERRILL

COLIN GREENALL IN THE PUMA PRODUCED KIT THAT LASTED FOR THREE SEASONS FROM 95–98.

The 1978–82 striped Umbro home kit went through some subtle changes during the four years it was in use. In 1980 the Umbro logo switched from white to red, and in 1981 the stripes became a little wider.

H 1978–79 to 1981–82

Design: UMBRO
Sponsor: BALDWIN TIMBERLAKE (81–82)

It is no coincidence that the most fondly remembered kits often accompany a momentous period in a club's history. This was definitely the case with the blue and white striped Umbro kit Wigan adopted in the 78–79 season as they at last achieved Football League status under manager Ian McNeill. It was a simple and classic design complete with blue collar and diamond trimmed shorts. Motor company Baldwin Timberlake became the side's first shirt sponsor in October 1981.

Worn in: The club's first ever league game vs Hereford (a 0–0 draw) in August 1978. Also the 3–1 win over Mansfield that sealed promotion for the club in 81–82.
Worn by: Eamon O'Keefe, Mickey Quinn.

A 1978–79, 1979–80
3 1980–81, 1981–82

Design: UMBRO
Sponsor: BALDWIN TIMBERLAKE (81–82)

The club's first league change strip was this yellow and green ensemble in a standard Umbro design, virtually identical to that also worn by both Newcastle Utd and Chelsea at roughly the same time. The famous Umbro diamond trim was also included on the shirt as well as on the shorts. Although replaced in 1980, the kit made several appearances as a third kit in the following two years.

Worn in: Good 2–1 away wins over Halifax in the 78–79 season and Peterborough the following year.
Worn by: Peter Houghton, Maurice Whittle, Tony Quinn, Frank Corrigan, Derek Brownbill.

3 1979–80
A 1980–81, 1981–82

Design: UMBRO
Sponsor: BALDWIN TIMBERLAKE (81–82)

This vibrant all-red kit was actually worn as a third kit in 79–80 during the Latics' impressive FA Cup run before being promoted to their regular away choice the following year. 81–82 also saw the shirt sometimes worn with the blue shorts from the home kit. The Umbro era coincided with a great period for the club, who were promoted to Division 3 at the end of the 81–82 season.

Worn in: Two important FA cup ties in 79–80: the stunning 1–0 win over Chelsea at Stamford Bridge in the third round followed by a 3–0 defeat to Everton in the fourth.
Worn by: Les Bradd, David Glenn, Neil Davids.

H 1982–83

Design: JSW
Sponsor: BULLDOG TOOLS

With the club now proudly playing in the third division, their kit was brought bang up to date with this trendy all-blue outfit by small sportswear company JSW. Fashionable white pinstripes adorned the fabric and a white V-neck replaced the old collar. A simple white stripe down each sleeve and the shorts completed the design. Bulldog Tools replaced Baldwin as shirt sponsor.

Worn in: Some fine home wins in an otherwise disappointing season: 4–0 over Southend Utd, 3–0 against Plymouth and 3–2 vs Sheffield Utd. Also the awful 2–1 defeat away to non-league Telford in the FA Cup 1st round.
Worn by: David Lowe, Steve Walsh, Archie Gemmill, John Butler.

The Wigan groundsman in the early 80s, Bill Mitchell, appeared frequently in matchday programme advertisements endorsing Bulldog Tools, the club's sponsors during the 82–83 season.

A 1982–83

Design: JSW
Sponsor: BULLDOG TOOLS

As the club struggled both on and off the pitch, they returned to yellow and green for their away colours and took to the field in this smart pinstripe kit clearly inspired by the Norwich City strip of the time. Player-manager Larry Lloyd, who had guided the side to promotion the previous season, was sacked in April 1983 and the club eventually finished the season in 18th place – just above the relegation zone.

Worn in: A rare away win this season: a 2–0 victory over Gillingham. Also an unfortunate defeat by the same score to Manchester City in the Milk Cup after drawing 1–1 with the First Division side at home.

Worn by: Kevin Sheldon, John McMahon, Jimmy Weston, Graham Barrow.

H 1983–84, 1984–85

Design: HOBOTT
Sponsor: HEINZ (84–85)

Hobott produced many kits for clubs in the lower divisions during the early 80s, including this all-blue affair for Wigan. Hobott's kits were known for their combination of vertical pinstripes (or shadow stripes as included on the Latics shirt) and dual piping running from the neck to the seam. This strip was worn unsponsored throughout 83–84, but also curiously made several appearances the following year when it appeared with the red logo of food giants Heinz, who had become the club's new sponsor in September 1984.

Worn in: A thrilling 3–2 triumph over a high-flying Wimbledon at Springfield Park and a good 3–0 win over Port Vale (both 83–84).

Worn by: Steve Johnson, Neil Bailey, Tony Kelly.

A 1983–84

Design: HOBOTT
Sponsor: NONE

The Latics – now under the guidance of manager Harry McNally, who had replaced Larry Lloyd in the summer of 1983 – sported one of the most unusual and colourful combinations of the time this season: a vibrant orange/amber and red ensemble. Featuring shadow stripes, red sleeves and a finely trimmed V-neck, the design only lasted one season and was treated with disdain by the fans, who were no doubt pleased when it did not feature in the Hobott comeback of 84–85.

Worn in: A superb 3–2 televised win away at Preston North End. Also defeats at Millwall (2–0) and Southend (1–0).

Worn by: Paul Comstive, Alex Bruce, Mike Newell, Kevin Langley.

H 1984–85

Design: UNKNOWN
Sponsor: HEINZ

Although the Wigan outfit now contained more blue than ever, the side entered a bit of a grey area with their kit supply. The club's new sponsorship deal with locally-based Heinz meant that, despite starting the 84–85 season in the previous year's Hobott kit, this rather basic blue design, complete with the Heinz logo, was introduced in September 1984. Then, towards the end of the season, the Hobott kit returned – now also complete with red Heinz logo! The Latics held their own in Division 3, eventually finishing the season in 16th place.

Worn in: A 4–2 thrashing of Orient and a fine 1–0 win over Bolton. Also the 3–1 win over Wrexham in the Freight Rover 1st round.

Worn by: Jimmy Mitchell, Paul Jewell.

Two variations exist of the 85–86 New Balance home shirt: one as illustrated below, and another that positioned the white band (which now also contained a curious '2000' logo) much higher on the chest.

A 1984–85, 1985–86

Design: UNKNOWN
Sponsor: HEINZ

Pinstripes returned to the Wigan wardrobe with this simple (and very tight-fitting!) white and black kit. Like the all-blue home outfit, no manufacturer's logo was present, although it was probably produced by American company New Balance, who supplied the club's kit the following season. The strip is probably best remembered for the heroics it inspired in the 84–85 FA Cup 3rd round match at Stamford Bridge, but it was also worn during the club's great unbeaten run the following year.

Worn in: The thrilling penalty shoot-out Northern Area final win over Mansfield in the 84–85 Freight Rover Trophy. Plus of course the fine 2–2 draw at Chelsea in that year's FA Cup.
Worn by: Colin Methven, Gary Bennett.

H 1985–86

Design: NEW BALANCE
Sponsor: HEINZ

Although the lack of club badge on all Wigan shirts this season met with the disapproval of fans, this kit is most famous for its appearance in the Freight Rover Trophy win over Brentford in June 1985. The outfit was produced by New Balance in one of the company's few ventures into English football apparel. The all-blue theme was continued, complete with shadow stripes, the only differences being the large white chest band that housed the Heinz logo and the addition of white V-neck and cuffs.

Worn in: The 3–1 Freight Rover Wembley win over Brentford. Also worn as a full-of-beans Latics side smashed five goals past Swansea, Darlington and Wolves in 85–86.
Worn by: Barry Knowles, Wayne Aspinall.

3 1984–85, 1985–86

Design: UNKNOWN
Sponsor: HEINZ

The last strip of this mysterious era in the club's kit history was this third choice all-green ensemble – a forerunner of the 86–87 away colour scheme. As with the other two kits worn in these seasons, the shorts and socks were pretty basic with no logos or trim of any description. Despite further financial troubles the club, now managed by Bryan Hamilton, who had taken over in March 1985, finished 4th in 85–86 – missing promotion to the second division by just one point.

Worn in: A 3–1 defeat at West Brom in the 84–85 Milk Cup plus a 1–0 defeat at Reading the following year.
Worn by: John Butler, Alex Cribley.

H 1986–87

Design: ERIMA
Sponsor: HEINZ

After the great 85–86 season there was a new sense of optimism at Springfield Park at the start of the following campaign. The club had a new manager in Ray Mathias, who replaced Bryan Hamilton, and a radical new kit design. Gone was the traditional blue, replaced by this modern-looking white shirt made by little-known company Erima. The shirt was completed with unusual blue bands across each shoulder and the return of the club badge – restoring the Latics' identity at last!

Worn in: The club's great FA Cup run this season, including the great 1–0 win over Norwich City in the 4th round. Plus the sad 3–2 defeat to Swindon in the play-offs.
Worn by: Paul Beesley, Mark Hilditch.

Local company Ellgren also produced apparel for Wigan's Rugby League side in the late 80s.

A 1986–87

Design: ERIMA
Sponsor: HEINZ

Away from home the Latics sported this all-green strip in a design that mirrored that of the home, complete with non-contrasting round neck, shoulder panels and chevron shadow pattern. The Erima shorts this season were in a very skimpy and lightweight athletic style. The shoulder panels obviously caused some problems for the designers on both this and the home kit, hence the unusually low positioning of the club badge. 86–87 saw another good season for the club, who finished 4th again and qualified for the inaugural play-offs this year.

Worn in: Solid wins this season over Port Vale (1–0) and Bolton (2–1).
Worn by: Chris Thompson, Andy Holden.

H 1987–88

Design: ELLGREN
Sponsor: HEINZ

Ellgren took over Wigan's kit production in 1987. Their first strip was only a slight move on from the previous design; the subtle changes included an extra blue stripe on each shoulder panel and the replacing of the crew-neck with a slick V-neck. The shorts were also updated to include a broad white stripe on each leg, and a white turnover appeared on the socks. Early versions of the shirt included extra trim on the cuffs and an embroidered 'Wigan Athletic' script instead of the badge.

Worn in: A good run of home wins from December through to March, including 3–1 over Walsall and a 4–0 thrashing of Aldershot.
Worn by: Bobby Campbell, Paul Cook, Alan Kennedy, Steve Senior.

A 1987–88, 1988–89

Design: ELLGREN
Sponsor: HEINZ

Yellow returned to the Latics' colour palette courtesy of Ellgren. An interesting kit, it saw a V-neck combined with red flashes to each sleeve completed with a subtle shadow pattern. Despite leading Division 3 at one point, the side eventually ended the 87–88 season in 7th place. The following season saw Mathias sacked and replaced by a returning Bryan Hamilton, who managed to save the club from relegation to Division 4.

Worn in: A thrilling 4–4 draw with Notts County on the opening day of the 87–88 season followed later by a 3–2 win over Bristol Rovers.
Worn by: Stuart Storer, David Hamilton.

H 1988–89

Design: ELLGREN
Sponsor: HEINZ

Like the shirt itself, Ellgren's second home kit divided the opinion of the Springfield faithful. With the club facing a relegation battle in the season ahead, this blue jersey with white diagonal chest panel was introduced. The shirt was tight-fitting and trimmed with delicate red piping. The red Heinz logo was obviously causing some legibility problems when positioned on a blue shirt (perhaps the reason for the side's recent preference for white home jerseys?) and was pushed up onto the cramped chest panel.

Worn in: A 3–0 win over Reading in the second home game of the season plus a fine 1–0 defeat of Cardiff City later in the season.
Worn by: Craig Ramage, Don Page.

A primary reason for the introduction of shadow-patterned materials, which grew ever more complex in the late 80s/early 90s, was to discourage the growing trend for counterfeit replica shirts.

H 1989–90, 1990–91

Design: ELLGREN
Sponsor: HEINZ

After several years of experimental home kits and with a more traditional style now sweeping over football fashion, Wigan took to the field in this debonair blue shirt complete with old-fashioned button-up collar and a subtle shadow pattern. Other changes included a new coat-of-arms-style badge in place of the familiar 'tree and crown' design and a new white Heinz logo giving it good stand-out on the blue fabric. Also worn with black shorts.

Worn in: The two defeats to mighty Liverpool in the 89–90 Littlewoods Cup: 5–2 and 3–0. Plus a cracking 4–1 win over Exeter (90–91).
Worn by: Ray Woods, Darren Patterson.

A 1989–90, 1990–91

Design: ELLGREN
Sponsor: HEINZ

Ellgren continued with a yellow and red change strip and simply updated it with the same collar and shadow fabric design of the home. Like the previous away kit, this was also worn with red shorts. After a dismal 89–90 season, the following year saw a vast improvement and the side finished the season in 10th place.

Worn in: A dire 6–1 defeat at Bristol Rovers in the 89–90 season. Also the battling 1–1 draw with First Division Coventry City in the 90–91 FA Cup 3rd round thanks to a last-minute Patterson goal. Sadly, the Latics lost 1–0 in the replay at Springfield Park.
Worn by: Alan Johnson, Peter Atherton.

H 1991–92, 1992–93

Design: MATCHWINNER
Sponsor: HEINZ

After four eventful years Ellgren departed Springfield Park and were replaced by football kit stalwarts Matchwinner. They introduced another simple and restrained all-blue outfit. The large collar remained and was now trimmed with red. The shorts included a standard Matchwinner asymmetrical trim design in the top corner. The fabric on all three kits this season included a swirling shadow pattern. The Heinz logo was updated to the design more commonly seen on their products.

Worn in: A 2–2 draw with Ipswich in the 92–93 Coca-Cola Cup. Plus the 2–0 home defeat to Plymouth that condemned the Latics to Division 3 (the old Division 4) in 92–93.
Worn by: Phil Daley, Gary Worthington.

A 1991–92, 1992–93

Design: MATCHWINNER
Sponsor: HEINZ

For the first time since the Umbro kit of the early 80s, the Latics turned out in a red change strip away from home. The design mirrored that of the home kit with, of course, a blue and white trim throughout. The coat-of-arms club crest remained. Although the Matchwinner kits were undoubtedly a good-looking set of outfits, they unfortunately coincided with Wigan's first ever relegation at the end of the 92–93 season and are therefore forever scarred in Latics fans' memories.

Worn in: The thrilling 3–3 draw at Birmingham City in 91–92. Also the 5–1 thrashing by West Brom at The Hawthorns in 92–93 that virtually sealed Wigan's fate that season.
Worn by: Gary Powell, Steve Cooper.

Other teams that sported the dazzling multi-coloured Matchwinner away design as worn by Wigan in 93–94 include Preston and Oxford.

3 1991–92, 1992–93

Design: MATCHWINNER
Sponsor: HEINZ

The club also sported this elegant all-white third kit in the early 90s. The design was simply that of the home and away, trimmed naturally with red and blue, and featuring the same shadow pattern that was included on the other strips. The shorts and socks from this outfit were interchangeable with those of the home where necessary. The side's poor performances in the 92–93 season inevitably led to the sad departure of manager Bryan Hamilton, who was replaced by Dave Philpotts.

Worn in: A good 1–0 win away at Burnley in the 92–93 season – a rare highlight in a poor campaign.
Worn by: Chris Makin, Dean Connelly, Chris Sharratt, Allen Tankard.

H 1993–94

Design: MATCHWINNER
Sponsor: HEINZ

Matchwinner, armed with a new logo, reinvented the Wigan home kit in 93–94 with dramatic results. After blue jerseys, white jerseys and blue and white jerseys, Inter Milan-inspired blue and black stripes were introduced at Springfield. Featuring a new style of button-up collar, diagonal shadow stripes and black shorts trimmed with white and blue, the powerful new strip once again divided the Wigan fans.

Worn in: A 6–3 goal-fest at home to Chester, plus a good 4–1 win over Mansfield and a 2–0 triumph over Gillingham in the last home game of the season.
Worn by: Peter Skipper, Greg Strong, Neil Morton, Dave McKearney.

A 1993–94

Design: MATCHWINNER
Sponsor: HEINZ

With the club preparing for a long season ahead in the basement of the Football League, the Springfield faithful felt that things couldn't get any worse. However, the introduction of this vibrant red, black and white away kit might just have changed their minds! One of the more unusual trends of the early 90s was the penchant for lurid away kits – the more outrageous the better. It has to be said that the club's fans were not happy with this daring and controversial outfit, which accompanied the side to their lowest ever league position of 19th in Division 3.

Worn in: Away defeats to Colchester (3–1), Chesterfield (1–0) and Carlisle (3–0).
Worn by: Andy Lyons, John Doolan.

H 1994–95

Design: MATCHWINNER
Sponsor: JJB SPORTS

Matchwinner's new home kit updated the blue and black striped affair from the previous season. The blue was now much lighter and the stripes a little wider. After ten years at Springfield Park as Wigan shirt sponsor, Heinz departed at the end of the 93–94 season and were replaced by JJB Sports, the successful sports chainstore launched by new Latics owner Dave Whelan. It was the start of a long and inspirational association with the club.

Worn in: Some good wins this season: 4–1 vs Darlington, 4–0 against Rochdale and 3–1 vs Exeter City, which helped earn the club a final position of 14th place.
Worn by: David Miller, Mark Leonard, Neill Rimmer, Matthew Carragher.

The club's biggest ever league win (a 7–1 home humbling of Scarborough in the wonderful 96–97 season) was achieved while wearing the strong Puma blue, white and green strip.

A 1994–95

Design: MATCHWINNER
Sponsor: JJB SPORTS

In the last season of their four-year deal with Wigan, Matchwinner introduced this stunning and adventurous new away kit. In a previously untried maroon and amber colour combination the shirt, with its minimal collar, thin shadow stripes and innovative shoulder flashes, was a really classy and restrained ensemble. Ex-player Graham Barrow arrived as manager in September 1994, replacing Kenny Swain.

Worn in: An unfortunate 2–1 defeat at Carlisle in the opening game of the season, followed by good 1–0 wins over Colchester and Gillingham.
Worn by: Jonathan Whitney, Ian Benjamin, Joe Jakub, Ian Kilford.

H 1995–96 to 1997–98

Design: PUMA
Sponsor: JJB SPORTS

With Dave Whelan's exciting Latics revolution gathering pace, sportswear giants Puma arrived in 1995 to supply the club kit. Their popular home shirt was one of the most distinctive jerseys worn by the club. It went back to the Ellgren era of white and blue shirts, but now added green to the palette, creating a brand-new colour scheme for the club.

Worn in: The 1–0 victory vs Colchester that confirmed Wigan's promotion, and the glorious 2–0 win over Mansfield that clinched the Third Division title for the club (96–97).
Worn by: The Three Amigos – Roberto Martinez, Jesus Seba, Isidro Diaz.

A 1995–96 to 1997–98

Design: PUMA
Sponsor: JJB SPORTS

The three-year Puma era was a momentous time for the club under the leadership of John Deehan, who led the club triumphantly up to Division 2. The German company's away strip was another strong outfit: all yellow, trimmed with blue and featuring a neat collar and thin vertical stripes. Another change saw the old 'tree and crown' badge reinstated. 97–98 was an anti-climax for the club, although they did eventually finish in a creditable 11th place.

Worn in: The solid 2–0 victory over Carlisle in 96–97. Also a 3–2 win over Chesterfield and the thrilling 4–2 defeat at Blackburn Rovers in the FA Cup third round (both 97–98).
Worn by: John Pender, Chris Lightfoot, Andy Farrell and the late Michael Millett.

H 1998–99, 1999–2000

Design: ADIDAS
Sponsor: JJB SPORTS

Puma's arch-rivals adidas took over the Wigan kit production in the eventful 98–99 season. It was a return to a more traditional blue shirt with the white panels reduced to under the arms and down each side. Green remained as a third colour, giving a vital lift to the overall appearance of the kit. It was worn in two brilliant seasons for the club, who reached the play-offs in both seasons the design was worn.

Worn in: The unbelievable last-ever league game at Springfield (98–99): the 3–1 win over Chesterfield that also confirmed the Latics' place in the Division 2 play-offs that year. Plus the vital 1–0 win over Millwall in the Division 2 play-off semi-final the following season.
Worn by: Colin Greenall, Stuart Barlow.

Although Wigan's home kit of 98–00 was worn in the side's first league game at the splendid new JJB Stadium (a 3–0 win over Scunthorpe), the side mysteriously wore their amber change kit for the official opening, the friendly vs Manchester Utd.

A 1998–99

Design: ADIDAS
Sponsor: JJB SPORTS

Adidas' first away kit for the club was a clean and fresh reversal of the home outfit – now in white and trimmed with green and blue – which allowed the shorts and socks to be worn with the home kit if necessary and vice versa. The adidas era also saw the coat of arms return once again to replace the 'tree and crown' design. As with the home kit, all badges and logos were placed centrally on the shirt and the club's initials were included on the socks for the first time.

Worn in: The second leg of the 98–99 play-off semi-final against Manchester City that ended in a desperately unlucky 1–0 defeat for Wigan.
Worn by: Graeme Jones, Kevin Sharp, Pat McGibbon, Scott Green, Carl Bradshaw.

A 1999–2000   3 2000–01

Design: ADIDAS
Sponsor: JJB SPORTS

This invigorating and popular amber and navy number was actually premiered in April 1999 in the Auto Windscreens Shield final

against Millwall – the season before it became the club's official away kit. A typically stylish adidas outfit, it included a pinstriped fabric, a simple collar and a more traditional rendering of the famous adidas three-stripe trademark.

Worn in: The wonderful 1–0 win over Millwall in the 98–99 Auto Windscreens final at Wembley courtesy of a last-minute Rogers goal. Also worn in the sad 2–1 defeat to Reading in the 00–01 play-off semi-final.
Worn by: Simon Haworth, Michael O'Neill.

H 2000–01, 2001–02

Design: ADIDAS
Sponsor: JJB SPORTS

The club made their next assault on the second division under the guidance of Bruce Rioch (who had replaced John Benson) in another slick all-blue adidas kit. Green was retained as an integral part of the trim and a collar returned to the shirt. The only real embellishments were the three-stripe trademark and a green horizontal stripe across the chest. The kit was actually previewed in the last game of the 99–00 season: the defeat to Gillingham in the Division 2 play-off final.

Worn in: The desperately unlucky 3–2 defeat to Gillingham in the 99–00 play-offs. Also the 0–0 draw with Reading in the following year's play-off semi-final first leg.
Worn by: Peter Beagrie, Arjan De Zeeuw.

A 2000–01

Design: ADIDAS
Sponsor: JJB SPORTS

As with the first adidas outfit, the club's next away design followed that of the home, but reversed out to all white. The white shorts and socks of this kit could also be worn with the home shirt when required. A poor run of results in February led to the departure of Rioch, and he was eventually replaced by ex-Manchester United star Steve Bruce. The 00–01 season saw the Latics make the play-offs for an incredible third year running after finishing 6th. But, unfortunately, they again stumbled at the final hurdle.

Worn in: Poor defeats against Oldham (2–1) and Peterborough (2–0).
Worn by: Lee McCulloch, Steve McMillan, Matt Jackson, Paul Dalglish.

The Patrick third strip of 02–03 was the first time the club had
worn an all-red kit since the Matchwinner away outfit of 91–93.

A 2001–02

Design: ADIDAS
Sponsor: JJB SPORTS

With Steve Bruce lured to Crystal Palace,
ex-Latics player Paul Jewell became the club's
manager in time for the 01–02 season. The last
kit of the four-year adidas deal was another
amber creation – this time trimmed with
contemporary black underarm and side panels,
a sleek futuristic V-neck and a new
interpretation of the trademark three stripes
across each cuff. Matched with black shorts
and socks, it was a fine-looking strip that
unfortunately failed to inspire the side to the
promotion they so desperately craved. The
club finished the season in a slightly
disappointing 10th place.

Worn in: A solid 2–1 win at Chesterfield.
Worn by: Lee Ashcroft, Paul Mitchell.

H 2002–03

Design: PATRICK
Sponsor: JJB SPORTS

Exit adidas – enter French sportswear company
Patrick. Their first home kit was not a million
miles away from the first adidas outfit, with its
large white side panels and fine green trim.
Topped with a minimal crew-neck and a little
restrained use of white piping, the strip graced
the backs of the Wigan side as they stormed
Division 2 and clinched the title at last. The
white socks returned, now adorned with a
trendy vertical green stripe and blue turnovers.

Worn in: An incredible Worthington Cup run
including wins against Fulham (2–1), WBA (3–1)
and a glorious 1–0 revenge win over Man City.
Also worn when the side collected the Division
2 trophy after the 1–0 win over Barnsley.
Worn by: Jason De Vos, Neil Roberts.

A 2002–03, 2003–04

Design: PATRICK
Sponsor: JJB SPORTS

Unlike the home kit, Patrick's first away effort
lasted for two seasons and brought back
memories of the white shirt from the mid-80s.
The shirt, which featured a similar basic cut to
the home version, was embellished with two
vertical navy stripes. An element that some
supporters felt looked a little cheap was the
white chest band sewn across the shirt to
house the JJB logo. Navy shorts and socks
(including a vertical stripe and the Patrick
logo) completed the outfit.

Worn in: An impressive 2–0 win over Oldham
at Boundary Park (02–03). Also a superb 3–1
triumph vs Ipswich Town the following year.
Worn by: Nathan Ellington, Andy Liddell,
Tony Dinning, Karl Duguid.

3 2002–03

Design: PATRICK
Sponsor: JJB SPORTS

As Wigan had found out many times over the
last few years, white shirts often cause colour
clash problems when playing against teams
who sport stripes. To compensate for the
problem, Patrick introduced this rather dashing
all-red outfit that featured in some vital games
in the 02–03 season, including a particularly
memorable game at Huddersfield! Similar in
style to the home shirt, the crew-necked jersey
featured white side panels and a broad white
stripe down each sleeve.

Worn in: The brilliant 1–0 win at Queens Park
Rangers (02–03) and the 0–0 draw at
Huddersfield that finally clinched that season's
Division 2 title for the Latics.
Worn by: Nicky Eaden, Ian Breckin.

Despite blue being one of the most popular colour choices for football kits, and stripes of course being a traditional football design, Wigan's blue and white stripes are unique in the 05–06 Premiership.

H 2003–04, 2004–05

Design: PATRICK
Sponsor: JJB SPORTS

With the club now playing in the First Division, Patrick launched this intimidating new home strip. It was a mixture of old and new, with pinstripes combining well with a very minimal and modern V-neck design matched with dynamic white panels across the shoulders. Green was reduced to just a little trim on the neck and two stripes on the socks turnover. After finishing in a respectable 7th place in their first season in Division 1, this strip was worn by the club as they steamrollered the 04–05 season, eventually finishing 2nd.

Worn in: The incredible 5–0 win over Crystal Palace (03–04). Plus the vital 1–0 win over Ipswich towards the end of the 04–05 season.
Worn by: Geoff Horsfield, Leighton Baines.

3 2003–04

Design: PATRICK
Sponsor: JJB SPORTS

Wigan reverted to the ever-popular amber/yellow away kit combination for their third kit for the 03–04 season, with the red shirt that had proved so lucky the previous year consigned to the history books. This new shirt brought back a more old-fashioned collar, teamed with a broad black horizontal chestband trimmed with white piping and black side panels. The black shorts featured the standard Patrick dual-stripe trim.

Worn in: The impressive 4–2 win over Wimbledon in one of the south London club's last games at Selhurst Park.
Worn by: Gary Teale, Ian Breckin.

A 2004–05

Design: PATRICK
Sponsor: JJB SPORTS

The sublime 04–05 season saw the club play away from the JJB Stadium in this threatening and mysterious all-black outfit, trimmed elegantly throughout with a rich gold. Featuring hi-tech fabric and a fashionable continental neck, it was the first time the side had sported a black strip and it played its part in some vital victories away from home as the side pushed for the Premiership. A new version of the JJB logo housed within an oval shield was also introduced.

Worn in: The two brilliant away wins at the start of the 04–04 campaign: 2–0 at Millwall followed by a 3–1 victory at West Ham.
Worn by: Jimmy Bullard, Jason Roberts, Gareth Whalley, Alan Mahon.

H 2005–06

Design: JJB SPORTS
Sponsor: JJB SPORTS

This is surely a kit that will go down in Latics history as being the one worn during one of the club's greatest matches – the 3–1 win over Reading that sealed the side's promotion to the Premiership for the first time. Premiered at that game, the last of the 04–05 season, the return to blue and white stripes for the first time since 1982 accompanies Paul Jewell's men as they take on their greatest challenge. The Latics fans love the shirt, which is the first worn by the club to actually be manufactured as well as sponsored by JJB as the company venture into the world of apparel production for the first time.

A 2005–06

Design: JJB SPORTS
Sponsor: JJB SPORTS

The club are also wearing their preferred change colour of amber during their momentous first season in the Premiership. The jersey features white-trimmed navy sleeves leading into panels that run down each side of the shirt. Rather than the angular design included on the home kit, this outfit favours a more relaxed curved trim throughout. Unlike the home kit, this shirt features a more conventional placement of the club badge and manufacturer's logo.

ACKNOWLEDGMENTS

I'd like to say a very very special thank you to the lovely Julie Hayman for all her support and for putting up with me doing this project for the past four years!

I'd also like to thank my big sister Helen and brother-in-law David and all my friends and family for all their encouragement and help.

Design opinions and advice were gratefully received from Matt Christmas, Rob Parker and all at The Design Practice, Ashford, Kent. A special thank you to Emma Goodman for being such an understanding and supportive manager.

Thanks also to: Julia Stanton, Claire Dunn and all at A & C Black, tutors and staff at The Kent Institute of Art and Design - Maidstone, The Society of Authors, Kent County Council Libraries, Furley Page Solicitors, Soccer Scene, Faith Warne, Laura Hitchcock, Simon Rosen, Natalie Wilson, Adam Barker, Stewart Bamford, Richard Owen, Carl McNally, Brian Porter, Richard Stanley, Mick Cooper, Carl at Wolves Stats, Claire Walton, Jeff Sechiari, David Poulton, Steve Westby, Frank Nicholson, Emma Heathcote, Doug Trotman, Iain Loe, John Collison and Roger Protz.

Sincere thanks to all the football clubs, sportswear companies and shirt sponsors who have so kindly allowed me to include their logos and intellectual property within my illustrations and who have helped me with my research. Without your help this project would not have been possible:

Joseph Cohen, Michelle Tierney, Phil Smith, Kate Linnell, Claire Walton, Steve Pain, Ken Beamish, Simon Marland, Danny Reuben, Emma Tedman, Rick Everett, Emma Wingfield, Andy Hosie, Ben Adcock, Marie-Louise Culbert, Ian Howard, Frank Lomas, Peter Draper, Graham Fordy, Steve Spark, Jason Stone, Tara Snowden, Lesley Callaghan, Clare Blakeman, Selwyn Tash, Stuart Hayton, Fran Jones, John Evans and Peter Stewart.

Barry Moore, Janet Wild, Arthur Hoeld, Tony Hutchinson, Mr Sekito, Peter Crawford, Julie Paul, Simon Bartle, Fabrizio Taddei, George Meudell and Peter Lawson, Ben Shuttleworth, Halldor Einarsson, Andy Reid, Samesh Kumar, John Woodfield, Domenico Sindico, Kevin Batchelor, Lawrence Turnbull, Paula Green, Simon Charlesworth, Ninz Sangha, Rick Becker, Tom Riden, Cheryl Burkett, Mike Thorpe, Gary Dixon, Steve Eden, Vicki Azmanova, Mark Freeman, Peter Dawson, Pat Thomas, Ribero International, Saj Khawaja, TFG Sports, Uhlsport, Nick Crook, Mike Taylor, Robert Ward and Graham Burke.

Jon Graham, Sue Thaw, Matthew Berry, L.Peters, Randall Hughes, Justine Wise, Ian Hannaford, Carlotta Zavanelli, Gareth Roberts, Jacqueline Malone, Steve Hughes, John Savage, Cath Eddleston, Stuart Elsom, Pipat Visuttiporn, Julie Jobling, Caroline Knight, Donna Cresswell, Louise Woodier, Mike Berriman, Sally Heppenstall, Peter Vaughan, Peter Maslyn, Steve Richardson, Carol Ware, Rupert Erskine, Bob Norton, Scott Munro, Jonathan Wall, Naomi Kotz, Alison Yaldren, Scott Stevens, Katie Martin, Steve Dyson, Anita-Lynne Henderson, Sylvia Robinson, Christophe Castagnera, John Brayford, Nick Melton, Hugh Robertson, Justin Smith, David Edwards, Paul Kenny, Tina Wilkinson, Roger Fearn, Lesley Britton, Alison Carley, Chris Houghton, Kate Chandler, Michael Brandt Jensen, Jezel Hardern, Mikio Yotsu, Stuart Mahoney, Emma Gale, John Edgar, Lynne Deegan, Phil Carling, Robbie Cowling, Lucy Squance, David Stanley, Sarah Jones, Graham Hughes, Nick Walter, Ken Wood, Simon Villaneuva, Jennie Drake, Rachel Dean, Alex Lee, Claire Ford, Jane Taylor, Elaine Weatherhead, Mark Craig, Dawn Crees, Karen Tipping, Paul Samuels, Victoria Bedford-Stockwell, Laura Cruickshank, Willem Majoewsky, Jenna Jensen, Kathryn Smith, Sarah French, Darren Caveney, Caroline Barratt, Tony Howarth, Mark Fisher, Faith Wootton, Mike Mainwaring, Tobias Musaeus, Chris Marking, David Osborne, Gloria Holme, Patricia Roche, Brian Trevaskiss, Jeremy Topp, Nunzia Varricchio, David Pinnington, Nicki Walker, Brian Seymour-Smith, Perry Jones, Gay Moseley, Matt Robinson, Iram Mirza, Dana Loftus, Chris Hayden, Andy Woon.

Thanks also to all the football clubs and other companies who have sponsored or manufactured kits who were kind enough to grant permission but, due to space restrictions, were not able to be included.

All logos, club badges and trademarks are the copyright of their respective owners and are used with kind permission.

Every possible effort has been made to contact all relevant copyright owners in the book. Anyone who has not been contacted for any reason is requested to write to the publishers so that full credit can be made in subsequent editions.

... and yes, I should get out more.

Magazines

Match, Shoot, Goal, Four Four Two, Total Football, 90 Minutes, Match of the Day, Design Week, Creative Review, United World, Roy of the Rovers – various issues from 1980 to 2005.

Matchday Programmes

Arsenal, Aston Villa, Birmingham City, Bolton Wanderers, Blackburn Rovers, Charlton Athletic, Chelsea, Coventry City, Crystal Palace, Derby County, Everton, Fulham, Ipswich Town, Leeds United, Liverpool, Leicester City, Liverpool, Manchester City, Manchester United, Middlesbrough, Newcastle United, Nottingham Forest, Portsmouth, Southampton, Southend United, Sunderland, Tottenham Hotspur, Watford, West Bromwich Albion, West Ham United, Wimbledon, Wolverhampton Wanderers – various issues from 1980 to 2005.

Catalogues

Umbro teamwear (1991, 1992, 1993) Replica World, Soccer Scene, Soccer Equipe, Charlton Athletic Merchandise 2001–02, Worthington Sports, Bourne Sports, Intersport, Fulham Merchandise 2003-04, Sportshoes Unlimited, Olympus Sport, Norwich City Merchandise 2002-03 and West Ham United Merchandise 2000-01.

Sticker Albums

Panini's Football 1986, 1988, Panini's Football League 1985, Merlin Premier League 1995, 1996, 1997, 1998, 2001, 2002, 2003, 2004, The Sun Soccer Collection 1989-90.

Newspapers

The Times, The Sunday Times, The Observer, The Guardian, The News of the World, The Sun.

Books

Shoot Annual 1980–1999, IPC Magazines.
Match Football Yearbook 1982, 1984, 1988, 1991.
Roy of the Rovers Annual 89, Fleetway Publications.
The Official Premier League Annual 1994, 1995, 1996, Grandreams Ltd.
Official Liverpool Annual 1990, Hamlyn.
The Match Annual 1992, Hamlyn.
The Sun Soccer Annuals 1986, 1988, Invincible Press Ltd.
Soccer Monthly Annual 1983, Fleetway.

The Topical Times Football Book 1982, 1984, 1985, 1988, 1991-94, 1997, DC Thompson & Co Ltd.
The Guide to the FA Carling Premiership, Stopwatch Publishing Ltd 1997.
A Guide to the Premier League, PRC Publishing 1998.
Superstars of the Premier League 1995-96, 1996-97, Parragon.
Official Football League Yearbook 1991, Valiant Sporting Books Ltd.
Official Premier League Yearbook 1992-93, published by Stanley Paul.
Football Memorabilia, Robert McElroy & Grant MacDougall, Carlton Books 1999.
FC Football Graphics, Jeremy Leslie and Patrick Burgoyne, Thames and Hudson 1998.
The Homes of Football, Stuart Clarke, Little, Brown and Company 1999.
Moving the Goalposts, Ed Horton, Mainstream Publishing 1997.
Daily Telegraph Football Chronicle, Norman Barrett, Carlton 1999.
The Hamlyn Illustrated History of Liverpool 1892–1998, Stephen F Kelly, Hamlyn 1998.
The Hamlyn Illustrated History of Manchester Utd, Tom Tyrell and David Meek, Hamlyn 1998.
Club Colours, Bob Bickerton, Hamlyn 1998.
The Sunday Times Illustrated History of Football, Chris Nawrat and Steve Hutchings, Hamlyn 1994.
The Soccer Tribe, Desmond Morris, Jonathan Cape 1981.
The Official Manchester United Illustrated Encyclopedia, Manchester United Books 1998.
The Official Arsenal Fans Guide, Keir Radnedge, Carlton 1997.
The Official Tottenham Hotspur Fans Guide, Gerry Cox, Carlton 1997.
Rothmans Football Yearbook 1985-86, Editor: Peter Dunk, Rothmans.
Team Shirts to Ticket Stubs, Nick Davidson, Watford Football Club 2002.
Saints in Stripes, Howard Bowden and Alan Gibson, Clash of Colours 2002.
Images of Sport – Charlton Athletic, Compiled by David Ramzan, Tempus Publishing 2001.
Flick to Kick, Daniel Tatarsky, Orion Books 2004.
Trainers, Neal Heard, Carlton 2003.
Opta Football Yearbook 2000-01, Compiling Editor Rob Bateman, Carlton 2000.
Kick Off 1996-97, Editor Mike Ivey, Sidan Press.
Kick Off 2002-03, Editor John Ley, Sidan Press.
Final Whistle 2004-05, Editors Johanne Springett and Mark Peters, Sidan Press.
The Who's Who of Wigan Athletic, Dean P.Hayes, Breedon Books 2004.
Wigan Athletic – The Football League Years, Dean P.Hayes, Sutton 2004.

BIBLIOGRAPHY

Selected Websites

Official websites of all the clubs featured in the book.
The excellent Footy Mad.net series of websites (www.footy-mad.co.uk)
http://norfox.net
www.premiershirts.net
www.prideofanglia.com
www.liverweb.org.uk
www.footballanorak.com
www.kopcollector.co.uk
http://hem.passagen.se/arsenalshirts/
www.geocities.com/chelseafcshirt/
www.footballculture.net
www.sporting-heroes.net
www.unitedmanchester.com/sport/
http://homepage.ntlworld.com/steveeyre/kits.htm
www.bcfc-archive.freeserve.co.uk/
http://onesunderland.com
www.depro.co.uk/sbs/
www.bluekipper.com
www.truegreats.com
www.the-citizen.org.uk
www.subside.co.uk
www.kitbag.com
www.footballshirtbible.co.uk
www.kitclassics.co.uk
www.yeoldetreeandcrown.34sp.com
www.laticsworld.co.uk
www.chilvers1.demon.co.uk/Wafc1.htm
www.cockneylatic.co.uk

www.truecoloursfootball.co.uk

Visit the *True Colours* website: use the timeline to trace trends in football fashion over the years, discover the stories behind special commemorative kits and some of the most controversial kits in history, test your knowledge of football kit design in our quiz (and have a chance of winning a print of one of the illustrations in this book) and use the discussion board to make any suggestions or comments about kits you've loved or loathed in the past.